The Art of Investing
Lessons from History's Greatest Traders

John M. Longo, Ph.D., CFA

THE
GREAT
COURSES®

PUBLISHED BY:

THE GREAT COURSES
Corporate Headquarters
4840 Westfields Boulevard, Suite 500
Chantilly, Virginia 20151-2299
Phone: 1-800-832-2412
Fax: 703-378-3819
www.thegreatcourses.com

John M. Longo, Ph.D., CFA

Professor of Professional Practice in the Finance
& Economics Department
Rutgers Business School

John M. Longo is a Professor of Professional Practice in the Finance & Economics Department at Rutgers Business School, part of Rutgers, The State University of New Jersey. He also has served for multiple years as a visiting professor of finance at EMBA-Global—the joint international Executive MBA program of Columbia Business School, London Business School, and The University of Hong Kong. A Chartered Financial Analyst (CFA), Professor Longo earned a B.A. in Computer Science and a B.A. in Economics as well as a Ph.D. and an M.B.A. in Finance, all from Rutgers University. He is a two-time award winner for innovative teaching at Rutgers Business School.

Professor Longo has 20 years of professional investment management experience. Since 2015, he has served as chief investment officer and portfolio manager for Beacon Trust, a registered investment advisor with 2.5 billion dollars under management. Beacon is a subsidiary of Provident Financial Services (NYSE: PFS), founded in 1839. Professor Longo served as chief investment officer and portfolio manager for The MDE Group from 2002 until its acquisition by Beacon Trust at the end of 2014. He also previously worked at Merrill Lynch as a vice president in a quantitative unit of the firm.

Professor Longo has appeared on CNBC, Bloomberg Television, Bloomberg Radio, Fox Business Network, BBC World News, WSJ.com, GreatInvestors.tv, The Insana Quotient with Ron Insana, and several other programs. He has been quoted in *The Wall Street Journal*, *Barron's*, *Thomson Reuters*, *MarketWatch*, *U.S. News & World Report*, *CNBC.com*, and dozens of other periodicals.

Professor Longo is the author/editor of *Hedge Fund Alpha: A Framework for Generating and Understanding Investment Performance*. He is a member of the editorial board of *The Journal of Performance Measurement*. Professor Longo also serves as an ad hoc book proposal reviewer for Columbia University Press and has served on the advisory board of Bloomberg's educational subsidary, Bloomberg Institute. On four separate occasions, he led college students to a personal visit with Warren Buffett. ■

Table of Contents

Introduction

Lecture Guides

Supplemental Material

Disclaimer

The financial information provided in these lectures is for informational purposes only and not for the purpose of providing specific financial advice. Financial investing carries an inherent risk that you will lose part or all of your investment. Investors must independently and thoroughly research and analyze each and every investment prior to investing. The consequences of such risk may involve, but are not limited to: federal/state/municipal tax liabilities, loss of all or part of the investment capital, loss of interest, and contract liability to third parties, and other risks not specifically listed herein. Use of these lectures does not create any financial advisor relationship with The Teaching Company or its lecturers, and neither The Teaching Company nor the lecturer is responsible for your use of this educational material or its consequences. You should contact a financial advisor to obtain advice with respect to any specific financial investing questions. The opinions and positions provided in these lectures reflect the opinions and positions of the relevant lecturer and do not necessarily reflect the opinions or positions of The Teaching Company or its affiliates. Pursuant to IRS Circular 230, any tax advice provided in these lectures may not be used to avoid tax penalties or to promote, market, or recommend any matter therein.

The Teaching Company expressly DISCLAIMS LIABILITY for any DIRECT, INDIRECT, INCIDENTAL, SPECIAL, OR CONSEQUENTIAL DAMAGES OR LOST PROFITS that result directly or indirectly from the use of these lectures. In states that do not allow some or all of the above limitations of liability, liability shall be limited to the greatest extent allowed by law. ■

The Art of Investing
Lessons from History's Greatest Traders

According to investing legend Warren Buffett, great investors are both born and made. Innate talent must be paired with hard work and honing investment skill to achieve truly outstanding results. One way to learn about investing is to study the backgrounds and strategies of some of history's greatest investors. Sir Isaac Newton wrote, "If I have seen further, it is by standing on the shoulders of giants." In this course, we'll examine the backgrounds and investment strategies of more than two dozen of the greatest investors who ever lived. By standing on the shoulders of the giants of the investing world, we will, at minimum, become more educated investors.

Personal background or history is important not only because it is sometimes fascinating, but also because it often plays a key role in the development of an investor's philosophy. For example, Warren Buffett's mentor, Benjamin Graham, lived through the Panic of 1907 as a young child and The Great Depression as an adult. These experiences led him to become a pioneer in value investing, an approach that involves buying investments at a steep discount. These experiences also helped him formulate a core part of value investing: margin of safety, or protection against downside risk.

John Templeton traveled the world as a young man and saw an expanded set of investment opportunities, a mindset perhaps best encapsulated by one of his most famous quotes, "If you search worldwide, you'll find more and better bargains than by studying only one nation." This vision led Templeton to pioneer the field of international investing and helped make investing in foreign firms almost as easy as it is to buy shares in Apple. Buffett, Graham, Templeton, and the many other great investors covered in this course developed an investment strategy based on their backgrounds, skill sets, resources, and personality types that ultimately led each of them to find enormous investment success.

This course will also serve as an educational primer on many different fields of investing, including stocks, bonds, commodities, mutual funds, hedge funds, and private equity. We'll examine different techniques applied in each of these investment sectors. The topics of risk, return, and the different types of investments are of fundamental importance. But, the topic of investment is important far beyond the obvious notion of making money. To many, it is about freedom— financial freedom. The freedom to live the life you want to live. The freedom to help your family, friends, community, and perhaps ultimately society.

We'll wrap up with a case study that touches on many of the concepts discussed in the course and develop an investment checklist designed to help you ask the right questions about your personal approach to investing and craft your own investment philosophy. ∎

1

Investing Skill, Strategy, and Temperament

When asked if a great investor is born or made, Warren Buffett said he thought it was a little bit of both. He gave the example of Tiger Woods in his prime. He said Tiger Woods was born with an aptitude for golf, but that Tiger honed his craft by hitting 500 golf balls a day. Buffett and I both believe that investing is part art and part science. One way to learn about investing is to study the backgrounds and strategies of some of history's greatest investors. Personal background or history is important because it often plays a role in the development of an investment philosophy.

Learning from Great Investors

> For example, Warren Buffett's mentor, Benjamin Graham, lived through both the Panic of 1907 and the Great Depression. These experiences led him to pioneer the investment approach known as value investing, which refers to buying sound investments at bargain prices. He learned to formulate a strategy called a margin of safety, or protection against downside risk.

> From a macro perspective, the financial markets play an integral role in the world we live in by helping to raise money for growing firms.

- Without financial markets, it would be almost impossible for a firm like Facebook to go from a startup run out of a dorm room to one valued at hundreds of billions of dollars in about a decade.

- Similarly, Home Depot, which pioneered the superstore home improvement concept and is one of the largest retailers in the world, started with two leased stores. Through the financial markets, it raised the money that enabled the company to open more stores and develop its concept. Today, Home Depot operates thousands of stores around the world, resulting in annual sales of about $100 billion.

> There's no single best way to become a successful investor, but many great investors follow several principles:

- The great traders and investors in this course typically find a strategy that matches their skill set and personality type.

- They work extremely hard and usually love what they do.

- Nearly all of them continue to work well after the point at which they become rich.

- They don't give up when things go wrong, and they learn from their mistakes.

Principles and Strategies

> When you start investing your own money or have someone manage your money for you, you'll have to ask yourself some tough questions. The first is whether you want to be an active investor, trying to outperform the market, or buy a handful of low-cost index funds and try to make money passively.

> Each approach has merit. Beating the market is tough, so buying and holding low-cost index funds that track the market as a

whole—or special sectors, like health care or technology—makes sense for a lot of people.

> The next question is what kind of asset you'd like to concentrate on. One approach is value investing: trying to buy stocks at a discount to their intrinsic value. Benjamin Graham developed this field of securities analysis during the first part of the 20th century.

> Value stocks tend to sell at a discount to the market because of certain problems: A stock like Apple, for example, appeared to be on the verge of going out of business before Steve Jobs returned in 1997.

> Another popular approach to picking stocks is called growth investing. Growth-oriented investors are less concerned about buying an asset at a discount. Instead, they seek leaders in an industry—the next Amazon. This school of thought was developed in the 1950s by Philip Fisher and Thomas Rowe Price.

> Growth and value are the main distinctions in strategy among stock investors, but other approaches are also available.

> Before the Great Depression, publishing audited financial statements was optional for companies. Without hard data, most investors traded on rumors and hot tips or relied on a ticker-tape machine that produced a thin strip of paper with a stock's symbol, its price, and perhaps the number of shares traded. Some investors were really good at "reading the tape," or figuring out the trend in security prices. Today, this approach can be viewed as an early form of technical analysis.

> Technical investors look for patterns in price and volume, believing that certain trends can be anticipated and will repeat themselves. Most believe in a phenomenon known as trend trading or momentum investing. If the trend is up, you'd buy. If the trend is down, you'd sell.

> Another way to differentiate stocks is by their size—that is, the amount you'd have to pay if you were to buy the entire firm, not simply one share.

  o Large companies tend to be more established, have a longer history, and may pay a dividend.

  o Some companies generate more money than they can reinvest profitably. Giving a dividend to their shareholders is one way to use this excess cash.

  o Dividend-seeking investors include many value investors and others who live off the income.

> Some analysts focus instead on small-capitalization, or small-cap, companies. Small-cap companies are usually valued at $1 billion or less.

- ○ Small companies typically outperform large companies by about 2% or 3% a year over time. They also introduce about 50% more risk into your portfolio than their large counterparts.

- ○ Risk refers to the volatility of returns in your investment portfolio, a statistical measure known as standard deviation. Small-cap stocks are also more volatile, and information about them may be scarce.

> The stock market gets most of our attention, but the bond market is much bigger. The bond market consists of government and corporate bonds as well as fixed-income securities tied to mortgages, student loans, and car loans.

> Most great investors tend to own concentrated portfolios of between 10 and 30 stocks. They tend to believe you can't follow many firms in detail because of limited time and attention. If they are correct in their analysis, this method might be the best way to maximize returns.

> Other great investors favor a much more diversified approach. Successful quantitative investors run dozens, if not hundreds, of different investing models managed by quantitative analysts, or quants, who are the card counters of investing. They make many small bets with the odds in their favor, the results adding up over time.

> Still other great investors use leverage, or borrowed money, as a key part of their investment strategy.

Patterns in Investing Strategies

> We can also discern other patterns in investing strategies: For instance, most investors tend to be focused on investments in their home country. Academics call this the home-country bias.

- Often, more information is readily available to us about our home country than about somewhere abroad.

- But the British-American investor John Templeton believed that chances to earn attractive returns increase with broader investment opportunities.

> At times, you can be your own worst enemy. Sometimes investors chase hot investments and buy near a peak. Then, when these hot investments cool off, they sell near the bottom, the classic misstep of buying high and selling low.

> A whole school of thought on the tendency of investors to make such mistakes is called behavioral finance. One investor, in particular, who made pioneering contributions in the field is David Dreman, known as a contrarian investor. He's willing to buy what is out of favor—like tobacco stocks, when they were being investigated by the government—knowing that the bad times affecting a particular stock or industry usually don't last forever.

Deeper Values

> For many wealthy investors, transmitting values—the beliefs that generated their wealth, such as hard work, persistence, and integrity—is as important as passing on the value of their wealth.

- Many of the great investors featured in this course have signed The Giving Pledge, a program set up by Bill Gates and Warren Buffett, under which the wealthy pledge to give away at least half of their fortunes. Among the signatories featured in this course are Carl Icahn, Bill Ackman, and Ray Dalio.

- Warren Buffett, for instance, once purchased a farm for his son Howard but charged him market-rate rent. Buffett believes that just handing someone a big check is not a way to build character or achieve lasting happiness.

> Financial freedom means different things to different people, and it doesn't have to include becoming a billionaire. A more modest goal to which nearly everyone aspires is a comfortable retirement. Becoming a more competent and knowledgeable investor will most likely help you in that regard and may also give you a greater sense of control over your financial future.

> During one of my meetings with Warren Buffett, he discussed the increase in the standard of living around the world, in part because of the role of the financial markets in providing capital to innovative firms that need it to grow. He said the average American today lives better than John D. Rockefeller, because we have better technology, better health care, and a host of other advances that were not available more than a hundred years ago. Investing and the financial markets are about the impact that successful investing and innovative firms can have on our lives—and on the world around us.

> Increasing your knowledge about investments is a way to increase your control of financial matters. It means being guided by wisdom, not fear, when bad things happen in the markets and in the economy.

Suggested Reading

Bodie, Kane, and Marcus, *Investments*.
Hagstrom, *The Warren Buffett Way*.

Questions to Consider

1. Do you think investment success is mostly art or science?

2. What was your first investment and how has your approach changed over time?

1

Transcript

Investing Skill, Strategy, and Temperament

I once asked Warren Buffett if a great investor is born or made. He said he thought it was a little bit of both. He gave the example of Tiger Woods in his prime. He said Tiger Woods was born with an aptitude for golf, but that Tiger honed his craft by hitting 500 golf balls A day. Buffett and I both believe that investing is part art and part science. So one way to learn about investing is to study the backgrounds and strategies of some of history's greatest investors.

That's what this course is all about. In this program, we'll examine the backgrounds and investment strategies of more than two dozen of the greatest traders who ever lived. Personal background—or history— is important because it often plays a key role in the development of an investment philosophy. For example, Warren Buffett's mentor—Benjamin Graham—lived through the Panic of 1907, as a young child; and later, the Great Depression as an adult. These experiences led him to pioneer the investment approach known as value investing, which refers to buying sound investments at bargain prices. And he learned to formulate a strategy called margin of safety, or protection against downside risk.

From a macro perspective, the financial markets play an integral role in the world we live in. The financial markets can help raise money for growing firms. Without financial markets, it would be almost impossible for a firm like Facebook to go from a start-up run out of a dorm room to one valued at hundreds of billions of dollars, in about a decade. A similar story unfolded for Google now Alphabet—and at firms like Home Depot, which pioneered the superstore home improvement concept, and is one of the largest retailers in the world. Home Depot started with just two leased stores. Through the financial markets, which you and I are able to invest in, it managed to raise the money that enabled the company to open more stores and develop the superstore concept. Today, Home Depot operates thousands of stores around the world, resulting in annual sales of about $100 billion.

There's no single best way to become a successful investor, just as there's no single best way to sing a song, or swing a baseball bat. But there are several principles that many great investors follow. The great traders and investors in this course typically find a strategy that matches their skill set and personality type. They work extremely hard, and usually love what they do for a living. Nearly all continue to work well after the point at which they become rich. They don't give up when things go wrong. and they learn from their mistakes. I'm going to tell a lot of stories about some very successful and pretty amazing men and women in this course. But we're going to do more than that. This course serves as a primer on many of the different fields of investing—including stocks, bonds, commodities, currencies, futures, mutual funds, hedge funds, private equity, and distressed assets. and we'll examine the different techniques applied to each of these instruments. It's basically a boot camp on investing.

So, who am I to stand on the shoulders of Benjamin Graham, and Warren Buffett and all these other great investment professionals to teach this course? Well, that's for you to decide. But I've been teaching investing courses as a professor of finance for more than 15 years. And I've been affiliated with some of the world's great institutions of learning, including Rutgers University, Columbia University, the London Business School, and the University of Hong Kong. I've also worked as a professional money manager for more than 20 years.

My first exposure to the stock market was at family gatherings when I was a boy, and where I'd hear my father and relatives talking about some of the popular stocks of the day, like AT&T and IBM. My family invested in the market, even though they didn't work in the financial services industry.

By the time I was I a teenager, I'd started saving money from various odd jobs—including a paper route, shoveling snow, cutting lawns, and working at McDonald's. And, like Tiger Woods with his golf clubs, I started investing.

I didn't know it back then, but when I bought my first stock, I was following one of the investment maxims of Peter Lynch, the famous portfolio manager at Fidelity Investments. Peter Lynch said, "Invest in what you know." The first stock I bought was Topps, a company that made collectible sports cards. I owned baseball cards and football cards as a boy, and I thought it might be a good investment. I didn't know it at the time, but I was also following an investing principle of Benjamin Graham, who viewed stock as the ownership of a business. That is, if you wouldn't want to own the business, you shouldn't buy the stock. I got lucky when my first stock doubled in value, and I was hooked.

Academics have a name for this phenomenon. It's called the house money effect. It means that if you are successful in an early experience with a risky endeavor, chances are you'll be more likely to stick with it. The billionaire investor Ray Dalio—who founded Bridgewater Associates, the largest hedge fund on earth—had a similar experience as a teenager. He bought an airline stock that also doubled in value. And he concluded that investing was easy. Of course, he learned it's not easy. That's what makes investing challenging and exciting. Every day is different.

I attended college at Rutgers University, where, as an undergraduate, I double-majored in economics and computer science. The economics courses related to my interests in the financial markets. And the courses I took provided a good foundation of how the markets worked. But they didn't cover what successful investors actually do. Between classes, I began reading all the major business publications. And the most popular fund manager featured in them was Peter Lynch of Fidelity Investments.

So Lynch became a role model for me. Later, I got interested in other great investors, too, like Warren Buffett—not only for their investment and business success but also because of the positive ways in which they lead their lives. I wanted to become an expert in investing, so eventually I pursued a Ph.D. in finance, also at Rutgers. My dissertation combined my academic background in computer science and economics and was related to using artificial intelligence to pick stocks.

With an advanced degree in hand, I started out as a quantitative analyst, or quant for short, at Merrill Lynch. A quant is an investor who builds financial models in an attempt to predict the direction of security prices. This approach stands in contrast to the seat of the pants stock picker, or an investor who pores over financial statements and talks to management or other people in the industry. This latter approach is known as fundamental analysis. I was a pretty good quant. But I realized that I wouldn't be a James Simons or a David Shaw, who are two of the pioneers and most successful practitioners of quantitative investment management.

And so my strategy evolved to owning high-quality stocks for the long-term, an idea I learned mostly from Warren Buffett's example. I complemented these relative safe investments with some higher-risk ones. The risky ones involved growth firms with a lot of potential—that's something I learned from growth-investing pioneers Philip Fisher and Thomas Rowe Price—and deep-value investments with high potential upside, something I learned from such experts as Benjamin Graham, Seth Klarman, and David Tepper—three of the best value investors ever.

Now, when you start investing your own money or have someone manage your money for you, you'll have to ask yourself some tough questions. The first is, Am I going to be an active investor, trying to outperform the market? Or should I buy a handful of low-cost index funds, and try to passively make money? There is merit to each approach. It's tough to beat the market. And so buying and holding low-cost index funds that track the market as a whole—or special sectors, like health care or technology—makes sense for a lot of people. It makes sense for almost all people, according to John Bogle, the founder of the three-plus trillion dollar Vanguard Group of mutual funds, whose company created the first index mutual fund.

But nearly all of the great investors whom we'll meet in this course would tell you there is also another way. That's active management, and it's typically what made them rich and famous. Active investing is predicated on trying to beat the market. Beyond thinking about whether you want to be a buy-

and-hold investor or an active investor, it's important to consider what type of assets you want to concentrate on. In stocks, there are different schools of thought.

One approach is value investing, which means trying to buy stocks at a discount to their inherent, or intrinsic, value. Benjamin Graham developed this field of securities analysis during the first part of the 20th century. And many others, including Warren Buffett, have added their own twist to it. Value stocks tend to sell at a discount to the market because of certain problems, or warts. Think a stock like Apple, which appeared to be on the verge of going out of business, before Steve Jobs's return in 1997. Value stocks remind me of one of my favorite *Twilight Zone* episodes from the 1960s. It was called "The Eye of the Beholder," and it featured a woman undergoing plastic surgery on her face. When the doctor and nurse remove the bandages, we see a beautiful woman—the actress Donna Douglass—who bears a resemblance to Marilyn Monroe.

You'd think the surgery would be viewed as a success. But the doctor and nurse recoil in horror. The camera closes in to reveal that the doctor and nurse have distorted pig-like faces. In that *Twilight Zone* episode, a pig-like face was considered beautiful while the Marilyn Monroe prototype was considered ugly. Beauty is always in the eye of the beholder. Value stocks might look ugly on the surface, but you never know. They might be really beautiful in the long run.

Another popular approach to picking stocks is called growth investing. Growth-oriented investors are not so concerned about buying an asset at a discount. Instead, they are looking for leaders in an industry—the next Amazon or Alphabet or Google. This school of thought was developed in the 1950s by Philip Fisher and Thomas Rowe Price. Growth and value are the main distinctions in strategy among stock investors. But there are other approaches, too.

Before the Great Depression—and before some of the financial regulatory reforms that came out of it, during the 1930s and 1940s—it was optional for companies to publish audited financial statements. Now that might be hard to imagine today, but back then, without hard data to rely on, most investors traded on rumors and hot tips. The only information that many investors had, came out of a ticker tape machine. The ticker tape machine produced a thin strip of paper with a stock's symbol, its price, and perhaps the number of shares traded. That's it. But some investors were really good at reading the tape or figuring out the trend in security prices. Today, this approach can be viewed as an early form of technical analysis. Technical investors look for patterns in price and volume, under the belief that certain trends can be anticipated, and repeat themselves.

Most investors who adhere to some form of technical analysis believe in a phenomenon known as trend trading—or momentum investing. If the trend is up, you'd buy. If the trend is down, you'd sell. Perhaps the greatest trend trader who ever lived was a man named Jesse Livermore who made and lost several fortunes during the first half of the 20th century. But the story didn't end all that well for Jesse Livermore. I'll save that one for another day.

Another way to differentiate stocks is by their size, large or small. By size, I mean the amount you'd have to pay if you were going to buy the entire firm, not simply one share. Large companies tend to be more established, have a longer history and may pay a dividend. A dividend is basically a check the company sends you in the mail. Some companies can generate more money than they can reinvest profitability. So giving a dividend to their shareholders is one way to use this excess cash. And there's a whole class of dividend-seeking investors, including many value investors and others who live off the income. John D. Rockefeller once, said, "Do you know the only thing that gives me pleasure? It's to see my dividends coming in."

The trouble with buying a stock in a large company like Exxon or Wal-Mart is that their size alone means it's unlikely you'll uncover information that the market doesn't already know. In other words, it will be harder to beat the market since everyone – be it Wall Street analysts, professional fund managers or individual investors—is already watching these firms like a hawk. So, some analysts focus instead on small capitalization—or small-cap companies. Small-cap companies are usually defined as firms valued at less than $1 billion dollars. Small companies typically outperform large companies over long periods of time by about 2 or 3% a year. These firms also introduce you to about 50% more risk into your portfolio than their large counterparts.

By risk, I'm referring to the volatility of returns in your investment portfolio, a statistical measure known as standard deviation. Risk can be good, and it can be bad. Finding a small-cap company that eventually turns into a large-cap company is like winning the lottery. But small-cap companies are also more volatile, and there may be a dearth of information about them. That said, the general lack of information about a smaller company may be precisely what allows you to uncover an undiscovered gem. Michael Burry, the hero of the Michael Lewis book, *The Big Short*— which was turned into a successful movie—originally earned his reputation by buying small companies.

The stock market gets most of our attention, but the bond market is bigger by far. And the bond market doesn't consist only of government and corporate bonds, but also fixed-income securities tied to mortgages, student loans, and car loans. Basically, anything that has cash flows can be turned into a bond, including music royalties. The late David Bowie helped pioneer a class of bonds called bowie bonds, which enabled artists to monetize the cash flows of their music publishing rights.

You probably hear the expression, "Don't put all your eggs in one basket." This is the essence of diversification. Most great investors tend to own concentrated portfolios of between 10 and 30 stocks. If they are correct in their analysis and they usually are, or they wouldn't be featured in this course, this might be the best way to maximize returns. These investors essentially argue that it's better to have a few eggs in a basket—and to watch the basket carefully—than it is to own hundreds of eggs, in many different baskets. They tend to believe that you can't follow many firms in detail because of limited time and attention.

Other great investors follow a much more diversified approach, like Vanguard founder John Bogle. And many of the successful quantitative investors—like James Simons—run dozens, if not hundreds, of different investing models. These tend to be managed by quants, who are like the card counters of investing. They make many small bets, with the odds in their favor, adding up over time.

Still other great investors—like the macro hedge fund manager, George Soros—use leverage, or borrowed money, as a key part of their investment strategy. Soros became famous in the investing world for betting against the British Pound in 1992. His fund earned a billion dollars in one day—by betting against the Bank of England.

Now, in addition to classifying investors as active or passive—and being focused on growth or value, stocks or bonds—we can also discern other patterns in investing strategies. For instance, most investors tend to be focused on investments in their home country. Academics call this the home-country bias. It's understandable. We're all more familiar with where we live than with some faraway place. It's akin to Peter Lynch's maxim about investing in what you know. And often, more information is readily available about our home country than somewhere abroad. But the British-American investor John Templeton—who founded a mutual fund company named after him—believed that one's chances to earn attractive returns increase with broader investment opportunities. As he put it, "If you search worldwide, you'll find more and better bargains than by studying only one nation." John Templeton is the one person most responsible for making international investing broadly available to us today. As a result, it's generally as easy to own many foreign stocks and bonds as it is to buy a share of Coca-Cola. We'll come back to that idea later in this course.

Now, sometimes you can be your own worst enemy when it comes to investing. A lot of investors chase hot investments and buy things near a peak. Then, when these hot investments cool off, you may be disposed to sell near the bottom. That is, you may be inclined to follow the classic misstep of buying high and selling low—the exact opposite of what you want to do. There's a whole school of thought on the tendency of investors to make such mistakes. It's called behavioral finance.

Many important thinkers have contributed to this field, including Nobel Laureate Daniel Kahneman, of Princeton University. One investor, in particular, who made pioneering contributions in the field is David Dreman.

Dreman is known as a contrarian investor. He's willing to buy what is out of favor—like tobacco stocks when they were being investigated by the government—knowing that the bad times affecting a stock or industry usually don't last forever. Here's where, by limiting your own mistakes, you might be able to profit from the mistakes of others.

Great investing isn't confined to one strategy, nor is it confined to one gender. In fact, academic studies find that women tend to have better investment performance than men. Women tend to be more patient. They tend to have a greater focus on downside risk. One woman named Hetty Green was an early value investor. Buying cheap and selling dear she called it. But she also earned the nickname the Witch of Wall Street for her stingy behavior. And, despite a fortune that would be worth as much as $4 billion today, Guinness World Records once listed her as the world's greatest miser.

I don't think it's a coincidence that many of the great investors featured in this course have signed the Giving Pledge—a program set up by Bill Gates and Warren Buffett, under which the wealthy pledge to give away at least half of their fortunes. Among those to do so, and who are featured in this course, are Carl Icahn, Bill Ackman, and Ray Dalio. For many wealthy investors, it's just as important to transmit values—the beliefs that generated their wealth—like hard work, persistence, and integrity—as it is to pass on the value of their wealth. Warren Buffett, for instance, once purchased a farm for his son Howard, but charged him market-rate rent. Warren believes that just handing someone a big check is not a way to build character or achieve lasting happiness.

Buffett's approach brings to mind the old proverb, "Give a man a fish, and you feed him for a day. Teach a man to fish, and you feed him for a lifetime." Of course, financial freedom means different things to different people. And it doesn't have to include becoming a billionaire. A more modest goal that nearly everyone aspires to is to have a comfortable retirement. Becoming a more competent and knowledgeable investor will most likely help you in that regard. Becoming a more knowledgeable investor may also provide you with a greater sense of control over your financial future.

Many states now require that financial literacy be taught in public schools. I think that's a good start. But I think that parents should also teach their children about financial matters. I originally learned this myself, second-hand. When I was a boy—I was in middle school—my father lost his job during the double-dip recession of 1980 and 1981–1982. Unemployment rose to the highest levels since just before World War II. At the time, my mother and father had one child in college and three more who hoped to get there. I didn't know much about the financial markets, back then. But I didn't like the feeling of what was going on, and not being able to make sense of it. Increasing your knowledge about investments is a way to increase your control of financial matters. It means being guided by wisdom, not fear when bad things happen in the markets and in the economy.

Things have come full circle for me, as I've taught my own young son about the basics of investing. We bought his first stock, Disney, when he was in second grade. Of course, my son didn't know anything about Disney's financial fundamentals. But he loved their resort experience. And I knew the company had strong fundamentals and had a great long-term track record. And so, just as when I purchased my own first stock, we were following Peter Lynch's maxim about investing in what you know. We've continued to purchase stocks for my son's college fund in subsequent years, like Apple because he likes the product. And in this way, I think that Benjamin Graham's concept of viewing stock as ownership in a business can also be communicated to children at a young age.

There are other ways to teach your children, grandchildren, or other family members about investing, too. You shouldn't feel compelled to follow a single approach, be it from Peter Lynch, Benjamin Graham, or any other investor. During one of my meetings with Warren Buffett, he discussed another thought—beyond the one about investors being born or made, and about Tiger Woods practicing with his golf clubs. This thought was about the increase in the standard of living around the world, in part because of the role of financial markets in providing capital to innovative firms that need it to grow.

Warren said the average American today lives better than John D. Rockefeller did, when he was the richest man in the world, at the turn of the last century. We have airplanes, televisions, computers, cell phones, better healthcare, and a host of other advances today that were not available more than a hundred years ago.

So, investing and the financial markets are about more than just the money. It's also about the impact that successful investing and innovative firms can have on our lives—and on the world around us.

2

Benjamin Graham and Value Investing

Benjamin Graham is known as the father of value investing, and he pioneered a rigorous, quantitative approach to security analysis. Graham started investing during the early 1900s. The landscape then was very different. For example, investing was not considered a respectable profession. It was viewed more like astrology or a game of chance—run by crooks and people with inside information. Using inside information was legal at the time. His groundbreaking investment strategy had its roots in his own personal hardship.

The Graham Effect

> Investors before Graham used an early form of technical analysis, making investment decisions based on stock price and volume changes. Before the days of Bloomberg terminals and Yahoo Finance charts, the ticker tape listed that information, which was all that many investors had with which to make an investment decision.

> Back then many investors viewed stock as little more than a vehicle to speculate. One of Benjamin Graham's seminal insights for securities analysis was in viewing stock as the ownership of a business.

> The point is this: The difference between Graham's strategies and some of the investment techniques used by his peers and predecessors is like the contrast between Babe Ruth and the home run hitters who came before him. It is not an exaggeration to say that Ben Graham changed the investing landscape forever.

Graham Mini-Biography

Benjamin Graham

> Benjamin Graham was born Benjamin Grossbaum in London in 1894. He moved with his family to New York when he was a year old. His father, Isaac, ran successful retail businesses selling high-end chinaware and figurines. The family led a comfortable life on Fifth Avenue in Manhattan.

> When Graham was 9 years old, his father died, and the business quickly went downhill. Then his mother, Dorothy, was wiped out trading stocks during the Crash of 1907.

> Graham was an excellent student and received a scholarship to Columbia University. After graduating second in his class in 1914, his Wall Street career began with the firm of Newburger, Henderson and Loeb. He quickly rose through the ranks and made partner at the age of 26.

> He left Newburger in 1923 to set up his own firm with business partner Jerome Newman. The investment vehicles related to this business agreement became known as the Graham Newman Partnerships.

> In 1928, he finally returned to Columbia to teach. His 1934 book, *Security Analysis*, which has since become known on Wall Street

as the bible of value investing, was created in large part from the lecture notes of his classes.

Graham Investment Philosophy

> One of Graham's principles was that if you had the money, you shouldn't buy a share of stock in a company unless you would be willing to buy the company itself.

  ○ With that caveat, you would certainly be interested in the firm's financials. Focus on the balance sheet, which lists assets on the left and liabilities and net worth on the right.

  ○ You probably would also want a business that had stood the test of time. For example, you might want to make sure it had survived a couple of recessions.

  ○ You probably would also like to buy the business at a discount to what you thought it was worth, just in case something went wrong or you miscalculated its value.

> Graham summarized these ideas into the concept margin of safety. He phrased it this way: "To have a true investment, there must be present a true margin of safety. And a true margin of safety is one that can be demonstrated by figures, by persuasive reasoning, and by reference to a body of actual experience."

> Graham focused on quantitative measures of value. He first looked at the value of existing assets, such as cash, inventory, and property, by examining a target company's financial statements. Next, Graham looked at current earnings. Lastly, and only in rare circumstances, he considered future profits, but only in the core competence area of a firm with a sustainable competitive advantage.

Mean Reversion

> The concept of mean reversion is a major underpinning of the value-investing philosophy. It means that past winners often become future losers, while past losers often become future winners.

> Graham was also early to recognize the role of market psychology in investing. Today, the field of investor psychology is known by academics and practitioners as behavioral finance.

> Value investments often occur because of market psychology, with fear and greed moving prices away from their long run or equilibrium prices.

Net–Net

> One of Graham's favorite value-oriented strategies to pick investments was to find companies selling for less than their cash-liquidation value. He called this deep-value strategy Net–Net.

   ○ Graham's Net–Net calculation started with the cash and cash equivalents item on a firm's balance sheet and then added a conservative portion of accounts receivable and inventory. Then he subtracted all liabilities.

   ○ He compared this aggregate amount of cash and hard assets to the stock market value of the firm. If the company was selling for less than market value, Graham would consider it a bargain under his Net–Net deep-value approach.

> He estimated that his Net–Net strategy provided his partnerships with returns of approximately 20% a year, double the market's historical return.

Northern Pipeline

> The investment that put Graham on the map was known as the Northern Pipeline Affair, a Net–Net investment. Northern Pipeline Company was one of Standard Oil's 34 spinoff companies. Its business involved transporting crude oil to a Standard Oil refineries.

> After the Supreme Court decision breaking up Standard Oil, Graham combed through the forms that energy firms filed with the Interstate Commerce Commission. He found that Northern Pipeline had $95 a share in railroad bonds and other liquid assets. Yet the stock was trading for only $65 a share, and it paid a hefty 9% annual dividend yield.

> ○ In 1926, Graham's partnership acquired roughly a 5% stake in Northern Pipeline, and he asked the company to distribute more cash to shareholders. Northern Pipeline's management wasn't pleased at being told what to do and actively avoided his requests.

> ○ In 1928, after contacting other shareholders and requesting their help, Graham put together proxies, or voting power, equal to 38% of Northern Pipeline's shares and was able to get himself appointed to the firm's board of directors.

> Over time he persuaded the company to pay out $70 a share in special or extra dividends. Coming in the midst of the Great Depression, it was a very attractive return from Graham and his partners.

Government Employee Insurance Company

> GEICO was Graham's most famous investment. GEICO wasn't Net–Net, but it had unique value, such as its superior business model of selling car insurance. Graham purchased almost half of the company for his investment partnerships in 1948, at a 10% discount to its book value.

> GEICO rode the wave of the post-World War II American automobile industry. Among its advantages was the clever business model of selling directly through the mail at discount prices. Drivers benefited from lower car insurance prices, while GEICO benefited from its lean infrastructure, avoiding the need to build a costly network of offices and salespeople.

Seven Defensive Investing Strategies

> Graham made a distinction between the enterprising investor and the defensive investor. The difference was based on the ability of the investor to put time and effort into the research process.

> For the defensive investor, Graham suggested 7 factors in selecting a common stock. Unlike his Net–Net strategy, there will almost always be a fair number of firms that meet these 7 criteria.

  ○ Adequate Size. Graham viewed adequate size in a target company as more than $100 million in 1971 dollars, or about $600 million today. He viewed traditional, government-regulated utilities as safer than industrial firms, so you could cut the adequate size threshold in half for utilities. Graham reasoned that larger firms are less likely to go out of business; that they probably have resources, scale, and experience to weather any storm.

  ○ Sufficiently Strong Financial Condition. Graham defined this term as current assets at least twice the size of current liabilities. He also thought total liabilities should not be higher than working capital (that is, current assets minus current liabilities).

  ○ Earnings Stability. Graham defined earnings stability as positive earnings for at least 10 consecutive years. This rule eliminates many cyclical firms and those younger than 10 years.

- A Strong Dividend Record. This criterion recommends 20 years or more of uninterrupted dividends. This rule eliminates most growth stocks, since the vast majority don't pay dividends.

- Organic Earnings Growth of at Least 33% over the Past 10 Years. This hurdle is not huge since the United States' Gross Domestic Product (GDP) historically grew at about 3% per year. But it does eliminate businesses that are stagnant or shrinking, even if they pay dividends or generate a lot of cash.

- A Moderate Price-to-Earnings Ratio. Graham defined this term to be the current price of the stock as not more than 15 times its average earnings over the past 3 years. This number makes sense to many investors, since the long-term P/E ratio for U.S. stocks is about 15.

- A Moderate Ratio of Price to Assets. Graham defined a moderate price-to-assets ratio as a firm trading for less than 1.5 times its book value. Book value is also known as accounting net worth. It's equal to all of the firm's assets minus all of its liabilities. This factor of less than 1.5 times book value also rules out most growth stocks since they often trade at a high multiple of Price to Book.

> In his later years, Graham suggested another simple value formula: Create a portfolio that consists of at least 30 stocks with P/E ratios less than 10 and debt-to-equity ratios less than 50%. Hold each stock until it returns 50%. If it doesn't achieve a 50% return after 2 years, sell it no matter what. Graham back-tested this formula and found it to earn about 15% a year over the previous half-century.

Graham's Legacy

> Benjamin Graham made seminal contributions to measuring value, viewing stock as the ownership of a business, and investing with a margin of safety. He made clear the distinction between speculation and investment: "An investment operation is one

which, upon thorough analysis, promises safety of principal and an adequate return. Operations not meeting the requirements are speculative."

> Many of the most successful investors of the 20th and early 21st centuries were hugely influenced by his work.

> Value investing requires analytical rigor, discipline, patience, and willingness to go against the crowd. Graham was able to follow this approach, and his investment firm posted annualized returns of about 20% per year from 1936 to 1956—roughly double that of the market.

Suggested Reading

Graham and Dodd, *Security Analysis.*
Graham and Zweig, *The Intelligent Investor.*

Questions to Consider

1. How would you describe the investment strategy of Benjamin Graham?

2. How would you define value investing?

2

Transcript

Benjamin Graham
and Value Investing

Benjamin Graham is known as the father of value investing, and he pioneered a rigorous, quantitative approach to security analysis. Value investing is the art of trying to buy an asset at a deep discount—like 50 cents on the dollar. As we'll see, his groundbreaking investment strategy had its roots in his own personal hardship.

Graham started investing during the early 1900s. The landscape then was a whole lot different than it is today. For one thing, investing wasn't typically thought of as a respectable profession. It was viewed more like astrology, or a game of chance—run by crooks and people with inside information. And using inside information was legal at the time. Before congress created the Securities and Exchange Commission in 1934—to regulate the financial markets after the Great Depression—it was optional for firms to produce audited financial statements, on a regular basis. It's even been said that Joe Kennedy—John F. Kennedy's father—was appointed as the first chairman of the SEC because he knew many of the tricks the scammers used to stack the deck in their favor.

Many investors at the time traded on rumors or hot tips. Joe Kennedy once said he knew it was time to get out of the market when he received stock tips from a shoe-shine boy. Other investors used an early form of technical analysis, making investment decisions based on stock price and volume changes. Back then, there were no computers. But there were stock ticker machines that produced quotes on thin strips of paper. Maybe you've seen photographs of a ticker tape parade after the World Series. Or perhaps you were a fan of the 1960s TV show *The Addams Family*. Gomez Addams— who played the debonair father in a ghoulish household—was often excited to read the ticker tape coming out of his home stock ticker machine.

Before the days of Bloomberg terminals and Yahoo Finance charts, the ticker tape listed all the information that many investors had with which to make an investment decision. And that was the stock symbol, price, change in price, and volume of shares traded. That's it. Benjamin Graham's contributions to security analysis were almost too numerous to mention, but one of his seminal insights was in viewing stock as the ownership of a business. Back then—and even today—many investors view stock as little more than a vehicle to speculate.

Graham was a successful money manager who taught at Columbia University in New York City, and who—with a fellow faculty member named David Dodd—wrote a book in 1934 called *Security Analysis*, which has since become known on Wall Street as The bible of value investing. At 725 pages, it is almost the size of the Bible. Warren Buffett later called a book by Graham—*The Intelligent Investor*, which was published in 1949—The best book on investing ever written. It is a bit slimmer at 640 pages and a more investor-friendly read.

The point is this, the difference between Graham's strategies and some of the investment techniques used by his peers and predecessors is like the contrast between Babe Ruth and the home run hitters who came before him. In 1920, Babe Ruth hit 54 home runs for the New York Yankees. Before Babe Ruth came onto the scene, the record for home runs in a single season was only half that, 27. In fact, in most years prior to Ruth, the single-season home run leader hit between seven and 12. In this session, we'll provide some background on Ben Graham and his pioneering work on value investing. We'll also discuss examples of his strategy in action. It's not an exaggeration to say that Ben Graham changed the investing landscape forever.

Benjamin Graham was born Benjamin Grossbaum in London, England, in 1894. He moved with his family to New York City when he was one-year-old. His father Isaac ran a successful retail business selling high-end dishes, or chinaware, and figurines. The family led a comfortable life on Fifth Avenue in Manhattan. They were well off enough to afford servants. But that all changed when Graham was nine years old and his father died. The business went downhill quickly. And Graham's mother, Dorothy, also known as Dora, was wiped out trading stocks during the Crash of 1907. The Wall Street Journal columnist Jason Zweig—who produced a revised version of Graham's classic, *The Intelligent Investor*—cites a powerful story that helped shape Graham's character, and ultimately his investment philosophy.

He relates that Graham once cashed a check for his mother at a local bank, and overheard someone say," Is Dorothy Grossbaum good for $5?" The family changed its name from Grossbaum to Graham after World War I, due to the discrimination that was common than against people of German and Jewish descent at the time. Graham was an excellent student and received a scholarship to Columbia University. After graduating second in his class in 1914, at the age of 20, he turned down a teaching position at the university since he felt the need to earn more money in order to help support his family.

Graham began his Wall Street career with the firm of Newburger, Henderson, and Loeb. He quickly rose through the ranks and made partner at the age of 26. He left Newburger in 1923 to set up his own partnership, which he ran by himself at first, and later with business partner Jerome Newman. The investment vehicles related to this business agreement became known as the Graham-Newman Partnerships. In 1928, he finally returned to Columbia to teach. And his 1934 book, *Security Analysis*, was created in large part from the lecture notes of his class.

One of Graham's principles was that if you had the money, and weren't willing to buy a company then you shouldn't be willing to buy a share of its stock, either. As he put it, "Every corporate security may be best viewed in the first instance as an ownership in, or a claim against, a specific business enterprise." With that in mind, you would certainly be interested in the firm's financials. Graham focused on the balance sheet, which lists assets on the left hand side and liabilities and net worth on the right. You'd probably also want to buy a business that had stood the test of time, at least in those days. For example, you might want to make sure the company had survived a couple of recessions. Or, as Warren Buffett said, "You only find out who is swimming naked when the tide goes out." You probably would also like to buy a business at a discount to what you thought it was worth, just in case something went wrong, or if you miscalculated its value.

Graham summarized these ideas into the concept margin of safety. He phrased it this way, "To have a true investment, there must be present a true margin of safety. And a true margin of safety is one that can be demonstrated by figures, by persuasive reasoning, and by reference to a body of actual experience." It's not a mystery why Graham had such a strong focus on margin of safety. Like many people of his generation, he was scarred by his family's loss of wealth, and by his own financial setbacks during the Great Depression. Between 1929 and 1932, his partnerships lost 70%. Graham focused on quantitative measures of value. He first looked at the value of existing assets—things like cash, inventory, and property. He did so by examining a target company's financial statements, and also other resources around at the time, such as the Moody's Manual. *Moody's Manual of Industrial and Miscellaneous Securities* combined research and data on a bunch of firms, especially railroads. It had a fanatical following. Warren Buffett once said, "People who want to relive their youth buy old Playboys. I buy old Moody's."

Next, Graham looked at current earnings. Lastly, and only in rare circumstances, he considered future profits. And only in the core competence area of a firm with a sustainable competitive advantage. Graham was aware of growth stocks, but he thought they were too risky since they might blow up. For example, a lot of Internet stocks like Webvan and CMGI went bankrupt or lost most of their value after the bubble popped. Back in Graham's day, many early-stage car and computer companies also went bust, despite the overall tremendous growth in their industries. Graham thought that the odds of finding the next blockbuster stock—like an Apple, Google, or Microsoft, in our time—was about as likely as winning the lottery. He said, "Of course, wonders can be accomplished with the right individual selections. But the average investor can no more accomplish this than to find money growing on trees."

The concept of mean reversion is a major underpinning of the value-investing philosophy. What do we mean by the phrase mean reversion in the context of stocks? It says past winners often become future losers, while past losers often become future winners. Graham himself said, "Over the long-run performance of both companies and share prices generally revert to the mean." What causes this 180-degree change? In a word, competition.

If you are at a firm that's on top, everyone is gunning for you, trying to take a piece of your market share and profits. These top firms are often trading at high valuations, so when things go wrong the stock has far to fall. On the other hand, if things are going poorly at a firm, it might have less competition, and you can often fix the problems. Investors probably don't expect much from these stocks. They've probably already been beaten down, so if things turn around there may be a lot of upsides.

Former General Electric CEO Jack Welch—a legend in Corporate America—put it this way. "GE will be #1 or #2 in every industry it competes in. Otherwise, we will try to fix it. If we can't fix it, we'll get out." So, some underperforming businesses can be fixed, while others can be exited, removing the drag on performance. Graham was also early to recognize the role of market psychology in investing. Maybe you have chased a stock that had great past performance, or sold stocks near a market bottom. If so, psychology has probably gotten the best of you. Graham put it this way, "The investor's chief problem – even his worst enemy – is likely to be himself."

Today, the field of investor psychology is known by academics and practitioners as behavioral finance. Some Nobel Prizes have been awarded to researchers in this field. Value investments often occur due to market psychology, with fear and greed moving prices away from their long run or equilibrium prices. Graham devised a widely cited analogy to explain market mood swings. He postulated a schizophrenic business partner that he called MR. Market. Each day, Mr. Market offered what he was willing to pay for your share of the business, or at what price he would sell you additional shares. Sometimes Mr. Market was in a bad mood, and the price was far too low. At other times, he would be euphoric and offer a very high price. Occasionally, the price was in line with your estimate of the value of the business. Graham said you should forget trying to change Mr. Market's mood and forget figuring out what drives him. Just recognize that he is schizophrenic, and try to buy low and sell high. The same strategy should apply to your investments.

If you don't like that analogy of market behavior, Graham had another one that is also widely cited. He said,

> The market is a pendulum that forever swings between unsustainable optimism which makes stocks too expensive and unjustified pessimism which makes them too cheap. The Intelligent Investor is a realist who sells to optimists and buys from pessimists.

So, according to Graham, stock prices deviate from their long-run fundamentals values due to too much optimism or pessimism. Intelligent investors must have the temperament to buy when sentiment is bad, and sell when sentiment is good.

It sounds good in theory. In practice, many investors don't have the stomach to do this, since it involves going against the crowd. Graham used a number of value-oriented strategies to pick investments. One of his favorites was to find companies selling for less than their cash liquidation value. He called this deep value strategy net-net. Graham's net-net calculation started with the cash and cash equivalent item on a firm's balance sheet, and then added a conservative portion—let's say 75%—of accounts receivable and inventory. Then he subtracted all liabilities.

He then compared this aggregate amount of cash and hard assets—let's say $100 million for example—to the stock market value of the firm. If the company was selling in the stock market for less than $100 million, Graham would consider it a bargain under his net-net deep value approach. He estimated that his net-net strategy provided his partnerships with returns of about 20% a year, double the market's historical return. There were a lot of net-nets around during the Great Depression. But, over time, it became much harder to find companies trading for less than their net cash on hand.

Occasionally, these firms exist even in today's market. But they tend to be money-losing companies with questionable long-term prospects.

The first investment that put Graham on the map was known as the Northern Pipeline Affair. It was a net-net type of investment. It was also an early example of activist investing, a strategy later made famous by Corporate Raiders such as Carl Icahn and Bill Ackman. In 1911, the U.S. Supreme Court ordered the breakup of John D. Rockefeller's Standard Oil under a federal antitrust lawsuit brought by the Justice Department. As a result, Rockefeller's industrial empire was split into 34 separate companies.

Northern Pipeline Company was one of Standard Oil's 34 sister companies. Its business involved transporting crude oil to a Standard Oil refineries. After the Supreme Court decision, Graham combed through the forms that energy firms filed with the Interstate Commerce Commission. Obviously, this sort of analysis requires a lot more work than following a hot tip or looking at a stock ticker tape. He found that Northern Pipeline had $95 a share in railroad bonds and other liquid assets. Yet the stock was trading for only $65 a share—and it also paid a hefty 9% annual dividend yield. Back then, it wasn't uncommon for stocks to pay dividend yields higher than bond yields. Conventional wisdom, up to the 1950s, was that stocks are paid after bonds and are riskier. Therefore, they should pay higher yields.

In 1926, Graham's partnership acquired roughly a 5% stake in Northern Pipeline. And he asked the company to distribute more cash to shareholders. Northern Pipeline's management wasn't pleased at being told what to do by Graham, and actively avoided his requests. In 1928, after contacting other shareholders and requesting their help, Graham put together proxies, or voting power, equal to 38% of Northern Pipeline's shares, and was able to get himself appointed to the firm's board of directors. Over time he persuaded the company to pay out $70 a share in special or extra dividends. Coming in the midst of the Great Depression, it was a very attractive return for Graham and his partners.

Geico, the car insurance company with the funny TV commercials, was Benjamin Graham's most famous investment. In case you wind up on the Jeopardy game show someday, Geico stands for Government

Employees Insurance Company. Geico wasn't a net-net investment, but it had unique value, like its superior business model of selling car insurance. Graham purchased almost half of the company in 1948 for his investment partnerships, at a 10% discount to its book value. Graham usually diversified widely, but in this instance, he put almost a quarter of his partnerships' assets into this single investment. He felt very good about it, even though he tried to negotiate some provisions that would provide him with an out—without suffering a large loss—if things went bad.

Geico rode the wave of the post-World War II American automobile industry. Among its advantages was its clever business model of selling directly through the mail, at discount prices. Drivers benefited from lower car insurance prices, while Geico benefited from its lean infrastructure, avoiding the need to build a costly network of offices and salespeople. The Graham-Newman Partnership's original $720,000 investment in 1948 would have been worth more than $500 million 25 years later. But Graham distributed the stock to his partners over time. Later, Warren Buffett bought all of Geico for his holding company, Berkshire Hathaway.

Graham made a distinction between the enterprising investor and the defensive investor. The difference wasn't based on risk tolerance, but rather on the ability of the investor to put time and effort into the research process. His strategies for the enterprising investor required a lot more time and research. Like his investment in Northern Pipeline, where he combed through a bunch of regulatory fillings and waged a proxy battle against the firm. His strategies for the defensive investor were more passive in nature and involved buying larger, high-quality stocks at a discount, and then holding them for the long-term until they reached fair value. Over time, Graham became known more for his defensive strategies.

For the defensive investor, Graham suggested seven factors in the selection of common stock. And unlike his net-net strategy, there will almost always be a fair amount of firms that meet these seven criteria. So you could call it an evergreen strategy. And because so many people followed Graham's original strategy of buying deeply undervalued companies, alternative value strategies became necessary. The market always trends toward becoming more efficient, sweeping away the easy money opportunities.

Here are the seven criteria. Number one is adequate size. Graham viewed adequate size in a target company as $100 million+ in sales in 1971 dollars, or about $600 million in sales today. That said, he viewed traditional, government regulated utilities as safer than industrial firms, so you could cut the adequate size threshold in half for utilities. Graham reasoned that larger firms are less likely to go out of business. They probably have resources, scale, and experience to weather any storm.

Number two is sufficiently strong financial condition. Graham defined sufficiently strong financial condition as current assets at least twice the size of current liabilities. He also thought that total liabilities should not be higher than working capital or current assets minus current liabilities. This factor seems obvious, but it would screen out a firm like Lehman Brothers. Lehman Brothers got its start in 1860, before the American Civil War. It survived the Great Depression, the Crash of 1987 and countless other financial panics. But it went bankrupt in 2008 during the financial markets crisis because other big banks cut off its credit, and its liquidity evaporated.

Number three is earnings stability. Graham defined earnings stability as positive earnings for at least 10 consecutive years. This rule eliminates many cyclical firms, and—by definition—firms that haven't been around for 10 years or more.

Number four is a strong dividend record—and preferably 20 years or more uninterrupted dividends. This rule eliminates most growth stocks since the vast majority of them don't pay dividends.

Number five is organic earnings growth of at least 33% over the past 10 years. This is not a huge hurdle since U.S. GDP historically grew at about 3% a year. But it does eliminate businesses that are stagnant or shrinking, even if they pay dividends or generate a lot of cash.

Number six is a moderate price-to-earnings ratio. Graham defined this by saying the current price of the stock should not be more than 15 times its average earnings over the past three years. This number makes sense to many investors since the long-term P/E ratio for U.S. stocks is about 15.

And finally, number seven, a moderate ratio of price to assets. Graham defined a moderate price-to-assets ratio as a firm trading for less than 1.5 times its book value. Book value is also known as accounting net worth. It's equal to all of the firm's assets minus all of its liabilities. The factor of less than 1.5 times book value also rules out most growth stocks since they often trade at high multiples of price to book.

So, Graham's evergreen strategy for value stocks can be summarized as adequate size, strong financial condition, earnings stability, a strong dividend record, earnings growth of at least 33% over the past 10 years, a moderate P/E ratio, and moderate price to assets. In his later years, Graham suggested another simple value formula. He suggested creating a portfolio of at least 30 stocks with P/E ratios below 10, and debt-to-equity ratios under 50%. Hold each stock until it returns 50%. And if it doesn't achieve a 50% return, sell it after two years no matter what. Graham back-tested this formula and found it to earn about 15% a year over the previous half century. A more recent study encompassing the 1976 to 2011 period found that the strategy held up, returning almost 18% a year, including capital gains and dividends, against an 11% total return for the Standard & Poor's 500 index.

I think value investing works because of the combination of market competition and investor psychology. Competition results in top firms falling back down to earth, and with underperforming firms fixing themselves. Basically, mean reversion. The psychology aspect is the hardest part to stick to. If money managers buy the leading firms of the day—say Apple, Starbucks, and the like—it's hard to get fired, at least when the going is good. The Wall Street expression, is "You can shake hands on the way down." Another one is that "It's warm in the herd." In contrast, if value managers stick their necks out and buy a stock with problems—and they blow up—the manager looks really stupid, and is more likely to get fired. And that is why I think the advantages of value investing will endure.

So, to wrap this up, Benjamin Graham made seminal contributions to measuring value, viewing stocks as the ownership of a business, and investing with a margin of safety. He made clear the distinction between speculation and investment. He defined it this way, "An investment operation is one which, upon thorough analysis, promises safety of principal and an adequate return. Operations not meeting the requirements are speculative." Many of the most successful investors of the 20th and early 21st centuries were hugely influenced by his work, including Warren Buffett and Charlie Munger and other legends such as John Templeton, Peter Lynch, Mario Gabelli, Charles Brandes, and Joel Greenblatt.

In 1937, Graham became one of the founders of The New York Society of Security Analysts. It's the largest group of security analysts in the world and did a lot to make security analysis a respected profession. The New York— and other societies like it—created what we know of today as The CFA Institute, which administers the Chartered Financial Analyst, or CFA, program. Having a CFA Charter is viewed as the gold standard credential for anyone who wants to become an investment analyst or money manager. I have a CFA and view it as one of my most important professional accomplishments.

So, as we've seen, value investing requires analytical rigor, discipline, patience and a willingness to go against the crowd. This approach is easier said than done. Many investors are unwilling to put up their money when it seems like the sky is falling. But Graham was able to follow this approach. And his investment firm posted annualized returns of about 20% a year from 1936–1956—roughly double the market's.

3

Warren Buffett:
Investing Forever

Warren Buffett had success written all over him at a young age, but his investment strategy began to take shape only after he met the value investor Benjamin Graham. Buffett initially embraced Graham's strict value investing strategy by looking at companies in a quantitative manner and trying to buy companies for the equivalent of 50 cents on the dollar. Buffett's contribution to the concept of value investing was to find high-quality companies selling at a discount and to let the moat around these companies protect his investment, enabling him to hold them for his favorite holding period—forever.

The Birth of Berkshire Hathaway

> Warren Buffett always ranks near the top of *Forbes*'s list of the richest people in the world, and virtually all of his net worth has been generated by investing. As the CEO of Berkshire Hathaway, his investment holding company, Buffett typically is paid $100,000 a year; unlike many hedge fund managers, Buffett doesn't skim off a large percentage of the investment profits he generates.

> Buffett had a nose for making money even as a young child growing up in Omaha. While still in elementary school, he sold

packs of Wrigley's gum and cans of Coca-Cola, both future investments for him. He bought his first stock at the age of 11 and filed his first tax return at the age of 13.

> After finishing his undergraduate degree at the University of Nebraska, he applied to Harvard and was rejected. It turned out to be a blessing in disguise, because he was accepted at Columbia and studied under the man who would change his investing life, the pioneer of value investing Benjamin Graham.

> When Graham decided to wind down his investment business, which Buffett had joined in 1954, Buffett set up his own investment business through a series of partnerships that were, in essence, hedge funds. In 1969, Buffett decided the stock market was overvalued and shut down the investment partnerships. He recommended 3 options to his partners at the time.

   ○ Take the cash from the liquidated partnerships.

   ○ Invest with his friend, the value investor Bill Ruane, of the Sequoia Fund.

   ○ Take shares in a company he controlled—Berkshire Hathaway.

> Buffett acquired Berkshire shares in 1962, when it was a struggling textile maker. The textile business never turned around, but Buffett used the cash flow to acquire other businesses. One of Berkshire's investing hallmarks was insurance, which historically accounts for the bulk of its profits.

   ○ An insurer has the use of every insurance premium for a period of time—from a day to months to forever—before it has to pay a claim on someone's behalf. This time-value of money, called the "float," is a boon to an investor like Buffett, who can put it to good use.

The Moat as a Competitive Advantage

> Eventually, Buffett moved away from Graham's strict approach. He continued buying companies at a discount, but his focus shifted to high-quality companies, especially those with a durable competitive advantage—what Buffett called a moat—a buffer around a company's core business that makes attack difficult for the competition. Two popular approaches to analyzing a company's moat are Porter's 5 Forces and Morningstar's Economic Moat Framework.

> Michael Porter is a Harvard Business School economist who in the 1980s developed a framework to help explain the impact of industry structure on performance, generally referred to as Porter's 5 Forces.

  o The threat of new entrants. Certain businesses require massive capital to get started. The Boeing and Airbus commercial-aircraft manufacturing business is a case in point. The harder it is for a new firm to enter a market, the greater the competitive advantage of the firms already in that market.

  o The threat of substitute products or services. Although some products have no substitute, most industries offer a variety of substitutes: Coke vs. Pepsi. The fewer substitute products or services, the greater the competitive advantage.

  o The bargaining power of customers. The Internet has given customers great power. Best Buy went from being a dominant company to one struggling to survive because customers could search for better prices on Amazon.com and other websites.

  o The bargaining power of suppliers. The less a firm is impacted by its suppliers, the greater its competitive advantage. The De Beers cartel of South Africa controls about 35% of the diamonds produced in the world. De Beers has extraordinary bargaining power when dealing with jewelry merchants. Conversely, clothes can be manufactured fairly cheaply in many places around the world, so companies like Nike have a lot of power in their supplier relationships.

- The intensity of competitive rivalry. Firms in the airline industry, such as U.S. Airways, went bankrupt because of intense competition. Conversely, the less intense the rivalry, the greater the competitive advantage.

> Morningstar, a firm known for its research on mutual funds, created a framework for its research rating based to a large extent on a company's moat. Like Porter, Morningstar identified 5 factors.

- The first factor is the network effect. Why do people shop at eBay? Because millions of items are for sale. Why do people join Facebook? Because nearly all of their friends are on it. Why do people shop at Amazon.com? For the huge selection as well as the millions of reviews. Morningstar believes a network effect occurs when the value of a company's service increases, as more people use the service.

- The second factor is intangible assets. A patent is an intangible asset that provides legal protection lasting up to 20 years. A brand name is an invaluable asset that can be hard to quantify, but easy to see in action.

- The third factor is cost advantage. The concept of a cost advantage can easily apply to many industries. For example, stories abound of Wal-Mart and Home Depot driving their smaller competitors out of business because they couldn't match the larger firms' low prices. Having a cost advantage also gives these companies the opportunity to raise prices without worrying about losing the bulk of their customers.

- The fourth factor is switching cost. Imagine if you had a new alarm system installed in your house. It would be expensive to switch it for a new system, even if the new system had lower monthly fees. The same concept applies to other products.

○ The fifth factor is efficient scale. Efficient scale relates to a niche market served by a small number of companies—in some cases, only one. For example, building a hospital is a massive undertaking, so there is likely to be only one in each town or county.

> Buffett came to believe that a better approach to value investing would be to buy high-quality companies with a moat around their businesses. His 1963 investment in American Express was perhaps his first major purchase in sync with this philosophy.

○ The story begins with salad oil. Though American Express is known today for its financial products, the firm has operated in a number of finance-related businesses. One was warehousing: Amex would lend money against the inventory of a company's goods, stored in a warehouse that Amex's employees could inspect.

○ Allied Crude Vegetable Oil Refining Corporation borrowed money against its inventory of salad oil. But the company committed fraud, filling huge barrels with water and sprinkling salad oil on top. Eventually, the fraud was uncovered, with the result that Allied Crude filed for bankruptcy.

○ Amex was on the hook for $150 million, or about $1.5 billion in 2015 dollars. In the wake of the salad oil scandal, Amex's stock fell 50%. Buffett thought this was a bad but temporary misstep and that the core business was intact and the damage to Amex's brand name would eventually be repaired.

○ Buffett bought 5% of American Express, 40% of his partnership's assets at the time. The result was that Buffett sold his partnership's shares in Amex about 5 years later at more than 5 times the profit. Berkshire has long since staked a new position in American Express and added to it over 25 years.

Boldness in a Crisis

> The epicenter of the financial markets crisis was the housing industry and the subprime mortgages lent to people with poor credit ratings. Bank risk managers reasoned that if the borrower couldn't pay the mortgage, they could simply take the house as collateral. They believed the house would rise in value so they wouldn't lose on a diversified portfolio of these loans. When consumers defaulted on their loans and real estate prices crashed, excessive leverage (debt-to-equity ratio) on the part of both consumers and banks led to financial disaster.

> Purchasing a house with a 20% down payment results in leverage of 5 to 1; many banks were leveraged at a ratio of 30 to 1 or more. The investment bank Bear Stearns was one of the first casualties of the housing and financial markets crisis. It was sold to JP Morgan for $2 a share. Lehman Brothers, an investment bank that had been around since 1860, declared the biggest bankruptcy ever.

> In this financial environment in September 2008, Buffett had the confidence to invest in Goldman Sachs and General Electric Capital Corporation. Buffett invested $5 billion in Goldman and $3 billion in GE convertible preferred stock with a 10% dividend. By March 2011, Buffett earned $3.7 billion in realized and unrealized profit on Goldman Sachs. By September 2011, he made at least $1.2 billion from his GE investment.

Some Losing Investments

> But even The Oracle of Omaha can make blunders. Buffett often refers to Berkshire's purchase of Dexter Shoe Company as one of his worst investments ever. In 1993, Berkshire paid $433 million for the Maine-based shoe company. Buffett's biggest mistake wasn't that Dexter's shoe business deteriorated rapidly. It was that he paid for the deal in Berkshire stock, which has risen exponentially since the purchase. He has rarely used Berkshire stock in future acquisitions and had a successful investment in the dominant casual shoe company, Nike.

> His investment in IBM was also criticized by some investors, who viewed IBM as a dinosaur in a technology world dominated by Google, Apple, Microsoft, Amazon, and the like. Buffett first started buying IBM in the first quarter of 2011. He invested more than $13 billion at a cost basis of $170 a share. Recently, IBM was trading at roughly $160 a share, resulting in a paper loss of more than $750 million.

> In the end, the numbers speak for themselves. In the 50 years after Buffett took over Berkshire in 1965, the S&P 500 was up

11,355%. In contrast, over the same period, Berkshire's stock was up an amazing 1,600,000%.

Suggested Reading

Lowenstein, *Buffett*.
Schroeder, *The Snowball*.

Questions to Consider

1. How would you describe the investment strategy of Warren Buffett?

2. What does Warren Buffett mean when he talks about a company having a "moat" around its business?

3

Transcript

Warren Buffett: Investing Forever

Warren Buffett is always ranked near the top of Forbes's list of the richest people in the world, and virtually all of his net worth has been generated by investing. What kind of personal wealth are we talking about? Well, tens of billions of dollars—give or take a dime or a dollar. As the CEO of Berkshire Hathaway—his investment holding company—Buffett is typically paid only $100,000 a year. And, unlike many hedge fund managers, Buffett doesn't skim off a large percentage of the investment profits he generates.

So how did he do it? Two words, value investing. And we'll come back to that in a moment. Buffett always had a nose for making money, even as a young child growing up in Omaha, Nebraska. While still in elementary school, he sold packs of Wrigley's gum and cans of Coca-Cola—both future investments for him. He bought his first stock at the age of 11. And Buffett filed his first tax return at the age of 13.

His father was a congressman, and Warren moved to Washington, D.C., during World War II. He got a paper route there delivering *The Washington Post* another future stock investment. At 14, he used the profits to buy farmland in Nebraska. As a teenager, he and a friend also bought pinball machines and put them in barbershops, splitting the profits with the shop owners. Buffett went to the Wharton School at the University of Pennsylvania, but got homesick and returned to the University of Nebraska to finish his undergraduate degree. He applied to Harvard for graduate school—and was rejected. It turned out to be a blessing in disguise, because he was accepted at Columbia University in New York City and studied under the man who would change his investing life, the pioneer of value investing, Benjamin Graham.

Buffett, although he had invested in the stock market since he was 11, had felt he was spinning his wheels with a variety of techniques until he came across Benjamin Graham's approach, which viewed stock as ownership in a business, and which sought to buy stocks at a discount from the underlying asset's intrinsic value. After Columbia, Buffett returned to Omaha and worked at his father's brokerage firm. He also kept in touch with Ben Graham and ended up joining his mentor in 1954. A couple of years later, Graham decided to wind down his investment business and so Buffett went home to Omaha, this time for good, to set up his own investment business. He did so through a series of partnerships that he managed, which were, in essence, hedge funds.

In 1969, however—before he was even 40 years old—Buffett decided the stock market was overvalued and shut down the investment partnerships. He recommended three options to his partners at the time. First, take the cash from the liquidated partnerships. Second, invest with his friend, the value investor Bill Ruane of the Sequoia Fund. Or third, take shares in a not very big company he controlled called Berkshire Hathaway. Berkshire, of course, would become one of the world's largest conglomerates. It would come to own Geico Insurance, Duracell, Dairy Queen, NetJets, and dozens of other businesses. Berkshire also amassed huge amounts of stock in Coca-Cola, Wells Fargo, Wal-Mart, Bank of America, Kraft, Heinz, American Express, and many others.

Buffett originally acquired Berkshire shares in 1962 under the framework of a typical Graham and Dodd type investment. I mentioned Benjamin Graham, but by Dodd, I am referring to David Dodd, a colleague of Graham's at Columbia. The two wrote the classic book, *Security Analysis*, known on Wall Street as the bible of value investing. Graham and Dodd focused on finding investments selling at a discount to the market, and which also generated positive cash flow. At the time, Berkshire was a struggling textile maker. The textile business never turned around, but Buffett used the cash flow to acquire other businesses. These new acquisitions snowballed into others. One of its investing hallmarks was insurance, which historically accounts for the bulk of Berkshire's profits. Think about your car insurance payment, which you mail in and never see again. The term float means an insurer has the use of your insurance premium for a period of time—from a day to months to forever—before it has to pay a claim on your behalf. The time-value of money is a boon to an investor like Buffett, who can put it to good use. Buffett likened Graham's value investing approach to a cigar butt—with at least a few puffs left in it.

Eventually, Buffett moved away from Ben Graham's strict approach to value investing to incorporate the strategies of the growth investor Philip Fisher, and Buffett's future business partner, Charlie Munger, who liked investing in high-quality companies for the long-term. He stayed true to Graham's approach of buying companies at a discount, but now his focus shifted to buying high-quality companies. Especially those companies with a durable competitive advantage—or what Buffett called a moat. A moat is just what it sounds like. It's a buffer around a company's core business that makes it very difficult for the competition to attack. Did you ever wonder why certain industries have a small number of competitors while others have hundreds of thousands? For example, there are two main commercial aircraft manufacturers in the world, Boeing, and Airbus. Want to create your own commercial jet company? Good luck; the odds of succeeding are slim Yet, there are more than 600,000 restaurants in America.

There are two popular approaches for determining if a company has a wide moat—Porter's 5 Forces and Morningstar's Economic Moat Framework. Michael Porter is a Harvard Business School economist who in the 1980s developed a framework to help explain the impact of industry structure on performance. Today, it's generally referred to as Porter's Five Forces. The first of Porter's Five Forces is the threat of new entrants. Certain businesses require a ton of capital to get started. The Boeing and Airbus commercial aircraft manufacturing business is a case in point. Automobile manufacturing is another example. The idea behind the force Porter called the Threat of New Entrants is this—the harder it is for a new firm to enter a certain market, the greater the competitive advantage of the firms already in that market.

The second of the forces is the threat of substitute products or services. Some products, say a patented drug, have no substitute. Most industries, however, have a variety of substitutes. Coke vs. Pepsi, Ford vs GM, Coffee vs. Tea, and the list goes on. The fewer substitute products or services, the greater the competitive advantage.

Porter's third force is the bargaining power of customers or buyers. The Internet has given customers great power. Best Buy went from being a dominant company to one struggling to survive due to customers searching for better prices on Amazon.com and other websites. When you're buying a product that many customers consider to be generic or replaceable, like a standard TV or a washing machine, price competition tends to be fierce, and you can often search around for a great deal. In other words, your bargaining power is very high. Conversely, if you want the latest smartphone or hot concert ticket, you will probably have to pay up. The weaker the bargaining power of customers, the greater the competitive advantage.

The fourth force Porter talks about is the bargaining power of suppliers. A great example of this is the De Beers cartel of South Africa, which amazingly controls about 35% of the diamonds produced in the world. De Beers has extraordinary bargaining power when dealing with jewelry merchants. Another example is OPEC. During its heydays in the 1970s and 1980s, when it controlled a huge chunk of the world's oil supply, giving the group great power. Conversely, clothes can be manufactured fairly cheaply at many places around the world, so companies like Nike have a lot of power in their supplier relationships. The bottom line is that the less a firm is impacted by its suppliers, the greater its competitive advantage.

Porter's fifth and final force is intensity of competitive rivalry. Firms in the airline industry, such as U.S. Airways, went bankrupt, often more than once, due to intense competition. The cell phone industry is very competitive, with smaller firms attacking the larger incumbents. Conversely, the less intense the rivalry, the greater the competitive advantage.

So Porter's Five Forces again are threat of new entrants, threat of new products or services, bargaining power of customers, bargaining power of suppliers, and intensity of competitive rivalry. Analyzing these forces can be invaluable in helping us to uncover the size of a company's moat. But Morningstar, a firm known for its research on mutual funds, went one better. Morningstar created a framework for its research rating to be based to a large extent on a company's moat. Like Porter, Morningstar identifies five forces, or what they call factors, that provide a company with a moat. Morningstar calls its first factor the network effect. Why do people shop at eBay? Because there are tons of items for sale. Why do people join Facebook? Because nearly all of their friends are on it. Why do people shop at Amazon.com? For the huge selection as well as the millions of reviews. Morningstar believes a network effect occurs when the value of a company's service increases, as more people use the service.

Morningstar's second moat-creating factor is intangible assets. Clearly, a patent is an intangible asset that provides legal protection lasting up to 20 years. A brand name is also an invaluable asset that can be hard to quantify, but easy to see in action. Putting the words Disney or Apple on a product is almost a license to print money.

Morningstar's third factor is cost advantage. The concept of cost advantage can easily apply to many other industries as well. For example, there are many stories of Wal-Mart and Home Depot driving their smaller competitors out of business because they couldn't match the larger firms' low prices. Having a cost advantage not only drives competitors out of business, but it also gives these companies the opportunity to raise prices without worrying about losing the bulk of its customers.

The fourth factor Morningstar identifies is switching costs. Imagine if you had a new alarm system installed in your house. It would probably be pretty expensive to rip it out and install a new system, even if the new system had lower monthly fees. Or consider the QWERTY keyboard system. It would take you quite a bit of time to learn another typing interface. The same concept applies to the products of many firms. For example, it might be a challenge to maintain your same level of productivity if you switched from

Microsoft software to another productivity suite, even if the other software were objectively better.

Morningstar's fifth factor is efficient scale. Efficient scale relates to a niche market served by a small amount of companies. In some cases, only one company. For example, most small to mid-size cities can support only one airport. The airport owner, in this case, would benefit from the efficient scale. The same logic applies to a hospital. Building a hospital is a massive undertaking, so there is likely only one in each town or small county.

So, Buffett came to believe that a better approach to value investing would be to buy—at a discount—high-quality companies with a moat around their businesses. Let's look at a few examples where he put this idea into action with incredible results. His 1963 investment in American Express is, perhaps, his first major purchase in synch with this philosophy. The story begins with an everyday food item—salad oil. American Express may be known today for its credit cards and travelers' checks but the firm has also operated in a number of other financial related businesses. One was called warehousing, where they would lend money against the inventory of a company's goods. These goods would be located in a warehouse that AMEX's employees could inspect.

So a company called Allied Crude Vegetable Oil Refining Corporation borrowed money against its inventory of salad oil. The main problem was that the company committed fraud, filling huge barrels with water and salad oil sprinkled on top. Eventually, someone blew the whistle and the fraud was uncovered, with the result that Allied Crude filed for bankruptcy. At the time, AMEX was on the hook for a good portion of the firm's borrowings— to the tune of $150 million, or about $1.5 billion in today's dollars. In the wake of the salad oil scandal, AMEX's stock fell 50%. Buffett thought this was a bad but temporary misstep by AMEX, and that its core business was still intact. It still had a moat around its traveler's check and charge card business and he felt the damage to its brand would eventually be repaired. Buffett bought 5% of American Express, a huge 40% of his partnership's assets at the time. The end result? Buffett sold his partnership's shares in AMEX about five years later at a more than five-fold profit. Buffet has long since staked a new position in American Express, and added to it over a quarter-century period, bringing to mind one of Buffett's most famous quotes, "My favorite holding period is forever".

Warren Buffett's purchase of Coca-Cola provides another telling example of his value plus moat strategy in action. He began buying Coke for Berkshire Hathaway in 1988. At the time, Coke was trading at a P/E of about 15, not outrageously cheap, but well below its historical average of 20 plus. P/E measures a stock's value by taking its price per share and dividing it by earnings per share. The lower the number, the cheaper the stock. Coke was selling at depressed levels for several reasons. First was the market crash of 1987 when the Dow Jones Industrial Average fell more than 22% in a single day. Second, Coke had made several missteps. Perhaps their most famous blunder was the new Coke debacle a few years earlier, which had customers clamoring for the taste of Coke's original classic formula.

In addition, Coke had purchased Columbia pictures, a business well outside its core competence. It ultimately sold Columbia to Sony at a profit but received sharp criticism for the box office bomb—you've probably forgotten it, by now—"Ishtar." Ishtar lost $40 million in 1987, a huge sum at the time.

Enter Warren Buffett. He correctly reasoned that any damage to the Coke brand was temporary and that its moat was still very wide. Buffett realized Coke's greatest asset is perhaps its marketing and distribution network, making it difficult for competitors to mount any real challenge, even if they had a better product. Buffett once famously remarked, "If you gave me $100 billion and said, 'Take away the soft-drink leadership of Coca-Cola in the world,' I'd give it back to you and say it can't be done".

The gross margins on Coke's products were huge—up to 80%—basically giving it a license to print money and generate a ton of free cash flow. Coke was also a play on the emerging markets consumer. Consumption tends to increase throughout the world as GDP and personal income increase. Buffett's original $1.2 billion investment in Coke, with additional occasional purchases, came to be valued in the neighborhood of $16 billion—plus billions more in dividends received.

Not everyone has the temperament to buy assets with problems when things look bleak. Were you dying to buy financial stocks during the financial markets crisis of 2008-2009? Probably not. Well, Warren Buffett was. He invested in Goldman Sachs, General Electric, and later, Bank of America. And as you might guess, he made a bundle. Buffett put one of his most famous maxims to work during the crisis. Namely, "Be fearful when others are greedy and greedy when others are fearful."

But first, a little context on what led us to the financial markets crisis. The epicenter was the housing industry, and subprime mortgage's lent to people with poor credit ratings. Perhaps the most famous type of subprime mortgage was the so-called ninja loans. No Income, No Job, No Assets? NO problem. Others call these liar loans since the borrower didn't have to verify the income or assets they put on the mortgage application. Bank risk managers believed that if the person can't pay the mortgage, we'll simply take the house as collateral. The house probably went up in value so we won't lose on a diversified portfolio of these loans.

Interest rates were low in the mid-2000s, and mortgage related products with subprime mortgages had higher yields than conventional prime, which were given to people with good credit ratings. If investors want something—in this case, higher-yielding investments—Wall Street bankers will give it to them. Wall Street has an expression, "When the duck is quacking, feed it."

Of course, we know the end of the story. Consumers defaulted on their loans and real estate prices crashed. Excessive leverage, on the part of both consumers and banks, led to financial disaster. Now, if you purchase a house with a 20% down payment this results in leverage of 5 to 1. But many banks were levered a ratio of 30 to 1 or more. Suppose you put $10,000 down on an apartment that costs $100,000. The bank has lent you $90,000, so the leverage, or debt to equity ratio, on this single home is 9 to 1. Suppose the house drops 10% in value to $90,000. Well, the $10,000 cushion the bank had protecting itself from a bad loan has now disappeared. The investment bank Bear Stearns was one of the first casualties of the housing crisis and financial tailspin from 2007–2009. It ended up being sold to J.P. Morgan for $2 a share. And Lehman Brothers, an investment bank that had been around since 1860, ended up declaring the biggest bankruptcy ever. Merrill Lynch might have gone bankrupt if it hadn't been bought by Bank of America. And AIG, one of the world's largest insurers, needed a bailout by the U.S. government. Likewise for the bank holding company Citigroup.

It was in this financial environment in September 2008 that Warren Buffett had the confidence to invest in Goldman Sachs and General Electric. Many people don't know that for many years GE received the bulk of its profits from its financial services arm, GE Capital. Buffett invested $5 billion in Goldman and $3 billion in GE convertible preferred stock with a 10% dividend. Preferred stock is a hybrid investment that has characteristics of a stock and a bond. So as long the firms didn't go bankrupt, and Buffett's multi-billion investment bought the firms time, he would get a very attractive 10% dividend each year. And if the stocks recovered, he would get to convert his preferred stock to common stock at the September 2008 price when he made the investment, resulting in an even bigger windfall. The end result? You guessed it. By March of 2011, Buffett earned a $3.7 billion realized and unrealized profit on Goldman Sachs. And by September 2011 he made at least $1.2 billion from his GE investment.

A few years later, Buffett made a similar investment in Bank of America, which was having problems recovering from the financial markets crisis. He invested $5 billion in Bank of America convertible preferred stock paying a 6% dividend, with the option to convert them into 700 million shares of common stock at any point within the next 10 years. The end result? Just 4 years later he turned in a $8.4 billion profit, in both realized dividends and unrealized capital gains. Buffett claims he came up with the idea to invest in Bank of America while he was in the bathtub. If that's true, it might have been the most profitable bath in history.

It's hard to think of a business that will be around longer than selling ketchup. Well, maybe funeral homes and tax services. You know the old saying on death and taxes. In 2013, Buffett partnered with the Brazilian private equity firm 3G Capital to buy Heinz for $28 billion. You probably know Heinz as the maker of ketchup, but it also sells hundreds of other products as well, such as Ore-Ida French Fries. Part of Buffett's success is that anyone would take his phone call to discuss a merger or investment.

He was usually viewed as a white knight since he generally leaves existing management in charge when he makes an investment.

So, even though Heinz was doing fine on its own when Buffett and 3G Capital came calling, Heinz's management was willing to listen. Buffett put in $4.5 billion in cash and invested another $8 billion in preferred stock of the new Heinz, which paid a 9% annual dividend. Roughly two years later, Buffett and 3G capital swapped their stake in Heinz for 51% of a new firm, merging Heinz with Kraft. Kraft is another huge, multinational food products firm. 3G Capital is a private equity firm, so naturally, debt financing was also part of the equation. The end result for Buffett? Quadrupling his money in about two years.

But even the Oracle of Omaha—as he is sometimes known—can make huge blunders. Buffett often refers to Berkshire's purchase of the Dexter Shoe Company as one of his worst investments ever. In 1993, Buffet paid $433 million for the Maine-based shoe company. Buffett's biggest mistake wasn't that Dexter's shoe business deteriorated rapidly. Instead, Buffett laments that he paid for the deal in Berkshire stock, which has since risen 12-fold or so since the purchase. Using some basic math, this means that Buffett paid the equivalent of $5.2 billion for a virtually worthless shoe company.

I think Buffett learned from this lesson since he rarely used Berkshire stock in future acquisitions, and had a successful investment in the dominant casual shoe company Nike. Buffett, like many investors, also had a disappointing experience in airline stocks. In 1989, he invested $358 million in the convertible preferred stock of U.S. Air. It appears he escaped relatively unscathed before U.S. Air went bankrupt, but it was still a disappointment. Buffett himself once said, "If a capitalist had been present at Kitty Hawk back in the early 1900s, he should have shot Orville Wright." Of course, the implication is that many investors have lost money in the many airlines that have gone bankrupt over the years.

Although Buffett is known mostly for his stock investments, he also invests in other securities, such as bonds. In 2007, he purchased $2 billion in the debt of a Texas utility known as Energy Future Holdings. The company was the subject of a leveraged buyout, or LBO, and choked on too much debt. Buffett's net loss on this investment was more than $900 million. His investment in IBM was also criticized by some investors, who viewed IBM as a dinosaur in a technology world dominated by Google, Apple, Microsoft, Amazon, and the like. Buffett first started buying IBM in the first quarter of 2011. He invested more than $13 billion in IBM at a cost basis of $170 a share. When I last checked, IBM was trading at roughly $160 a share, resulting in a paper loss of more than $750 million, at the time.

Back to the big picture, Warren Buffett had success written all over him at a very young age. But it wasn't until he came across the value investor Ben Graham that his investment strategy began to take shape. Buffett initially embraced the strict value strategy of Graham by looking at companies in a quantitative manner and trying to buy companies for the equivalent of 50 cents on the dollar. Buffett's contribution to the concept of value investing was to find high-quality companies selling at a discount. And to let the moat around these companies protect his investment, enabling him to hold them for his favorite holding period—forever.

In the end, the numbers speak for themselves. In the 50 years after Buffett took over Berkshire in 1965, the S&P 500 was up 11,355%. In contrast, over the same period, Berkshire's stock was up an amazing 1.6 million percent.

4

Fisher and Price:
The Growth-Stock Investors

Philip Fisher and Thomas Rowe Price Jr. are the two individuals most associated with growth investing as a valid and important investment strategy. In extreme cases, growth stocks have the potential to go up 1000% or more from inception. Occasionally, you'll find a growth stock in the bargain-basement bin. But, usually, it's up to you to make the assessment that a growth stock will keep growing, and that paying a somewhat high price today is a good gamble for a stock that is headed higher.

Growth Stocks

> A growth stock is like a first-round draft pick: A lot is expected and it is in great demand, so it usually sells at a high price. One reason is that a stock can split.

  ○ You might own 100 shares of a stock trading at $50 a share, for a total of $5000.

  ○ After a 2-for-1 stock split, you would now own 200 shares of the stock at $25 a share, but the aggregate value would remain the same: $5000.

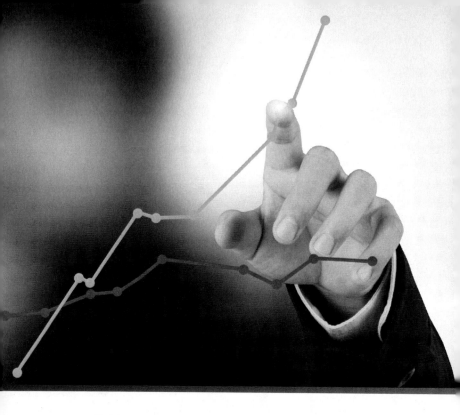

> Relying on price alone might not be a meaningful way to differentiate between growth and value stocks. Thus, analysts look at other measures of valuation. The two most common are the price-to-earnings ratio (P/E) and the price-to-book ratio.

  ○ The P/E ratio is the price of a share divided by its annual earnings per share. If the P/E of the market is at 15, any stock with a P/E of less than 15 would be considered a value stock, while a stock with a P/E higher than 15 would be considered a growth stock.

  ○ The price-to-book ratio is the price per share of the stock divided by the book value—that is, the accounting value or net worth figure on the balance sheet—per share.

- A high price-to-book ratio suggests a growth stock: It's valued in part on its future potential. A low price-to-book ratio indicates a value stock: It might be undervalued relative to its intrinsic worth.

> Another way to differentiate growth from value stocks is the average valuation level of the market. Anything above the current market average is considered to be a growth stock, while anything below average is considered a value stock.

Philip Fisher

> Philip Fisher was born in San Francisco September 8, 1907. He attended Stanford University and earned a bachelor's degree in economics. In 1931, he set up his own investment advisory firm, Fisher & Company, retiring in 1999 at the age of 91.

> For many years, Fisher taught an investments course at Stanford, and his location in the San Francisco and Silicon Valley area positioned him to become an early investor in several venture capital and private equity investments.

> Philip Fisher is probably best known for his bestselling book, *Common Stocks and Uncommon Profits,* in which he lays out his investment philosophy.

Investment Strategy

> As a growth investor, Fisher looked for companies with the potential to significantly grow sales for several years into the future. The quality of a firm's sales force was one of the factors that Fisher assessed. A firm that grows sales at a faster rate than the industry is one sign of a good quality sales organization.

> Fisher was also one of the first investors to conduct rigorous fundamental analysis, which goes beyond looking at a company's

financials to include talking to management, competitors, suppliers, former employees, and others.

> Fisher looked at the integrity of a target company's management. Signs of quality management included the following factors:

    ○ Management talks freely to investors about its affairs when things are going well and when they're not.

    ○ The firm is able to keep growing when a product has run its course. Can they come up with a new and improved version? Or pivot to selling a somewhat related product?

    ○ The company's research and development function, or R&D is robust. Does a significant part of a company's sales come from new products?

> Profit margins differ dramatically by industry. For example, supermarkets might have profit margins in the low single digits, while software or pharmaceutical firms often have profit margins greater than 20%. Growth stocks typically have above-average profit margins.

> Fisher would often ask a company's management what it was doing to maintain or improve its profit margins relative to its competitors, and he liked companies that had a focus on profits for the long term.

> Fisher advocated owning a relatively small number of investments in a portfolio—roughly 30. He felt that owning too many stocks made it impossible to watch all the eggs in all the different baskets. He felt that buying a company without a detailed understanding of the business could be riskier than limited diversification.

> Fisher also believed that when finding attractive investments is hard, the market as a whole might be overvalued; you should consider taking some money off the table.

T. Rowe Price

> Thomas Rowe Price Jr. was born in born in Glyndon, MD, March 16, 1898. He earned a bachelor's degree in chemistry from Swarthmore.

> After a brief stint as a chemist at DuPont, Price realized that his passion was in the financial markets, and he joined the Baltimore brokerage firm of Mackubin Goodrich, today known as Legg Mason. He worked his way up to become the firm's Chief Investment Officer, but he wanted to develop his ideas about growth stocks.

> After a disagreement with the other executives at the firm, he left in 1937 to set up T. Rowe Price Associates. He charged a fee for his investment services, in contrast to the commission approach that was widespread at the time.

> Price produced tremendous long-term returns. If you invested $1000 in his recommended stocks in 1934—with dividends reinvested—it would have grown to $271,201 by the end of 1972 during which time $1000 invested in the market as a whole grew to only about $66,000.

Investment Strategy

> Price is probably best known for his life-cycle approach to investing. He felt that the risks of owning a stock increase when the industry it competes in matures. He wanted to buy stocks when earnings were increasing or accelerating. The industry life cycle typically has 4 stages.

  ○ A period of rapid and increasing sales growth. For example, think about the early stages of the Internet, when many startups occurred and the aggregate industry experienced exponential growth.

- A period of stable growth. Consolidation tends to occur during this phase. Smartphones are one example. Even after cell phones had been around a while, the ability to turn a phone into a mini-computer with millions of apps resulted in stable growth with a limited number of firms capturing the lion's share of the profits.

- Slowing growth or maturity. Coca-Cola's stock might be an example. Today, it might be too big and its market too saturated to consistently grow at double-digit rates.

- Minimal or negative growth. The industry revenues and earnings are in relative decline. The railroads were an example of this factor after being eclipsed by the automobile, but they found a second life in transporting increased commodities, rather than people.

> Price's preferred hunting ground was the stable growth phase since it is more predictable and less volatile than the startup phase.

> Within the growth-stock universe, Price differentiated between two types of growth. The first is cyclical, where the magnitude of the industry's growth is tied strongly to the economy. For example, during the 1950s auto sales grew sharply.

> The other type is stable growth. In this case, sales are not highly dependent on the specific phase of the economic cycle. For example, health care stocks can grow strongly during a recession.

> Price also looked at a range of criteria:

- Superior research and development activities likely to spur future growth. 3M—a stock Price held for 33 years—is one company known for its R&D and innovation.

- Avoidance of cutthroat competition. Firms that engage in teamwork are more likely to be stable and around for the long term.

- Relative immunity from government regulation. This criterion knocks out several industries, including utilities, financial services, and energy.

- Low total labor costs but fair employee compensation. Costco made a reputation for generating great growth in its stock price while paying above-average wages to its employees relative to other firms in the industry.

> Besides high growth in sales and earnings per share, Price also wanted stocks with at least a 10% return on invested capital. Return on invested capital can be calculated a few ways, but one popular approach divides net income by capital, basically the value on its balance sheet of its debt and equity.

> Many industries are defined by a sort of Darwinian process of elimination for achieving high profits. Price recognized this dynamic and suggested finding the most promising company or companies in a growth industry. He also provided some insight on how to determine when a firm was losing its edge.

- Companies lose patents and new inventions may make old inventions obsolete. For example, Pfizer's stock price struggled for years after its best-selling cholesterol drug, Lipitor, went off patent.

- The legislative or legal environment can get worse for a firm, affecting its ability to grow. For example, defense firms are largely dependent on the federal budget.

- The costs of labor and raw materials also affect a firm's profitability significantly. For example, the price of jet fuel is one of the largest costs to running an airline.

Conclusion

> Philip Fisher and T. Rowe Price Jr. helped establish growth investing as a valid strategy, and their focus on the long term or, more accurately, the very long term, was novel at the time.

> Fisher's book, *Common Stocks and Uncommon Profits,* was one of the first bestsellers on the subject of personal finance and played a part in transforming the stock market from a playground for the rich into a legitimate arena for savings and investments.

> T. Rowe Price thought that investing in a leading company in a fast-growing industry was like sailing with the wind at your back. He fleshed out his ideas by carefully looking at sales growth, earnings growth, profit margins, and return on invested capital. He bought leaders and held them for long periods of time—several decades in some cases.

> Price's philosophy of putting customers' interests first was a novel idea when he established his firm in the 1930s, and his method of doing business won out. His excellent investment performance added great value to his clients. And today his namesake firm, T. Rowe Price, manages roughly $750 billion.

Suggested Readings

Fisher, *Common Stocks and Uncommon Profits.*
Train, *Money Masters of Our Time.*

Questions to Consider

1. How would you describe the investment strategies of Philip Fisher and T. Rowe Price?

2. How would you define growth investing?

4

Fisher and Price:
The Growth-Stock Investors

Warren Buffett once described himself as 85% Benjamin Graham and 15% Philip Fisher. Many of us are familiar with the value investing pioneer Benjamin Graham. But who was Philip Fisher? Well, Philip Fisher was a pioneer of growth investing, which is a separate school of portfolio analysis from value investing.

Fisher and another man, Thomas Rowe Price Jr., are probably the two individuals most associated with the emergence of growth investing as a valid and important investment strategy. You probably have some intuition about what growth stocks are—a young Microsoft, Apple, Amazon, or Facebook. In extreme cases, growth stocks have the potential to go up 1000% or more from inception. A growth stock is like a first-round draft pick in the NFL or NBA. A lot is expected of the pick, and it's in great demand, so it usually sells at a high price. And by high price, we typically don't refer to the cost of a single share, but rather the valuation of the company as a whole.

Why? Well, for one reason, a stock can split. You might own 100 shares of a stock that was trading at $50 a share, for a total of $5,000. After a 2-for-1 stock split, you would now own 200 shares of the stock that is, twice as many at a price of $25 a share, only half as much. But, the aggregate value would remain the same, $5,000. And because your investment is still valued at $5,000, you can't say it dropped 50% in value. My point is that relying on price alone may not be a meaningful way to differentiate between growth and value stocks. So analysts typically look at some other measures of valuation to differentiate growth from value stocks. The two most common approaches are the price-to-earnings ratio and the price-to-book ratio.

The price-to-earnings, or P/E, is the price per share divided by its annual earnings per share. For example, if a stock sells for $10 a share, and its annual earnings come to $1 a share, its price-to-earnings Ratio, or P/E, can be computed as ten. In the same way, the price-to-book ratio is the ratio of the price per share of the stock divided by the book value per share. Book value is the accounting value—or net worth figure—on the balance sheet. It is the total of a firm's assets, minus its liabilities. A high price-to-book ratio, suggests a growth stock meaning it's valued in part on its future potential, while a low price-to-book ratio indicates a value stock meaning, actually, that it might be undervalued relative to its intrinsic worth.

To differentiate growth from value stocks, analysts look at the average valuation of the market as a whole. Anything above the current market average is considered to be a growth stock, while anything below the average is considered a value stock. So, if the P/E of the market is currently at 15, any stock with a P/E of less than 15 would be considered a value stock, while a P/E higher than 15 would be considered a growth Stock. In practice, most value and growth indexes are updated between quarterly and annually, so a stock won't flip-flop between a growth index and value index every day.

The market isn't stupid. usually, a company with strong growth prospects trades at a high P/E. Alphabet, previously known as Google, rarely if ever traded at a price-to-earnings multiple below the market as a whole, even during the Great Recession of 2007–2009. Occasionally, you'll find a growth stock in the bargain-basement bin. But, usually, it's up to you to make the assessment that a growth stock will keep growing and that paying a somewhat high price, today, is OK for a stock headed higher. And the two investors who laid the groundwork for this artful assessment were Philip Fisher and T. Rowe Price.

Philip Fisher was born in San Francisco on September 8, 1907. He attended Stanford University and graduated with a bachelor's degree in Economics. Fisher started out at Anglo-London Bank and then had a brief stint at a brokerage firm. As the Great Depression began to take hold, he lost his job at the brokerage. And so, in 1931, he set up his own investment advisory firm, Fisher & Company. For the most part, he worked alone in a sparsely furnished office. Fisher served in the Army Air Corps during World War II, decades before it became today's Air Force. But he ran his investment firm for an extraordinarily long time, before and after his military experience, prior to finally retiring in 1999, at the age of 91.

For many years, Fisher also taught an investments course at Stanford's Graduate School of Business. And his location in San Francisco and Silicon Valley helped him to become an early investor in several venture capital and private equity investments. Fisher's son, Ken Fisher, became a very successful investor in his own right, and an investment columnist for Forbes magazine. Ken runs Fisher Investments, an investment firm with tens of billions of dollars under management.

Ken said that his father suffered from Asperger's Syndrome, a high-functioning form of autism. But in some ways, the Asperger's condition may have helped his father's investment career. Individuals with autism tend to prefer to spend time alone, rather than in social situations. Ken recalls his father spending hours on end in solitude, deep in thought—no doubt much of it on investment-related matters. Philip Fisher is probably best known for his bestselling investment book, *Common Stocks and Uncommon Profits*, in which he lays out his investment philosophy.

As a growth investor, Fisher looked for companies with the potential to significantly grow sales for several years into the future. For example, he was managing money during the years when the automobile industry experienced its greatest growth. Most households went from having no cars to one or two. Sometimes a product is so good it can sell itself—like the iPhone or an Oreo cookie. More often than not, though, a product is sold through some sort of sales force.

So, assessing the quality of a firm's sales force was one of the things that Fisher looked at. A firm that grows sales at a faster rate than the industry is one good sign of a quality sales organization. Fisher cited IBM as one example of a company with an excellent sales organization. And from the 1950s through the 1970s, IBM was considered a star growth stock in the stock market. Fisher was also one of the first investors to rigorously conduct fundamental analysis—which goes beyond looking at a company's financials. He called this approach the scuttlebutt method or business grapevine. It involved starting with a company's financials, but also talking to management, competitors, suppliers, former employees, and so forth. Fisher looked at the integrity of a target company's management. For example, he posed the question of "Does the management talk freely to investors about its affairs when things are going well, but clam up when troubles and disappointments occur?"

Another sign of quality management is a firm's ability to keep growing when a product has run its course. Can they come up with a new and improved version? Or pivot to selling a somewhat related product? For example, continuing with our IBM example, the firm went from selling mostly hardware to a company that was focused on selling computer services.

Another sign of quality management that Fisher looked at was a company's research and development function, or R&D. Did a significant part of a company's sales come from new products? Or was the company basically a one trick pony? Some companies are dominated by a single personality. But Fisher liked companies that had depth in management. Some companies have strong or important unions. For example, when analyzing airline stocks, the relationship of the pilots' union with management historically was important. So, Fisher would look at the relationship between management and labor.

Fisher's focus on high-quality stocks and strong management is how he came to influence Buffett's evolution away from Graham's strict value approach. Buffett introduced himself to Fisher after reading his book, *Common Stocks and Uncommon Profits*. Buffett said, "When I met him, I was impressed by the man and his ideas. A thorough understanding of a business, by using Phil's techniques ... enables one to make intelligent investment commitments." When Buffett's investment holding company, Berkshire Hathaway, takes over a firm, it usually leaves the existing management alone. Of course, to do this, you have to believe in the integrity and talent of the management team. One of Buffett's most famous quotes is that his favorite holding period is forever. I think he learned the value of long-term thinking at least partially from Fisher, who once wrote, "If the job has been correctly done when a common stock is purchased the time to sell is—almost never."

Fisher practiced what he preached. One of his most successful investments was in Motorola, which he purchased in 1955 and held until his death 49 years later. Other multi-decade holdings by Fisher included Dow Chemical and Texas Instruments. Of course, long-term holding periods for strong-performing stocks have the added benefit of postponing—and potentially eliminating—capital gains taxes. Growth stocks typically have above-average profit margins. For example, Microsoft has historically had operating profit margins of more than 25%. Not surprisingly, Fisher liked companies with above-average profit margins. Now, profit margins differ dramatically by industry. For example, supermarkets might have profit margins in the low single digits, while software or pharmaceutical firms often have profits margins greater than 20%. So, while you might prefer to invest in one industry, technology, let's say, over another, food service, you need to look at profit margins not only from industry-to-industry but also within industries, relative to the firm's competitors.

Fisher would often ask a company's management what it was doing to maintain, or improve, its profit margins relative to its competitors. Fisher liked companies that had a focus on profits for the long-term. Management can sometimes play games, and pump up short-term earnings, but that usually just takes away earnings from future periods. Kind of like robbing Peter to pay Paul.

One famous example of accounting irregularities involved the kitchen-appliance firm Sunbeam. Back in the late 1990s, it gave retail customers big incentives to purchase the company's electric blankets over the summer, and its barbecue grills over the winter, both prior to their normal cycles. As BusinessWeek magazine wrote at the time, "By booking these sales before the goods were delivered, Dunlap helped boost Sunbeam's revenues by 18% in 1997 alone. In effect, he was shifting sales from future quarters to the current one." The process of trying to inflate sales for the short-term through incentives or other means is known as channel stuffing.

Soon enough, Sunbeam was facing follow-on losses, huge layoffs and the CEO lost his job. The Securities and Exchange Commission brought a civil fraud lawsuit against some of the company's top officers, eventually culminating in fines and other penalties. Sunbeam had problems recovering from the accounting scandal and declared bankruptcy in 2001.

Fisher advocated owning a relatively small number of investments in a portfolio— roughly 30. He felt that owning too many stocks made it impossible to watch all the eggs in all the different baskets. He felt that buying a company without a detailed understanding of the business could be riskier than limited diversification. Fisher also discussed when to sell a stock. One reason when to sell is when the facts about a company change. For example, Kodak was once a great company but the profitability of its core film product virtually disappeared, after digital film and phone cameras came on the market. A second reason to sell could be a loss of faith in management, or in the growth prospects of the firm or industry. Fisher also felt that when the attractiveness of investments are hard to find, it might signify that the market as a whole is overvalued and that you should consider taking some money off the table.

T. Rowe Price Jr. was born in born in Glyndon, Maryland, on March 16, 1898. His father was a doctor and this probably had something to do with his early interest in science. He earned a bachelor's degree in chemistry from Swarthmore College in a Philadelphia suburb. After a brief stint as a chemist at DuPont, Price realized that his passion was in the financial markets. So, he joined the Baltimore brokerage firm of Mackubin Goodrich, which today is known as Legg Mason. Price worked up his way to become the firm's chief investment officer. Price wanted to develop his ideas about growth stocks. And so, after a disagreement with other executives at the firm, he left in 1937 to set up T. Rowe Price and Associates. And he charged a fee for his investment services, in contrast to the commission approach that was widespread at the time.

The fee-based approach—which is common today—sees the investment manager's compensation go up as the value of the account rise. In contrast, commissioned salespeople have the incentive to sell—and keep selling—to generate commissions. The fee-based approach is also consistent with Price's investment philosophy of holding growth stocks for the long term. He said, "If we do well for the client, we will be taken care of."

Price produced tremendous long-term returns. One thousand dollars invested in his recommended stocks in 1934—with dividends reinvested—grew to $271,201 by the end of 1972 during which time $1,000 invested in the market as a whole grew to only about $66,000. This type of performance is due not to luck but rather to talent and extremely hard work. Price worked long hours for nearly all of his adult life. He got up at 5 a.m. and worked a full day, even into his 80s.

As a fund manager, Price was most closely affiliated with the T. Rowe Price Growth Stock Fund that he established in 1950. IBM was a core holding. A $1,000 investment in this fund in 1950 would have increased—with dividends and capital gains reinvested—to $22,837 by the end of 1972. A similar investment in the market grew to about $18,000 over the same period.

Price stepped down from the active management of his firm around 1970, ultimately selling it to other employees, but he continued to manage his personal account until his death in 1983 at the age of 85.

In some respects, Price was a precursor to Peter Lynch of the Fidelity Investments mutual fund family. Lynch is known for his great performance, and for saying that amateur investors can do as well as professionals by finding good companies they know, and holding them for the long-term. Price said,

> Even the amateur investor who lacks training and time to devote to managing his investments can be reasonably successful by selecting the best-managed companies in fertile fields for growth, buying their shares and retaining them until it becomes obvious they no longer meet the definition of a growth stock.

Philip Fisher and T. Rowe Price both liked buying growth stocks with rapidly rising sales and earnings. These were their preferred metrics. Decades later, analysts came to focus on measures such as above-average P/E and price-to-book ratios to differentiate growth from value. Furthermore, Price is probably best known for his life cycle approach to investing. He thought that companies and industries had life cycles. And he felt the risks of owning a stock increase when the industry it competes in becomes mature. He wanted to buy stocks when earnings were increasing or accelerating.

The industry life cycle typically has four stages. The first is a period of rapid and increasing sales growth. For example, think about the early stages of the Internet industry, when there were many startups and the aggregate industry experienced exponential growth. The second stage is a period of stable growth. There tends to be consolidation during this phase. Smartphones are one example. Even after cell phones had been around a while, the ability to turn your phone into a mini-computer with millions of apps resulted in stable growth with a limited number of firms, like Apple and Samsung capturing the lion's share of the profits. The third phase is slowing growth or maturity. Coca Cola's stock might be an example. Today, it might be too big, and its market too saturated, to consistently grow at double-digit rates. The last phase is minimal or negative growth, where the industry revenues and earnings are in relative decline. The railroads are one example of this after being eclipsed by the automobile. But, then they found a second life in transporting an increased amount of commodities across the nation, rather than people. The buggy whip, however, never recovered. Price's preferred hunting ground was the stable growth phase since it is more predictable and less volatile than the start-up phase.

Within the growth-stock universe, Price differentiated between two types of growth. The first is cyclical, where the magnitude of the industry's growth is tied strongly to the economy. For example, during the 1950s auto sales grew sharply. This was the heyday of General Motors or GM, and it was regarded as one of the best growth stocks during this decade by investors. However, GM wasn't immune to the business cycle, so its sales and earnings growth varied more widely during recessionary periods.

Similar stories can be found during the strong growth years of Home Depot, Wal-Mart, and Honeywell. These firms also grew rapidly but had noticeably smaller increases in sales and earnings during recessionary periods. Honeywell was one of Price's core holdings—he held it for more than 34 years. The other type of growth according to Price is stable growth. In this case, sales are not highly dependent on the specific phase of the economic cycle. For example, healthcare stocks can still grow strongly during a recession. The pharmaceuticals giant Merck & Company was one of Thomas Price's holdings for more than 32 years. He tended to favor stable growth firms unless he could get the cyclical firms at an attractive discount.

Price also had other methods of selecting growth stocks. He looked at a range of criteria. Like Fisher, he wanted firms with superior research and development activities since this was likely to spur future growth. 3M—a stock Price held for 33 years—is one company known for its R&D and innovation. You're probably familiar with some of its products like Scotch Tape and Post-It Notes. Fisher also preferred firms that didn't promote—and avoided—cutthroat competition. He felt that firms that engage in teamwork are more likely to be stable and around for the long-term. And he wanted companies that were relatively immune from government regulation. This would knock out several industries, including utilities, financial services, and energy.

And Price wanted firms that paid their employees well but had low total labor costs. A retailer like Costco might be an example. Costco made a reputation for generating great growth in its stock price while paying above-average wages to its employees, relative to other firms in the retail industry. Besides high growth in sales and earnings per share, Price also wanted stocks with at least a 10% return on invested capital or ROIC. Return on invested capital can be calculated a few ways, but one popular approach takes net income and divides this by the company's capital, which is basically the value on its balance sheet of its debt and equity.

Also like Fisher, Price preferred to invest in companies with high-profit margins, since profitable growth—once achieved—is sustainable, while a loss leader or meager profit margin model is difficult to sustain unless you are the low-cost producer or seller. Many industries are defined by a sort of

Darwinian winner-take-all process of elimination for achieving high profits. Think about Microsoft in computer operating systems and productivity software, Alphabet or Google in search, and Facebook in social media. Price recognized this dynamic and suggested finding the most promising company or companies in a growth industry. He also provided some insight on how to determine when a firm was losing its edge—beyond looking for a simple deceleration in sales and earnings growth.

For instance, Price recognized that management performance is key in most industries. If management changed for the worse, that would be a red flag. And if competition were to intensify or a market was to become saturated, that wouldn't bode well, either, for a growth stock that usually trades at lofty levels.

Here's another insight, companies lose patents and new inventions may make old inventions obsolete. For example, Pfizer's stock price struggled for years after its best-selling drug, Lipitor, went off patent. And the legislative or legal environment can get worse for a firm, impacting its ability to grow. For example, defense firms are largely dependent on the federal budget. The costs of labor and raw materials also impact a firms' profitability significantly. For example, the price of jet fuel is one of the largest costs to running an airline.

In addition to all of these many factors, Price recognized the need for more qualitative analysis. In most management classes they teach a strategic framework called PEST or STEP analysis. These acronyms stand for Political Economic Social Technological. Price anticipated this form of analysis decades earlier when he said,

> Because the economic or business cycle runs concurrently with a company's life cycle, it is difficult to determine in advance when earnings power is on the decline. Research and an understanding of social, political, and economic trends should enable one to recognize the change in the long-term earnings trend of a business.

So, Philip Fisher and T. Rowe Price Jr. were the fathers of growth investing. They helped establish this school of portfolio analysis as a valid school of investing, and their focus on the long-term, or more accurately, the very long term, was novel at the time. Fisher's book, *Common Stocks and Uncommon Profits*, was one of the first bestsellers on the subject of personal finance and played a part in transforming the stock market from something of a casino, or playground for the rich, into a legitimate mainstream arena for savings and investments. He influenced the average investor and the great Warren Buffett. If you look at many of Berkshire Hathaway's top holdings over the years—Coca-Cola, Wal-Mart, Procter and Gamble, Kraft Heinz, each of them held for multi-year periods—I'd conclude that Fisher's influence on Buffett is a lot greater than that of his original mentor, Benjamin Graham.

In turn, T. Rowe Price thought that investing in a leading company in a fast-growing industry was like sailing with the wind at your back. Price fleshed out his ideas by carefully looking at sales growth, earnings growth, profit margins, and return on invested capital. He bought leaders and then held them for long periods of time—several decades or more, in some cases. And Price's philosophy of putting customers' interests first was a novel idea when he first established his own firm in the 1930s. At the time, churn and burn or pump and dump tactics were common—and they still exist today.

But Price's method of doing business won out. His excellent investment performance added great value to his clients. And today his namesake firm, T. Rowe Price, manages roughly three-quarters of a trillion dollars.

5

Harry Markowitz's Modern Portfolio Theory

Not until the 1950s did we have a rigorous way of measuring risk. A young graduate student named Harry Markowitz published an article in *The Journal of Finance* related to his doctoral dissertation at the University of Chicago. Markowitz made the immense contribution of putting risk on equal footing with return. His work in this area won him a Nobel Prize in Economics. Before Markowitz, risk played second fiddle to return. People took kind of a shotgun approach when trying to reduce risks by diversifying across assets, companies, and industries, in an imprecise manner.

Developing the Markowitz Portfolio Theory

> Modern portfolio theory has its roots in Markowitz's work in the early 1950s. It's still called modern portfolio theory all these decades later because changes in investment thought over the past 50 years have been incremental or evolutionary, rather than radical.

> Many great accomplishments in life start out with what appears to be a random series of coincidences. Markowitz was looking for a dissertation topic in the early 1950s. He was waiting outside his advisor's office when he met a stockbroker.

- The broker suggested that Markowitz write his dissertation on something related to the stock market. Markowitz's advisor thought the idea had merit and sent him to discuss possible topics with the dean of the business school, who recommended a book called The Theory of Investment Value, by John B. Williams.

- The essence of this book is still taught in finance classes: The price of a stock is equal to the value of its future dividends, adjusted for the time value of money. That is, a dividend of $1 today is worth more than a dividend of $1 in the future.

- Markowitz concluded that if you followed Williams's logic, you would wind up with a portfolio of a small number of stocks because everything else had an inferior return. But in practice, Markowitz knew, people diversified their portfolios fairly widely.

> The book, *Introduction to Probability,* by James Uspensky, profoundly influenced Markowitz's thinking. Its formula for the variance of a weighted sum essentially is used to calculate the variance of a portfolio—a popular measure of risk.

> Markowitz also learned about the production possibility frontier concept, which posits that an economy makes tradeoffs in what it produces. It can produce a lot of one good and nothing of another or some combination. Markowitz now had the idea to create a frontier that made a tradeoff between risk and return.

Variance and Correlation

> Although there is no uniform way of measuring risk, many economists focus on measures of volatility. The standard deviation—the square root of variance—is one widely used measure of volatility. Markowitz used standard deviation as his primary measure of risk, but he recognized the possibility of using other measures of risk as well, such as returns below a certain threshold.

> Markowitz had the further insight that the risk of a portfolio is primarily based on the interaction of the portfolio's holdings, not on the risk of the securities individually or in isolation. He arrived at this insight, in part, from the formula on variance in Uspensky's book.

    ○ According to Markowitz's Portfolio Theory, two securities that are very risky in isolation—say a retail stock in Singapore and a health care stock in Brazil—might have less risk than two blue chip stocks in the United States because the U.S. stocks probably move in tandem because of their dependence on the U.S. economy.

    ○ In contrast, retail sales in Singapore probably have little to do with health care in Brazil. One may zig, while the other zags. This lack of common movement reduces the overall risk of the portfolio.

    ○ The mathematical term for the way two assets move with or against each other is correlation, a number that ranges between negative one and positive one. Two securities with a positive correlation move in lockstep: When one goes up, the other goes up, and they have little diversification. The art of picking a diversified portfolio is to select securities that have low correlation and positive expected returns.

The Optimal Portfolio

> Markowitz's remaining challenge was to find the best portfolio for any particular person: an optimal portfolio. Markowitz returned to the notion of the production possibility frontier and imagined a graphed curve that shows the range of portfolios that maximize return for a given level or tolerance of risk.

> Markowitz called this curve the efficient frontier. Any portfolio below the efficient frontier is inefficient, and no rational person would select it because it would yield a lower return and/or higher risk than another possible portfolio.

> Risk tolerance is estimated by an indifference curve that measures willingness to trade off outcomes—in this case risk and expected return. The optimal portfolio for you is the place where your indifference curve matches the efficient set of portfolios.

William Sharpe

> What if all investors tried to maximize their returns according to their risk tolerance? William Sharpe set out to find the answer in his own Ph.D. dissertation. It described a way to simplify the calculation of efficient portfolios that were the output of Markowitz's Portfolio Theory.

> He continued to think about what prices would look like in equilibrium if everyone tried to maximize the returns for a given level of risk. Sharpe's insight was that the only risk worth paying for is risk that can't be diversified away—that is market risk, or what academics call beta.

> Sharpe developed a model showing that the expected return on any risk asset is equal to the risk-free rate of interest plus the market risk of the asset (beta) times the market risk premium as a whole. The model is known as the Capital Asset Pricing Model or CAPM.

Capital Asset Pricing Model (CAPM)

> The risk-free rate, say a fixed-income security issued by the government, is virtually free of default. It should be the minimum hurdle for any investment to pass.

> To this risk-free rate add beta. The average beta of the market as a whole is one. Therefore, stocks with a beta lower than one are less risky than the market. Stocks with a beta greater than one are riskier than the market.

> The market risk premium is the expected return on the market minus the risk-free rate. The market premium is tied to market psychology, so it can expand or contract. On average, it tends to be around 6% or 7%.

> According to the theory, a portfolio of high beta stocks yields a high return. When the market goes up, such portfolios tend to outperform the market and low beta portfolios tend to underperform the market. But when stocks go down, portfolios of low beta stocks tend to lose less than high beta portfolios.

> Sharpe published the Capital Asset Pricing Model in 1964, and since that time other academics have been finding chinks in its armor. Perhaps the most important paper published on this topic was by Eugene Fama and Ken French.

- They found that with data going back to the early 1930s, the CAPM worked pretty well. It showed a straight line relationship between risk and return, as predicted by the theory.

- But for the period from 1966 to the present, the theory held up less well. High beta stocks returned less than expected and low beta stocks returned more than expected. In some respects, the theory was turned upside-down: Many low-risk investments outperformed many high-risk investments.

> Given these results, Fama and French set out to better explain the relationship between risk and return. They found two factors that mattered greatly: size and style.

- Size is the market value or market capitalization of the firm. It equals the stock price times the number of shares outstanding. Over long periods, small cap stocks outperform large cap stocks. This finding makes intuitive sense, since small firms are nimbler and can grow quickly from a smaller base.

- Style refers to growth or value. Value stocks historically return more than growth stocks over long periods because growth stocks tend to be glamorous, and investors often bid them up. Eventually, some run into competition or have missteps and fall back down to earth. Since not much is expected of value stocks, they often fix their problems and show a surprise upside.

> Professors Fama and French used the price-to-book variable to differentiate between growth and value. The price part of the ratio is the market capitalization that measures size. The book part of the ratio in the denominator is the net worth item on the balance sheet.

- Book value equals all the assets on a firm's balance sheet minus all its liabilities. A firm with a lower than average price-to book-ratio is considered to be a value stock, while a firm with a higher than average price-to-book ratio is considered to be a growth stock. The historical average price-to-book ratio of the Standard and Poor 500 is about 2.5.

> Combining the two factors results in the following historical results:

  ○ Small cap value stocks usually have the best performance over long periods.

  ○ Large cap growth stocks usually have the worst performance over long periods. In the short run, investors might gravitate toward the safety of large cap growth stocks, especially during times of market distress, but over the long term, fear usually fades, and these investments tend to provide lower returns.

Momentum and Liquidity

> Momentum investors buy stocks that have been rising and sell or sell short investments that have been falling. In the short run, say a year or less, researchers have found that momentum works. High flyers keep flying and losers keep falling.

> Liquidity refers to the ability to sell an asset quickly and at fair market value: Your house is probably not liquid, but blue-chip stock, U.S. Treasury bonds, notes, and bills are liquid.

  ○ Researchers have found that over long periods, investors get paid to own illiquid assets. These assets are basically another type of risk.

  ○ During times of distress, the opposite usually holds. That is, people gravitate towards the safety of liquid investments.

> According to the theories and empirical evidence, if you want to make the most money, buy illiquid, small cap, value stocks that have upward momentum. The stocks that tend to have the lowest return are the most liquid, large cap growth names, with downward momentum.

> But if you follow this approach, be prepared to hold onto your hat when the market is falling, because in the short run you will lose the most money with this kind of security.

Suggested Readings

Bernstein, *Capital Ideas*.
Markowitz, *Portfolio Selection*.

Questions to Consider

1. How would you describe Harry Markowitz's approach to selecting an optimal portfolio?

2. According to the Capital Asset Pricing Model why is market risk more important when forecasting stock returns than company specific risk?

5

Transcript

Harry Markowitz's Modern Portfolio Theory

How do you pick a portfolio? Warren Buffett said, "The formula for value was handed down from 600 B.C. by a guy named Aesop. A bird in the hand is worth two in the bush." Buffett felt that Aesop understood the tradeoffs between risk and return. And the notion of a portfolio doesn't only apply to financial securities. Ancient farmers had to decide what crops to plant and ultimately harvest—wheat, corn, grapes for wine, and so forth.

So, the notion of not putting all of your eggs in one basket goes back hundreds of years. And the saying is attributed to many people, including the writer Miguel de Cervantes in his classic novel, *Don Quixote*—or *The Ingenious Gentleman Don Quixote of La Mancha*. Shakespeare, in *The Merchant of Venice*, also writes about diversifying across assets and across time. But it wasn't until the 1950s that we had a rigorous way of measuring risk when a young graduate student named Harry Markowitz published an article in *The Journal of Finance* related to his doctoral dissertation at the University of Chicago. Markowitz made the immense contribution of putting risk on equal footing with return. His work in this area won him a Nobel Prize in Economics. Before Markowitz, risk played second fiddle to return. People took kind of a shotgun approach when trying to reduce risks by diversifying across assets classes, companies, and industries, in an imprecise manner.

So modern portfolio theory has its roots in Markowitz's work in the early 1950s. And it's still called modern portfolio theory all these many decades later. Why? Because changes in investment thought over the past 50 years have been incremental or evolutionary in nature, rather than radical. In this lecture, we will discuss the key aspects of modern portfolio theory, its creators, and the implications for investors.

Harry Markowitz was born in 1927 and grew up in Chicago. He earned his undergraduate degree, master's degree, and Ph.D. in Economics from the University of Chicago school, which is known for its world-class Economics Department. It boasts the greatest number of Nobel Prize winners in economics of any university, including Milton Friedman and Friedrich Hayek. Many great accomplishments in life start out with what appears to be a random series of coincidences. Markowitz was looking for a dissertation topic in the early 1950s. And he was waiting outside his advisors' office when he ran into a man who was a stockbroker.

The broker suggested that Markowitz write his dissertation on something related to the stock market. Markowitz's advisor, Jacob Marschak, thought the idea had some merit, and sent him to discuss possible topics with the Dean of the Business School, Marshall Ketchum, who was the editor of The Journal of Finance at the time. Ketchum told him to read a book called The Theory of Investment Value by John B Williams. The essence of this book, published in 1937, is still taught in most finance courses today. Williams suggested that the price of a stock is equal to the value of its future dividends, adjusted for the time value of money.

By time value of money, I mean that a dividend of $1 today is worth more than a dividend of $1 in the future. You could get the $1 dividend today, put it in the bank and earn some interest on it. So you need to make an adjustment. Markowitz went to the library one afternoon to read Williams's book. He concluded that if you followed Williams's logic, you would wind up with a portfolio of a small amount of stocks because everything else had an inferior return. But, in practice, Markowitz knew people didn't put all their eggs in one basket, and that they diversified their portfolios fairly widely.

During that same afternoon, Markowitz found a book in the library called *Introduction to Probability* by James Uspensky, which would profoundly change his thinking. It contained a formula for the variance of a weighted sum. This is essentially the formula for calculating the variance of a portfolio—a popular measure of risk. This might have been one of the most productive afternoons in the history of economic thought. In his economics courses, Markowitz also learned about a concept called a production possibility frontier. The production possibility frontier says that an economy makes tradeoffs in what it can produce. It can produce a lot of one good and nothing of another, or some combination of the two. A famous textbook called *Economics* and written by the Nobel Laureate Paul Samuelson talks about an economy trading off the production of guns versus butter.

So, Markowitz now had the idea to create a frontier that made a tradeoff between risk and return. Risk used to be almost an afterthought prior to Markowitz Theory. In equilibrium, you could have a portfolio with little to no risk and a small expected return, or a lot of risk with a high expected return. Or some combination in between. When talking about returns that occur in the future, we talk about expected returns, since almost anything can occur. After the fact, we can measure actual or realized returns.

Now, although there is no uniform way of measuring risks, many economists focus on measures of volatility. The standard deviation is one widely used measure of volatility. Markowitz used variance and its square root, standard deviation, as his primary measure of risk. But he recognized the possibility of using other measures of risk as well, such as returns below a certain threshold. Markowitz had the further insight that the risk of a portfolio is primarily driven on the interaction of the portfolio's holdings, and not the risk of the securities individually—or in isolation. He was able to get this insight, in part, from seeing the formula on variance from Uspensky's book.

Often you'll hear someone say, "Tell me something I don't know." According to Markowitz Portfolio Theory, two securities that are very risky in isolation—say a retail stock in Singapore and a healthcare stock in Brazil—might have less risk than two blue chip U.S. stocks. Why? Because U.S. stocks probably move in tandem due to their dependence, in part, on the U.S. economy. In contrast, retail sales in Singapore probably have little to do with healthcare in Brazil. One may zig, while the other zags. This lack of common movement reduces the overall risk of the portfolio.

The mathematical term for the way two assets move with each other, or lack thereof, is called correlation. Correlation is a number that ranges between negative one and positive one. If two securities have a positive correlation, they move in lockstep with one another. When one goes up, the other goes up. One example of a correlation is the price of gold and the price of the exchange-traded fund GLD. If two securities are correlated at—or close to—positive one, then they don't provide you with much diversification. So the art of picking a diversified portfolio is to select securities that have little relationship with one another while still having positive expected returns.

Let's look at a simplified example to illustrate the huge importance of correlation. Suppose there were only two companies in the entire stock market. One firm sells suntan lotion by the beach. The other firm, also located on the beach, sells umbrellas. When it's sunny out, the suntan lotion firm makes a lot of money. Let's say it gives its stockholders a return of 20% when the sun shines. But when it rains it's unable to sell any suntan lotion and the company loses money due to its fixed costs of labor and running the factory. Let's say its shareholders lose 10% when it's raining. In contrast, when it rains, the umbrella company's making a lot of money. Let's also assume it makes 20% in this case. But when it is sunny out, few people are buying umbrellas, except those trying to shield themselves from the sun. So, in the case of sun or shine, the shareholders of the umbrella company lose 10% to be consistent with the loss from suntan lotion company.

Let's assume that the probability of rain and shine are both 50%. Now, here is the magic of correlation. If you put all of your money in one company, your wealth is entirely dependent on something you have no control over— the weather. However, if you put half your money in the suntan lotion stock and half your money in the umbrella company stock, you are guaranteed a profit, rain or shine. In this hypothetical example, the correlation between the suntan lotion and umbrella company is negative one. When one stock goes up, the other always goes down, and vice versa. So, one of Markowitz's important contributions was in solving the riddle of the risk of a portfolio. He found that correlation drives risk, while the risk of securities in isolation is of far lesser importance.

Markowitz's remaining challenge was to find the best portfolio for any particular person. A so-called optimal portfolio. Well, there are almost an infinite number of possible portfolios that you can select. There are tens of thousands—if not hundreds of thousands—of investments, and you can hold these investments in different proportions or weights. So how can we narrow this down to a single portfolio for each investor?

Well, at the University of Chicago, Markowitz took a mathematically oriented economics course that showed him how to differentiate between efficient and inefficient outcomes. So going back to the notion of the production possibility frontier, imagine a graphed curve that describes the range of efficient outcomes. That is a curve that shows the range of portfolios that maximize return for a given level or tolerance of risk. Markowitz called this curve the efficient frontier. Any portfolio below the efficient frontier is inefficient, and no rational person would select it because you would have a lower return and/or higher risk than another possible portfolio.

How do you know what your risk tolerance is? In practice, you can get an estimate by taking a risk questionnaire. Economists like to measure your willingness to trade off things—in this case risk and expected return—with something called an indifference curve. That is, your happiness would be the same with a low risk and low return portfolio, or a slightly higher return and risk portfolio. So, the optimal portfolio for you is the place where your indifference curve matches the efficient set of portfolios. Your specific optimal portfolio might contain a bunch of blue-chip stocks combined with some safe bonds. My specific optimal portfolio could consist of a bunch of technology and foreign stocks, combined with real estate and international bonds. But your portfolio and mine are both efficient and maximize the expected return for the risk you and I are willing to take. And that is the takeaway from Markowitz Portfolio Theory. The theory was such an advance from the prior portfolio management work in economics and finance that future Nobel Laureate, Milton Friedman initially opposed awarding Markowitz a Ph.D. in Economics. He said it wasn't economics, but it was something different.

Do people use Markowitz Portfolio Theory in practice? It is used widely by institutions at the asset-allocation level. Asset allocation is your mix of stocks, bonds, and cash. Sometimes you can add other asset classes like hedge funds, private equity, and real estate. It is not so widely used for picking individual stocks because of an issue called sensitivity analysis. That is, if the inputs to the Markowitz Model—such as the expected return and standard deviation of stocks—are volatile, then the output is also volatile. Sensitivity analysis can result in your portfolio this month looking a lot different than the recommended portfolio that you had last month. If this happens, many investors might be reluctant to use the approach because of the high transaction costs and taxes associated with trading in and out of different investments. But fortunately, portfolios tend to be more stable when you are looking at broad asset classes and not individual stocks. This is the main reason why Markowitz Portfolio Theory has found a greater following in asset allocations than in picking individual stocks.

What if all investors behaved the way that Markowitz suggested? That is, what if everyone tried to maximize their returns, given their risk tolerance. William Sharpe set about to find the answer to this question in the early 1960s in developing his own Ph.D. dissertation. Sharpe's dissertation developed a way to dramatically simplify the calculation of the efficient portfolios that were the output of Markowitz's Portfolio Theory. And Sharpe continued to think about the portfolio management problem. He pursued the path of what things might look like if everyone followed Markowitz Portfolio Theory. In other words, what would prices look like in equilibrium if everyone tried to maximize their returns for a given level of risk?

There were other researchers working on the same topic independently around the same time. But Sharpe published first, so he got most of the credit and—like Markowitz—eventually won a Nobel Prize. Sharpe's insight was that the only risk that is worth paying for is risk that can't be diversified away. So, if you put all of your money in a biotech stock with no earnings, that's risky. But you shouldn't be rewarded for taking on this crazy risk since much of the company specific risk can be diversified away. As you expand the portfolio, from one stock to two all the way to the 50,000 plus around the world, you still have risk. For example, you know the market goes up and down every day, and sometimes it crashes like in October 1987.

Even if you own a world index fund, there is still risk. The risk that can't be diversified away is called market risk, or what academics call beta. Sharpe developed a model showing that the expected return on any risk asset—such as IBM stock—is equal to the risk-free rate, such as a U.S. Treasury bill, plus the market risk of IBM, times the market risk premium as a whole. The risk model is known as the Capital Asset Pricing Model or the acronym CAPM for short.

Let's break down the three parts of the model into more basic terms. The risk-free rate, say a bank CD backed by federal deposit insurance or a fixed-income security issued by the government, is virtually free of default. It should be the minimum hurdle for any investment to pass. Otherwise, why would you want to own a risky investment when you can get something risk-free with a higher return? To this risk-free rate, we are going to add something related to the riskiness of the individual stock, and the riskiness of the market as a whole. The riskiness of the individual stock, as I said, is called beta. It turns out that the average beta of the market as a whole is one. So stocks with a beta of less than one are less risky than the market. For example, utilities and food and beverage stocks usually fall into this category. Stocks with a beta greater than one are riskier than the market. Technology, financial, and biotech stocks often fall into this category.

The third factor relates to the riskiness of the market as a whole. Economists call it the market risk premium. It starts with the expected return on the market. We then subtract the risk-free rate of interest. So, if the expected return on the market is 10%, its long-term historical average, and the risk-free rate of return is 2%, the market risk premium is 8%. The market risk premium is tied to market psychology, so it can expand or contract like an accordion. When people are greedy, it shrinks to something like 2% or 3%. When people are fearful, it expands to something like 10% or 12%. On average, it tends to be around 6% or 7%.

To summarize, the CAPM says the expected return on any asset is equal to the risk-free rate of interest plus the market risk, or beta, of an individual asset times the market risk premium. According to the theory, if you want a high return you should load up on a portfolio of high beta stocks. If you can't stomach the risk, then the beta of your portfolio should be on the lower side.

Does CAPM work? Well, it does add some value. When the market goes up, portfolios of high beta stocks tend to outperform the market. Portfolios of low beta stocks tend to underperform the market. But there is no free lunch. So when stocks go down, portfolios of low beta stocks tend to lose less than portfolios of high beta stocks. Most stocks have positive beta since they are all part of the same economic boat. That is, the United States and/or the global economy.

Sharpe published the Capital Asset Pricing Model in 1964, and since that time other academics have been finding chinks in its armor. Perhaps the most important paper published on this topic was by two famous professors at the University of Chicago at the time, Eugene Fama and Ken French. They found that if you start with data going back to the early 1930s, the CAPM worked pretty well. There was basically a straight line relationship between risk and return, as predicted by the theories.

But if you looked at the period shortly after CAPM was published, from 1966 to the present, the theory didn't hold up as well. High beta stocks returned less than expected and low beta stocks returned more than expected. In some respects, the theory was turned upside down since a lot of low-risk investments outperformed many high-risk investments. And not just for the short-term but over long periods of time, as well. Given these results, Fama and French set about to find some factors that might better explain the relationship between risk and return. They found two that mattered greatly, size and style.

Size is measured as the market value or market capitalization of the firm. It equals the stock price times the number of shares outstanding. They found that over long periods of time, small cap stocks outperform large cap stocks. This makes intuitive sense since small firms are nimbler, they can grow quickly, and they're growing from a smaller base. Many large companies can become bloated or inefficient, and eventually run into the law of large numbers. That is, the bigger you get, the harder it is to grow, especially at the same percentage rate.

The second factor—style—places stocks either in a growth bucket or value bucket. They found that value stocks historically return more than growth stocks do over long periods of time. That's because growth stocks tend to be glamor, or star, stocks. Investors often bid them up too much. Eventually, some of these stocks run into competition, or have missteps and fall back down to earth. In contrast, value stocks have problems and are already beaten down. One Wall Street expression is "You can't get hurt if you fall out of the basement." Since not much is expected of these stocks, they often fix their problems—and surprise us to the upside.

Professors Fama and French used price-to-book to differentiate between growth and value. The price part of the ratio is the market value, or market capitalization, a term that measures size. The book part of the ratio in the denominator is the net worth item on a balance sheet. In other words, book value equals all of the assets on a firm's balance sheet minus all of its liabilities. A firm with a lower than average price-to-book ratio is considered to be a value stock, while a firm with a higher than average price-to-book ratio is considered to be a growth stock. The historical average price-to-book ratio of the S&P 500 is about 2.5.

Putting the two factors—size and style—together results in the following historical results. Small cap value stocks usually have the best performance over long periods of time. Large cap growth stocks usually have the worst performance over long periods of time. In the short run, of course, investors might gravitate towards the safety of large cap growth stocks, especially during times of market distress. However, over the long-term, fear usually fades and these investments tend to provide lower returns.

The mutual fund research service, Morningstar, has popularized the term style box. It's a picture that shows a fund by its size and style dimensions. If you have bought a mutual fund before, you know that many of them have the term large cap, small cap, growth or value in their names. So now, you know some of the backstory on these terms. Fama and French's two-factor model, size and style, explains the historical relationship between risk and return pretty well. But they and other researchers have continued to refine the approach.

The three-factor model adds beta back to the equation. In more recent years, researchers have added two new variables into the mix, momentum and liquidity. The notion of momentum, or trend following, has been around for more than 100 years. Jesse Livermore, a great trader in the first half of the last century, was one of its most successful practitioners. Momentum investors buy what has been going up in the recent past, and sell—or sell short—investments that have recently been falling. In the short-run, let's say periods of one year or less, researchers have found that momentum works. High flyers keep flying and losers keep falling.

Liquidity refers to the ability to sell an asset quickly and at fair market value. So, your house or apartment is probably not liquid. But stock in AT&T or IBM is liquid. U.S. Treasury bonds, notes, and bills are very liquid. Researchers have found, once again over long periods of time, that investors get paid to own illiquid assets. It is basically another type of risk. During times of distress, the opposite usually holds. That is, people gravitate towards the safety of liquid investments.

So, the current state of Modern Portfolio Theory is that you should consider risk to be an equal partner with return. The risk is driven by the interaction or correlation among the investments in your portfolio. Markowitz Portfolio Theory offers a strong foundation for obtaining portfolios this way. Professors Sharpe, Fama, French, and others have done a lot to explain the relationship between risk and return. The risk-free rate of interest should be the minimum threshold for any risk asset. Beyond this low hurdle, investors should get compensated in the long run for taking on additional types of risk.

The additional risk factors that researchers have zoomed in on include market risk, also known as beta; size, measured as the market value of the stock; style, measured as growth or value; momentum, or the recent trend in price, and liquidity, which measures how quickly you can sell an asset at fair market value.

According to the theories and empirical evidence, if you want to make the most money, buy illiquid small cap value stocks that have upward momentum. The stocks that tend to have the lowest return are the most liquid large-cap growth names, with downward momentum. But if you follow this approach, be prepared to hold onto your hat when the market is falling, because in the short run you will lose the most money with this kind of security.

If all this sounds too theoretical for you, I'm not surprised. But don't worry, there are a lot of practical applications. Many index funds and ETFs, or exchange-traded funds, are organized by the large cap, small cap, growth, and value themes. Other ETFs focus on momentum. One of the largest firms in the space is Dimensional Fund Advisors, or DFA for short, with something on the order of $400 billion in assets under management. Not surprisingly, Professors Fama and French serve on the firm's Board of Advisors.

6

John Bogle, Index Mutual Fund Pioneer

I ndex funds are mutual funds that track the performance of specific index, like the 30 stocks in the Dow Jones Industrial Average. They're not sexy, and they're unlikely to help you get rich quickly, but today they account for more than 20% of all mutual fund assets. An exchange-traded fund, or ETF, is an investment that is constructed like a mutual fund but trades like an individual stock. The theoretical underpinning of the value provided by index funds is intense competition.

Making the Market versus Beating the Market

> Because investors will act on important information when they come across it, market prices usually reflect all relevant information. Such a market is said to be efficient. An entire theory attaches to this thought process, called the efficient market hypothesis. Its roots go back to 1900 and the doctoral dissertation of French mathematician Louis Bachelier, who argued that prices typically follow a random pattern.

> The concept of efficient markets is upsetting to many active fund managers. It basically says that a monkey throwing darts at the stock pages of *The Wall Street Journal* will select a portfolio

that performs about as well as one chosen by professional fund managers. The reason is that investors compete intensely; over time, competition swallows all the easy money opportunities. Only new information impacts the price of a stock, and that is, by definition, unpredictable.

> Noble laureate Eugene Fama breaks the efficient market hypothesis into 3 forms, or information sets:

  o Weak-form efficiency, wherein investors can't consistently beat the market using historical price and volume data.

  o Semi-strong form efficiency, wherein investors can't consistently beat the market using any public information; not only the historical price and volume information, but also a company's financial statements, and whatever other information is available.

  o Strong-form efficiency, wherein investors can't consistently beat the market using any information, whether historical price and volume data; public information; or private, inside information.

> The bulk of the academic studies of the efficient-market hypothesis find that the market is both weak form and semi-strong form efficient, but that the market is not strong-form efficient. Rather than citing a laundry list of academic studies, perhaps the best "proof," of weak and semi-strong market efficiency is the performance of professional fund managers. Most can't beat a simple index, despite their advantages.

> An index tracks a basket of stocks. The oldest is the Dow Jones Industrial Average, which tracks the performance of 30 blue chip stocks. Index funds have very low trading costs, since they essentially buy and hold forever. The typical cost of an index fund is about 0.2%, and sometimes much less. Some index funds charge no fee, with the sponsoring company hoping to make money by also selling the customer some other product or service.

○ An index fund helps answer at least two important questions. The first is, "How did the market do today?" You need to measure market performance to answer that question.

○ The second is, "How is my portfolio doing?" To answer that question, you probably want to compare the performance of your portfolio to a benchmark like a market index such as the S&P 500.

> A quantitative group within Wells Fargo created the first index fund in 1971. It was an equal-weighted index based on a group of large stocks trading on the New York Stock Exchange. Equal weighted means the price changes in the smallest stock have the same impact on the index returns as the price changes in the largest stock.

> John Bogle, the founder and retired CEO of the Vanguard Group created the first index mutual fund in 1975. This landmark fund, based on the performance of the S&P 500, changed the financial landscape in ways that Bogle probably never imagined.

John Bogle

> John Bogle was born May 8, 1929, in Montclair, NJ. His family, like many others at the time, lost most of their wealth during the Great Depression. Nevertheless, he attended the Blair Academy on a scholarship. He also worked at a series of jobs to help pay for school expenses. Bogle attended Princeton University, also on scholarship, where he studied economics. One afternoon, in the Princeton library, Bogle came across a *Fortune* magazine article titled "Big Money in Boston."

> Mutual funds, as we know them today, had originated in Boston in 1924, and most of the funds at the time operated in that region. Bogle decided to write his senior thesis on mutual funds. His thesis found that the average mutual fund didn't outperform the market, and he suggested that the industry would be best served by lowering sales charges and management fees.

> Princeton alumnus Walter L. Morgan—the founder of the Wellington Fund—read Bogle's thesis and offered him a job. By the mid-1960s, he made it clear that Bogle was in line to run the firm. Bogle officially became president of Wellington in 1967 and CEO in 1971. Wellington was an actively managed investment firm—it did not follow the passive management strategy of index investing that Bogle prescribed—and it remains so to this day.

  ○ The late 1960s were a bull market in U.S. stocks, and the funds that did the best employed momentum and high turnover strategies. They owned names like Xerox, Polaroid, and IBM and other well-known growth stocks. The investment mindset at the time was that these companies were so strong that they could be successfully bought regardless of their price. The thinking, which was eventually shown to be flawed, is that these companies could grow their way out of any problems.

  ○ Wellington's performance in the mid-1960s was disappointing and, in 1966, Bogle made the decision to merge with Thorndike,

Doran, Paine and Lewis. The go-go stocks began to fall a short time later and ran into a terrible bear market during the 1973–1974 period, when the S&P 500 fell by about half.

Vanguard

> Vanguard was not organized as a traditional for-profit corporation, but rather as a mutual share company. Vanguard returns all its profits to the mutual funds it administers. This practice results in lowering expense ratios even beyond the relatively low costs of index fund-based investing. In a mutual form of ownership, the shareholders are the owners.

> Vanguard quickly expanded into running its own funds: first active, then passive (or index) funds and still offers many actively managed funds that account for about one-quarter to one-third of the firm's assets. But even these are relatively low cost, and the net profits from the management fees of running the funds accrue to the shareholders of the funds. With about $3 trillion in client assets, Vanguard is a major presence in the mutual fund industry today.

> At the end of 1975, when Vanguard launched the first index mutual fund, some critics said that trying to market average returns was un-American. Bogle was hoping to raise $150 million at the launch, but raised only $11.3 million, and it would be another decade before the fund had any material competition in index based investing. But over time, people couldn't argue with the fund's performance, tax efficiency, and bargain-basement fees.

Advice for Investors

> John Bogle stepped down as CEO of Vanguard in 1995 and left its board in 1999. He has written about 10 books, in which he lays out his investment philosophy. Bogle cautions against paying a lot of money for financial advice. Although not denying that some investors could benefit from using advisors, for example,

to prevent them from doing irrational things with their money, he questions how much value advisors can add to performance.

> Bogle believes that past fund performance may offer some predictive value in establishing the risk of a fund, and its long-term consistency, but it should not be overrated or overemphasized. For example, a fund that owns mostly utility and consumer staples stocks is likely to have less risk than the market as a whole over long periods, assuming the fund doesn't materially change its strategy or types of holdings.

> Bogle also suggests that we be somewhat wary of star mutual fund managers. For every Peter Lynch or John Neff who consistently generate strong returns, many one- and two-hit wonders call a dramatic market turn and later badly underperform.

> Bogle cautions awareness of the law of large numbers for actively managed funds. That is, the bigger a fund gets, the harder is it to outperform. One reason is that large funds are generally tilted towards large stocks that are widely followed; the manager is unlikely to uncover something unknown by the market, generally a precondition for outperformance.

> For nearly all investors, Bogle suggests a long-term buy and hold approach. He advises looking at your portfolio once a year so you can have the miracle of compound interest and returns work in your favor without the urge to make too many changes.

> John Bogle and Vanguard also played a leading role in two other low-cost, index-oriented strategies. These are target (or horizon date) funds, and tax-advantaged funds.

  ○ The typical horizon-date fund looks at your planned retirement date. Let's say you are 40 and plan to retire in 20 years. Because you still have a long time to retirement, your asset allocation in a horizon fund will consist mostly of equity index funds. As you gradually approach retirement age, the horizon fund will increase your allocation to fixed-income index funds, because they tend to be steadier, and decrease your exposure to more variable equity investments.

○ If you have assets in a taxable account, it might be possible to get a slightly better outcome using tax-loss harvesting. Let's say you have a diversified portfolio of investments, and one of your stocks is Goldman Sachs. Suppose Goldman Sachs's stock is down 15% for the year to date. Tax-advantaged funds would look to sell Goldman Sachs when it was down, take the capital loss, and match it against capital gains in the same account or elsewhere. Estimates vary, but a rule of thumb is that the tax-advantaged fund can add about 1% per year, on an after-tax basis, over a regular index fund held in a taxable account.

> Index funds are best suited for people who don't have a background in financial investments or who are too busy to devote time to picking individual securities or funds. The efficient market hypothesis is not set in stone. Examples of people and strategies that appear to outperform the market as a whole occur on a regular basis. But outperformance is hard to achieve and indexing is simple—and tough to beat.

Suggested Reading

Bogle, *Common Sense on Mutual Funds*.
Rostad, *The Man in the Arena*.

Questions to Consider

1. How would you describe the investment strategy of John Bogle?

2. Do you think passive or active investment strategies are a better route to financial security?

6

Transcript

John Bogle, Index Mutual Fund Pioneer

What if I told you I had a simple, low-cost investment strategy that would enable you to outperform about 90% of all professional fund managers over the long run? By long run, I mean 10 plus years. And no, I'm not talking about a Bernie Madoff-like strategy.

I'm talking about index funds. Index funds are mutual funds that track the performance of a specific index, like the 30 stocks in the Dow Jones Industrial Average. Why don't more people buy them? Well, they're not sexy, and they're unlikely to help you get rich quickly. But today they account for more than 20% of all mutual fund assets. An exchange-traded fund, or ETF, is an investment that's constructed like a mutual fund but trades like an individual stock. One ETF that tracks the Standard and Poor's 500 index trades something like an incredible 155 million shares a day.

In this session, we'll discuss what index funds are, how they're created, and their theoretical underpinnings. We'll also discuss the seminal role that john bogle, the founder of the mutual fund titan Vanguard, played in bringing index funds to the public. The theoretical underpinning of the value provided by index funds is intense competition. There is a story in the leading investments textbook that goes something like this.

> Two professors are walking down the street. One is a finance professor, the other is a history professor. A $20 bill is lying on the

street. The finance professor walks by while the history professor stoops down to pick it up. The history professor says, "Why didn't you try to pick up the $20 bill?" The finance professor says, "If it was real, someone would have picked it up already."

The point of the story is that people aren't going to leave money lying on the ground. If investors come across important information, they will act on it. So market prices usually reflect all relevant information. A market that has this characteristic is said to be an efficient market. There is an entire theory attached to the thought process, which goes by the name of the efficient market hypothesis or EMH for short. A Nobel Prize in Economics was awarded to Eugene Fama, a finance professor at the University of Chicago, mainly because of his work in this field.

The roots of the efficient market hypothesis go back to 1900 and the Ph.D. thesis of a French mathematician named Louis Bachelier. In his *Theory of Speculation*, Bachelier argued that prices typically follow a random pattern or what is often called a random walk today. The term random walk has a colorful history. One version of the story says it came from a mathematician trying to model the behavior of a drunken person who was trying to find his keys at night beneath a dim streetlight. He would take a step in one direction, and then another direction, and then another with no discernible pattern.

The concept of efficient markets is upsetting to many active fund managers. It basically says that a monkey throwing darts at the stock pages of The Wall Street Journal will select a portfolio that performs about the same as highly educated and compensated professional fund managers. The reason, of course, is that investors compete intensely, and, over time, this takes all of the easy money opportunities away. So it is new news that impacts the price of a stock. And new news is, by definition, unpredictable.

A theory has to be testable. Otherwise, it's just talk. In order to make the efficient market hypothesis testable, you need to specify the information that you are using to pick the investments. Noble Laureate Eugene Fama breaks the efficient market hypothesis into three forms or information sets. He calls the first information set weak-form efficiency. If the market is weak-form efficient, it means investors can't consistently beat the market using historical price and volume data. I emphasize the word consistently since almost anyone can get lucky for a while. Consistency is a sign of skill and not luck.

Technically, academics try to measure excess returns—or returns greater than the risk you're taking—but the phrase beating the market is more intuitive, and so I will stick with it.

Strategies that look for patterns in stock prices using past price and volume data comprise the investment school of thought called technical analysis. And a popular strategy in technical analysis is momentum trading. Momentum strategies buy what has gone up recently and sell or sell short what has gone down. Its roots are in crowd psychology. One of the worst feelings for an investor is to be wrong and alone. By engaging in momentum trading, you are following the crowd. And if you are wrong, you have plenty of company and can rationalize, to yourself or a client, that everyone else had the same stocks.

The second form of the efficient-market hypothesis is called semi-strong form efficiency. If the market is semi-strong form efficient it means you can't consistently beat the market using any public information. This includes not only historical price and volume information, but also a company's financial statements, and whatever else information is out there on the Internet, or CNBC, and so forth. It basically implies that what most professional fund managers are doing is a waste of time, since they rely on public information. So, now you can see more clearly why most fund managers—except index fund managers, of course—hate the theory.

The third and final form of the efficient-market hypothesis is called strong-form efficiency. If the market is strong-form efficient it means you can't consistently beat the market using any information, be it historical price and volume data, public information, or private, inside information. Now, trading on inside information—to the explicit disadvantage of outsiders—can be illegal, but corporate insiders always have private information about their companies, and legally are entitled to certain windows when they can trade in their own stock, for example.

So, what does the evidence say about the efficient-market hypothesis? The bulk of the academic studies find that the market is both weak and semi-strong form efficient, but that the market is not strong-form efficient. Rather than citing a laundry list of academic studies, perhaps the best proof, so to speak, of weak and semi-strong for market efficiency is the performance of professional fund managers. Most can't beat a simple index despite their advantages. Namely, they are highly educated, have many informational resources and get a large bonus – often in the millions of dollars – if they beat their benchmark. Corporate insiders and, yes, members of Congress, have been found to earn superior returns based on inside information. It's somewhat easy to see why corporate insiders may earn superior returns, due to their private information about the companies they work for. But folks in Congress?

Well, imagine that you were a congressperson and knew in advance of public disclosure that there was going to be a large increase in the defense budget. It doesn't take a rocket scientist to make money trading in defense stocks, like Lockheed Martin or General Dynamics. Well, the gravy train for Congress on insider trading may be over. The Stop Trading on Congressional Knowledge Act—the bill's acronym spells S-T-O-C-K—is now law, restricting the ability of Congress members to lawfully trade on private, governmental information.

One of the takeaways from the efficient-market hypothesis is that there is a relationship between risk and return, in the long run. So, if you want higher returns, you're probably going to have to take on more risk. The efficient-market hypothesis first got widespread attention in the mid-1960s and early 1970s. Of course, it was only natural that someone would try to turn the implications of the theory into a product. So creating a fund based on an index was a natural place to look.

The oldest, and among the best known to the investing public, is the Dow Jones Industrial Average. It tracks the performance of 30 blue-chip stocks, such as Apple, Microsoft, Coca-Cola, Wal-Mart, and Home Depot. Index funds have very low trading costs since they essentially buy and hold forever. The typical cost of an index fund is about 2/10 of 1%, and sometimes much less. I have seen some index funds charge no fee, with the sponsoring company hoping to make the money by also selling the customer some other product or service.

An index fund manager is like the equivalent of the Maytag repairman. That is, stock index fund managers don't have much to do. The average number of annual changes in the Dow's index membership is about 5% per year, which means that the average stock stays in the index for about 20 years. An index fund helps answer at least two important questions. The first is, "How did the market do today?" You need an index fund to measure market performance to answer that question.

A second important question is "How is my portfolio doing?" To answer that question, you probably want to compare the performance of your portfolio to a benchmark like a market index. Let's say you own a diversified portfolio of large U.S. stocks, and that an appropriate benchmark is the S&P 500. For example, if the S&P 500 increased 5% over the year, and your portfolio was up 10%, you probably did a great job. However, if the S&P 500 was up 20% and your portfolio was only up 5%, you probably did a lousy job.

A quantitative group within Wells Fargo created the first index fund in 1971. It was an equal-weighted index based on a group of large stocks trading on the New York Stock Exchange. Equal-weighted means each stock in the index has the same effect, or importance when computing a return on the overall index. For example, if there were 100 stocks in an equal-weighted index, each stock would count for 1% when computing the returns of the overall index. So the price changes in the smallest stock have the same impact on the index returns as the price changes in the largest stock. The Wells Fargo fund was marketed to institutions such as pension funds, and not to individual investors. But a couple of years later, Burton Malkiel, a professor of economics at Princeton University, published his bestselling book *A Random Walk Down Wall Street*. In it, Malkiel called for the creation of index funds for the general public. John Bogle, the founder and retired CEO of the Vanguard Group created the first index mutual fund on December 31, 1975. This landmark fund, which was based on the performance of the S&P 500, changed the financial landscape in ways that Bogle probably never imagined.

John Bogle was born on May 8, 1929, in Montclair, New Jersey. His family, like many others at the time, lost most of their wealth during the Great Depression. Nevertheless, he attended an exclusive prep school, the Blair Academy in Blairstown, New Jersey, on a scholarship. He also worked a series of jobs to help pay for school expenses, such as delivering newspapers, working at the post office and a bowling alley, and serving food. Bogle attended Princeton University, also on scholarship, where he studied economics. One afternoon, in the Princeton library, Bogle came across a *Fortune* magazine article called "Big Money in Boston."

The year was 1949, and the article discussed the small, but rapidly growing, mutual fund industry. Mutual funds, as we know them today, had originated in Boston a quarter century earlier, in 1924. And most of the funds at the time operated in that region. Bogle decided to write his senior thesis on mutual funds. He called it, "The Economic Role of the Investment Company." His thesis found that the average mutual fund didn't outperform the market. And he suggested the industry would best be served by lowering sales charges and management fees. It would be decades before he created the first index mutual fund, but his thesis suggests that the seeds of how he would run Vanguard were sowed during his time at Princeton.

Princeton alumnus Walter L. Morgan—the founder of the Wellington Fund—read Bogle's thesis, and offered him a job. Morgan wrote to his employees, "Largely as a result of his thesis, we have added Mr. Bogle to our Wellington organization." Morgan went on to mentor Bogle, and, by the mid-1960s, he made it clear that Bogle was in line to run the firm. Bogle officially became President of Wellington in 1967, and CEO in 1971. Now, Wellington was an actively managed investment firm—meaning it did not follow the passive investment strategy of index investing that Bogle prescribed—and it remains an active manager to this day.

The late 1960s were known as the go-go years in the mutual fund industry. There was a bull market in U.S. stocks and the funds that did the best employed momentum and high turnover strategies. Some of the aggressive growth managers at the time included Gerry Tsai at Fidelity Investments, and the later The Manhattan Fund; and Fred Carr of The Enterprise Fund. They owned names like Xerox, Polaroid, and IBM and other well-known growth stocks. The investment mindset at the time was that these companies were so strong that they could be successfully bought, regardless of their price. The thinking, which was eventually shown to be flawed, is that these companies could grow their way out of any problems. But, to use a Wall Street expression, "No tree grows to the sky." In other words, a bull market can't last forever.

Wellington's performance in the mid-1960s was disappointing, and, in 1966, Bogle made the decision to merge with one of the go-go firms in Boston, Thorndike, Doran, Paine, and Lewis. However, the go-go stocks began to fall a short time later and ran into a terrible bear market during the 1973–1974 period, when the S&P 500 fell by about half. The merger of Wellington and Thorndike, Doran went sour as the market tipped. Bogle was fired as CEO in 1974, but he maintained a cordial relationship with the firm.

That's when he formed Vanguard, and he was able to negotiate an agreement to perform administrative work, but not investment management, for the Wellington Funds. The name Vanguard comes from a series of boats in the British Royal Navy with a distinguished history. Of course, the word vanguard also means the leader or forefront of a movement.

One huge contribution Bogle made was in the way he set up Vanguard. It wasn't organized as a traditional for-profit corporation but rather as a mutual share company. That's right, a mutual fund company organized as a mutual share company. It means that Vanguard returns all its profits to the mutual fund which it administers, which winds up lowering expense ratios even beyond the relatively low costs of index fund–based investing. In a mutual form of ownership, the shareholders are the owners. It's somewhat common in the insurance industry, but to this day remains virtually unheard of in the investment management space.

At Vanguard, Bogle championed the notion of being a fiduciary, which means managing a client's assets solely in the best interest of the client. He also called it stewardship, and an approach of the people, by the people, for the people. Bogle's emphasis on putting the investor first—and being a fiduciary, being a steward—and his emphasis on low-cost, tax-efficient index funds, resulted in some calling him by the nickname,

Saint Jack. And no doubt, Bogle's strong Christian faith helped shape his personal investment philosophy. He became wealthy running Wellington and Vanguard, but he could have been a billionaire many times over if he ran Vanguard as a traditional for-profit company. He has a fan club that goes by name of Bogleheads.

So, Vanguard began its existence as sort of a back-office type mutual fund firm but quickly expanded into running its own funds. First active, then passive or index funds. Some people are surprised to learn that Vanguard still offers many actively managed funds. It's true, they account for about one-quarter to one-third of the firm's assets. But even these are relatively low cost, and the net profits from the management fees of running the funds accrue to the shareholders due to Vanguard's mutual form of ownership. With about $3 trillion in client assets, Vanguard is a major presence in the mutual fund industry today. But at one time, this appeared to be far from inevitable.

At the end of 1975, when Bogle and Vanguard launched the first index mutual fund—then called the First Index Investment Trust —people made fun of the idea. They called it Bogle's Folly. Some investment-management critics said that trying to market average returns was un-American. Bogle was hoping to raise $150 million at the launch but raised only $11.3 million. And it would be another decade before the fund had any material competition in index-based investing. But, slowly, over time, people couldn't argue with the index fund's performance, tax efficiency and bargain-basement fees. Plus, with Bogle preaching his gospel, he won a lot of converts.

While Bogle hit a home run with index funds, his vision isn't perfect. For instance, he isn't a fan of a variation of the index fund, known as exchange-traded fund or ETF. ETFs, hold baskets of stocks, bonds or commodities, and trade actively. Typically they track an index. But Bogle thinks they encourage investors to speculate, or adopt a trading mentality, rather than invest for the long-term. And yet, ETFs are today a $3 trillion business. And Vanguard, run today by a different management team, is now a sizeable player in the ETF market.

John Bogle, who stepped down as CEO of Vanguard in 1995—and left its board in 1999—has written about 10 books. His bestselling one is called *Common Sense on Mutual Funds*, in which he lays out his investment philosophy. Of course, he starts out with the advice of selecting low-cost index funds. Bogle also cautions against paying a lot of money for financial advice. He doesn't deny that some investors could benefit from using advisors, for example, to prevent them from doing irrational things with their money. But he questions how much value advisors can add to performance.

One of the most important problems investors encounter is chasing top-performing funds and then later cashing out when the funds inevitably fall back down to earth, buying high and selling low. Bogle says not to overemphasize past fund performance, though he says that performance may offer some predictive value in establishing the risk of a fund and its long-term consistency. For example, a fund that owns mostly Utility and Consumer Staples stocks, like Con Edison, Coca-Cola and Procter and Gamble, is likely to have less risk than the market as a whole, over long periods of time. That assumes the fund doesn't materially change its strategy, or types of holdings, over time.

Bogle also suggests that we be somewhat wary of star mutual fund managers. For every Peter Lynch or John Neff who consistently generate strong returns, there are many one- and two-hit wonders who might call a dramatic market turn, and later badly underperform. In addition, Bogle made us more aware of the law of large numbers for actively managed funds. That is, the bigger a fund gets, the harder it is to outperform. One reason is that large funds are generally tilted towards large stocks like IBM, Johnson & Johnson, and AT&T. These stocks are widely followed, and therefore the manager is unlikely to uncover something that's not known by the market—generally a precondition for outperformance.

With very large funds in mind, Peter Lynch coined the term diworseification. That is, diversifying beyond a certain limit can actually detract from your results. Bogle says don't own too many funds since they will probably overlap and result in unnecessary fees and transaction costs. For nearly all investors, Bogle suggests a long-term buy and hold approach. He advises not to peek at your portfolio on a regular basis, but rather to look at it once a year—and, ideally, not much more than that—so that you can have the miracle of compound interest and returns work in your favor, without the urge to make too many changes. John Bogle and Vanguard also played a leading role in two other low-cost, index-oriented strategies. These are target or horizon date funds, and tax-advantaged funds.

The typical horizon-date fund looks at your planned retirement date. Let's say you're 40 and you plan to retire in 20 years. Because you still have a long time to retirement, your asset allocation in a horizon fund will consist mostly of equity index funds. As you gradually approach retirement age, the horizon fund will increase your allocation to fixed-income index funds because they tend to be steadier and decrease your exposure to more variable equity investments.

Now, you might have thought that once an index fund's returns were in, it wasn't possible to improve on the result. However, if you have assets in a taxable account, it might be possible to get a little bit better outcome. The trick lies in what is called tax-loss harvesting. Let's say you have a diversified portfolio of investments, and one of your stocks is Goldman Sachs. Suppose Goldman Sachs is down 15% for year-to-date. Tax-advantaged funds would look to sell Goldman Sachs when it was down and to take the capital loss so that you could match it against capital gains in the same account or elsewhere.

You could then replace Goldman with a competitor that moves in tandem, such as Morgan Stanley. And if you want to put Goldman back in your portfolio, you can do it after the 30-day wash sale rule has expired. A wash is the sale of a security to realize a loss, but one that is purchased back within 30 days. The IRS disallows losses for wash-sale transactions, so most taxable investors wait at least 30 days to repurchase a security that had losses in their account. In most instances, the replacement stock would not have moved so much in the interim, so even if it were up you wouldn't get hit with a large tax bill if you wanted to switch back to Goldman. Estimates vary, but the rule of thumb is that the tax-advantaged fund can add about 1% per year, on an after-tax basis, over a regular index fund held in a taxable account.

So, the index fund is a staple of modern day investments. There is an index fund for almost anything you can think of. Want to track the bond market? One popular index is the Barclay's Aggregate, symbol AGG. Worried about inflation? There is the Treasury Inflation Protected securities, symbol TIP. Want to track the performance of a foreign stock market like Germany? There is an index fund for it, symbol EWG.

Who are index funds best suited for? Well, practically everyone, I suppose, but especially people who don't have a background in financial investments, or people who are too busy to devote a lot of time to picking individual securities or funds. Index funds are the ultimate set it and forget it investments.

The efficient market hypothesis is not set in stone. There are examples of people and strategies that appear to outperform the market as a whole, on a regular basis. But outperformance IS hard to achieve, and indexing is a simple and tough to beat. Investors largely have John Bogle to thank for the index fund revolution. Without having to pick a single stock, he changed the investment world forever.

7

Small-Cap Stocks: More Risk, More Reward

Numerous academic studies have found that over long periods, small-cap stocks tend to outperform large-cap stocks by wide margins. That said, small stocks sometimes also experience huge volatility swings, especially in declining markets. A small-cap stock is generally held to be one valued at less than $1 billion. A stock with a market cap of less than $100 million is called a micro-cap. A company with a market cap of less than $50 million is called a nano-cap.

Small-Cap Fundamentals

> Studies find that small-cap stocks historically provide higher returns than large-cap stocks by an incremental 2 to 3 percentage points per year. Though it might not sound like much, these fractional gains can add up to very large differences over time. Small-cap stocks historically provide higher returns than large-cap stocks because, according to several measures, they are riskier.

> The first measure is market risk, known as beta, which measures the risk of one investment against the market as a whole. Small-cap stocks tend to be more volatile and usually have a higher level of beta than large-cap stocks. The small firms are generally less

established, have shakier financials, and do not pay a dividend, and therefore exhibit higher market risks.

> In addition, small-cap stocks have higher liquidity risk. A liquid asset is one that you can sell quickly and at fair market value. A liquidity risk entails the danger of trading into or out of an asset with a narrow investor base.

> Small-cap stocks also are under-followed by analysts and financial reporters. The lack of coverage means less information about these neglected stocks, which is a negative to investors who want some hand-holding. We can refer to this as information risk. Wall Street firms often have little incentive to follow small-cap stocks because bankers who employ research analysts typically get paid a percentage of the size of the deals they work on.

> These risks might be a negative from some perspectives, but they can also be positive. Higher risk investments generally result in

higher realized returns, but capturing the extra risk premium often takes a long time, often more than a decade.

Passive Small-Cap Strategies

> The easiest way to invest in small-cap stocks is through an index fund or an exchange-traded fund or ETF. The first small-cap index was created in 1984 by Frank Russell and Company and is known as the Russell 2000 Index. This index created an opportunity for investors to become active in the small-cap market without having to individually research and select small stocks.

> It is the most widely followed small-cap index today. More than 90% of small-cap investment managers use the Russell 2000 as benchmark. Standard and Poor, or S&P, also has a small-cap index of 600 names, but it hasn't gained as much traction as Russell's.

> In the early 1990s, Eugene Fama and Ken French provided further insight into the large- versus small-cap performance discrepancy. They verified the finding that small-cap outperforms large-cap over long-periods. But they combined this finding with another, which is that value typically outperforms growth over long periods.

> Fama and French don't view their findings as the Holy Grail of investing. Rather, they think small firms and value firms have higher risks, such as being more prone to bankruptcy, and that's why they have higher returns.

Warren Buffett Cameo

> Warren Buffett is well-known for his investing prowess. But earlier in his career, Buffett managed much smaller amounts of capital, and had incredible success with small-cap stocks. He has often said that managing large sums of money results in a performance disadvantage. It forces him to hunt for large firms to have a meaningful impact on his portfolio's overall performance.

- In one interview, Buffett said that if he were managing only a million dollars instead of tens of billions, he would guarantee returns of 50% a year because he would have no constraints on a target's size and would not have to worry, when taking a position, about his investment's impact on the price.

- Buffett once was asked where individual investors should look for investments. Buffett replied that he thought small-cap stocks were great hunting grounds because large institutions can't invest there, practically speaking.

> Buffett's most famous small-cap investment was in Berkshire Hathaway. Today, Berkshire is one of the largest companies in the world, with a market cap in the hundreds of billions of dollars, but it started life as a textile maker. Buffett started buying Berkshire in 1962, at a price of $7.60 a share. Even then, Buffett could see that textile manufacturing was a declining business in the United States, but he saw value in the firm in the form of its working capital, real estate, plants, and equipment.

> Buffett paid $14.86 a share to gain control of Berkshire in 1965. At the time, Berkshire had net working capital of $19 a share plus valuable property. The genius of Buffett was to use its cash flow to help buy other companies—such as The Washington Post, See's Candy, Coca-Cola, and GEICO insurance, a business that generated a lot of cash itself—either outright or in part through their stock.

Peter Lynch Cameo

> Another famous investor who did well with small-cap stocks is Peter Lynch. He turned Fidelity Investments' Magellan Fund into the largest mutual fund in the world by the time he stepped down. A $1000 investment in Magellan when Lynch started there in 1977 had turned into $28,000 by his retirement 13 years later.

> A significant part of Lynch's outperformance was due to his investment in small-cap firms. And even after Magellan became large—with an investment portfolio in the tens of billions of dollars—Lynch didn't completely abandon small caps.

> Lynch coined the investment term tenbagger, which refers to a stock that increases 10 times or more from the original purchase price. Dunkin' Donuts is one of Lynch's most famous tenbaggers. The relevant point is that it is much easier for a small-cap stock to become a tenbagger than it is for a large one.

> Lynch has shared his thoughts on the small-cap market in several of his books. He suggests that with small companies, you are better off to wait until they turn a profit before you invest. This point might seem obvious, but it's important because small money-losing firms sometimes go out of business.

> Lynch also suggests looking for niche companies. Many large companies today started out as niche players. Microsoft began as a firm that developed programs for the BASIC computer language. One of its first big breaks was creating the operating system MS-DOS for the IBM personal computer.

  ○ MS-DOS eventually came to dominate the operating system market. But Microsoft also expanded into the business-software marketplace with MS-Office. The lesson from Lynch is that a small-cap company can eventually dominate its niche and expand to related fields.

  ○ One way to determine if a stock has been "discovered," so to speak, is to look at the percentage of the stock owned by institutions. This statistic can easily be found at no cost on many financial websites.

  ○ As a rule of thumb, if institutional ownership is less than 50%, the stock is not widely followed by larger investors such as mutual funds, hedge funds, and pension funds. A small-cap stock can quickly turn into a mid-cap stock when institutions get on board.

> Lynch likes small companies that have proved that their concept can be replicated. Starbucks is a good example of what he means:

  o Starbucks had a concept—a coffee shop that provides a unique experience.

  o The concept began in Seattle, and was developed in one region, the Northwest, before being rolled out nationwide.

  o If Peter Lynch saw a concept like this that could be replicated across the country—and the firm was profitable—he'd be inclined to invest in it.

> Lynch thinks the opportunities abound to find small-cap investments. He says, "The average person is exposed to interesting local companies and products years before professionals."

Michael Burry Cameo

> If you've read the book or seen the movie called *The Big Short* you probably recognize the name Michael Burry. He was one of the first to recognize the bubble that occurred in the U.S. housing market, and he made an enormous amount of money by betting that the housing market would collapse. He did so by using a complicated derivative instrument called a credit-default swap.

> Although Burry is most famous for that trade, a big part of his financial success can be traced to his investments in small-cap stocks.

> Burry considers himself a value investor and a disciple of value-investing pioneers Benjamin Graham and Warren Buffett. His investment in Hyde Athletic Industries back in 1997 is a good example of his approach to small caps.

- ○ Hyde Athletic was a maker of athletic footwear. When Burry bought the stock it was selling at a deep discount and less than its net working capital—what Graham called a net-net. Furthermore, the company was growing rapidly.

- ○ Burry bought the stock for around $5 a share, when its market cap was $31 million. But based on its net working capital alone, the company was worth at least $37 million. Hyde Athletic eventually changed its name to Saucony, its most popular brand, which today has a rabid following among runners. And Burry says he made a 50% return on this small-cap investment.

Conclusion

- > Small-cap investing can offer excellent long-term investing possibilities. The easiest way to get exposure to small-caps is by investing in an index fund, which typically are well diversified and relatively inexpensive. You could also invest in one of the many actively managed small-cap mutual or exchange-traded funds.

- > A common strategy is to invest in a basket of small, young firms in a rapidly growing industry and then, as the evidence becomes clearer, sell the laggards and put the sales proceeds into the winner—or winners.

- > Buffett, Graham, and Burry focused on deep value. They reasoned that the deep value in neglected stocks would eventually be realized by the market. Or you could take the Peter Lynch approach, and focus on small companies that are profitable, have a niche, and can eventually replicate their product on a larger scale.

- > Many small and risky investments end up losing money, and going out of business. But those that turn out to be winners sometimes return multiples on the initial investment. In baseball a good hitter is one who can make a hit in 1 of 3 at-bats. In the same way with small-cap stocks, you don't need to bat a thousand to generate a winning long-term return.

Suggested Reading

FTSE Russell, "The Russell 2000® Index."
Gannon, "Warren Buffett."

Questions to Consider

1. How does investment in small and mid-cap stocks differ from investing in large cap stocks?

2. Why do the stocks of small companies historically outperform large ones, over long periods of time?

7

Transcript

Small-Cap Stocks:
More Risk, More Reward

A heavyweight boxer would likely pulverize a flyweight boxer. But in investing, David sometimes beats Goliath. Numerous academic studies have found that—over long periods of time—small-cap stocks tend to outperform large-cap stocks. And by wide margins. That said, small-cap stocks sometimes experience huge volatility swings, especially in declining markets. And many investors can't stomach this kind of uncertainty.

A small-cap stock is generally held to be one valued at less than $1 billion. For instance, if the price of a stock is $10 a share—and a firm has 50 million shares outstanding—then its market capitalization would be $500 million, and that would be considered a small-cap company. A stock with a market cap of less than $100 million is called a micro-cap. And if that's not small enough, a company with a market cap of less than $50 million is called a nano-cap, which means very small.

Many famous stock pickers—including Warren Buffett, Peter Lynch, and value investors Joel Greenblatt and Seth Klarman—have made lots of money investing in small-cap stocks. Inevitably, however, as the size of their portfolios became quite large, they skewed their holdings to emphasize larger firms. That's because it's a lot easier to put large sums of money to work in big firms. If you manage $10 billion and buy a $100 million company that doubles in price, it has a 1% impact on the portfolio return, barely a rounding error. Plus, you probably wouldn't buy the entire $100 million of the company's stock, only a fraction of it. That would further limit the returns on a $10 billion portfolio. And if—like Buffett—you are managing more than $100 billion, it would be like a grain of sand on the beach.

So, most great investors have bought small-cap stocks at one time or another, but few focus exclusively in this area. And that can be an advantage for you. In this lecture, we will explore the world of small-cap investing, and discuss a range of strategies from investors in this sometimes-overlooked space.

Why do small-cap stocks historically provide higher returns than large-cap stocks? Studies find they tend to earn an incremental 2 or 3 percentage points more per year than bigger stocks. And though it might not sound like much, these fractional gains can add up to very large differences over time. The answer, in short, is that small-cap stocks historically provide higher returns than large-cap stocks because they are riskier, according to several measures.

The first measure is market risk, known as beta. Beta essentially measures the risk of one stock investment against the market as a whole. For example, technology or biotechnology stocks tend to be more volatile than food or utility stocks. Small-cap stocks also tend to be more volatile, and usually have a higher level of market risk or beta than large-cap stocks. These firms are generally less established, have shakier financials, and often do not pay a dividend, and, therefore, exhibit higher market risks. In addition, small-cap stocks have higher liquidity risk. A liquid asset is one that you can sell quickly and at fair market value. So a liquidity risk entails the danger of trading into, or trading out of, an asset with a narrow investor base.

A U.S. Treasury bill is liquid. Stock in General Electric is liquid. Stock in a small-cap stock is usually not liquid. One way to measure liquidity is by looking at trading volume. Trading volume in General Electric averages about 30 million shares a day. By comparison, trading volume in many small-cap stocks is often less than 50,000 shares a day. When institutional investors inject large amounts of money into a company or withdraw it, the act can very easily push the price of the stock up or down. So it's hard for institutional investors to quickly establish a position in a small-cap stock without affecting its price.

Small-cap stocks are also under-followed by analysts and financial reporters. There is less information about these neglected stocks due to the lack of coverage, which is a negative to investors who want some handholding. We can refer to this as information risk. Wall Street firms often have little incentive to follow small-cap stocks. That's because bankers who employ research analysts typically get paid a percentage of the size of the deals they work on. So a 5% fee for issuing a billion dollars worth of equity—something a large-cap company like Tesla might do—would be a lot more lucrative for an investment bank than would be helping a small-cap firm issue $100 million dollars' worth of equity. So bankers are more inclined to pour research resources into larger sources of fees than smaller ones.

Now, the risks we've just taken into account—market risk, liquidity risk, and information risk—might be a negative from some perspectives, but they can be positive from another perspective. Higher risk investments generally result in higher realized returns. That's primarily why small-cap stocks historically return 2 or 3% more a year than do large-cap stocks. But it often takes a long time to capture that extra premium. Often more than a decade.

For example, during the internet bubble in the late 1990s, large technology stocks like Dell, Microsoft and Amazon did very well. Small-cap stocks, especially those outside the tech sector, typically couldn't keep pace, and their indexes underperformed large-cap stock indexes five years in a row. So, it takes patience to be a small-cap investor. And you need to be able to stomach the volatility. Small-cap stocks historically exhibit about 40% to 50% greater volatility than large-cap stocks do. And, of course, this often comes during down markets. This brings to mind a Wall Street expression, "You don't know your risk tolerance until you live through a bear market."

Let's look at some small-cap strategies, both active and passive. And let's start with the passive. The easiest way to invest in small cap is through an index fund, or an exchange-traded fund—known as an ETF, for short. Index funds and ETFs are basically baskets of stocks. The first small-cap index was created in 1984 by Frank Russell and Company. It is known as the Russell 2000 Index.

Out of a universe of 3000 stocks, Russell established the first widely referenced small-cap index in 1984 by creating a basket of the lower or smaller 2000 stocks. By lower or smaller I mean as determined by market cap. With this, index funds—and later, exchange-traded funds—created an opportunity for investors to become active in the small-cap market without having to individually research and select small stocks. The index is rebalanced, or reconstituted, each June. The rebalance process accounts for changes in firm size, and for firms leaving the index due to mergers or bankruptcies, as well as firms entering the index due to initial public offerings or spinoffs. The companies in the Russell 2000 Index usually range in size from a couple of hundred million dollars in market cap all the way up to $5 billion. But the average valuation of a stock in the index is about a billion dollars.

The Frank Russell Company was started by its namesake out of Tacoma, Washington, in 1936. It began as a brokerage firm. And Frank's grandson, George Russell, is the one who really developed the firm. George graduated from Harvard Business School in 1958 and was thrust into running the company a few months later after his grandfather's unexpected death. George grew the firm, especially in the area of institutional investment consulting. One of the common things consultants do is measure performance. There were well-known stock indexes for large firms, such as the Standard & Poor's 500 and Dow Jones Industrial Average, but there was nothing for small-cap stocks. Hence, the birth of the Russell 2000 Index. It is the most widely followed small-cap index today. More than 90% of small-cap investment managers use the Russell 2000 as their benchmark. Standard and Poor's, or S&P, also has a small-cap index of 600 names, but it hasn't gained as much traction as Russell's.

In the early 1990s, Eugene Fama at the University of Chicago, and Ken French, then at Chicago—and now at Dartmouth College—provided further insight into the large versus small-cap performance discrepancy. They verified the finding that small cap outperforms large cap over long periods of time. But they combined this with another, which is that value typically outperforms growth over long periods of time. Academics typically differentiate between value and growth by metrics such as price to earnings and price to book. The price to earnings or P/E ratio is measured as the price of a stock per share, divided by the earnings per share. Stocks that have above-average P/E, typically higher than 15, are considered growth stocks. Stocks with a below-average P/E are considered value stocks.

The numerator of the price to book ratio is also the price of a stock. And the denominator, or book value, is the same as the wet worth, or shareholder equity figure, on the balance sheet. It's measured by starting with all of the assets of the firm and then subtracting all liabilities. A firm with an above-average price to book ratio, typically higher than 2.5, is considered a growth stock. Firms with a price to book value of less than average are considered value stocks.

Fama and French don't view their findings on small-cap and value investments as the holy grail. Rather, they think small firms and value firms have higher risks, such as being more prone to bankruptcy, and that's why they have higher returns. The Fama-French findings were put into action by the investment firm Dimensional Fund Advisors or DFA for short. DFA was set up in 1981 by two of Fama's students from the University of Chicago, David Booth and Rex Sinquefield. You might recognize the Booth name. Later, he donated $300 million to the University of Chicago, and they named their business school after him. DFA put many of the ideas of Fama and French to work across a range of products, including many low-cost index funds. Fama and French also serve on the Board of Directors and act as consultants to DFA. And today, the firm manages in excess of $400 billion for clients.

Now, Warren Buffett is well-known for his investing prowess in large firms such as Coca-Cola, American Express, and Wells Fargo. But earlier, in his long and storied career, Buffett managed much smaller amounts of capital and had incredible success with small-cap stocks. He's often said that managing large sums of money results in a performance disadvantage. It forces him to hunt for elephants, or large firms, to have a meaningful impact on his portfolio's overall performance. In one interview, Buffett said that if he were managing only a million dollars—instead of tens of billions of dollars—he would guarantee that he could achieve returns of 50% a year since he would have no constraints on a target's size, and not have to worry about his investment's market impact on the price, when taking a position.

Buffett once was asked where individual investors should look for investments. Buffett replied that he thought small-cap stocks were great hunting grounds because large institutions can't invest there, practically speaking. He gave the example of investing in small-cap stocks in South Korea, where the price-to-earnings ratios of many firms was only three times earnings, at the time—about 80% cheaper than the values of large U.S Stocks.

Berkshire's acquisition of See's Candy in 1972 provides a good case study on Buffett's approach to small caps. See's Candy is a California-based maker of chocolates and other confectionary items. It was founded in 1921 by Charles See. The company had a great product and a loyal following. And Buffett had a second home in California. He also loved the product, after it was brought to his attention back in 1971 by his business partner, Charlie Munger. Buffett thought there was a lot to like about See's. The product tastes great. It is a consumable, which ensures recurring revenues. It has a fanatical following and great brand name. It has the ability to raise prices. And the company requires little R&D or capital expenditures to keep the business going. It's also hard for a firm like Amazon.com to displace it.

In sum, it's a great business. But the high-end chocolate business is never going to be a huge industry, like the auto industry or the cell phone industry. So, it is destined to stay relatively small, and therefore would be under the radar screen of large fund managers. Besides, See's was a private, family owned business. And, as the principals of the firm got up in age, they decided to sell the firm to Berkshire for $25 million. At the time, See's was doing about $30 million in annual revenue and generating $4.2 million a year in profits. Well, fast forward a few years, and the business is doing about $400 million a year in sales and about $100 million a year in profits. Its cumulative profits since Buffett bought the firm are more than $1.5 billion.

Buffett's most famous small-cap investment was in Berkshire Hathaway itself. Today, Berkshire is one of the largest companies in the world, with a market cap in the hundreds of billions of dollars. But Berkshire started out in 1839 as a textile maker. And although textiles were once a thriving business in America, the business was—like many manufacturing industries—gradually outsourced overseas. Berkshire was also headquartered in the New England area and operated most of its plants there. That was a pricey area to operate factories, especially as the services industry in the Northeast prospered.

Buffett first started buying Berkshire in 1962, at a price of $7.60 a share, for his own investment firm, which he had then called the Buffett Partnership. Even then, Buffett could see that textile manufacturing business was a declining business in the United States. But he saw value in the firm, in the form of its working capital, real estate, plants, and equipment. He also held out hope that the company would be able to turn around, or at least stabilize its declining fortunes. Buffett paid $14.86 a share to gain control of Berkshire in 1965. At the time, Berkshire had net working capital of $19 a share—that is, current assets minus current liabilities—plus valuable property, its plant, and equipment. So, Buffett was getting the company for basically nothing.

And because Berkshire had more than enough capacity to handle its declining business, it didn't require a lot of new capital expenditures. The business threw off a lot of cash. And although Berkshire eventually left the textile business, the genius of Buffett was that he used its cash flow to help buy many other companies, either outright, or in part through their stock. These included companies such as The Washington Post, See's Candy, Coca-Cola, Dairy Queen, Burlington Northern, and Wells Fargo, and especially Geico insurance, a business that generated a lot of cash itself. Ultimately, through wise capital-allocation decisions, Buffett turned a small-cap company into one of the largest in the world.

Another famous investor that did well with small-cap stocks is Peter Lynch. He turned Fidelity Investments' Magellan fund into the largest mutual fund in the world by the time he stepped down. A $1000 investment in Magellan when Lynch started there in 1977 had turned into $28,000 by his retirement 13 years later. A significant part of Lynch's outperformance was due to his investment in small-cap firms. And even after Magellan became large—

with an investment portfolio in the tens of billions of dollars—Lynch didn't completely abandon small caps. He wound up owing more than 1000 stocks in Magellan. It was only by investing in such a large number of small-cap stocks that he was able to get them to have a meaningful effect on Magellan's returns. And he had the resources of Fidelity to help him find and monitor all of these companies.

Lynch coined the investment term tenbagger, which refers to a stock that increases 10 times or more from the original purchase price. Dunkin Donuts is one of Lynch's most famous tenbaggers. The relevant point is that it is a lot easier for a small-cap stock to turn into a tenbagger than it is for a large one. For example, if a stock starts with a market cap of $1 billion, a tenbagger increase turns it into $10 billion stock. That's a 900% total return. By comparison, a company that starts with a market cap of $10 billion needs to go up to $100 billion to be a tenbagger. That's a pretty rare bird.

Lynch has shared his thoughts on the small-cap market in several of his books, including *One Up on Wall Street* and *Beating the Street*. He suggests that "With small companies, you are better off to wait until they turn a profit before you invest." This might seem like an obvious point, but it's an important point since small money-losing firms sometimes tend to go out of business. Being profitable improves your chance to fight another day, as well as to invest in future growth.

Lynch also suggests looking for companies with niches. Many large companies today started out as niche players. Microsoft began as a firm that developed programs for the BASIC computer language. One of its first big breaks was creating the operating system MS-DOS for the IBM Personal Computer. MS-DOS eventually came to dominate the operating system market for computers. But Microsoft also expanded into the business-software marketplace with MS-OFFICE, including Word, Excel, PowerPoint, and so forth. So, the lesson from Lynch is that small-cap companies can eventually dominate its niche, and expand to related fields.

Lynch liked to find companies off of Wall Street's radar screen. An Apple, General Electric, or Johnson & Johnson is not going to sneak up on any fund managers. Everyone knows about them. But most fund managers don't know all of the 5000-plus stocks in the U.S. and the more than 50,000 globally. There are just too many to follow in detail. One way to determine if a stock has been discovered, so to speak, is to look at the percentage of the stock owned by institutions. This statistic can easily be found at no cost on many financial websites. As a rule of thumb, if the percentage of institutional ownership is less than 50%, then it is not widely followed by larger investors such as mutual funds, hedge funds, and pension funds. Institutions tend to move in herds, so once institutions pile in, others are likely to follow. A small-cap stock can quickly turn into a mid-cap stock when the institutions get on board.

Another investment consideration is this. Lynch likes small companies that have proven that their concept can be replicated. Starbucks went public in 1992, a couple of years after Lynch stepped down from running Magellan. But it's a good example of what he means by replication. Starbucks had a concept—a coffee shop that provides a somewhat unique dining experience—that began in Seattle and then was then developed in one region of the country—the Northwest—before being rolled out nationwide. If Peter Lynch saw a concept like this that could be replicated across the country—and the firm was profitable—he'd be inclined to invest in it. Lynch thinks the opportunity to find small-cap investments abounds. He says, "The average person is exposed to interesting local companies and products years before professionals."

If you've read the book or seen the movie called *The Big Short* you probably recognize the name Michael Burry. He was one of the first people to recognize the famous bubble that occurred in the U.S. housing market in the mid-2000 period. And he made an enormous amount of money by betting that the housing market would collapse. He did so by using a complicated derivative instrument called a credit-default swap. Although Burry is most famous for that trade, a big part of his financial success can be traced to his investments in small-cap stocks.

Burry was a medical doctor who traded at night and at other times outside of his work hours. He had a passion—or some might say obsession—for the stock market. He self-diagnosed himself with a high functioning form of autism called Asperger Syndrome. Adding to Burry's unique personal character is the fact that he has one glass eye. Burry considers himself a value investor, and a disciple of value investing pioneers Benjamin Graham and Warren Buffett. Burry's investment in Hyde Athletic Industries back in 1997 is a good example of his approach to small-cap stocks. Hyde Athletic was a maker of athletic footwear. When Burry bought the stock it was like when Buffett first bought Berkshire Hathaway. That is, it was selling at a deep discount, and less than its net working capital—what Graham called a net-net. Furthermore, the company was growing rapidly.

In a November 1997 post on the Silicon Investor website, Burry wrote,

> That they are growing sales when other shoe companies are floundering is a testament to me of the sublime power of the Saucony brand. To be growing sales at a 24% clip, have a tiny PSR or price-to-sales ratio, and be a net-net, this has to be a stock value investors would love. The only problem is management, but they seem to be doing a better job, and I like the way they are refocusing.

Burry bought the stock for around $5 a share when its market cap was $31 million. But the company was worth at least $37 million based on its net working capital, alone. Hyde Athletic eventually changed its name to Saucony, its most popular brand, which today has a rabid following among runners. And Burry says he made a 50% return on this small-cap investment.

So, small cap investing can offer excellent long-term investing possibilities. The easiest way to get exposure to small caps is by investing in an index fund, which typically are well diversified and relatively inexpensive. You could also invest in one of the many actively managed small-cap mutual or exchange-traded funds. Or maybe there's a local version of See's Candy that you know about, and Wall Street doesn't. A common strategy is to invest in a basket of small, young firms in a rapidly growing industry and then, as the evidence becomes clearer, reinvest in the winner. By reinvest, I mean sell the laggards and put the sales proceeds in the winner—or winners. For example, during the early years of the worldwide web, there were a bunch of search engines—Alta Vista, Lycos, Infoseek, Ask.com, Yahoo, and ultimately Google. So a strategy along the basket line of logic would be to invest equally in all the search firms when the internet was in its infancy, and then to reinvest later when it became clear which firms were gaining market share.

You could also take a page out of the playbook of some of the great investors, including Warren Buffett, Peter Lynch, Benjamin Graham, and Michael Burry. They used different approaches. Buffett, Graham, and Burry focused on a deep value approach. They reasoned that the deep value in neglected stocks would eventually be realized by the market. Or you could take the Peter Lynch approach, and focus on small companies that were profitable, had a niche, and the ability to eventually replicate their product on a larger scale.

Many small and risky investments end up losing money, and going out of business. But those that turn out to be winners sometimes return multiples on the initial investment. You can be a good hitter in baseball by making a hit in only one out of every three times you get up at the plate. In the same way with small-cap stocks, you don't need to bat a thousand to generate a winning long-term return.

8

John Templeton, Global Treasure Hunter

Sir John Templeton, one of the pioneers of global investing, said, "If you search worldwide, you will find more bargains and better bargains than by studying only one nation." And Templeton didn't just speak these words, he lived them, traveling all over for most of his 95 years, in search of great opportunities. In his early twenties, Templeton was a Rhodes scholar. This opportunity gave him the chance to tour throughout much of Europe and planted some of the earliest seeds of his views on global investing.

John Templeton

> John Templeton's investment style did not fit neatly into a style box. He often talked about searching for bargains, which would indicate a value mindset. However, he called his original and most famous fund the Templeton Growth Fund, with an emphasis not on buying at a discount, as under-value investing, but rather investing in a company's potential.

> Templeton was one of the early proponents of what is known today as socially responsible investing: That is investing in a way that

is consistent with personal beliefs. Templeton avoided stocks that operated in the alcohol, tobacco, and gambling industries.

American Depository Receipt

> A global fund refers to one that invests anywhere in the world. By comparison, an international fund is one that invests only outside your home country.

> In the United States, a particular type of security, called an American Depository Receipt or ADR, allows you to buy many foreign stocks easily.

  ○ ADRs basically work like this. JP Morgan or Bank of New York—the two largest players in the space—buy Sony shares on the Nikkei stock exchange. They put the equivalent of a U.S. dollar wrapper around this block of Sony stock, such that it is priced in U.S. dollars, pays dividends in U.S. dollars, and is listed to trade on an American stock exchange.

  ○ ADRs are negotiable certificates that represent an interest in the shares of a non-U.S. company, are deposited with a U.S. bank, and trade on the major U.S. stock exchanges. You trade it just as you trade IBM in your brokerage account.

> The Sony ADR tends to closely track the price of Sony stock in Japan, adjusted for currency differences. If any difference gets too wide, short-term traders, known as arbitrageurs, make the discrepancy go away. They buy the cheap security and sell or, more accurately, sell short its more expensive equivalent.

  ○ Selling short is a way of making money if a security falls in price. The typical investor first buys and then sells. Selling short involves the same transaction but in the reverse order: The stock is sold first and purchased later—hopefully at a lower price. If you sold the stock short for $50, and then bought it back later for $40, you made a gross profit of $10.

The Rise of the Global Economy

> U.S. stocks account for only about half of the value of global stock markets. Many products that we know and love are made by foreign companies. Nestle is a Swiss company. Novartis, another Swiss enterprise, is one of the largest pharmaceutical firms in the world. Toyota is a Japanese automaker. Daimler, the owner of Mercedes Benz, is a German company. All of these firms have ADRs that trade on American stock exchanges

> By some estimates, China's economy will be twice as big as that of the United States by 2050. That is, China will be as big as the United States and the European Union combined. Thus, investing only in the United States might seem a bit short-sighted.

> Wider selection is perhaps the most important benefit of international investing. But the increased diversification that results from international investing can also produce the extremely important benefit of lowering the overall risk of your portfolio because local economies around the world don't move in complete sync.

> Of course, international investing has its share of risks, too. Perhaps the most obvious is currency risk. Most of Alibaba's profits are from China. If China's currency plunges versus the

dollar, its profits will be lower for U.S.-based investors, potentially hurting the price of Alibaba on U.S. stock exchanges. The reverse could also be true.

> Some countries place capital controls on foreign investment, restricting the ability to move money into or out of the country. A worst-case scenario is a country expropriating or nationalizing foreign assets, but most countries are fairly stable and tend to respect foreign property rights, and the potential benefits of international investment outweigh the risks.

> Even so, most people suffer from what behavioral economists call the home country bias. Investors typically put roughly 90% of their investible assets in their home country. Some financial planners suggest placing a significant percentage of investible assets abroad.

Templeton Background

> John Templeton was born in Winchester, Tennessee, in 1912. Following in his brother's footsteps, he entered Yale in 1930, during The Great Depression. Shortly after, Templeton's father told him he could no longer help to pay for his education, forcing the young man to work to supplement the two scholarships that defrayed his tuition. Templeton graduated near the top of his class and went on to win a Rhodes scholarship to study at Oxford

> In 1936, he and a friend spent 7 months traveling to 24 different countries. Templeton knew he wanted to go into the investment business, and his education and travel provided him with a wealth of experiences that would ultimately be useful to him.

> Although in later years he would avoid taking on debt, in 1939 he borrowed money to buy 100 shares in each of 104 companies that were selling at $1 a share or less (including 34 companies that were in bankruptcy). Only 4 turned out to be worthless, and he turned large profits on the others when U.S. industry rebounded

as a result of World War II. His roughly $10,000 initial investment turned into about $40,000 4 years later.

> In 1940 he purchased an investment firm that would become known as Templeton, Dobbrow & Vance and called himself an investment counselor. Templeton quickly realized that the economics of running a mutual fund were better than running an investment advisory firm; in 1954, he set up the Templeton Growth Fund and, in 1962, sold his stake in the traditional investment counseling business.

> The mutual fund industry grew rapidly during the 1950s, and the Templeton Growth Fund expanded into an entire family of funds. With so many funds, usually at least one would be performing well. Templeton relocated to the Bahamas in the early 1960s, renouncing his American citizenship, and felt that the solitude of living there provided him with a competitive edge when picking stocks.

Templeton's Investing Philosophy

> Templeton felt that the best performance is produced by a person, not a committee. Committees have a tendency to focus their views similar to a consensus, which Templeton believed would not result in market beating performance. At worst, it can result in groupthink, wherein a number of professionals working together and trying to minimize conflict make an irrational or dysfunctional, decision.

> As an investment advisor, Templeton followed what's called the Yale method of asset allocation, a strategy of mean reversion or rebalancing by trimming winning asset classes and adding to underperforming asset classes. The Yale method that Templeton used is different from what is known today as the Yale Model employed by Yale University's endowment.

> Templeton once said, "For all long-term investors, there is only one objective. Maximize total return after taxes." This is an important point: Taxes are often the largest transaction cost for

most investors. One way Templeton tried to reduce taxes was by holding his investments for the long term—about 4 years, representing investor turnover of about 25% a year—compared to an average holding period of about one year—100% turnover—for most actively managed stock funds today.

> Templeton generally avoided stocks yielding the highest dividends because those companies often had problems, putting the dividend at risk of being cut. He preferred dividend growth over the absolute level of the dividend itself, and he thought stocks that paid no dividends had more upside potential. This view differs from that of Graham and other traditional value investors.

Templeton Preferences for Foreign Investment

> Templeton preferred to invest in countries that exhibit the following characteristics:

  ○ Less government ownership. State-owned enterprises might have an advantage against stockholder-owned firms if the government makes the rules.

  ○ Less government regulation. He believed strongly in the efficiency of the free market system.

  ○ Less quarrelsome unions. Unions might be less efficient than the free market.

  ○ Lower taxes. They encourage investment, which should ultimately lead to growth.

  ○ Firms with higher research and development budgets.

  ○ The ethic of the people is to be honest and reliable. Investing in a stock is the equivalent of trusting the firm with your money. Corruption results in inefficient markets.

- The people are farsighted rather than short-sighted. Farsighted people often have better long-term results.

- Citizens exhibit higher rate of savings. Savings often find their way into the stock market.

Conclusion

> John Templeton changed the world of investing forever. He was the person likely most responsible for persuading many of us to invest on a global basis. He was also one of the earliest practitioners of socially responsible investing. He had an investment record of outperformance for more than 50 years. In this respect, perhaps only Warren Buffett can compare.

> Templeton demonstrated that investors with a long-term focus don't have to listen to the day-to-day noise that emanates from Wall Street. He was the epitome of a flexible investor, making money with value stocks, growth stocks, domestic stocks, and international stocks. He had the temperament to remain optimistic when it looked to others that the sky was falling.

Suggested Reading

Davis and Nairn, *Templeton's Way with Money*.
Proctor, *The Templeton Touch*.

Questions to Consider

1. How would you describe the investment strategy of John Templeton?

2. What are some of the advantages of owning international investments?

8

John Templeton,
Global Treasure Hunter

Sir John Templeton, one of the pioneers of global investing, once said, "If you search worldwide, you will find more bargains and better bargains than by studying only one nation." And Templeton didn't just speak these words, he lived them, traveling all over for most of his 95 years, in search of great opportunities. When he was in his early 20, Templeton was a Rhodes scholar. This opportunity to study in England, and receive a master's degree in law from Oxford University, provided him with the opportunity to tour throughout much of Europe. And these experiences planted some of the earliest seeds on his views on global investing.

Templeton didn't have an investment style that you could neatly fit into a style box. He often talked about searching for bargains, which would indicate a value mindset. However, he called his original, and most famous fund, the Templeton Growth Fund, with an emphasis not on buying at a discount, as in value investing, but rather investing in a company's potential. Every $10,000 invested in the Templeton Growth Fund Class A in 1954, at inception, would have grown with dividends reinvested to $2 million by 1992 when he sold his Templeton Funds business to the Franklin Group. A similar investment in the Standard & Poor's 500 index of large U.S. firms would have grown to less than $500,000 over the same period.

Besides being a great investor, Templeton donated more than $1 billion to various charitable causes. He also established the Templeton Prize for

Religion, whose winners have included Mother Theresa, Desmond Tutu, and the Dalai Lama. The monetary value of the prize is inflation adjusted to be worth more than the Nobel Prize. Templeton believed that many characteristics consistent with his own religious faith—including discipline, thrift, stewardship, dealing with adversity, humbleness, and clarity of thought—contributed to his performance as an investor. Often, he would begin investment meetings with a prayer because he believed it would help him think more clearly, and avoid stupid mistakes.

Templeton was one of the early proponents of what is known today as socially responsible investing. That's investing in a way that is consistent with your personal beliefs. Templeton avoided stocks that operated in the alcohol, tobacco, and gambling industries. In this lecture, we'll talk about John Templeton's great evolution into a great investor, his investment strategy, and the mechanics and importance of global investing, broadly.

A global fund refers to one that invests anywhere in the world. By comparison, an international fund is one that invests outside of your home country. So if you live in America, an international fund would buy non-American securities, while a global fund could buy American and non-American securities. It's pretty easy to invest globally today. You can buy an international mutual fund or an ETF—that is, an international exchange-traded fund—just about anywhere you can buy stock. Many exchange-traded funds are themselves country funds. For example, TUR is an exchange-traded fund for Turkish stocks. EWI is an ETF for Italian stocks. EWG is an ETF for German stocks. And there are dozens of other country ETFs.

But what if you wanted to buy an individual foreign stock? That's pretty easy, too, at least for most large foreign stocks. In the United States, there is a particular type of security, called an American Depository Receipt, or ADR, that allows you to buy many foreign stocks. ADRs basically work like this. JP Morgan or Bank of New York—two of the largest players in the space—go to a foreign market and buy a block of the stock. Let's say they buy Sony shares on the Nikkei stock exchange. They take this block of Sony stock and put the equivalent of a U.S. dollar wrapper around it, such that it is priced in U.S. dollars, pays dividends in U.S. dollars, and is listed to trade on an American stock exchange.

In other words, ADRs are negotiable certificates that represent an interest in the shares of a Non-U.S. company, and which are deposited with a U.S. bank. And ADRs trade on the major U.S. stock exchanges. For example, SNE is the ADR symbol for Sony. GSK is the ADR symbol for the British drug maker GlaxoSmithKline. You would trade it just like you trade IBM in your brokerage account. There are hundreds of other ADRs from many countries around the world. You can find them on adr.com, or elsewhere, and search by country, region, or sector.

The bank creating the ADR gets a small fee, say one-quarter of 1% of the assets of the certificate per year. Of course, Sony has to agree to this as well.

And by listing on an American exchange, Sony must file an annual report called a 20-F, using U.S. Generally Accepted Accounting Principles. From Sony's perspective, it's probably worth it since their stock can now more easily get on the radar screen of U.S. and other investors. The Sony ADR tends to closely track the price of Sony stock in Japan, adjusted for currency differences. If any difference gets too wide, short-term traders, known as arbitrageurs, make the discrepancy go away. They will buy the cheap security and sell, or more accurately, sell short, its more expensive equivalent.

Selling short is a way of making money if a security falls in price. The typical investor first buys and then sells later. Selling short involves the same transaction but in the reverse order. That's why it has the slightly different nomenclature of selling short and not simply selling. So, the stock is sold first and then purchased later—hopefully at a lower price. If you sold the stock short for $50, and then bought it back later for $40, you made a gross profit of $10.

You might be wondering how you can sell something that you don't yet own. This is how, the brokerage firm where your account is held gets the shares from another client, and then lends them to you the short seller, in this example. The transaction is usually seamless. The investor who loaned you the shares is typically not even aware of the transaction. The brokerage keeps track of everything.

What if you want to trade a foreign security that doesn't have an ADR? Back in Templeton's day, that was much harder. You had to open a brokerage account in a foreign country. And if you traded in a dozen countries, you might have to open up a dozen different brokerage accounts, unless your broker operated on a global scale. And then you needed the accounting systems to consolidate all of that. This wasn't an easy task in the 1950s and 1960s when Templeton got started. But today, the process is much more streamlined. Some brokerage firms let you create one global account to trade on many exchanges around the world. And they usually handle the payment of any foreign taxes. One service that I've seen lets you trade in more than 100 markets in 24 different countries from a single brokerage account.

U.S. stocks account for only about half of the value of global stock markets. Many products that we know and love are made by foreign companies. For example, Nestle is a Swiss company. Novartis, another Swiss enterprise, is one of the largest pharmaceutical firms in the world. Toyota is a very well-known Japanese automaker. Daimler, the owner of Mercedes-Benz, is a German company. Royal Dutch Shell is based in the Netherlands but incorporated in England and Wales. All of these firms have ADRs that trade on American stock exchanges. And, of course, there is China with globally recognized firms such as Alibaba, an e-commerce company that is something like eBay and Amazon.com. By some estimates, China's economy will be twice as big as that of the United States by 2050. That is that China will be as big as the U.S. and the European Union combined. So, to simply invest in the U.S. might seem a bit short sighted.

A wider selection is perhaps the most important benefit of international investing. It's like picking between the best wines of California, France, Spain, and Italy. But the increased diversification that results from international investing can also produce the extremely important benefit of lowering the overall risk of your portfolio. The basic idea is this, India might be growing while the U.S. is in a recession. Singapore might be growing while Brazil is in a recession. Local economies around the world don't move in complete sync. So these broader choices might have the added benefit of reducing overall portfolio risk.

But, of course, international investing has its fair share of risks, too. Perhaps the most obvious is currency risk. Most of Alibaba's profits are in China. So, if China's currency, the Renminbi—or Yuan—plunges versus the dollar, its profits will be less for U.S.-based investors, potentially hurting the price of Alibaba on U.S. stock exchanges. And the reverse can also be true. If the Yuan were to rise against the dollar, a stake in Alibaba might turn positive for U.S.-based investors. Now, some countries place capital controls on foreign investment, restricting your ability to move money into—or out of—the country. A worst-case scenario is when a country expropriates or nationalizes, foreign assets. This happened in Iran after the Shah fled from power in 1979. But most countries are fairly stable and tend to respect foreign property rights. So, the risks of international investment are often outweighed by the potential benefits.

Even so, most people suffer from what behavioral economists call the home country bias. The typical person puts 90% of their investible assets in their home country. That means as an American citizen, I'd be likely to put 90% of my investible assets in U.S. investments. If I were Canadian, I'd tend to put 90% of my assets in Canadian investments. But some financial planners suggest that you place a significant percentage of your investable assets abroad. John Templeton innately understood the benefits of global investing, and, due to his pioneering work, we are all able to benefit from his insights today.

John Templeton was born in Winchester, Tennessee, in 1912. Following in his brother's footsteps, he attended Yale University. But shortly after entering Yale in 1930, during the Great Depression, Templeton's father told him he could no longer help to pay for his education. This forced the young man to work to supplement the two scholarships that defrayed his tuition. He also made money off of his wealthier Yale classmates with his poker winnings. Templeton was an excellent student at Yale. He was elected president of Phi Beta Kappa, the academic honor society, and graduated near the top of his class. He went on to win a Rhodes Scholarship, meaning he had an opportunity to study at Oxford.

Beginning in 1936, he and a friend spent seven months traveling around the world—to 24 different countries—on a shoestring budget. At this point,

Templeton knew he wanted to go into the investment business, and his educational and travel activities provided him with a wealth of experiences that would ultimately be useful to him. He began his career on Wall Street in 1938, working for Fenner & Beane, one of the predecessor firms of Merrill Lynch. He then took a job as secretary/treasurer at an oil exploration firm in Texas called National Geophysical Company.

The experience of living through the Great Depression was probably instrumental in forging Templeton's frugal and thrifty behavior. As his career progressed, he tried to save money even on mundane things like office supplies. He furnished his New York City apartment with second-hand furniture. Frugality doesn't necessarily mean cheap. We know that Templeton was very generous with his fortune, giving nearly all of his wealth away to charitable causes. But Templeton did look for investment bargains. One of his most famous sayings was, "The time of maximum pessimism is the best time to buy, and the time of maximum optimism is the best time to sell."

He had one opportunity to buy during rampant pessimism in 1939 when war broke out in Europe. Although in later years he would avoid taking on debt, in 1939 he borrowed money to buy 100 shares in each of the 104 companies that were selling at $1 or less including 34 companies that were bankrupt. Only four turned out to be worthless, and he turned large profits on the others when U.S. industry rebounded, as a result of World War II. His roughly $10,000 initial investment turned into about $40,000 four years later.

But Templeton always wanted to run his own business. So in 1940 he purchased an investment firm that would become known as Templeton, Dobbrow & Vance. It was what we would today call a registered investment advisor. Templeton called himself an investment counselor. And in 1954, Templeton set up the Templeton Growth Fund. In the interim, however, he was hit by a terrible personal tragedy. His wife Judith Folk, whom he'd married in 1937, and who was the mother of the couple's three children, died in a motorbike accident in 1951, leaving Templeton with primary childcare responsibilities. He remarried to a woman named Irene Reynolds Butler in 1958 and the couple remained married until her death in 1993.

Templeton quickly realized that the economics of running a mutual fund were better than running an investment advisory firm. Mutual funds are more scalable, meaning they are easier to ramp up. Consider it this way, if you are an investment advisor, you might have the time to meet with 100 clients a year. But with a mutual fund, you could have thousands or more shareholders, many of whom would pay a sales charge up to 7% or more up front. So, Templeton set up his Growth Fund, and, in 1962, sold his stake in the traditional investment counseling business.

In the interim, the mutual fund industry grew rapidly during the 1950s— in concert with the economic boom of the post-World War II Years—and Templeton's Fund group expanded into an entire family of funds. With so many funds, usually at least one would be performing well. He originally domiciled the business in Canada, which had lower dividend and capital gains taxes than the U.S. did at the time. But Templeton relocated to the Bahamas in the early 1960s, renouncing his American citizenship in favor of British citizenship. He loved the Bahamas and felt that the solitude of living there provided him with a competitive edge when picking stocks—similar to Warren Buffett making his investment fortune at his home in Omaha, instead of on Wall Street. For many years, Templeton operated with a small staff, managing his Growth Fund with a single research assistant, Mark Holowesko, who eventually became the portfolio manager of the Growth Fund after Templeton retired.

Although it would be a mistake to characterize Templeton strictly as a quantitative investor, he did like to quantify upside and downside potential. Back in 1984, Mark Holowesko's first assignment was to quantify the downside risk for Union Carbide's stock in the wake of a disaster in Bhopal, India, where at least 3000 people died after a natural gas leak. Templeton felt that the best performance is produced by a person, not a committee. Committees have a tendency to focus their views on a consensus, which Templeton believed would not result in market-beating performance. At worst, it can result in groupthink, where a number of professionals working together—and trying to minimize conflict—make an irrational, or dysfunctional, decision.

For example, some so-called active managers wind up with a portfolio that looks like an index fund. Known as closet indexing, or index hugging, the fund charges high active management fees but looks and performs like an index fund. As an investment advisor, Templeton followed what was known as the Yale method of asset allocation. It is basically a strategy of mean reversion, or rebalancing by trimming winning asset classes and adding to underperforming asset classes.

So, if he started with a mix of 50% stocks and 50% bonds, and the stocks went up by 10% over the course of a year—while the bonds were flat—he would generally reduce his equity exposure by 10%, and increase his fixed income exposure by 10%. In essence, this mean-reversion strategy is an exercise in buying low and selling high. The Yale method of asset allocation that Templeton is different than what is known today as the Yale model or endowment model employed by David Swensen, the Chief Investment Officer of Yale University's endowment. Swensen is known for a portfolio that consists of mostly alternative investments, like hedge funds, private equity, and real estate.

Now, Templeton once said that "For all long-term investors, there is only one objective. Maximize total return after taxes." This is an important point since taxes are often the largest transaction cost for most investors. But taxes are virtually ignored by most professional fund managers since they are usually compensated on pre-tax performance. One way that Templeton tried to reduce taxes was by holding his investments for the long-term. The average holding period in his Growth Fund was about four years, representing investor turnover of about one-in-four, or 25 percent. This compares to an average holding period of about one year—100% turnover—for most actively managed stock funds today.

An important part of Templeton's investment-vetting process was estimating a company's earnings five years into the future. This was Templeton's variation on the intrinsic value approach popularized by value investing pioneer Benjamin Graham. Graham had a greater focus on the value of current assets, and a lesser focus on future earnings. There's little evidence of any relationship between earnings and stock prices over the short-term. However, Templeton said, In the long-run, the stock market indexes fluctuate around the long-term upward trend of earnings per share. Empirical studies bear him out. Templeton's focus on a five-year time frame allowed him to buy traditional growth stocks. That is smaller firms that would likely grow into to larger firms. But the time frame also allowed him to buy struggling—not fatally flawed—companies that could eventually rebound.

Templeton generally avoided the highest dividend-yielding stocks since these companies often had problems, putting the dividend at risk of being cut or reduced. He preferred dividend growth over the absolute level of the dividend itself. And he thought stocks that didn't pay dividends had more upside potential. This view differs from that of Graham and other traditional value investors. Templeton's search for bargains often led to a contrarian investment approach. One of his many investment maxims or principles, was, When any method for selecting stocks becomes popular, then switch to unpopular methods. He also thought it was impossible to produce superior performance unless you did something different from other investors. He said, If a particular industry or type of security becomes popular with investors, that popularity will always prove temporary and when lost, won't return for many years.

Templeton was one of the earliest institutional investors in Japan. He started there in the early 1950s, through his personal account, and placed client money there a few years later. But in doing so, Templeton also took the time to understand the nuances of Japanese company accounting. Many Japanese firms operate what is called a Keiretsu structure, where a parent firm like Mitsubishi owns pieces of other firms. So, the Mitsubishi keiretsu might control an automotive company, mining company, shipping, oil and gas company, and a financial services firm.

Templeton invested in the Japanese firm Hitachi. The parent company appeared to be traded at a price-to-earnings level in the mid-teens. No great bargain on the surface. But when Templeton consolidated the earnings of all of its member companies, he realized that Hitachi was trading at single digit P/E levels, a huge bargain. This kind of logic resulted in the Templeton Growth Fund having more than 50% of its assets in Japanese stocks for a while. His holdings in Japanese stocks were one of the most important reasons for his great long-term performance and cemented his reputation as a superstar global investor. Templeton exited Japanese stocks a bit too soon—before their meteoric rise in the late 1980s—but he largely avoided the crash in Japanese stock prices that began around 1990, and the long period of deflation that followed.

Templeton's optimistic outlook on life played a role in his ability to be a contrarian investor. For instance, during the early 1980s, stocks were out of favor due to high levels of inflation and two recent recessions. The market was selling at a P/E level in the single digits, about half its long-term average. Templeton went on the TV show *Wall Street Week* in 1982 and forecast that the U.S. stock market would go up 400% over the next 10 years. He thought corporate earnings would double, and the market multiple would also expand back to its historical levels. He turned out to be right—within nine years—cementing his guru status. Templeton had an extensive business network and often interviewed management as one part of his investment process. His favorite question to ask executives was, If you were going to buy shares, and you couldn't buy shares in your own company, which one of your competitors, suppliers, or customers would you buy, and why?

Well, you might have your own question, like what kind of countries did Templeton like to invest in? The answer is that he preferred to invest in countries that exhibit the following characteristics. Countries with less government ownership because state-owned enterprises might have an advantage against stockholder-owned firms if the government makes the rules. He liked countries with less government regulation since he believed strongly in the efficiency of the free market system. He liked countries with less quarrelsome unions, once again since unions might not be as efficient as the free market system. He liked countries with lower taxes since they would encourage investment, which should ultimately lead to growth. He liked countries that had higher research and development budgets since R&D often results in future growth. He liked countries, where the ethic of the people is to be honest, and reliable since investing in a stock, is the equivalent of trusting the firm with your money. Corruption also results in inefficient markets. He liked countries where the people were farsighted rather than short sighted since farsighted people often have better long-term results. He liked countries where citizens exhibited a higher rate of savings since savings often find their way into the stock market.

John Templeton changed the world of investing forever. He was the person most likely responsible for getting many of us to invest on a global basis. He was also one of the earliest practitioners of socially responsible investing. He had an investment record of outperformance for more than 50 years. In this respect, perhaps only Warren Buffett can compare.

Like Frank Sinatra, Templeton did it his way. He invested primarily from his island paradise in the Bahamas, and in a manner that was consistent with his personal beliefs. That said, living in the Bahamas as a British citizen also saved him an estimated $100 million in income taxes when he eventually sold his mutual fund company to Franklin.

But his investments and charitable contributions also turned John Templeton into Sir John Templeton—at the hands of Queen Elizabeth—in 1987. Templeton demonstrated that investors with a long-term focus didn't have to listen to the day-to-day noise that often emanates from Wall Street. He was the epitome of a flexible investor, making money with value stocks, growth stocks, domestic stocks, and international stocks. He had the temperament to remain optimistic when it looked to others that the sky was falling.

And he demonstrated an incredible work ethic, putting in full work days well until his 80s. And he continued to manage his foundation's portfolio until his death at the age of 95.

9

David Dreman,
Contrarian Money Manager

Studies by Dreman and others have found that professional research analysts frequently fall prey to what is now known as optimism bias. They tend to be too optimistic about a company's prospects while failing to take into account what can go wrong, such as failure to execute or increasing competition. Dreman also came to believe that political and financial crises caused investors to sell stocks too hastily—what he considers is precisely the wrong reaction. Dreman advises buying during a panic, and not selling.

The Making of a Contrarian

> David Dreman's father, a commodities trader who operated a small brokerage firm, often told David that brokerage firms published flawed and incorrect research, possibly planting the seed for Dreman to become a wealthy and well-regarded contrarian—an investor who goes against the crowd.

> As a contrarian, Dreman bought tobacco stocks after the out-of-favor industry agreed to pay the U.S. government $206 billion across 25 years. The agreement settled a series of lawsuits from the damage that tobacco products cause consumers and related

health care costs incurred by the government. Dreman believed that people wouldn't stop smoking, and the industry's legal liability was now fixed at a finite (and affordable) cost.

Investor Psychology

> Security prices rarely move in a straight line. Instead, they may swing wildly because of the instability of market events and human emotions. In part, that's because fear and greed are inextricable expressions of human nature, and human emotions are closely tied to what is known as bull and bear market behavior.

  ○ Bulls fight with their horns—moving upward—signifying the market rising, usually at least 20% from a bottom. Bears fight with their claws—moving downward—representing the market falling, usually at least 20% from a peak. A market correction occurs when stock prices retreat about 10%.

> Over a recent 20-year period, the average investor returned 2.5% a year, compared with 6% annual returns for bonds and 10% gains for stocks, according to a report J. P. Morgan and the research firm DALBAR. Two decades' worth of data demonstrate that the average investor is beaten by the market every single year. The reason, stated plainly, is that the typical investor chases performance.

> If you look at individual stocks, you will periodically find examples of extreme price movements that can be explained principally by crowd psychology—sometimes leading to bubbles and busts—and not necessarily from any rational movements in the securities' intrinsic value.

Behavioral Finance

> What if there were a way to profit from the mistakes of others? In the emerging field of behavioral finance—the name that economists give to market psychology—learning how to profit

from the fallibilities of others is a primary objective. Another is to be more aware of one's own failings and to limit them going forward.

> Few investors have done more to advance the field of behavioral finance than David Dreman, who has written 5 books on the topic and is the money manager at his own firm, Dreman Value Management. Dreman is also a cofounder of the respected *Journal of Behavioral Finance*, and for decades he's written an investment column for *Forbes* magazine—appropriately titled "The Contrarian."

> The list of mistakes that investors seem to make regularly is long. One of the most common biases is the disposition effect. It means that typical investors hold onto losing investments long after they should: They want to at least break even, and they may feel that a paper loss is not the same as a realized loss.

  ○ The flipside is that many investors sell their winning investments too soon. Imagine owning a young Microsoft and selling after a 50% gain. You would have missed out on a 10-fold gain or more. Microsoft had its initial public offering on March 13, 1986, at a price of $21 a share. The stock has split something like 9 times and gone up more than 68,000% since.

  ○ One way to limit the impact of the disposition effect is to review certain fundamental measures of performance that may explain why a stock goes up or down—or be about to. If the fundamentals have changed for the worse, maybe you should consider selling.

> Investors tend to overreact to information. They often place more weight on what has happened recently and less on what happened in the more distant past. Mathematically, they weight things in a nonlinear manner. This behavior helps explain why many successful investors are contrarian in their outlook and strategy. They are willing to go against the grain and buy out-of-favor investments if they see fundamental value underneath the bad news.

> Investors also tend to suffer from optimism bias. They believe they are better investors than they actually are. For example, investors tend to underestimate the role of competition on their investments. They also tend to trade too much—acting on information that is already widely known and unlikely to add much value.

> Another typical mistake is representativeness bias. Investors may confuse a good company with a good investment. It's easy to say what a good company is. It's one that consistently increases sales

and profits. Saying it is a good investment is another story. A good investment goes up more than the market on a risk-adjusted basis.

> Most people are stubborn in their investment approaches. Once they've made up their minds about an investment, they tend to agree with information that supports their views and ignore information that conflicts with them. Economists call this behavior confirmation bias.

> Studies find that the average investor feels that losing $1 hurts twice as much as gaining $1 helps them. Economists call this weighting the value of gains and losses function. The implication is that investors really hate losses and should hold well-diversified portfolios to reduce risk. It also suggests why, as humans, we have a proclivity to lean toward "star" stocks that are expensive by almost any valuation metric. Investors tend to fear value stocks because they have problems. They extrapolate into the future that the current good or bad news will continue.

Dreman Strategy

> Some famous investors used price-trend analysis to time individual investments and the market. In contrast, David Dreman focuses on company fundamentals, such as valuation levels and industry standing, as well as on how other investors perceive the company's stock.

> Nowadays a ton of information is available to consider: financial statements, analysts' reports, press articles, bulletin board fodder, and so forth. We've all heard of the term information overload. Dreman says investors should respect the difficulty of working with a mass of undigested information because few can use it all successfully.

> Rather, he prefers the expression "in-depth profits"—knowing about a smaller number of companies in great detail: their product lineup, their ability to fend off competition, and their management

team's skill. When you are faced with too much information on a single company, focus most of your attention on the factors that drive sales, earnings, and profit margins.

> With regard to overcoming the tendency to harbor investment biases—most specifically, the optimism bias—and to make recurring investment mistakes, Dreman recommends making downward adjustments to analysts' earnings forecasts for a company. That is, if the analysts' consensus estimate for Coca-Cola's earnings is $2 a share, would you still want to buy the stock if it earned only $1.50?

> Because he is a contrarian, Dreman thinks that stocks everyone loves are more likely to run into problems: new competition, poor execution, or complacency. Conversely, if everyone hates a stock, maybe the firm can fix its problems. If it's a bad business, maybe some of its competitors will be leaving, gradually turning the economics from unfavorable to favorable for the survivors. Still, Dreman cautions that market reappraisals of favored and out-of-favor stocks tend to occur at a glacial pace. Thus, for a contrarian, an important personal characteristic is patience.

> As for the qualities that Dreman looks for in companies to invest in, he likes to buy solid or quality companies with high dividends and low price-to-earnings ratios, price-to-cash flow, and/or price-to-book value—at least 30% less than the market as a whole.

> No uniform definition exists to describe a quality company, but it usually has several characteristics: It's likely to have been in business for a while, to be profitable, to pay a dividend at least 0.5% higher than the average for the market as a whole and with a history of rising payouts, and to have strong management.

> Dreman prefers to hold a more concentrated portfolio than the typical mutual fund or index fund. He advises investing equally in 20 to 30 stocks, diversified among 15 or more industries. In his

opinion, this strategy balances diversification with his ability to follow the companies in detail.

> While taking losses sometimes is unavoidable, you should also know when to take your winnings. The best poker players don't stay at the table until their luck runs out. Dreman offers some advice on when to sell.

  ○ He recommends selling a stock when its P/E ratio (or other contrarian indicator) approaches that of the overall market, regardless of how favorable its prospects may appear, replacing it with another contrarian stock. Dreman's approach is always to be a disciplined value investor.

> One of the largest firms that tries to systematically capitalize on investor mistakes is LSV Asset Management, based in Chicago, with more than $80 billion in assets under management. The principals state that the fundamental premise on which LSV's investment philosophy is based "is that superior long-term results can be achieved by systematically exploiting the judgmental biases and behavioral weaknesses that influence the decisions of many investors…"

> Another investment firm to rely on behavioral finance as a core component of its investment strategy is Fuller and Thaler in California's Silicon Valley with about $5 billion under management. The firm is mid-sized but maintains important investment advisory relationships with much larger partners. Its founders are so committed to the ideas of behavioral finance that they've registered the trademark: The Behavioral Edge.

> People have known about the impact of market psychology on security prices for a long time. For example, the economist John Maynard Keynes once described the markets as being moved by animal spirits and not by reason. But over the past few decades, the field of behavioral finance has made great strides in

documenting the mistakes of investors. But not all investors make the same mistakes.

> David Dreman recognized that being a contrarian was the best way for him to make money. But not everyone has the temperament to be a contrarian. One of the worst feelings is to be wrong and alone. If you're wrong picking a stock that everyone loves, you are unlikely to get fired—even if that stock comes crashing down.

Suggested Readings

Dreman, *Contrarian Investment Strategies*.
———, *Psychology and the Stock Market*.

Questions to Consider

1. How would you describe the investment strategy of David Dreman?

2. What investment biases do you think you are most susceptible to and how do you plan to correct them?

9

Transcript

David Dreman, Contrarian Money Manager

David Dreman was born in Winnipeg, Canada, in 1936. His father, Joseph Dreman, was a commodities trader who operated a small brokerage firm and eventually became one of the leaders of the Winnipeg Commodity Exchange, which today is known as ICE Futures Canada. Many times, Joseph Dreman told his son David that brokerage firms published flawed and incorrect research. This may have planted the seeds for David Dreman to go on to become a wealthy, and well-regarded contrarian—an investor who goes against the crowd.

After graduating from the University of Manitoba, Dreman went to work in investment research positions at the brokerage firms of Rauscher Pierce and J&W Seligman. He also was a senior editor for the Value Line Investment Service when Value Line was among the few widely followed information resources available to investors. Dreman set up his own shop in 1977. And he had a formative experience early in his career that helped to shape his investing philosophy. In 1969, Dreman followed the crowd that was then piling into growth stocks. These stocks, like Hewlett-Packard and Electronic Data Systems, were trading at very high multiples of such valuation metrics as sales, earnings, and cash flow.

On the whole, these companies were long on potential but had little in the way of current earnings. Dreman said, "I invested in the stocks du jour and lost 75% of my net worth." This painful lesson caused him to investigate the effects of crowd psychology on investing. Studies by Dreman and others found that professional research analysts frequently fall prey to what is known as the optimism bias. They tend to be too optimistic about a company's prospects while failing to take into account things that can go wrong, such as the failure to execute or increasing competition. Dreman also came to believe that political and financial crises caused investors to sell stocks too hastily. He thinks this is precisely the wrong reaction. Like Warren Buffett, Dreman advises buying during a panic, and not selling.

Dreman put his money where his mouth is. He bought tobacco stocks such as Philip Morris and R.J. Reynolds after the out-of-favor industry agreed to pay the U.S. government $206 billion across 25 years. The agreement settled a series of lawsuits on the damage that tobacco products cause consumers and related healthcare costs incurred by the government. About owning Philip Morris, Dreman once said, "You've got to have a Teflon bottom to take the heat on this stock." But Dreman believed that people wouldn't stop smoking, and the industry's legal liability was now fixed at a finite and affordable cost. He turned out to be right. In this lecture, we'll explore the world of behavioral finance by analyzing some of the average investor's most common biases—and mistakes. We'll also examine how David Dreman and others turn the average investors' mistakes into profits for themselves.

Security prices rarely move in a straight line. Instead, they may swing wildly due to the instability of market events, and human emotions. In part, that's because fear and greed are inextricable expressions of human nature. And these human emotions are closely tied to what is known as bull and bear market behavior. Even most financial professionals don't know why the animals bull and bear represent dramatic moves in security prices. But I can answer that for you. bulls fight with their horns—moving in an upward direction. So bulls signify when the market rises, usually at least 20% from a bottom. By comparison, bears fight with their claws in a downward direction. So, on Wall Street, bears represent when the market falls, usually at least 20% from a peak. And a market correction is when stock prices retreat about 10%.

Here's a problem with human psychology that you might have a very close, personal relationship to. The average investor performs terribly compared to the market as a whole. And the reason is firmly rooted in investor psychology. What's my basis for this conclusion? Well, over a 20-year period, the average investor returned only 2.5% a year. Compared with 6% annual returns for bonds—and 10% gains for stocks, according to a report I've read by J.P. Morgan and the research firm Dalbar.

This isn't some kind of fluke. Two decades worth of data demonstrate that the average investor is beaten by the market every single year. The reason for this, stated plainly, is that the typical investor chases performance. We tend to buy investments that were hot in the past. And when these winning investments inevitably fall in the not-too-distant-future, the investor panics, and ends up selling near a bottom. In essence, the typical investor buys high and sells low. That's the exact opposite of we want to do—and what winning investors accomplish.

Warren Buffett said it best when he observed, "Be fearful when others are greedy, and be greedy when others are fearful." For example, Buffett invested about 40% of the investment partnership assets in the stock of American Express in 1963. American Express's stock had suffered in the wake of an accounting fraud at a company that it had backed with credit. Despite this misstep, Buffett thought that American Express' core business—its charge cards and traveler's checks—was still in good shape. American Express rebounded from the accounting scandal, and its stock went up tenfold within Buffett's purchase ten years later.

Buffet was also willing to invest in Goldman Sachs preferred and common stock during the Great Recession of 2007–2009. At the time, many financial stocks appeared to be vulnerable following Lehman Brothers into bankruptcy. And the investment paid off bigtime. It returned about $3.6 billion on a $5 billion investment, over roughly a five-year period. If you look at individual stocks, you will periodically find examples of extreme price movements that can be explained principally by crowd psychology—sometimes leading to bubbles and busts—and not necessarily from any rational movements in the securities' intrinsic value.

I'll offer you an example, JDSU Uniphase, or JDSU for short. During the Internet bubble, bulls referred to JDSU as the Intel of the internet. JDSU made fiber-optic equipment. Within the span of a few years, its share price went from $2 or $3 a share to more than $1000 a share. But as you probably guessed, after the Internet bubble popped, the share price crashed back to around $2 or $3 a share. It eventually regained its footing, and split into two companies that today operate under different names, but combined are well below the $1000 price peak. Bubbles continue to be recurring conditions almost everywhere around the world. I can think of a Chinese stock by the name of Beijing Baofeng Technology whose share price went up 40 times in the span of three months.

Back in the early 1700s—in one of the earliest and best-known incidents of a securities bubble with widespread fallout—the British government granted a joint-stock company called the South Sea Company a monopoly on Great Britain's trade in South America. The words monopoly and strong projected growth combined to whip investors into a speculative frenzy. The effect was to increase the company's stock price almost 10-fold in less than a year, from about £100 to £1000. Then—you guessed it—the stock price crashed back, even lower than its pre-bubble levels.

The English philosopher, astronomer, and mathematician Sir Isaac Newton—who developed the Universal Law of Gravitation—discovered gravity for himself as a result of this investment. By the year 1720, Newton had lost about £20,000 on the South Sea Company. That would be the equivalent to about four-and-a-half million dollars today. Investigations exposed a web of bribery, corruption, and deceit that led to some prosecutions of some South Sea Company officials and government officials. Newton reportedly said, "I can calculate the movement of stars, but not the madness of men."

But what if there were a way to profit from the mistakes of others? In the emerging field of behavioral finance—which is the name that economists give to the topic of market psychology—learning how to profit from the fallibilities of others is a primary objective. Another is to be more aware of one's own failings—and to limit them going forward. Think of it as heightened self-awareness about our own tendencies to make certain kinds of mistakes, like chasing winning investments while the price is rising, and panicking when the market is falling.

Many investors throughout history have recognized the role of psychology in setting prices and in their own investment performance. Value-investing pioneer, Benjamin Graham wrote that "The market is a pendulum that forever swings between unsustainable optimism which makes stocks too expensive and unjustified pessimism which make them too cheap. The Intelligent Investor is a realist who sells to optimists and buys from pessimists." Two Nobel Prize winners in economics—Daniel Kahneman, a professor of psychology at Princeton's Woodrow Wilson School, and Robert Shiller, an economics professor at Yale—have focused much of their academic research in the area of behavioral finance.

But few investors have done more to advance the field of behavioral finance more than David Dreman, who has written five books on the topic and is the money manager at his own firm, Dreman Value Management. Dreman is also co-founder of the respected *Journal of Behavioral Finance*, and for decades he's written an investment column for *Forbes*—appropriately titled "The Contrarian." His books have such titles as *Psychology and the Stock Market*, published in 1977; *Contrarian Investment Strategy, The Psychology of Stock Market Success*, in 1980; *The New Contrarian Investment Strategy* in 1982; *Contrarian Investment Strategies: The Next Generation* in 1988; and *Contrarian Investment Strategies: The Psychological Edge*, in 2012.

There's a laundry list of mistakes that investors seem to make on a regular basis. Let's discuss some of the most prominent ones, and tie them to some real events. One of the most common biases, or mistakes, is called the disposition effect. It means that the typical investor holds onto losing investments long after they should because they want to at least break even. And they may feel that a paper loss is not the same as a realized loss. The flipside is that many investors sell their winning investments too soon. Imagine owning a young Microsoft, Netflix, or Google and selling after a 50% gain. You would have missed out on a 10-fold gain or more. For example, Microsoft had its initial public offering on March 13, 1986, at a price of $21 a share. The stock has split something like nine times and gone up more than 68,000% since.

One way to limit the impact of the disposition effect is to review certain fundamental measures of performance that may explain why a stock goes up or down. If the fundamentals have changed for the worse, maybe you should consider selling. If your investments are in a taxable account, it might make sense to realize that loss and deduct it against future gains. This strategy is called tax-loss harvesting. Not only are you able to shelter some earnings by taking losses on investments you no longer want to hold, but it beats having to look at the loss every month on your brokerage statement.

As the value investor Benjamin Graham signaled in his reference to the pendulum, investors tend to overreact to information. They often place more weight on what has happened recently, and less weight on what happened in the more distant past. Mathematically, they weight things in a nonlinear manner. But for purposes of shorthand, most of us might find it easier to remember, simply, that the typical market participant overreacts today. And this behavior helps to explain why many successful investors, like David Dreman, are contrarian in their outlooks and in their strategy. They are willing to go against the grain and buy out-of-favor investments if they see fundamental value underneath the bad news. The German banker Nathan Rothschild—who was the patron of the European financial dynasty—is reported to have once said, "The time to buy is when there is blood in the streets."

Investors also tend to suffer, as I mentioned at the outset, from optimism bias. They believe they are better investors than they actually are. Now, I think it's good to be optimistic, but it's bad if it consistently costs you money. For example, investors tend to underestimate the role of competition on their investments. They also tend to trade too much—acting on information that's already widely known, and unlikely to add much value.

Another typical mistake is what's known as representativeness bias. In this, investors may confuse a good company with a good investment. It's pretty easy to say what a good company is. It's one that consistently increases sales and profits. So, most people would consider companies like Coca-Cola, Wal-Mart, Apple, and Procter & Gamble to be strong companies. However, saying they are a good investment is another story. A good investment goes up more than the market, on a standalone or risk-adjusted basis.

When considering individual stocks, you should look at how they are valued. This might be by looking at a price-to-earnings ratio, a price-to-book ratio, or some other valuation yardstick. The price to earnings ratio is measured as the price of a stock per share, divided by its earnings per share. The price to book ratio is the market value of a stock divided by the net worth, or book value, shown on the firm's balance sheet. Value stocks are often defined as having below-average price to earnings or price to book ratios. Conversely, growth stocks trade at higher-than-market levels on these metrics.

Most people are stubborn in their investment approaches. Once we've made our minds up about an investment, we tend to agree with information that supports our views and ignore information that conflicts with it. Economists call this behavior confirmation bias. Studies find that the average investor feels that losing $1 hurts twice as much as gaining $1 helps. Economists call this weighting the value of gains and losses function. The implication is that investors really hate losses, and should hold well-diversified portfolios to reduce risk. It also suggests why, as humans, we have a proclivity to lean towards star stocks that are expensive by almost any valuation metric. Investors tend to be afraid of value stocks because they have all sorts of problems or warts. They extrapolate into the future that the current good or bad news will continue.

One way to think about these biases is as if they were part of our own personal human genome. A treatment plan for me might differ from someone else like you, even if we share the same condition. So, to overcome our tendencies to make certain investment mistakes, we might want to adjust our choices and safeguards based on our own personal vulnerabilities.

Some famous investors such as Jesse Livermore—who was known as the Great Bear on Wall Street, and was prominent during the first half of the last century—used price trend analysis to time individual investments and the market. In contrast, David Dreman focuses on company fundamentals, such as valuation levels and industry standing, as well as on how other investors perceive the company's stock. Dreman says he never tries to time the market, or use trend following, or technical analysis. He thinks that these techniques usually just cost investors money.

And, these days, there is a flood of information to consider, financial statements, analysts' reports, press articles, bulletin board fodder, and so forth. We've all heard the term information overload. Dreman says investors should respect the difficulty of working with a mass of undigested information because few can use it successfully. Rather, he prefers the expression in-depth profits. This can be interpreted as knowing a smaller amount of companies in great detail. For example, knowing their product lineup, ability to fend off competition, and the skill of the firm's management team. And when you are faced with too much information on a single company, focus most of your attention on the factors that drive sales, earnings, and profit margins.

Now, with regard to overcoming our human tendency to harbor certain investment biases—most specifically, the optimism bias—and to make recurring investment mistakes, Dreman recommends that as investors we make downward adjustments to analysts' earnings forecasts for a company. So, if the analysts' consensus estimate for the Coca-Cola's earnings are $2 a share, would you still want to buy the stock if they earned only $1.50 a share?

Analysts tend to move in a herd. Many seem to love or hate a stock at the same time. Dreman thinks that favored stocks underperform the market while out-of-favor companies outperform the market. Because he is a contrarian, he thinks that stocks everyone loves are more likely to run into problems in the future. It could be new competition, poor execution, or complacency. And because he is a value investor, he will simply avoid stocks, such as most market darlings, that he views as expensive.

Conversely, if everyone hates a stock, not much is expected of it. Maybe the firm can fix its problems. If it's a bad business, maybe some of its competitors will be leaving, gradually turning the economics from unfavorable to favorable for the survivors. Dreman puts it this way, "Industry laggards often tighten their belts, improve their management and find ways of increasing their market share or developing new products, which results in their continued outperformance of the market for long periods." Still, Dreman cautions that market reappraisals of favored and out-of-favor stocks tend to occur extremely slowly—at what he calls a glacial pace. So, for a contrarian, an important personal characteristic is patience. And—as Dreman says—"Patience is a crucial but rare investment commodity."

As for the qualities that Dreman looks for in companies to invest in, he likes to buy solid or quality companies with high dividends and low price-to-earnings ratios, Price-to-cash flow, and/or price-to-book value. By low, he means at least 30% less than the market as a whole. Now, there is no uniform definition of what a quality company is, but it usually has several characteristics. It's likely to have been in business for a while, to be profitable, to pay a stock dividend, and to have strong management. In the context of dividends, Dreman likes to see a yield at least one-half of 1% higher than the average for the market as a whole—and with a history of rising payouts. In other words, he likes an attractive dividend yield and the potential for dividend growth. And Dreman—like many successful investors—prefers to hold a more concentrated portfolio than the typical mutual fund or index fund. Dreman advises investing equally in 20 to 30 stocks, diversified among 15 or more industries. In his opinion, this balances diversification with his ability to follow the companies in detail.

Of course, being a contrarian doesn't always work. Dreman bought financial stocks during the recession of 2007–2009. Among his holdings at the time were Citigroup, Washington Mutual, and Fannie Mae. These investments significantly impacted his performance. One of the largest funds he managed, the DWS Dreman High Return Fund, lost 45.5% in 2008, even worse than the S&P 500's drop of 37% that same year. During times like these, it's not easy to be a contrarian. Dreman said It's very hard to go against the crowd. Even if you've done it most of your life, it still jolts you.

While taking losses sometimes is unavoidable, you should often also know when to take your winnings. The best poker players don't stay at the table until their luck runs out. So Dreman offers some advice on when to sell. He recommends selling a stock when its P/E ratio or other contrarian indicator approaches that of the overall market, regardless of how favorable its prospects may appear. He advises replacing it then with another contrarian stock. In this, Dreman's approach differs from the advice of Peter Lynch, who once managed Fidelity Investments' Magellan fund, and who tended to hold on to good companies even if they appeared to be expensive. Dreman's approach is always to be a disciplined, value investor.

One of the largest firms that tries to systematically capitalize on investor mistakes is LSV Asset Management, based in Chicago, with more than $80 billion in assets under management. Its initials come from the surnames of the three university professors who founded the firm, Josef Lakonishok of the University of Illinois, Andrei Shleifer of Harvard University, and Robert Vishny of The University of Chicago. The principals state that the fundamental premise on which LSV's investment philosophy is based is that

> Superior long-term results can be achieved by systematically exploiting the judgmental biases and behavioral weaknesses that influence the decisions of many investors. These include the tendency to extrapolate the past too far into the future, to wrongly equate a good company with a good investment irrespective of price, to ignore statistical evidence and to develop a mindset about a company.

Another investment firm to rely on behavioral finance as a core component of its investment strategy is Fuller & Thaler in California's Silicon Valley with about $5 billion under management. Founder and principal Russell Fuller is a former academic who is the firm's chief investment officer. Its other namesake, Richard Thaler, is a professor of behavioral science, economics and finance at the University of Chicago's Booth School of Business, and a co-director—with Robert Shiller—of the Behavioral Economics Project at the National Bureau of Economics Research. Fuller and Thaler's firm is mid-sized but maintains important investment advisory relationships with much larger partners such as J.P. Morgan. Its founders are so committed to the ideas of behavioral finance that they've registered the trademark, The Behavioral Edge. And, as their website plainly states, "Investors make mental mistakes that can cause stocks to be mispriced. Fuller & Thaler's objective is to use our understanding of human decision-making to find these mispriced stocks and earn superior returns."

Years ago, the cartoonist Walt Kelly penned a long-running comic strip whose title character, Pogo, famously pronounced, "We have met the enemy and he is us." The same can be said of many investors. We tend to repeatedly make the same mistakes, like chasing performance and panicking when prices inevitably drop.

The first takeaway from behavioral finance—as Dreman, LSV, and Fuller & Thaler all demonstrate—is to identify one's own investing mistakes, and to be aware of others' vulnerabilities, as well. You might start by keeping a journal of your investments, why you went into them, and why you exited them. Are there any discernible patterns that might help you going forward?

People have known about the impact of market psychology on security prices for a long time. For example, the economist John Maynard Keynes once described the markets as being moved by animal spirits and not by reason. But over the past few decades, the field of behavioral finance has made great strides in documenting the mistakes of investors. Investors like David Dreman and academics like Daniel Kahneman, Amos Tversky, Robert Shiller, and Richard Thaler all have made enormous contributions to the field.

They have cataloged mistakes that investors are prone to make, like the disposition effect, optimism bias, overreaction bias, representativeness bias, confirmation bias, and many others. But not all investors make the same mistakes.

David Dreman recognized that being a contrarian was the best way for him to make money. But as he also said, :If contrarian strategies work so well, why aren't they more widely followed?" Not everyone has the temperament to be a contrarian. One of the worst feelings is to be wrong and alone. If you're wrong picking a stock that everyone loves, you are unlikely to get fired—even if that stock comes crashing down.

10

Peter Lynch:
Invest in What You Know

Peter Lynch managed Fidelity Investments' Magellan Fund from 1977 to 1990. During his 13-year tenure, a $10,000 stake in the fund would have grown to $280,000. Over the same period, the S&Ps 500 stock index roughly tripled, increasing 214%. Under Lynch, the Magellan fund never lost money over a calendar year, and it beat the S&P 500 11 out of 13 years. During that time, the size of the portfolio he managed grew from $18 million to $14 billion. Lynch was once the most successful mutual fund manager in the world, and then he retired at his peak.

The Investment Universe

> A mutual fund is an investment managed for the mutual benefit of its shareholders. A mutual fund such as Magellan offers the same portfolio of investments for all its shareholders. Large investors, or institutions, usually belong to a class of shares paying lower fees than small investors do. These fees may include management fees, marketing fees, and administration fees.

> The expense ratio is the "all in" number that expresses the fees you pay as a percentage of your overall investment.

> Research analysts often break the investment universe into different categories they call style boxes. The main distinctions are between growth, value, large cap, and small cap.

  ○ Growth firms trade at above-average valuations relative to the market as a whole. For example, their price to earnings or price to book ratios may be higher than the S&P 500's. By comparison, value firms trade at below-average multiples.

  ○ Growth investors are often trying to find rapidly growing smaller firms that have the potential to become large firms like the next Amazon. In contrast, value investors search for stocks trading at a low price relative to the company's earnings or cash flow or paying an above-average dividend.

  ○ Value stocks are companies that typically are growing sales and earnings more slowly than growth firms. They also might be going through some problems, explaining why they may be trading at below-average valuations.

- ○ Small-cap companies are valued at less than $1 billion. By comparison, large cap firms are those with a market capitalization—or market price times total shares outstanding—of $1 billion or more.

Lynch's Background

- > Lynch worked as a caddy to help support his family after his father's death. He found that it paid better than delivering newspapers, and being a caddy provided him with his first real exposure to the stock market: Businessmen, doctors, and lawyers naturally discussed the stock market while they were out on the golf course.

- > He joined Fidelity Investments in 1965 and became a full-time analyst in 1969, covering the metals and chemicals industries. In between, Lynch got his M.B.A. at the University of Pennsylvania's Wharton School and served in the Army for 2 years before launching his storied career at Fidelity. Lynch eventually headed Fidelity's research department before getting the chance to run Magellan.

Research Is Knowledge

- > Lynch gets upset when people say his strategy was to "invest in what you know," as if that's all there is to it. Research is essential. Lynch would follow up on his own common sense and instincts with rigorous fundamental analysis. That meant looking at a company's financials, talking to management, and talking to competitors in the industry.

  - ○ Listen to the quarterly earnings conference calls that firms host for analysts and investors.

- Listen to or view public presentations at conferences and elsewhere to get an impression of management's credibility over time.

- Find a recording of a firm's conference call on the investor relations portion of its website. You frequently can find earnings call transcripts and other information.

- Try calling a firm's investor relations department. These professionals tend to be more accessible than the company's CEO or CFO.

- Buy a single share of a company's stock, and attend its annual shareholders meetings. Most firms permit shareholders to ask questions at these annual meetings.

> Lynch rarely invested in a firm with a lot of debt. One of his maxims was, "Companies that have no debt cannot go bankrupt." Of course, bankruptcy is the worst-case investment scenario for the buyer of a stock, since the stock price almost always goes to zero. A few ways of assessing the bankruptcy risk of a firm include the following:

- Look at a company's credit rating. Standard and Poor, Moody's, Fitch, and other credit-rating services evaluate the debt of most public companies. A bond rated below BBB– is considered high-yield or junk. If you are a stock investor, you'll want to have a high level of conviction before investing in a company with a junk credit rating.

- Look at a number of ratios that measure creditworthiness: the debt to equity, debt to assets, and debt to income ratios. You can find most of these ratios at popular financial websites.

> Although Lynch didn't like firms with a lot of debt, there were some exceptions. One of his biggest winners was buying Chrysler stock in 1982, as the automotive company teetered on the edge of

bankruptcy. The stock was trading at $2 a share and it was losing money, but Lynch liked the product line.

- ○ Chrysler invented the minivan, a huge hit. He was a fan of its CEO, Lee Iacocca, and he thought the rumors of Chrysler's bankruptcy were greatly exaggerated, especially since the company had just sold its military tank division to General Dynamics, for $1 billion in cash.

- ○ The U.S. economy was just then emerging from a deep recession so he thought the auto industry was headed for a cyclical upturn. Lynch turned out to be right, as the stock eventually went up more than 10-fold. That's what Lynch calls a tenbagger.

> Lynch made money across the investment universe. When Magellan was small, he could count on small-cap stocks to help deliver outsized performance. Small-cap companies are valued at less than $1 billion. By comparison, large cap firms are those with a market capitalization—or market price times total shares outstanding—of $1 billion or more.

> Small stocks historically deliver higher returns than large stocks because they are riskier, but also because they are followed less intensively by Wall Street. You are more likely to uncover information on small cap firms that is not yet widely known by the market.

> Yet Lynch's superior performance continued even when Magellan ballooned in size, and he tilted towards larger firms: companies like IBM, Ford, Merck, and General Electric. Starting in the mid-1980s, Lynch also invested about 10% to 20% of Magellan's assets in international stocks, names like Unilever, Volvo, and Royal Dutch Shell.

> Part of Peter Lynch's mantra of investing in what you know is that you probably have some unique insights into the industry that you work in, or worked in. He says, "Your investor's edge is not

something you can get from Wall Street experts. It is something you already have. You can outperform the experts if you use your edge by investing in companies or industries you already understand."

Buying in Bulk

> Lynch had a portfolio liked to buy baskets of companies in an entire industry. His logic was that when you are looking at small firms or a new industry, you might not know which will emerge as winners. Therefore, if you are right on the industry at large—and buy a basket of its stocks—then the winners will go up in multiples; if you avoid borrowing, you won't lose more than 100% of your investment in the failures.

> Peter Lynch retired before the Internet boom, but as an example of investing in baskets of stocks, think about all the search engines that once existed: Alta Vista, Lycos, Infoseek, Yahoo!, and others. The eventual winner turned out to be Google, which came to be valued in the hundreds of billions of dollars. But if you'd bought a basket of all the leading candidates at the time, you would have wound up ahead even if all the other search engines went to zero.

> Lynch generally avoided hot stocks in hot industries, preferring companies that appeared to be dull, mundane, or out of favor, or which hadn't caught the fancy of Wall Street. He thought they shared several characteristics:

    ○ They tended to be low-cost operators with penny-pinching managers in the executive suite.

    ○ They avoided going into debt.

    ○ They rejected the corporate caste system and didn't pit white-collar workers against blue-collar workers.

    ○ Their workers tended to be well paid, with stakes in the companies' future.

> These kinds of companies seemed to find niches and grow faster than average.

> Although not everyone has the resources that Peter Lynch had at Fidelity, he suggested a number of tips that the rest of us can use.

  o He looked for companies that consistently bought back their own shares. If a company buys back its own shares, it tells the market that it thinks its stock is undervalued.

  o A company buyback also tends to keep away short sellers who are betting the stock price will fall. Many companies also buy back stock to offset the shares given to employees as compensation.

> Look for companies that started out with little or no institutional ownership. If the amount of institutional ownership is less than 50% of the total number of shares outstanding, the institutions haven't piled in yet. Once the institutions pile in, the stock price can take off.

> Lynch viewed insider buying by management as a positive sign. Corporate insiders should know more about the firm than almost anyone else. Most corporate directors get the bulk of their compensation from their company's stock. For them to buy on top of that sends a very strong signal.

> On the other hand, insiders sell for various reasons: to pay taxes or diversify their portfolios, for example. But if corporate insiders sell a large portion of their holdings, it may be cause for concern.

> If you are getting nervous about a rising stock price, hold at least a portion of the stock if the business is still solid, even if you think it might be overvalued. Lynch believed in investing in companies, not in the stock market. He tried to ignore short-term fluctuations, viewing market declines as an opportunity to buy stock in

companies he liked. In the long term, there is a 100% correlation between the success of a company and the success of its stock.

> Even so, you can't simply invest in what you know. Successful investing requires research. Before buying a stock, look at a company's financials, its competitive position in the industry, and its management. One of his rules is, "Never invest in anything that you can't illustrate with a crayon."

Suggested Reading

Lynch, with Rothchild, *Beating the Street.*
———, *One Up On Wall Street.*

Questions to Consider

1. How would you describe the investment strategy of Peter Lynch?

2. Which industries do you think you have a core competence or competitive advantage in?

10

Peter Lynch:
Invest in What You Know

Peter Lynch was once the most successful mutual fund manager in the world—and then, he retired, at his peak. Lynch managed Fidelity Investments' Magellan Fund from 1977 to 1990. During his 13-year tenure, a $10,000 stake in the fund would have grown 28-fold to $280,000. Over the same period, the Standard & Poor's 500 stock index roughly tripled, increasing 214%.

Under Lynch, the Magellan fund never lost money over a calendar year, and it beat the S&P 500 11 out of 13 years. And during that time, the size of the portfolio he managed grew more than 750-fold, from just $18 Million to $14 billion, when Lynch stepped down. Magellan was the largest mutual fund in the world by that time. One out of every 100 Americans were invested in it. Lynch also managed a $1 billion Fidelity pension fund with even better performance.

So why did he retire? Well, there were a few reasons. Lynch's father had died at the age of 46 due to cancer. He got sick when Peter was seven, and died when his son was 10. Lynch himself had three daughters and he said that he wanted to be around them while they grew up. He regretted missing many of their school and athletic events. He also wanted to spend more time with his wife, Carolyn. At Fidelity, Lynch kept a grueling work schedule. On Monday through Saturday, he would leave for work at 6 a.m. and stay at the office until around 8 p.m. Toward the end of his tenure, he even worked on Sundays before going to church. And, as the fund got larger, he eventually was investing in more than 1500 different companies.

If you've ever seen a picture of Lynch, you probably know he had a head shock full of white hair, even when he was in his early 40s. The pressure of managing so much money might have played a role in his early retirement. But he also had a great deal of financial security. His salary was said to be at least $3 million a year. More importantly, he reportedly held a 6% ownership stake in Fidelity Investments. In the early 1990s, that would probably have been worth tens of millions of dollars. Today, it would be worth hundreds of millions of dollars.

Ultimately, Lynch had nothing left to prove. He'd built the largest mutual fund in the country with incredible performance. In this lecture, we'll survey Peter Lynch's personal background, his investment strategy, and his most important message, "Invest in what you know." That is, the average person probably knows more about the industry they work in than most Wall Street professionals do. This knowledge can be a starting point for making money.

A mutual fund is exactly what it sounds like, It's an investment managed for the mutual benefit of its shareholders. You might invest in a mutual fund as part of your retirement plan; or through a 401k or IRA; or as part of your basic savings. A mutual fund, such as Magellan, offers the same portfolio of investments for all of its shareholders. So, if you put in $10,000—and I put in $5,000—you will have twice as many shares as me, but we will both own the same investments, with the same returns. We each own pro-rata portions of the fund. Now, that said, sometimes the funds have different share classes. Large investors, or institutions, usually belong to a class of shares paying lower fees than small investors do. These fees may include management fees, marketing fees, and administration fees. Some funds also come with a sales charge called a load that's paid to the seller of the fund. No-load funds avoid this sales charge and generally have better net performance even though the pre-fee returns of load and no-load funds tend to be similar.

If the fees sound confusing to you, you are not alone. The expense ratio is the all-in number that expresses the fees you pay on a percentage basis.

That is, as a percentage of your overall investment. Actively managed stock funds have an average expense ratio on average of about 1%. Actively managed bond funds have an average expense ratio of 0.5% or 50 basis points. You might be asking, What is a basis point? Well, 100 basis points equal 1%. It sounds like a little, but it can add up as a cost. Index funds are a lot cheaper. An index fund is a mutual investment with a portfolio selected to match the components of a market index, such as the S&P 500. They usually have an expense ratio of 0.2% or 20 basis points or even less.

Now, most mutual funds trade only once a day—at 4 pm—after the market closes even though the basket of assets they own, like shares of Ford Motor, trades all day long. By way of contrast, an investment that looks something like a mutual fund—called an exchange-traded fund, or ETF—trades throughout the day. That is its price changes continuously to reflect the updated values of its underlying assets. And this intraday trading feature is one reason why they—the ETFs—became increasingly popular in recent years.

Research analysts often break the investment universe into different categories they call style boxes. The main distinctions are between growth, value, large-cap, and small-cap. The definitions vary from firm to firm, but growth firms trade at above-average valuations, relative to the market as a whole. For example, their price to earnings or price to book ratios may be higher than the S&P 500's. By comparison, Value firms trade at below-average multiples. Growth investors are often trying to find rapidly growing smaller firms that have the potential to become the next large firm like Apple or Amazon. In contrast, value investors search for stocks trading at low prices relative to the company's earnings or cash flow, or they pay an above-average dividend. Value stocks are companies that are typically growing sales and earnings more slowly than growth firms. They also might be going through some problems, explaining why they may be trading at below-average valuations.

Peter Lynch was born on January 19th, 1944 in Newton, Massachusetts, a Boston suburb. His father was a math professor at Boston College, and, later became an auditor for a large insurance firm, John Hancock. Peter worked as a caddy at an affluent Boston-area country club to help support his family, after his father's death. He found that it paid better than delivering newspapers and being a caddy provided him with his first real exposure to the stock market. He caddied for a bunch of businessmen, doctors, and lawyers, who, naturally, discussed the stock market while they were out on the golf course. Lynch said, "Those years on the golf course were a great education, the next best thing to being on the floor of the exchange." Lynch attended Boston College and invested his caddy money in his first stock, The Flying Tiger Line. He bought 100 shares at $8 a share, and it went up all the way to the mid-80s.

Later, he joined Boston-based Fidelity Investments in 1965, as a summer intern. He beat out 100 applicants for the job. But, he had an edge. He had been a caddy for Fidelity's President, D. George Sullivan. Lynch became a full-time analyst in 1969, covering the metals and chemicals industry. In between, Lynch got his MBA at the University of Pennsylvania's Wharton School, and served in the Army for two years, before launching his storied career at Fidelity. At Penn, Lynch also met his wife Carolyn, who was a sophomore, majoring in Physics and Physiology. While Lynch was in the Army he wrote Carolyn a postcard every day and the couple married in 1968. Lynch worked for eight years as an analyst—and eventually headed Fidelity's research department—before getting the chance to run Magellan. The fund was incubated with the founding family's own money in 1963 and didn't open its doors to the public until 1981.

The value-investing legend Warren Buffett has often talked about investing in his own circle of competence. That is, if you work as an engineer, you probably know more about engineering stocks than the average Wall Street Analyst does. Maybe not so much on the financials, but more about the trends and direction in the industry. So, Buffett—who was an expert on finance and insurance—famously avoided technology stocks, even though Microsoft co-founder, Bill Gates, became one of his best friends. However, Buffett and Lynch make the point that your circle of competence is likely different than their circle of competence.

Lynch gets upset when people say that his strategy is, invest in what you know as if that's all there is to it. It isn't. You have to do more than simply invest in what you know. Lynch would follow up on his own common sense and instincts with rigorous fundamental analysis. That meant looking at a company's financials, talking to management, and talking to competitors in the industry. Lynch says that when he was at Fidelity, he spent the bulk of his time talking to people—on the phone, or in person—trying to get a better understanding of their specific firms and industries.

Let's look at some stocks that Lynch and Magellan owned over the years. Dunkin Donuts, for instance, was founded in the Boston area and went public in 1968. Lynch bought Dunkin' Donuts because, as a starting point, he liked the coffee. But he followed up his initial interest in the stock by looking at its financials and talking to management. While it might be hard for the average person to talk to the management of a publicly traded firm, there are some things that you can do. You can listen to the quarterly earnings conference calls that firms host for analysts and investors. You can listen to—or view—some public presentations at conferences and elsewhere, to get an impression of management's credibility over time. You can also find a recording of a firm's conference call on the investor relations portion of its website. And you frequently can find earnings call transcripts and other information. You can also try calling a firm's investor relations department. These professionals tend to be more accessible than the company's CEO or CFO. And you can buy a single share of a company's stock, and attend its annual shareholder's meetings. Most firms permit shareholders to ask questions at these annual meetings.

Here's another example of a Magellan investment, Peter Lynch's wife, Carolyn, liked L'eggs pantyhose, so he bought stock in its parent company, Hanes, after putting in the requisite legwork. Yes, pun intended. Eventually, Consolidated Foods, later known as Sara Lee, bought L'eggs. Magellan fund holders experienced a 30-fold rise in Hanes's stock price. However, Lynch rarely invested in a firm with a lot of debt. One of his maxims was, "Companies that have no debt, cannot go bankrupt." Of course, bankruptcy is the worst-case investment scenario for the buyer of a stock since the stock price almost always goes to zero.

Now, there are a few ways of assessing the bankruptcy risk of a firm. The first is to look at a company's credit rating. Standard and Poor, Moody's, Fitch and other credit-rating services evaluate the debt of most public companies. A bond rated below BBB- is considered high yield or junk. So, if you are a stock investor you'll want to have a high level of conviction before investing in a company with a junk credit rating. You can also look at a number of ratios that measure creditworthiness, for example, the debt-to-equity, debt-to-assets, and debt-to-income ratios. You can find most of these ratios at popular financial websites. And there is a model for forecasting bankruptcy risk, known as the Altman Z-score, developed by Edward Altman, a finance professor at New York University. Think of it as a FICO score for corporate bonds.

So, Lynch didn't like firms with a lot of debt, but there were some exceptions. One of his biggest winners was buying Chrysler stock in 1982, as the automotive company teetered on the edge of bankruptcy. The stock was trading at only $2 a share, at the time, and it was losing money. But Lynch liked the product line. Chrysler invented the minivan, which, of course, turned out to be a huge hit. He was a fan of its CEO, Lee Iacocca, who was previously president of Ford and had helped launch the Ford Mustang. And he thought the rumors of Chrysler's bankruptcy were greatly exaggerated, especially since the company had just sold its military tank division to the defense firm General Dynamics, for $1 billion in cash. The U.S. economy was just then emerging from a deep recession so he thought the auto industry was headed for a cyclical upturn.

Lynch turned out to be right, and the stock eventually went up more than 10-fold. That's what Lynch calls a tenbagger. Chrysler was later sold to Daimler, the parent company of Mercedes-Benz, for about $60 a share, and today it is controlled by an arm of the Italian automaker, FIAT. But Lynch made money across the investment universe. When Magellan was small, he could count on small-cap stocks to help deliver outsized performance. Small-cap companies are valued at less than $1 billion. By comparison, large-cap firms are those with a market capitalization—or market price times total shares outstanding—of $1 billion or more.

Since there are more than 5,000 stocks trading on U.S. exchanges—and more than 50,000 around the world—sometimes there are even finer distinctions. The term microcap refers to firms with values of less than $100 million. The term mid-cap usually refers to firms with market values between $1 billion and $10 billion. Occasionally you'll even hear the term SMID, which means a fund that invests in small and midcap firms alike. And sometimes you'll hear the term megacap, which usually refers to the largest firms, typically valued at more than $50 billion. Anyway, small-cap stocks historically deliver higher returns than large stocks because they are riskier, but also because they are less intensively followed by Wall Street. You are more likely to uncover information on small-cap firms that is not yet widely known by the market. Yet Lynch's superior performance continued even well after Magellan ballooned in size, and he tilted towards larger firms, companies like IBM, Ford, Merck, and General Electric.

Starting in the mid-1980s, Lynch also invested about 10% to 20% of Magellan's assets in international stocks, in names like Unilever, Volvo, and Royal Dutch Shell. Now, as I've tried to indicate, part of Peter Lynch's mantra of investing in what you know is that you probably have some unique insights into the industry that you work in, or worked in. Lynch said, "Your investor's edge is not something you can get from Wall Street experts. It is something you already have. You can outperform the experts if you use your edge by investing in companies or industries you already understand."

One reason why Lynch had a portfolio with more than 1000 stocks besides Magellan's huge size is that he liked to buy baskets of companies in an entire industry. So he would buy baskets of financial companies, auto companies, restaurants, and the like. His logic was that when you are looking at small firms or a new industry, you might not know which one, or ones, will emerge as winners. You only know for certain only in retrospect. So if you are right on the industry at large—and buy a basket of its stocks— then the winners will go up in multiples, and, if you avoid borrowing, you won't lose more than 100% of your investment in the failures.

Peter Lynch retired before the Internet boom but as an example of investing in baskets of stocks, think about all the search engines that once existed, Alta Vista, Lycos, Infoseek, Yahoo, and so forth. The eventual winner turned out to be Google, now known as Alphabet, which came to be valued in the hundreds of billions of dollars. But if you'd bought a basket of all the leading candidates at the time, you would have wound up ahead even if all the other search engines went to zero.

Lynch generally avoided hot stocks in hot industries. He was suspicious of companies with growth rates of 50% to 100% a year. They wouldn't be able to keep it up, or they'd attract too much competition. Rather, Lynch preferred companies that appeared to be dull, mundane, out of favor, or which hadn't yet caught the fancy of Wall Street. He thought that these companies frequently shared several characteristics, they tended to be low-cost operators with penny-pinching managers in the executive suite; they avoided going into debt; they rejected the corporate caste system and didn't try to pit white-collar workers against blue-collar workers. Their workers tended to be well paid, with stakes in the companies' future. And these kinds of companies seemed to find niches, and grow faster than average.

Now, not everyone has the resources that Peter Lynch had at Fidelity, where he was supported by a large staff of analysts. Plus, almost any company executive would take a meeting with him. Still, he suggested a number of tips that the rest of us can use when buying a stock. For instance, Lynch looked for companies that consistently bought back their own shares. If a company buys back its own shares, it basically says to the market that it thinks its stock is undervalued. It usually has plenty of other options for the money, like building new projects or even buying another firm. If a company like Apple buys back billions of dollars worth of its shares, then it also tends to keep short sellers away. Short sellers are investors who are betting the stock will fall. Many companies also buy back stock to offset the shares given to employees as compensation. So, I would consider a noteworthy buyback as one that retires a number of shares equivalent to all the stock given to executives each year, plus at least 5% of shares outstanding.

In the era when Lynch was prominent, he liked to buy companies that started out with little, or no, institutional ownership. Institutions are banks, insurers, and pensions, for example. If the amount of institutional ownership is less than 50% of the total number of shares outstanding, then institutions haven't piled in yet. But once the institutions pile in, the stock price can really take off. It also helps for a company to have a recognized institutional sponsor. If Warren Buffett or Peter Lynch buy a stock, it quickly gets on the radar screen of other professional money managers. And, as more money managers buy the stock, a herding effect develops. You can find out which stocks money managers own by looking at a form with the Securities and

Exchange Commission called the 13F. All institutional investment firms with more than $100 million in assets under management have to file this form on a quarterly basis. There is a 45-day lag between the calendar and filing date. So, the December 31 holdings of a manager are revealed around February 14th or 15th of the following year.

Now, looking at stocks from another perspective, Peter Lynch viewed insider buying by management as a positive sign. Corporate insiders know more about the firm than almost anyone else. On the other hand, insiders sell for various reasons. Maybe they have to pay taxes. Maybe they want to purchase a new home. Maybe they are diversifying their portfolios. But if corporate insiders sell a large portion of their holdings, it may be cause for concern.

That said, insiders buy for only one reason, over the long term, to make money. Most corporate directors get the bulk of their compensation from their company's stock. For them to buy on top of that sends a very strong signal. If more than one insider buys, it sends an even stronger signal. Lynch, like other great investors—including Jesse Livermore, Benjamin Graham, Warren Buffett, and David Dreman—recognized the importance of having the right mindset to be successful. He said, "The key to making money in stocks is to not get scared out of them." Lynch also said "Everyone has the brainpower to make money in stocks. Not everyone has the stomach". And, at another point, he said, "You won't improve results by pulling out the flowers and watering the weeds."

Now, investors tend to experience regret when they miss buying a stock that subsequently goes up sharply, especially stocks they followed closely. Say, a young Starbucks, Facebook, or Apple, when Steve Jobs returned to the company. Lynch has another saying, "You don't have to kiss all the pretty girls." In other words, you don't have to pick all of the big winners in the stock market. Just a few can make a huge difference to your portfolio if you hang on. I'm sure we all have stories of buying a stock and selling it too soon. I once owned Netflix and Tesla and watched in envy as the stocks went up multiples of what I had sold them for. But Lynch has some good advice if you are getting nervous about a rising stock price. He said, If the story is still good and earnings keep growing, then, of course, it can go higher. In other words, hold at least a portion of the stock if the business is still solid, even if you think it might be overvalued. Lynch, after all, is the father of the tenbagger.

Like Benjamin Graham, Lynch believed in investing in companies, not in the stock market. He tried to ignore short-term fluctuations, viewing market declines as an opportunity to buy stocks that he liked. He also thinks no one can consistently predict what happens to the economy, market or interest rates, in the short run. But in the long-term, there is a 100% correlation between the success of a company and the success of its stock. Make no mistake. Peter Lynch had a tremendous ability to pick stocks. He estimates he purchased more than 15,000 stocks over the course of his career. He led one of the most successful mutual funds in history, Fidelity Magellan, for more than a decade with outstanding performance. And his investment advice resonated with individual investors because he gave us hope. He told us we actually have an edge over Wall Street professionals when it comes to what we know, and where we work, and because, sometimes, we're the early ones to use the products or services of a firm with national, or international, potential.

Even so, Lynch says you can't simply invest in what you know. Successful investing requires more than that. Before buying a stock, Lynch says you should look at a company's financials, its competitive position in the industry, and its management. And he reminds us that the average person spends more time doing research on a refrigerator that we might be interested in purchasing, than in a stock we might also like to buy. But, stock investing shouldn't be too complicated, Lynch says. One of his rules is, "Never invest in anything that you can't illustrate with a crayon." What this means is that if you don't really understand what the company does, and can't illustrate it with a crayon, then you are more likely to make a mistake.

So, the next time you see what you think might be the next Starbucks, Facebook, Amazon, or Costco, you can always take a page out of Peter Lynch's playbook to investigate further. Can the concept grow nationally or internationally? Are the financials good? How is the competitive landscape? Hey, if the answers are positive, maybe—just maybe—you've discovered the next tenbagger.

11

The Bond Kings: Bill Gross, Jeffrey Gundlach

The global bond market is more than twice as large as the stock market. It also plays a more central role in the lives of most people. The mortgage on your home, your student loan, your car loan are all tied to the bond market. Federal, state, and local governments finance themselves through the bond market. The assets in Social Security are tied to it, and the global economy almost melted down in 2008 because of the bond market—not the stock market.

Gross and Gundlach

> Bill Gross was crowned a "bond king" because of his storied career with the Pacific Investment Management Company, better known as PIMCO. That is, until their well-publicized breakup. Gross managed the firm's huge Total Return bond fund, which peaked with almost $300 billion in assets under management. In the more than 25 years that Gross ran the fund, it outperformed its benchmark by about 2% a year. That's a big deal in the bond world—especially with a fund so large.

> Jeff Gundlach earned his stripes as the top bond manager at Trust Company of the West, or TCW. Like Gross, Gundlach ultimately

had a contentious departure. Under Gundlach, TCW's Total Return Bond Fund finished in the top 2% of all funds in its class for the 10 years before he left. Less than 7 years after starting over at his own firm, he had more than $100 billion in assets under management.

> Bill Gross and Jeff Gundlach share a focus on 3- to 5-year investment horizons and top-down analyses that take the big picture of the economy into account. Bill Gross is adept at investing worldwide, while Jeff Gundlach has a special expertise in U.S. mortgage bonds and in relative-value analysis.

Bonds and Risks

> A bond is like an IOU backed by legal rights. The issuing party, typically a company or government entity, usually offers to pay interest, known as the coupon payment, in order to borrow money from investors. Eventually, it returns the money borrowed—known as the face, par, or principal value—along with interest. And since the amount and timing of the cash flows on bonds are usually known, they are called fixed-income securities. When investing in bonds, you should be aware of several important risks.

> Interest-rate risk. When interest rates go up, traditional bonds fall in value because the bond is viewed as riskier and is valued less. When interest rates fall, traditional bonds usually rise in value because the risk is perceived to be lower.

> Reinvestment rate risk. When rates rise, the coupons and maturing face value or bond principal can be reinvested at higher rates in newer securities, drawing investor interest away from the older instrument.

> Default risk. If a bond defaults, it may be forced into bankruptcy, and the bondholders may seize the assets of the issuer—often after a long and protracted bankruptcy court battle.

> Liquidity risk. A liquid asset is one that can be sold quickly, and at fair market value. A U.S. Treasury Bill is very liquid. Your house is not. During times of market distress, such as the Great Recession in 2008, illiquid assets often take a big hit. In the bond market, they tend to be bonds that have less trading volume; bonds with low credit ratings; emerging markets bonds; and bonds with wide bid-ask spreads—the difference in price between when you buy and when you sell.

Bill Gross

> Bill Gross was born April 13, 1944, in Middletown, Ohio. He wanted to go to college on the East Coast, and Duke offered him an academic scholarship. Gross majored in psychology and always had a knack for numbers. While in school, he was in a car accident. During his recovery, he read a famous gambling book titled *Beat the Dealer*.

> After graduation, he enlisted in the Navy, but first he went to Las Vegas for 4 months, where he made a living as a gambler, using the gaming strategy he'd read about. Gross would use many concepts from gambling, such as developing strategies for making decisions with incomplete information, in his future investment activities.

> After the Navy, Gross went on for his M.B.A. Although he wanted to be a stock trader, he joined the Pacific Mutual Life Insurance Company as a credit analyst. A short time later, Pacific Mutual created a new firm to focus on mutual funds: Pacific Investment Management Company, or PIMCO. Gross joined the new unit and eventually took it over with a couple of business partners.

Gross's Investment Strategy

> Gross believes that successful investment over the long run, whether in bonds or in equities, depends on developing a long-term outlook and acquiring the right mix of securities within an asset class. In addition, he believes that 3- to 5-year forecast

horizons force an investor to avoid the near-term fluctuations that lead to panic and bad investment decisions. This focus makes him a top-down investor.

> The expected return on a bond over its term should be pretty close to its yield to maturity—that is, the return from the coupon payment and the capital gain or loss on the instrument, together known as the bond's total return. Gross focuses on yield-to-call estimates, as opposed to yield-to-maturity calculations, when estimating the most probable total return on a bond held until maturity.

> In the search for yield, Gross also suggests exploring international bonds, particularly in emerging nations. They may also provide additional diversification. But a word of caution: International bonds also have currency risk. If an American investor invests in a foreign bond the foreign currency falls versus the dollar over your investment horizon, you may lose money, on a total return basis, when you try to convert your investment back to U.S. dollars.

> In short, Gross's impressive record in the bond markets has not been achieved with a single strategy but rather by being flexible, global, and long-term oriented.

> In 2000, the German insurance giant, Allianz AG paid $3.5 billion to acquire 70% of PIMCO, which had grown to be the largest bond shop in the world. But Gross butted heads with the other members of PIMCO's management team. Compounding the infighting was the lagging performance of Gross's main investment vehicle, the PIMCO Total Return Fund.

Jeff Gundlach

> Jeffrey Gundlach was born October 30, 1959, and grew up in a middle-class family near Buffalo. He was a strong student with near-perfect SAT scores, and he was admitted to Dartmouth College, where he majored in math and philosophy. Later, he entered Yale's Ph.D. program in applied math.

> Two years later, Gundlach disagreed with his advisor on the topic of his Ph.D. dissertation, dropped out of Yale, and headed to Los Angeles to be a drummer in a rock band. After a couple of years, he found himself broke and looking for a job when he saw a TV show that counted down the top paying jobs in the world and listed investment banker as number 1. Gundlach decided that he would be an investment banker.

> Gundlach didn't know the difference between an investment banker—who focuses on mergers and acquisitions and IPOs—and investment managers, who manage money on behalf of clients. But TCW hired him, thinking that his math background would provide a good foundation for him in the bond market. Gundlach was a quick study and thrived at TCW. He spent 24 years at the firm before being fired in 2009.

> His dispute was with TCW's management and the French parent company, Société Generale. Among other things, the firm accused Gundlach of attempting to steal confidential client and trading information that he could use to launch his own firm.

> Gundlach went on to found Doubleline Capital with about 45 former TCW colleagues who'd helped him run his funds at TCW. But, before his departure, Gundlach amassed one of the best bond records in the industry. Morningstar nominated him as Fixed Income Manager of the Decade. He lost out to Bill Gross.

Gundlach Investing Strategy

> Gundlach believes that if you buy bonds during periods of illiquidity and drops in price, you are likely to profit after the fear subsides and normalized market-levels return. Gundlach has made money investing in all sorts of bonds and other financial instruments. But he is perhaps best known for his investments in mortgage-backed securities.

> Fannie Mae and Freddie Mac are government-sponsored entities backed by the credit rating of the U.S. government and designed to facilitate the functioning of the mortgage market. In 1981, Fannie Mae issued the first mortgage-backed security. Think of it as a bond in which the cash flows are a group of individual mortgage payments rolled into a single security.

> Usually they trade at close to AAA or AAA- ratings while providing a slightly higher yield than U.S. Treasury securities. Gundlach specializes in buying securities that appear to give a higher return than their credit risk might indicate.

> Like Gross, Gundlach usually starts with a top-down view and sets a macroeconomic horizon of about 3 years when he enters a position. He is occasionally willing to make shorter term trades

with horizons of less than a year, and he gives careful thought to how he enters and exits positions. When Gundlach says that his firm is a liquidity provider, he means is that he's a reliable buyer of certain bond instruments when the sellers have to sell.

> When conducting his top-down analysis, Gundlach looks at a few variables. One is the yield curve—a graph of the relationship between time to maturity and yield to maturity. The yield curve typically slopes upward, with long-term interest rates higher than short-term rates.

> Gundlach also looks at what is happening in the economy. Gross domestic product growth might be a useful measure of how the economy is doing as a whole. But he also looks at the credit cycle, which refers to bank lending and customer-default rates. Historically, as the economy approaches recession, credit gets tight and defaults go up.

> This top-down analysis—taking into account the general state of the economy, liquidity in the debt market, and borrower health—gives Gundlach a sense of the credit and interest rate risk in his portfolio.

> Then Gundlach and his team turn to a bottom-up analysis for bonds, which might include looking at loan-level details and specific geographic areas. They check relative value among different credit sectors in fixed-income, at horizons of about 3 years and do a rich/cheap analysis on the various bond sectors, including emerging and foreign markets.

> Gundlach has one of the best batting averages in the investment world. He claims to be right about 70% of the time, which—if true—is phenomenal in a business where being right just over half of the time would make you an all-star.

Suggested Reading

Gross, *Bill Gross on Investing*.
Laing, "The King of Bonds."

Questions to Consider

1. How would you describe the investment strategy of Bill Gross and Jeff Gundlach?

2. How does bond investing differ from stock investing?

11

Transcript

The Bond Kings: Bill Gross, Jeffrey Gundlach

How would you pick the greatest bond manager ever? In my view, the answer might be a toss-up between Bill Gross and Jeff Gundlach; the old guard and the new guard. Both men share similarities in focusing on three- to five-year investment horizons, and top-down analyses, that take the big picture of the economy into account. But, they are also different. Bill Gross is adept at investing worldwide, while Jeff Gundlach has a special expertise in U.S. mortgage bonds and in relative-value analysis.

The global fixed-income or bond market is more than twice as large as the stock market. It also plays a more central role in the lives of most people. The mortgage on your home is tied to the bond market. If you have a student loan, it's tied to the bond market. If you have a car loan, it's tied to the bond market too. Federal, state and local governments also finance themselves through the bond market. The assets in social security are tied to the bond market. And the global economy almost melted down in 2008 because of the bond market—not the stock market.

The nuances of the bond market are largely unknown to most investors. Many of us might know about bond yields, and the principal, or face value of a bond, but little else. The difference in returns between a top-quartile bond manager and bottom-quartile bond manager is usually only 2-3% per year. But this difference adds up over time, and that's important because bonds are the bedrock of most pension funds and retirement plans. Bill

Gross was crowned as bond king due to his long and storied career with the Pacific Investment Management Company, better known as PIMCO, in Newport Beach, California. That is, until their well-publicized breakup. Gross managed the firm's huge total return bond fund, which peaked with almost $300 billion in assets under management. In the more than 25 years that Gross ran the fund, it outperformed its benchmark by about 2% a year. That's a big deal in the bond world—especially with a fund so large.

Jeff Gundlach earned his stripes as the top bond manager at Trust Company of the West, or TCW, in Los Angeles. Like Gross, Gundlach ultimately had a contentious departure. But, under Gundlach, TCW's total return bond fund finished in the top 2% of all funds in its class for the 10 years prior to his leaving. And less than seven years after starting over at his own firm, he had more than $100 billion in assets under management. A bond is like an IOU backed by legal rights. The issuing party—typically a company or government entity—usually offers to pay interest, known as the coupon payment, in order to borrow money from investors. Eventually, it returns the money borrowed—known as the face, par, or principal value— along with interest. And since the amount and timing of the cash flows on bonds are usually known or fixed, they are called fixed-income securities.

There are three or four important RISKS to be aware of when investing in bonds. The first is interest-rate risk. When interest rates go up, traditional bonds – that is those that pay a fixed coupon payment – fall in value. And the reverse is true. When interest rates fall, traditional bonds usually rise in value. Stated otherwise, when rates go up, the bond is viewed as riskier. And it's usually valued less. Of course, the reverse is true when rates fall. It's considered less risky. So you would pay more for it. And the price should rise.

A related risk is known as the reinvestment rate risk. It works in the exact opposite direction. When rates rise, the coupons and maturing face value or bond principal can be reinvested at higher rates in newer securities, drawing investor interest away from the older instrument. And, of course, when rates fall, these cash flows can be reinvested at lower rates. It's kind of like if you had a Certificate of Deposit or CD, that matured. If rates went up, you'd be pleased your next CD would get a higher yield. If rates went down, you'd probably be disappointed that your next CD would be earning a lower rate of interest.

Default risk is a third important type of risk affecting bonds. If a bond defaults, it may be forced into bankruptcy, and the bondholders may seize the assets of the issuer – often after a long and protracted bankruptcy court battle.

Bond analysts typically make a distinction between investment-grade bonds—those rated AAA to BBB-minus —and high-yield, or junk, bonds, which are rated below BBB-minus. Some investors, like pension funds, are often restricted from owning junk bonds. Now, when investment grade bonds default they historically pay about 70 cents on the dollar. When junk bonds default, they historically pay about 20 to 30 cents on the dollar. Of course, the deals on specific cases may be a lot better, or worse. The percentage of what you get, versus what you are owed, is called the recovery rate.

A fourth risk when dealing with bonds is called liquidity risk. A liquid asset is one that can be sold quickly, and at fair market value. A U.S. Treasury Bill is very liquid. Your house is not. During times of market distress, like during the Great Recession in 2008, illiquid assets often take a big hit. In the bond market, they tend to be bonds that don't have a lot of trading volume; bonds with low credit ratings; emerging markets bonds; and bonds with wide bid-ask spreads. A bid-ask spread is the difference in price when you buy versus sell a bond. Think of buying a car and trying to turn around and sell it. You might buy a car off the lot today for $30,000, but if you try to sell it back right away, you'd probably be lucky if you could get $25,000 for it. Fortunately, the bid-ask spread in most bonds is not that bad. But, for most retail investors, the spread tends to be wide enough that active trading usually doesn't make sense.

One more point, A lot of investors think they can't lose money in bonds if they hold them to maturity, and there is no default. However, even if the bond matures without defaulting, you still might suffer a loss on a purchasing power basis. That is, if your bond returns 2% and inflation is 3%, your standard of living has gone down by 1%.

Bill Gross was born on April 13, 1944, in Middletown, Ohio. His father was a sales executive at a steel company, and his mother was a homemaker. When Gross was about 10, his father transferred to San Francisco, taking the family with him. Gross wanted to go to college on the East Coast, and looked at a number of schools, including Cornell, Princeton, and Duke. Duke offered him an academic scholarship and had one of the top-ranked basketball programs. At 6 feet tall, he was a good high school basketball player, but he didn't make the Duke basketball team. Gross majored in psychology at the university, and always had a knack for numbers. Now, while in school, Gross got in a car accident. So, during his hospital stay, he read a famous gambling book by Ed Thorpe called *Beat the Dealer*.

Upon graduating in 1966, he enlisted in the Navy, rather than taking the risk of getting drafted and being put on the front lines at Vietnam. But before going to boot camp, he went to Las Vegas for four months, where he made a living as a gambler. Often, he played 16 hours or more a day, seven days a week. Gross said, the *Beat the Dealer* gaming strategy he read about, worked so well that casino bosses often asked him to leave, due to his winnings. Gross turned $200 into $10,000 during that summer. Gross would use many of the concepts from gambling—such as developing strategies for making decisions when dealing with incomplete information—in his future investment activities.

After coming out of the Navy, Gross went on to UCLA for his MBA. And, although Gross wanted to be a stock trader, he joined the Pacific Mutual Life Insurance Company as a credit analyst. A short time later, Pacific Mutual created a new firm to focus on mutual funds. It went by the name of Pacific Investment Management Company, or PIMCO. Gross joined the new unit, and eventually took it over with a couple of business partners. Gross believes that successful investment over the long-run whether in bonds or equities "rests on two foundations. The ability to formulate and articulate a secular, or long-term, outlook, and, having the correct structural composition within one's portfolio over time."

By structural composition, he means the right mix of securities within an asset class, be it stocks or bonds. Gross believes that three- to five-year forecast horizons force an investor to avoid the near-term emotional whipsaws of fear and greed. He says that "such emotions can convince any investor, or management firm, to do exactly the wrong thing, during irrational periods in the market." Gross goes so far as to practice yoga on a daily basis to help clear his mind, and to minimize the temptation of being swayed by short-term market movements. While three- to five-year investment horizons allow investors to avoid worrying about the latest employment report, Fed meeting or CNBC talking head, Gross says that forecast periods longer than five years represent guesswork, better left to fortune tellers than to serious investment analysts.

Gross's focus on long-term trends as the starting point for his analysis makes him a top-down investor. The opposite approach, called bottom-up, starts by looking at the credit quality of individual bond issuers. Gross says the expected return on a bond over its term should be pretty close to its yield to maturity, which includes the return from the coupon payment and the capital gain or loss on the instrument. These two parts together are known as the bond's total return. Sometimes investors are unclear why a bond's price might differ from its face value. For example, a bond with a face value of $1000 might be trading in the market for $1100, or even $900. Well, when a bond is first issued it generally trades close to its face value, or par. That's usually, $1000, but it's $100 for some bonds. The bond's coupon payment is fixed, but market interest rates—the yield to maturity in the case of a bond— change just about every day.

There is a good shorthand trick to tell if a bond should be trading at par; or at a discount to par; or at a premium to par. Here it is. If the coupon rate on the bond equals its yield to maturity, the bond should sell at par, or face value. If the coupon rate is higher than the yield to maturity, then it should sell at a premium to par. If one bond pays a coupon of 5%, and bonds with similar risk offer a coupon of 4%, then you might be willing to pay more for it. The reverse is also true. If the coupon rate is lower than the yield to maturity, it should sell at a discount to par. So if a bond pays a coupon of 5% and bonds of similar risk offer a coupon of 6%, you would want to pay less than face value for it.

Bonds are affected by certain factors, beyond interest rates, which we can refer to as secular trends. They include demographics, monetary policy, fiscal policy, trade balances, strength or weakness of the currency, and political trends. Gross provides some suggestions on how to become aware of secular trends. He suggests reading books on economic history. One that I like, was written by Carmen Reinhart and Kenneth Rogoff, called *This Time Is Different: Eight Centuries of Financial Folly*. It talks about how economic growth is reduced when economies are deleveraging, which means reducing debt. Deleveraging is usually accomplished by selling assets. And when that happens in a hurry, like in 2008, panic often ensues. Gross also recommends subscribing to periodicals and services that provide macroeconomic research. They help give him ideas for his big picture or top-down views. He cites a couple of institutional services that he uses. One is written by Ray Dalio, whose Bridgewater Associates is the largest hedge fund in the world.

He also mentions Evercore ISI's Ed Hyman, who was voted Wall Street's top economist by the financial magazine, *Institutional Investor*, for 35 consecutive years. While these services can be expensive, comments of well-known thought leaders, like Ray Dalio and Ed Hyman, can often be found on the internet for free. Gross focuses on yield-to-call estimates, as opposed to yield-to-maturity calculations, when estimating the most probable total return on a bond if you hold it until maturity. By call, I mean the issuer of the bond has the right to call in the bond and pay it off early. Kind of like you having the ability to refinance your mortgage if rates drop sharply below your current rate. In the search for yield, Gross also suggests exploring international bonds as alternatives to domestic offerings, particularly in emerging nations. They also might provide additional diversification. But, a word of caution, international bonds also have currency risk. That is, if you are an American investor and invest in a foreign bond, let's say in the United Kingdom, if the British Pound falls versus the Dollar over your investment horizon, you may lose money on a total return basis when you try to convert your investment back to U.S. Dollars.

Gross has had considerable success over the years investing in emerging-markets bonds and provides some specific advice on where to look. First, he says, look at economies with strong projected long-term growth—4% or higher, according to his rule of thumb. Next, look for a stable political environment. He cautions against investing in countries that are highly indebted. If a country has a sovereign debt-to-GDP ratio of less than 60% then Gross views that as a good sign, lowering the chance of default. Gross also prefers emerging markets with trade surpluses, not deficits. Moreover, a persistent trade deficit might not be sustainable in a developing country, as the government, and its people will eventually have to pare spending and pay down their debts. Like the international investing pioneer, John Templeton, Bill Gross also favors countries with high rates of savings and legal systems that emphasize property rights. In short, Gross's impressive record in the bond markets has not been achieved with a single one trick pony strategy but rather by being flexible, global, and long-term oriented.

In 2000, the German insurance giant, Allianz AG paid $3.5 billion to acquire 70% of PIMCO, making Gross a very wealthy man. He also pulled down a hefty salary estimated to be anywhere from $50 million a year to more than $200 million a year. PIMCO had grown to be the largest bond shop in the world, but Gross butted heads with other members of PIMCO's management team. Compounding the infighting, at the end, was the lagging performance of Gross's main investment vehicle, the PIMCO Total Return Fund. So, Gross jumped ship to Janus to manage the tiny Janus Global Unconstrained Bond Fund. But he didn't have to move to Janus's headquarters in Denver. Instead, he was able to manage money for Janus from California, with a small staff of analysts and traders.

Now, there is more than one way to skin the bond cat. So let's look at another master of the craft, Jeff Gundlach. Jeffrey Gundlach was born on October 30, 1959, and grew up in a middle-class family in the Buffalo, New York, area. His father was a chemist, and his mother a homemaker. Gundlach's uncle, Robert, worked for Xerox and is regarded as the inventor of the modern copier. Jeff Gundlach was a strong student with near-perfect SAT scores and was admitted to Dartmouth College, where he majored in math and philosophy. Later, he entered Yale's Ph.D. program in applied math.

Two years later, Gundlach got into a dispute with his advisor on the topic of his Ph.D. thesis. While today he is regarded as a rock star of the bond universe, Gundlach originally aspired to be a real rock star. After the argument with his advisor, he dropped out of Yale and headed to Los Angeles to be a drummer in a rock band called Radical Flat. The band never took off, and, after a couple of years, he found himself broke and looking for a job. That's about when he saw an episode of the TV show, "Lifestyles of the Rich and Famous." The show counted down the top paying jobs in the world and listed Investment Banker as number 1. So, Gundlach decided that he would be an investment banker.

He looked in the phone book and sent his resume to 23 investment firms. At the time, Gundlach didn't know the difference between an investment banker—which focuses on mergers and acquisitions and IPOs—and investment managers, who manage money on behalf of clients. One firm out of the 23, TCW, responded to Gundlach. It hired him, thinking that his math background would provide a good foundation for him in the bond market. Gundlach was a quick study and thrived at TCW. He spent 24 years at the firm before being fired in 2009.

His dispute was with TCW's management, and the parent company, France-based Societe Generale. Among other things, the firm accused Gundlach of attempting to steal confidential client and trading information, that he could use to launch his own firm. Gundlach went on to found Doubleline Capital with about 45 former TCW colleagues who'd helped him run his funds at TCW. But, before his departure, Gundlach amassed one of the best bond records in the industry. Morningstar nominated him as Fixed Income Manager of the Decade. He lost out to Bill Gross.

When questioned about his trading strategy, Gundlach once said,

> I don't often know where my ideas come from. Maybe it's the fact that I'm obsessively regimented in my analysis, borderline autistic. But whether it's bond selection or asset allocation, we can do it better than just about anybody around.

I think he has a little bit of Warren Buffett in him. Just as Buffett said "be fearful when others are greedy and greedy when others are fearful," Gundlach says, "I want fear. I want to buy things when people are afraid of it, not when they think it's a gift being handed down to them." He believes that if you buy bonds during panics—periods of illiquidity and drops in price—you are likely to profit after the fear subsides, and normalized market-levels return.

Gundlach has made money investing in all sorts of bonds and other financial instruments. But he is perhaps best known for his investments in mortgage-backed securities. In 1981, Fannie Mae—one of the government-sponsored entities designed to facilitate the functioning of the mortgage market—issued the first Mortgage-Backed Security. Think of it as a bond, where the cash flows are a bunch of individual mortgages rolled up into a single security. In turn, government-sponsored entities, such as Fannie Mae and Freddie Mac, are formally and informally backed by the credit rating of the U.S. government. Usually, they trade at close to AAA or AAA-ratings while providing a little bit higher yield over U.S. Treasury securities. And Gundlach specializes in buying securities that appear to give a higher return than their credit risk might indicate. Of course, it is a lot harder than simply buying Fannie or Freddie Mortgage-Backed Securities or almost anyone could do it.

Like Gross, Gundlach usually starts with a top-down or macro view and sets a macroeconomic horizon of about three years when he enters a position. But, sometimes he is willing to make shorter-term trades with horizons of less than a year. And he gives careful thought to how he enters and exits positions. He says, "We try to be liquidity providers and get paid for that." What Gundlach means is that he's a reliable buyer of certain bond instruments when other sellers have to sell. And he continues, "That's one of the things that tend to support outperformance over time—buying when other people need to sell. That's always been part of our strategy." Gundlach also argues that the federal reserve has an outsized influence on short-term market movements, so he watches Fed behavior closely despite his long-term investment horizon.

When conducting top-down analysis, Gundlach looks at a few variables. One item he looks at is the yield curve—both the shape and level of it. The yield curve is a graph of the relationship between time to maturity and yield to maturity. The yield curve typically slopes upward, with long-term interest rates higher than short-term rates. And, if rates are low, then there is a long-term tendency for them to eventually trend back up. That is, rates are usually low because of a weak economy, or some sort of financial crisis, which is the exception rather than the norm when looking at long time horizons.

Gundlach also looks at what is happening in the economy. For example, gross domestic product growth might be a useful measure of how the economy is doing as a whole. But he also looks at the credit cycle. The credit cycle refers to bank lending and customer-default rates. Historically, as the economy approaches recession, credit gets tight and defaults go up. This top-down analysis—taking into account the general state of the economy, liquidity in the debt market and borrower health—gives Gundlach a sense of the credit and interest rate risk in his portfolio.

Then, Gundlach and his team turn to the bottom-up analysis for bonds. This might include looking at loan-level details, and specific geographic areas they want to be exposed to. Gundlach says,

> When we look at relative value amongst different credit sectors in fixed-income, we are looking at horizons that are about three years—in line with our history. We basically do a rich/cheap analysis on all of the various bond sectors in the U.S., using emerging markets and non-U.S., as well. We try to have a view out at least 18 months to three years.

Gundlach doesn't always get it right. In a *Barron's* interview in early 2011, he thought that would be a tough year for stocks and suggested the S&P 500 could fall from its then level of 1300 all the way to 500, within two years. Instead, the S&P 500 increased modestly in 2011 and 2015. And it went up double digits each year in 2012 through 2014. Gundlach has one of the best batting averages in the investment world. He claims to be right about 70% of the time, which—if true—is phenomenal in a business where being right just over half of the time would make you an all-star investor.

So, bonds are a staple of most investors' portfolios. As a fixed-income investment, they pay steady streams of principal and interest to term. Many people and institutions live off of this income. Investment-grade bonds often increase in value when stocks plummet, or markets panic, providing excellent diversification and stability benefits. Investment-grade bond funds also provide good liquidity and transparency.

And bond funds typically come with very modest fees. Most active bond funds charge about a half of a percent per year against the assets under management, in contrast to active stock funds that usually charge 1% a year or more. And moving up from there, hedge funds and private equity funds usually charge 1 to 2% of assets along with taking 20% of the profits.

So bonds can be a good deal. And to have someone the caliber of Bill Gross or Jeff Gundlach manage the bond portion of your portfolio at such a low cost—that could be a great deal.

12

Sovereign Wealth Funds: Singapore

W hy should we care about sovereign wealth funds? The answer is because they control more financial assets than hedge funds and private equity funds combined, amounting to more than $7 trillion. Many governments view these funds strategically to help support their own political and economic agendas. As sovereign wealth funds grow in size and importance, they have come to play larger roles both in their own countries' affairs and in market battles between traditional, independent companies and state-owned and -controlled companies.

Sovereign Wealth Funds

> On February 27, 1981, the deputy prime minister of Singapore— Dr. Goh Keng Swee—announced a plan to establish a government-owned investment corporation for the benefit of the population of the island city-state. Its source of funds would be foreign-exchange reserves—reserves beyond what the central bank needed to manage the country's exchange rate. Its objective: capital appreciation.

> Today, dozens of countries, most of them commodity rich, are pouring billions and trillions of dollars into government-run funds

designed to benefit their domestic economies and populations while unleashing new and sometimes conflicting forces in world markets.

> Sovereign wealth funds have become increasingly popular and powerful on the one hand, and potentially controversial on the other. However, it's important to underscore the fundamental tension between the public good that such funds were intended for and potential pitfalls, such as state interests over private needs and the designs of managed markets over free ones.

> The U.S. Treasury Department defines a sovereign wealth fund as "A Government Investment Vehicle which is funded by foreign exchange assets and which manages those assets separately from the official reserves of the monetary authorities, (the Central Bank and reserve-related functions of the Finance Ministry)."

> The distinction is intended to clarify the difference between official reserves managed by a country's central bank, with short-term horizons, focused on liquidity and security, and the longer horizons associated with, for example, national pension systems.

> Three main drivers behind the creation and growth of sovereign wealth funds are balance of trade, economic stability, and the desire of sovereign nations to diversify their assets.

> The International Monetary Fund further classifies sovereign wealth funds in 5 categories, according to their form and function:

  ○ Stabilization funds are formed to insulate a state budget and economy from commodity price volatility and external shocks. These investments sometimes are designed to move in the direction opposite the commodity prices against which a government wishes to insulate its economy.

  ○ Savings funds are designed to transform nonrenewable assets into financial assets that can be shared across generations. Examples include the Abu Dhabi Investment Authority.

These portfolios are invested primarily in equities and other growth investments.

○ Development funds allocate state resources to high-priority socioeconomic projects such as infrastructure.

○ Pension reserve funds, as in Australia, Ireland, and New Zealand, invest in equities and other investments to offset rising retirement liabilities.

○ Reserve Investment Corporations are more complex funds designed to earn higher returns on foreign reserves or to reduce the negative carrying costs of holding them. They may invest in equities and alternative investments to achieve higher returns.

> Axiomatic in the United States and the United Kingdom is that the goal of an investment fund is to appreciate in value and maximize shareholder wealth. In other countries, other stakeholders also

receive important consideration, including customers, employees, the local community, and the government itself.

> Many countries run budget surpluses that can come from taking in more in tax receipts and other revenues than what goes out in the form government spending or from trade surpluses. An international trade transaction—for example, the United States buys oil from Saudi Arabia—involves several components.

  ○ The balance of payments includes all payments and obligations to foreigners balanced against all payments and obligations received from foreigners. The balance of payments must balance.

  ○ If one country runs a persistent trade deficit with another, something must happen on the other side of the international ledger to square it away. The typical transaction of the country with the trade surplus is to invest trade proceeds in securities or some other asset. Thus a trade deficit is usually offset by a positive financial account—including holdings such as foreign investments in stocks, bonds, commodities and real estate— or capital account balance including holdings such as foreign direct investment, which can include physical investments in equipment, buildings, and factories.

  ○ The purchase of Saudi Arabian oil thus may be balanced by a purchase of U.S. Treasury securities.

The Singapore Story

> Though it has little in the way of natural resources, Singapore's economy is diverse, with a strong position in technology-related firms, financial services, biotechnology, and chemicals.

> Per capita, it ranks among the 10 richest countries in the world; it is one of the few countries with a triple-A credit rating; and it

routinely ranks near the top of surveys as the most pro-business, and least corrupt.

> Singapore's sovereign wealth fund, conceived and first managed by Dr. Goh, played a key role in its growth from an emerging market to a developed market in a single generation.

> The monetary authority of Singapore is the Central Bank; one of its duties is maintaining the stability of Singapore's currency, the Singapore dollar. This balancing act can best be achieved with the help of foreign exchange reserves.

  ○ If the government wanted to support the Singapore dollar, it could sell some of its reserves of euros and Japanese yen to buy its dollars.

  ○ If it wanted to weaken its currency to make domestic industry more competitive in foreign markets, it would sell its own dollars and buy foreign currencies.

> A brief history of the fund described the idea as "far-sighted, original and bold." Not only did it foresee that Singapore would have balance of payments surpluses for years to come; it broke with the convention of vesting reserves management solely in the Central Bank, and it conveyed confidence that Singapore would be able to overcome its lack of local expertise in global investment management.

> Goh also saw that Singapore's persistent trade surplus could be put to better use other than buying low-yielding government securities and gold. Thus, the Government of Singapore Investment Corporation, or GIC, was born.

> The real impact comes from what the country does with the returns on its portfolio. The Singaporean government is permitted by charter to take up to 50% of net investment returns to supplement the government budget. This figure amounts to more than $10 billion a

year, or about 20% of the total budget, used to support the economy and for social purposes such as education and health care.

Sovereign Wealth Funds in Action

> Offsetting all the good that well-run sovereign wealth funds are capable of doing for their constituent populations, some concerns remain prominent. In contrast to the relative transparency of public pension funds, sovereign wealth funds are opaque. They often will not show their holdings, and usually provide only a rough estimate of the assets they have under management. Yet nations may have good reason for wanting to keep secret the details of their sovereign wealth funds.

  ○ For example, other investors might want to use that information against them when betting against a country's currency, as George Soros did by shorting the British pound sterling in September 1992. Soros made $1 billion by getting that trade right.

  ○ Five years later, speculators attacked Thailand's Bhatt currency, causing it to lose 30% against the U.S. dollar. The Thai currency crisis spread to other Asian nations—it became known as the Asian flu—and to Russia, creating turmoil throughout the global financial system.

> Another concern of some Western policymakers is the way sovereign wealth funds could use their assets to support critical or unfriendly agendas. Norway's sovereign wealth fund, the largest in the world, decided on ethical grounds to divest its ownership of any company that derives more than 30% of its revenues from coal.

> China, in particular, has used state-owned companies and its sovereign wealth fund to acquire rights to natural resources abroad that might be useful to domestic industry and its own population.

> Broad concerns about the lack of transparency, potential control of foreign resources, and investment decisions based not entirely on for-profit grounds led several sovereign wealth funds to sign a set of 24 voluntary guidelines known as the Santiago Principles.

> The Santiago Principles are partly designed by the International Monetary Fund; signatories include China, Qatar, Singapore, Russia, and the United States. The United States is represented by the state of Alaska Permanent Fund, which derives its endowment mainly from state oil revenue. Notably absent were Norway and Saudi Arabia.

> Most large sovereign wealth funds are owned by commodity-oriented countries. Saudi Arabia is a case in point about what happens when their resources, such as oil, run out. Oil accounts for 90% of the country's tax revenues and 85% of its export earnings.

> Because of the ineffectiveness of OPEC and the rise of non-OPEC oil and alternative energy sources, Saudi Arabia has lost pricing power over the global energy markets. A key part of Saudi Arabia's proposed solution to this problem is to dramatically expand its sovereign wealth fund, the Public Investment Fund.

> Saudi Arabia's sovereign wealth fund has been estimated at about $150 billion, with plans for the fund to increase to $2 trillion or more. The plan for Saudi Arabia's diversification is spelled out in Vision 2030. The centerpiece is the initial public offering of Saudi Aramco, which would allow the kingdom to monetize at least a portion of its vast energy holdings. Ownership of Saudi Aramco would be transferred to the Fund. The plan calls for roughly 50% of the assets to be invested internally, supporting areas outside the energy sector, like the defense industry, with growth potential. The remaining 50% would be invested outside of Saudi Arabia, with a global focus.

> This vision, if realized, raises an issue about the nature of competition as government-related entities play larger roles in

global markets than in the recent past. Will the playing field be level and how effective can the government be in playing a role in private industry?

Conclusion

> In less than a decade, sovereign wealth funds doubled to more than $7 trillion, substantially enough to be recognized as investment behemoths in the financial markets.

> With size comes influence. From this perspective, sovereign wealth funds might become like to activist hedge funds, but their motives may be different from those of activist hedge funds, whose goal is to maximize the stock price.

> These issues raise the question of how the global economy will evolve. Foreign governments are buying firms outside of their national territories. Yet cross ownership might also encourage nations to work together, taking the global economy to new heights—or to new conflicts.

Suggested Readings

International Working Group of Sovereign Wealth Funds, "Sovereign Wealth Funds."
Orchard, *Safeguarding the Future*.

Questions to Consider

1. How would you define a sovereign wealth fund?

2. Why are sovereign wealth funds becoming increasingly important in the global financial landscape?

12

Transcript

Sovereign Wealth Funds: Singapore

On February 27, 1981, the deputy prime minister of Singapore—Dr. Goh Keng Swee—announced a plan to establish a government-owned investment corporation. It was for the benefit of the entire population of the island city-state, located just off the southern tip of Malaysia. Its source of funds would be foreign-exchange reserves. That is excess reserves beyond what the central bank needed to manage the country's exchange rate. It's objective capital appreciation.

At the time, the idea of a Sovereign Wealth Funds was barely a glimmer in a few corners around the globe. Kuwait established the first such fund in 1953, to help the Gulf state stabilize its economy from fluctuating oil prices. Three years later, the Gilbert Islands—today known as Kiribati—located in the west-central Pacific Ocean—followed suit. They formed the Revenue Equalization Reserve Fund to manage royalties from local phosphate mines.

Today, dozens of countries, most of them commodity rich, are pouring billions—and now trillions—of dollars into government-run funds designed to benefit their domestic economies and populations while unleashing new, and sometimes conflicting, forces in markets around the world.

So why should we care about Sovereign Wealth Funds ? Well, the answer is because they control more financial assets than hedge funds and private equity combined, amounting to more than $7 trillion. And these funds are viewed strategically by many governments to help support their own political and economic agendas. As Sovereign Wealth Funds grow in size and importance they have come to play larger roles in their own country's affairs and in market battles between traditional, independent companies such as Apple and Exxon, and state-owned and controlled enterprises like Gazprom in Russia and China's PetroChina and Bank of China.

In 2007, the Government of Singapore Investment Corporation—commonly known as GIC—paid $9.7 billion for a 7.9% stake in the Swiss bank UBS. In 2008, it paid $6.9 billion for a 9.9% stake in Citigroup, half of which it later sold for a huge profit. Another Singaporean wealth fund called Temasek bought a controlling stake in the Thai telecom company, Shin Corporation—including control of space satellites relied upon by the Thai military. This investment produced such a popular outcry in Thailand, that the prime minister—whose family had owned the telecom company—was forced to resign.

So, as you can see, Sovereign Wealth Funds have become increasingly popular—and powerful—on the one hand, and potentially controversial on the other. In a moment, I'll offer a more complete definition of what a Sovereign Wealth Funds is, and describe the various roles it takes domestically and in global markets. But, I also want to underscore the fundamental tension between the public good, that funds such as the Government of Singapore Investment Corporation were designed for— for developing state economy and public infrastructure, including roads, airports, and classrooms and teachers—to potential pitfalls, such as state interests over private needs. And the designs of managed markets over free ones. International Monetary Fund researchers have sized up such concerns this way, "Anxieties about Sovereign Wealth Funds can be divided into two main categories, domestic concerns about effectiveness and foreign concerns about influence."

Or, as former Indiana Senator, Evan Bayh, told the U.S. Congress,

> A lack of transparency that characterizes many Sovereign Wealth Funds undermines the theory of efficient markets at the heart of our economic system. In addition, unlike private investors, pension

funds and mutual funds, government-owned entities may have interests that will take precedence over profit maximization.

So what is a sovereign wealth fund? The Treasury Department defines a Sovereign Wealth Funds as "A government investment vehicle which is funded by foreign exchange assets, and which manages those assets separately from the official reserves of the monetary authorities," the Central Bank and reserve-related functions of the Financial Ministry. The distinction is intended to clarify the difference between official reserves—managed by a country's central banks with short-term horizons, focused on liquidity and security—and the longer-term horizons associated with, for example, national pension systems.

The International Monetary Fund further classifies Sovereign Wealth Funds in five categories, according to their form and function. First are stabilization funds, which are formed to insulate a state budget and economy from commodity price volatility and external shocks. Examples include Chile's Economic Stabilization Fund and Russia's Oil Stabilization Fund. They invest largely in liquid assets, mostly in the form of bonds. These investments are sometimes designed to move in the opposite direction of the commodity prices a government wishes to insulate its economy against.

Second are savings funds, which are designed to transform non-renewable assets, again like oil, into financial assets that can be shared across generations. Examples include the Abu Dhabi Investment Authority. These portfolios are invested primarily in equities and other growth investments. Third are development funds, which allocate state resources to high-priority socio-economic projects, such as infrastructure. For example, roads, bridges, and tunnels. Fourth are pension reserve funds—as in Australia, Ireland, and New Zealand—which invest in equities and other investments to offset rising retirement liabilities. Fifth are Reserve Investment Corporations, which are more complex funds designed to earn higher returns on foreign reserves or to reduce the negative carrying costs of holding them. They may invest in equities and alternative investments to achieve higher returns, such as in South Korea and Singapore's Government Investment Corporation.

So that's a snapshot of what Sovereign Wealth Funds look like. In practice, they can look and act quite differently across markets, and across countries. In the United States and the United Kingdom, it is largely taken for granted that the goal of an investment fund is to appreciate in value and maximize shareholder wealth. But in other countries, other stakeholders also receive important consideration, including customers, employees, the local community, and the government itself. This splintering of objectives between profit, on the one hand, and diverse groups of people, on the other, might very well come to alter the global financial landscape. Especially, with the trillions of dollars behind the Sovereign Wealth Funds . In this lecture, we'll examine the history of Sovereign Wealth Funds , and how they operate. In particular, we will look at the case of Singapore, and its sovereign wealth fund. And we'll wind up by discussing the role of Sovereign Wealth Funds in the global economy today, and how those interests may evolve in the future.

It might seem strange to some Americans, but many countries actually run budget surpluses. These surpluses can come from taking in more tax receipts—and other revenues—than what goes out in the form government spending. Another form of surplus comes from trade surpluses. Net exports are one of the components of Gross Domestic Product or GDP; the others being consumption, investment, and government spending.

Let's take a step back and see what goes into an international trade transaction, like when the U. S. buys oil from Saudi Arabia. First, the balance of payments must balance. The balance of payments is simply all payments and obligations to foreigners, against all payments and obligations received from foreigners. So, if the U.S. runs a persistent trade deficit with Saudi Arabia, something must happen on the other side of the international ledger for things to be squared away. Otherwise, it's like a balance sheet not balancing. The typical transaction of the country with the trade surplus is to invest the trade proceeds in securities, or some type of investment. So, a trade deficit is usually offset by a positive financial account or capital account balance.

The Financial Account includes things like foreign investments in stocks, bonds, commodities and real estate. The Capital Account includes things like Foreign Direct Investment or FDI. FDI can include physical investments in equipment, buildings, and factories. It's active investing, rather than simply owning a passive bunch of securities. So, the U.S. purchase of Saudi Arabian oil may be balanced on their end by a purchase of U.S. Treasury securities. In fact, more than a third of all U.S. Treasury debt is owned by foreign governments, mostly China and Japan. And when a foreign government purchases a U.S. Treasury security, these securities count—like cash—toward its foreign exchange reserves.

The three main drivers behind the creation and growth of Sovereign Wealth Funds are balance of trade flows, economic stability, and the desire of sovereign nations to diversify their assets. Commodity-producing countries and export-driven economies often oversee some of the largest Sovereign Wealth Funds in the world, the largest is Norway's Government Pension Fund. It has more than $850 billion, according to research by the Sovereign Wealth Fund Institute. Others include the Kuwait Investment Authority, established in 1953, the Abu Dhabi Investment Authority, established in 1976, the Government of Singapore Investment Corporation formed in 1981, and the China Investment Corporation, established in 2007.

All told, there are some forty odd Sovereign Wealth Funds today, with about half their assets belonging to energy-exporting countries. The hand of Sovereign Wealth Funds was strengthened after the financial markets crisis of 2007–2008. Many global banks were weakened from the crisis and came hat-in-hand to the Sovereign Wealth Funds , looking for capital infusions. The Sovereign Wealth Funds were viewed as deep-pocketed investors, with long horizons. Now, in addition to investing in publicly traded stocks, bonds, and government securities, Sovereign Wealth Fund have also made venture capital investments in private firms like Uber, Airbnb, Snapchat, and Xiaomi, the Chinese cell phone maker. And sometimes Sovereign Wealth Funds purchase companies or properties outright. Dubai's Sovereign Wealth Funds once owned Barney's, the luxury clothing retailer. Qatar's Sovereign Wealth Fund owns the London office building that serves as the global headquarters for HSBC Bank.

So, let's look more closely at the Singapore example. Singapore is a beautiful country with a tropical climate, wonderful people, and, I think it has the best zoo in the world. Singapore's population of roughly 5 and a half million is about the same as Minnesota's or Wisconsin's, even though its land area measures only about 275 square miles—which is about half the size of Los Angeles. And though it also has little in the way of natural resources, Singapore's economy is diverse, with a strong position in technology-related firms, financial services, biotechnology, and chemicals. And it ranks among the 10 richest countries in the world, on a per capita basis. It's also one of the few countries with a AAA credit rating. And the country routinely ranks near the top of surveys as the most pro-business, and least corrupt.

Lee Kwan Yew, known as the father of Singapore, led the country to independence from its colonial ruler, Britain, and its temporary federation partner of Malaysia. Lee remained in power as Prime Minister for more than 3 decades. And, it is often said, that he took Singapore from an emerging market to developed market in a single generation. Singapore's Sovereign Wealth Funds played a key role in this. Freddy Orchard, a former fund official, provides a nice account of this in his book, safeguarding the future. Orchard writes that the fund was conceived and first managed by Dr. Goh—who we met at the beginning of this lecture—the deputy prime minister and chairman of the state monetary authority.

The Monetary Authority of Singapore is the Central Bank, like the Federal Reserve in the United States. And one of the monetary authority's jobs is to maintain the stability of Singapore's currency, the Singapore dollar. This is a balancing act that can be best achieved with the help of foreign exchange reserves. For example, if the government wanted to support the Singapore dollar, it could sell some of its reserves of Euros and Japanese yen to buy its dollars. On the other hand, if it wanted to weaken its currency—to make domestic industry more competitive in foreign markets—it would sell Singaporean dollars and buy foreign currencies.

In the long run, market forces determine the currency's value. But in the short-run, central banks have a lot of buying power, and usually get their way.

So what happens when a country has more money than it needs to stabilize its currency? For Dr. Goh, the answer was to create a Sovereign Wealth Fund.

In his brief history of the fund, Freddy Orchard writes, "The idea it expressed was far-sighted, original and bold." Far-sighted because it foresaw that Singapore would have a chronic balance of payments surpluses for years to come; original because it broke with the convention of vesting reserves management solely in the central bank; and bold because it conveyed confidence that Singapore would be able to overcome the lack of local expertise in global investment management.

Goh also saw that Singapore's persistent trade surpluses could be put to better use other than buying low-yielding government securities and gold which provided little to no income stream. Thus, the Government of Singapore Investment Corporation, or GIC, was born. "This massive project was undertaken in such haste," Orchard writes, "that Goh dispatched a deputy to New York to find American fund managers prepared to work overseas on short notice, in some cases within a week."

Today, Singapore puts about 80% of its money with its own investment professionals and takes an active investment management approach. And the returns have been good. If you take the value of Singapore's Sovereign Wealth Fund assets, divided by the number of its citizens over a 20-year-period, that comes out to about $91,000 a person. By comparison, if you take the U.S. Social Security Trust Fund assets of $2.5 trillion, divided by the U.S. population, that comes out to about $7,800 per person. But the real impact comes from what the country does with the returns on its portfolio. The Singaporean government is permitted, by charter, to take up to 50% of the net investment returns to supplement the government budget. This figure comes out to more than $10 billion a year, or about 20% of the total budget. And this money is used to support the economy and for social purposes.

For example, Singapore's K-12 school system typically ranks among the best in the world on standardized tests. The government also provides its citizens with free Wi-Fi access. And Singapore's healthcare system is among the most efficient in the world. The country spends less than 5% of its GDP on healthcare, while in the U.S. the figure is closer to 17%. And life expectancy in Singapore is about 82 years compared to about 79 in the U.S. The jobs situation also is quite good. Singapore's unemployment rate typically averages about 2%. Even during the global recession from 2007–2009, its unemployment rate peaked at less than 5%, which was half the 10% unemployment rate in the United States at its peak in October 2009.

Now, in addition to all the of good that Sovereign Wealth Funds are capable of doing for their constituent populations, some concerns remain prominent, as former Sen. Bayh expressed to Congress. In contrast with the relative transparency of public pension funds, Sovereign Wealth Funds are criticized for their opaqueness. They often will not show their holdings, and usually provide only a rough estimate of the assets they have under management. Now, there might be good reason for a country wanting to keep secret the details of its Sovereign Wealth Fund. For example, other investors—like hard-nosed hedge fund traders —might want to use that information when betting against a country's currency.

The billionaire, George Soros, made his claim to fame by shorting the British pound sterling right before its exit from the European Exchange Rate Mechanism, a precursor to the Euro in September 1992. Soros made $1 billion by getting that trade right. Five years later, speculators attacked the Thai's Bhatt currency, causing it to lose 30% against the U.S. dollar. The Thai currency crisis spread to other Asian nations—it became known as the Asian flu—and to Russia, creating turmoil throughout the global financial system.

Another concern of some Western policymakers is the way in which Sovereign Wealth Funds could use their assets to support critical, or unfriendly, agendas. Norway's Sovereign Wealth Fund, the largest in the world, decided to divest—on ethical grounds—its ownership in any company that derived more than 30% of its revenues from coal. China, in particular, has used state-owned companies, and its Sovereign Wealth Fund, to acquire rights to natural resources abroad, that may be useful to domestic industry and its own population. For example, in 2011, China's Sovereign Wealth Fund purchased a 25.8% stake in South Africa's

Shanduka Group, a diversified firm with interests in coal, timber, and other natural resources. And in 2005, the state-owned China National Offshore Oil Corporation tried to buy the American energy exploration company, Unocal. The bid valued Unocal attractively at $16–$18 billion.

But CNOOC—as China National Offshore is known—dropped its bid amid opposition in the U.S. Congress. And Unocal was eventually sold to Chevron, an American firm. Ultimately, broad concerns about the lack of transparency, potential control of foreign resources, and investment decisions not based entirely on for-profit grounds led several Sovereign Wealth Funds to sign what are known as the Santiago Principles.

The Santiago Principles are a set of 24 voluntary guidelines partly designed by the International Monetary Fund, and whose signatories include China, Qatar, Singapore, Russia, and the United States. The U.S. is represented by the state of Alaska Permanent Fund, which derives its endowment mainly from state oil revenue. Notably absent were Norway and Saudi Arabia.

The four key objectives of the Santiago Principles are to one, help maintain a stable global financial system and free flow of capital investment; two, comply with all applicable regulatory and disclosure requirements in the countries in which they invest; three, invest on the basis of economic and financial risk and return-related considerations. And, four, have in place a transparent and sound governance structure that provides for adequate operational controls, risk management, and accountability.

Now, as I mentioned earlier, most large Sovereign Wealth Funds—with the notable exceptions of Singapore and China—are owned by commodity-oriented countries. So, what happens when their resources, such as oil, run out? Let's look at the case of the Kingdom of Saudi Arabia. A report from The Harvard Belfer Center entitled, *A Stable and Efficient Fiscal Framework for Saudi Arabia* notes that oil accounts for 90% of the country's tax revenues and 85% of its export earnings. The report goes on to note that Saudi Arabia has lost pricing power over the global energy markets, due to the ineffectiveness of OPEC and the rise of non-OPEC oil, and alternative energy sources. A key part of Saudi Arabia's proposed solution to this problem is to dramatically expand its Sovereign Wealth Fund, called the Public Investment Fund, or PIF.

Bloomberg once estimated that the size of Saudi Arabia's Sovereign Wealth Fund was about $150 billion. But there were plans are for the fund to increase in size to more than $2 trillion dollars or more, which would make it the largest traditional Sovereign Wealth Fund by a factor of more than two to one. The vision for Saudi Arabia's diversification away from its overemphasis on oil is spelled out in an 84-page document called Vision 2030, spearheaded by Deputy Crown Prince Mohammed bin Salman. The centerpiece of the plan is the initial public offering, or IPO, of Saudi Aramco, the largest oil company in the world, both in terms of revenue and reserves. This would allow the Kingdom to monetize, at least a portion of, its vast energy holdings.

Ownership of Saudi Aramco would be transferred to the Public Investment Fund. Additional assets for the fund would come from the sale of government-owned real estate to private investors. The plan also calls for roughly 50% of the assets to be invested internally, supporting areas outside the energy sector with growth potential, like the Defense Industry. The remaining 50% would be invested outside of Saudi Arabia, with a global focus. Deputy Crown Prince Mohammed bin Salman has said "The Private Investment Fund will be the main engine for the whole world and not only for the region. There will be no investment, movement or development in any region of the world without the vote of the Saudi sovereign fund."

This vision, if realized, raises an issue about the nature of competition as government-related entities play larger roles in global markets than in the recent past. Will the playing field be level and how effective can the government be in playing a role in private industry? Let's look at the United States as one example. In America, the government owns and operates various entities that compete with private-sector in areas such as mortgage finance, transportation, package distribution, among others. Two enterprises it controls are AMTRAK the National Railroad Passenger Corp., and the U.S. Post Office. Both have had disappointing results in terms of a track record of profits. And the government-sponsored mortgage firms like Fannie Mae and Freddie Mac basically imploded during the Great

Recession and needed a bailout. So from that perspective, the evidence is not good.

On the other hand, Singapore is a country with few natural resources, but one that nevertheless has reinvented itself into a model of success. The Singaporean government controls several successful firms, including Singapore Airlines and the largest bank in the country, DBS Group. And a portion of the profits from its Sovereign Wealth Funds helped pay for the nation's infrastructure, paving the way for a strong economy, and a high standard of living for its citizens.

OK, we've covered a lot of ground with a topic that you might not be very familiar with. So let's summarize some things. Sovereign Wealth Funds are basically investment portfolios funded with national budget and trade surpluses and managed for the benefit of a government and its people. Originally, the funds invested primarily in government bonds and gold. But, over time, they became increasingly invested in publicly traded stocks, bonds and real estate; and in the ownership of natural resources, and other types of directly controlled assets. Most Sovereign Wealth Funds are controlled by countries with commodity-oriented economies—Norway, Saudi Arabia, Qatar, and Kuwait. Notable exceptions are China and Singapore. In less than a decade, Sovereign Wealth Funds have doubled in size to more than $7 trillion. They can't keep up this rate of growth indefinitely, or else they would come to own virtually everything.

But they've already grown substantially enough to be recognized as investment behemoths that play large roles in the financial markets. With size comes influence. From this perspective, Sovereign Wealth Funds might become akin to activist hedge funds, and play roles in the futures of the companies they invest in. But their motives may also be different than those of activist hedge funds, whose goal is to maximize the stock price. Outside of the U.S. and the U.K, it is not all about maximizing the stock price or shareholder wealth. Other stakeholders are also considered, including employees, customers, the surrounding community, and of course, the government.

This raises an issue of how the global economy will evolve. We know the world has become increasingly flat, to use the language of *The New York Times* columnist Thomas Friedman, with more companies from around the world competing more readily on a global scale. But, the investment world, too, is becoming flatter. Foreign governments are buying firms outside of their national territories. And yet cross-ownership might also encourage nations to work together, taking the global economy to new heights—or to new conflicts. We can hope that the more our pocketbooks are tied together, the greater the incentive we'll have to work together.

13

The First Hedge Fund: A. W. Jones

The term "hedge" in a financial context means to reduce risk. Specifically, a hedge is an investment designed to reduce exposure to price movements by transferring risk. Although no uniformly agreed definition of a hedge fund exists, a good working definition is a private investment vehicle that charges two types of fees: an asset-based fee assessed as a percentage of assets under management and a profit-sharing or incentive fee taken from the fund's earnings, if any.

A. W. Jones

> The story of Alfred Winslow Jones, the father of the hedge fund industry, hardly suggests he would become one of the most important figures in the history of investment management.

> He graduated from Harvard in 1923 and for the next decade traveled the world as a steamship's accountant, a member of the U.S. Foreign Service, and an observer in Spain during the Spanish Civil War.

> In the late 1930s, Jones pursued a Ph.D. in sociology at Columbia, and in 1941, he completed his dissertation, which served as the

basis for a textbook on sociology. Some excerpts also came to be published in *Fortune* magazine.

> Jones went on to work for *Fortune* as a writer and editor from 1941 to 1946, and then freelance. One article he wrote in 1949, "The Fashions in Forecasting," is said to have spurred his interest in setting up his own money-management firm.

The Birth of the Hedge Fund?

> That same year, Jones and 4 friends established A. W. Jones & Co. The firm started with $100,000 in capital. Jones put in $40,000, and was named managing partner. A. W. Jones & Co. was organized as a limited partnership rather than a mutual fund and thus was exempt from oversight by the SEC as long as the number of investors it served was limited to 99 or fewer and they were deemed to be affluent.

> Most managed investment vehicles—including mutual funds and exchange-traded funds—charge asset-based fees. Actively managed stock funds usually charge about 1% per year. By comparison, index funds and exchange-traded funds charge much less: usually in the neighborhood of 0.1% per year.

> Hedge funds typically charge 1% or 2% of assets, plus a percentage of the profits they earn on your investment. The standard profit sharing fee is 20%, but some funds take as much as 50%.

> Jones consciously avoided regulation and took 20% of the profits. He also dynamically adjusted the long to short ratio of his fund, meaning that sometimes he would be more long than short, other times more short than long, and other times about neutral between his long and short positions.

> These 3 characteristics—limiting regulation, taking 20% or more of the profits and dynamically adjusting the long to short ratio—describe the bulk of hedge funds today.

> Hedge funds managers know that they have no idea what the market is going to do, but they have confidence that company A (let's call it Ford) is better than company B (let's call it GM). By buying Ford and selling GM short, they essentially remove the market effect on these stocks and keep only the company-specific effects.

Leverage, Carry Trade, and Arbitrage

> Small spreads between long and short positions can become large spreads through various strategies that hedge funds employ, like using leverage (or borrowing money) and the carry trade.

> Many hedge funds use leverage to increase risk and expected returns. The amount of leverage varies widely by the type of hedge fund, but it can be 30 to 1 or more. More typical is a leverage of 2 to 1 or 3 to 1 in the aftermath of the 2008 financial crisis, when

heavy borrowing from investment and commercial banks and magnified losses destroyed some firms.

> The unit of investment and commercial banks that deals with hedge funds is typically called the prime brokerage unit. The prime brokerage unit wires the money and handles the trading back-office functions when a hedge fund makes a trade. Since the prime brokerage unit is a source of funding or liquidity for hedge funds, especially during times of market distress, the funds have a strong incentive to maintain good relations with their prime brokers.

> Banks are leveraged by their very nature. A local bank is leveraged about 10 to 1. It can lend $9 or $10 for each dollar it has in capital, expanding credit in the economy. Some Wall Street investment banks used to be leveraged at more than 30 to 1 before the financial markets crisis of 2007–2009. After the crisis, Congress passed the Dodd-Frank Act, which reduced the leverage of banks by to a maximum of 15 to 1.

> Still, well-capitalized banks have plenty of leverage to offer hedge funds. From the bank's perspective, if it lends money to the funds, the fund managers have to pay interest and they are likely to trade more, generating commissions for the bank. These loans are secured by the assets of the fund, so on balance they are pretty safe.

> In the carry trade, an investor seeks not only to borrow money, but to find the cheapest money available. A fund can then invest that borrowed money elsewhere at higher returns.

> Many hedge fund strategies also engage in a type of trade called arbitrage.

  ○ In this trade, you made 5% no matter whether the market went up or down—a strategy that tries to minimize market risk, but you still retain company-specific risk.

> Arbitrage extends the law of one price to two different securities—and even entire portfolios of securities—where both sides, the longs (the buyers) and shorts (the sellers) have the same general risk characteristics, but different expected returns. Arbitrage strategies always involve buying the cheaper item and selling short the expensive item.

A. W. Jones's Strategy

> If Jones's investors gave him $10 million in capital and he had $20 million in long investments and $5 million in short investments, the difference between his long and short assets would be a positive $15 million. This represents a net exposure ratio of 1.5 when dividing the positive $15 million investment position against his $10 million in capital provided by investors. In this example, Jones would be bullish on the market, and also leveraged on a gross basis of 2.5 to 1, signifying even greater conviction in his position. If Jones was $20 million short and $5 million long, this would result in a $15 million net short position. And it signifies a net exposure ratio of minus 1.5—and conviction for the bearish case.

> Jones dynamically adjusted his long and short exposure as well as his use of leverage regularly. Jones, like most hedge fund managers, tended to be more long than short. Part of the reason is that the market usually trends up. Most equity managers are short about 50 cents for each dollar that they are long.

> *Fortune* magazine's Carol Loomis wrote an article many years ago, "The Jones Nobody Keeps Up With." This profile, published in April 1966, also provided hedge funds with perhaps their first mainstream attention. It noted that Jones's partnership returned a 670% profit to investors in the previous 10 years. The best-performing mutual fund over the same period, The Dreyfus Fund, returned 358%.

Fund of Funds

> A. W. Jones wasn't known for his stock-picking ability per se, but he harvested ideas from a vast network of brokers and other investors, and he offered generous commissions as a way of getting good investment ideas. This flow of ideas was at least one reason for Jones's strong investment performance.

> Jones stopped running the fund according to its original approach sometime before or around 1984. By that time, the partnership had evolved into what is known as a fund-of-funds structure, which, instead of owning individual security positions, invests in other hedge funds. The fund-of-fund approach has its pros and cons.

> Perhaps the best attribute of a fund of funds is a diversified portfolio. Today, most hedge funds have a minimum investment of $1 million. Unless you're a really rich person, it would be difficult to own a diversified portfolio of hedge funds.

> In contrast, most funds of funds require a minimum investment of $500,000 or less. The managers of a fund of funds typically also perform substantial research and due diligence on the external hedge fund managers they select. It would be hard for most individuals to replicate this research on their own. Funds of funds sometimes also advertise the ability to get investors into very selective hedge funds of top managers that might be closed to individuals.

> The main disadvantage of a fund-of-fund structure is a second layer of fees. The most common fee structure for a fund of funds is 1% of assets and 10% of profits. So adding this to the common fee structure of the underlying hedge fund—that is 2% of assets and 20% of profits—results in a total fee structure 3% of assets and 30% of profits. It takes a very strong investment performance to overcome all these fees, and hedge funds can be tax inefficient because of the short-term capital gains they produce.

Conclusion

> Today, more than 12,000 hedge funds manage in excess of $3 trillion. Hedge funds have become mainstream, at least for high net worth investors and institutions—including the pension funds of many rank and file workers.

> At the same time, since the financial markets crisis of 2007–2009, the SEC requires greater regulation of hedge funds. U.S. funds that manage more than $100 million must register with the SEC as registered investment advisors. Being a registered investment advisor subjects a firm to inspection and requires periodic reporting of its assets and client base.

> However, the SEC does not impose diversification and leverage limits on hedge funds, as it does for mutual funds and pension funds. In other words, hedge funds can still pretty much do what they want with their investments, as long as it is disclosed in the operating documents sent to their investors.

> Jones had the foresight to realize that many investors disliked the wild gyrations of the stock market that are characteristic of a traditional buy-and-hold investment approach. Jones tempered market volatility by offsetting his long purchase positions with short sale positions, and he realized that he could even profit from a decline in the market if he were net short.

> Jones also added leverage to the equation, an aspect generally prohibited in mutual funds and pension funds except in small amounts. Leverage gives managers the ability to increase the amount of conviction to their investment ideas. And over more than a 30-year period, Jones's partnership earned positive returns more than 90% of the time.

Suggested Reading

Loomis, "The Jones Nobody Keeps Up With."
Mallaby, *More Money Than God.*

Questions to Consider

1. How would you describe the investment strategy of A. W. Jones?

2. How would you define a hedge fund?

13

Transcript

The First Hedge Fund: A. W. Jones

A. W. Jones, the father of the hedge fund industry, has a background that hardly suggested he would become one of the most important figures in the history of investment management. Jones was born on September 9, 1900, in Melbourne, Australia. His father was an executive at General Electric and moved his family to America when Jones was four. He graduated from Harvard in 1923 and went to work on a steamship—taking an administrative role in helping manage the ship's finances and supplies. This job enabled him to travel around the world. Jones joined the U.S. Foreign Service—a unit of the State Department—and, in the early 1930s, was vice consul at the U.S. Embassy in Berlin, when Adolf Hitler was in the process of rising to power. In 1936, he traveled throughout Spain in the midst of its Civil War, working for the Quakers as an observer, monitoring civilian relief efforts.

In the late 1930s, Jones pursued a Ph.D. in Sociology at Columbia University in New York. And in 1941, he completed his dissertation on *Life, Liberty, and Property, A Story of Conflict and a Measurement of Conflicting Rights*. This dissertation served as the basis for a textbook on sociology. Some excerpts also came to be published in *Fortune* magazine. Jones went on to work for *Fortune* as a writer and editor from 1941–1946, and on a freelance basis afterward. One article he wrote in 1949, called "The Fashions in Forecasting," is said to have spurred his own interest in setting up his own money-management firm.

That same year, Jones—at the age of 48—and four friends established A. W. Jones & Co. The firm started with just $100,000 in capital. This would be about $1.7 million today. Jones put in $40,000 and was named the managing partner. Now, A. W. Jones & Co. was organized as a limited partnership as opposed to a mutual fund. At the time, this allowed the firm to be exempt from oversight by the Securities and Exchange Commission in Washington, so long as the number of investors it served were limited to 99 or fewer and were deemed to be affluent. That made it arguably the first hedge fund.

Jones operated his hedge funds under a two-part model. First, he'd start with his investments that he thought were going up in value, which we can think of as long market-value investments. These investment ideas might come from Jones and his team, or through his extensive networks of contacts. He'd then subtract from that total the dollar value of his investments he thought were going to fall in value, known as short market-value investments, which might be obtained in the same fashion. If the difference were positive, he was more bullish on the market than bearish. If the difference was negative, he was more bearish than bullish. If the difference was about zero—or if the long dollar amount roughly equaled his short dollar amount—he was neutral on the market.

The second part of his model focused on leverage. He'd take the difference between the long and short value investments and divide this figure by his fund's net capital. Net capital is what the investors would have left if the firm sold all of its assets and paid off its debts. Now I'll circle back, in a bit, to what A. W. Jones did with this model. In this lecture, we'll discuss a range of hedge fund strategies and industry features. We'll also look more closely at Jones's investment strategy and his impact on the hedge fund industry.

The term hedge in a financial context means to reduce risk. Specifically, a hedge is an investment designed to reduce exposure to price movements—by transferring risk. But, what if I told you that many hedge funds don't try to reduce risk and instead increase it? Although there is no uniformly agreed definition on what is a hedge fund, a good working definition is that it is a private investment vehicle that charges two types of fees, an asset-based fee which is assessed on a percentage of assets under management and a profit-sharing, or incentive, fee which is taken out of the firm's earnings, if any. Nearly all managed investment vehicles—including mutual funds, and exchange-traded funds, or ETFs—charge asset-based fees. Actively managed stock funds usually charge you about 1% a year, or $1000 per year on a $100,000 investment. By comparison, index funds and exchange-traded funds charge a fraction of this, usually in the neighborhood one-tenth of 1% per year, or $100 on that same $100,000 investment.

Hedge funds typically charge a lot more, 1 or 2% of assets, resulting in a $1000 to $2000 fee in this $100,000 example. It's relatively more expensive in a hedge fund supposedly because you're getting expert management. Hedge funds also take a percentage of the profits that they earn on your investment. The standard profit sharing fee is 20%, but some funds charge as much of 50%. So, if a fund starts the year with $100 million under management, and the value increases to $120 million by the end of that same year after deducting the asset-management fee it is owed, the fund would have made a gross profit for its investors of $20 million. Typically, the fund managers will then take another 20% of this investment—$20 million— or $4 million in incentive pay. So, after adding the $2 million in asset-based fees to the $4 million in profit-sharing fees, the hedge fund manager could expect to see $6 million for managing the investment.

So now you understand why the top-paid hedge fund managers like David Tepper, James Simons, and Ken Griffin, running tens of billions of dollars or more, can make more than a billion dollars in a single year. No one knows for sure who set up the first hedge fund. There were so-called commodity pools and other investment partnerships around in the early 1900s. A commodity pool is basically an unregulated fund. Investors would pool their money together. Initially, the focus was on commodities, like corn, wheat, and sugar, but the concept could apply to stocks and other assets. The funds of many investors pooled together could have more influence than the funds of a single individual, no matter how well-heeled, sometimes with disastrous consequences.

It's been said that the Panic of 1907 was set off by a commodity pool of investors who tried to corner or manipulate the copper market. Warren Buffett's mentor, Benjamin Graham managed a well-known partnership of his own during the 1926–1956 period. It followed many strategies that hedge funds typically perform, like going long or short on their investments which is a bet that the asset will rise or fall in price, respectively and taking a percentage of the profits. Buffett himself operated an investment partnership from the late 1950s through the late 1960s.

Nevertheless, most researchers, such as hedge fund author, Sebastian Mallaby, credit Alfred Winslow Jones—A. W. Jones—as the person most responsible for launching the hedge fund industry shortly after World War II. Jones consciously avoided regulation and took 20% of the profits—commensurate with the same share of profits that Phoenician ship captains received about 2000 years ago, after completing successful journeys. Jones also dynamically adjusted the long/short ratio of his fund. By dynamically adjust, I mean that sometimes he would be more long than short, other times he would be more short than long, and other times about neutral between his long and short positions. These three characteristics—limiting regulation, taking 20% or more of the profits and dynamically adjusting the long/short ratio—describe the bulk of hedge funds today. And that's why Mallaby, and others, put Jones as the originator of the hedge fund.

Maybe you were invested during the popping of the internet bubble in the early 2000s or during the Great Recession in 2007 and 2008. Most stock price indexes fell about 50% from top to bottom around these periods. Many investments, like Internet stocks and financial firms, fell a lot more. In many cases all the way to zero. Well, many hedge funds think along the following lines. They say, I have no idea what the market is going to do, but I have confidence that company A let's call it Ford is better than company B let's call it GM. By buying Ford and selling GM short, you essentially remove the market effect on these automotive stocks and keep only the company-specific effects. Let's drill down on this trade to see better how it works. We'll consider two environments—a bull market and a bear market.

Suppose your analysis has led you to believe that Ford is a better stock than GM. This analysis might involve looking at the companies' financial statements, their product lineup, talking to people in the industry, and a host of other techniques. Now let's say we are in a bull market, and Ford's stock goes up 20%. In a bull market, a rising tide usually lifts all boats—and carmakers—so GM's stock probably went up too. Let's say it went up 15%.

When you sell short, the returns are mathematically computed with a negative or minus sign. So the spread between Ford and GM during this bull market scenario is 5% that is, Ford's 20% gain less GM's 15% increase. So the spread, again, is 5%.

In a bear market, both stocks probably fell. Once again, let's assume that your research is correct and that Ford continued to outperform GM on the downside. Assume that Ford fell 15% and GM fell 20%. The spread remains a positive 5% based on the difference between Ford's 15% decline, as opposed to GM's 20%. So in this trade, you made 5% no matter whether the market went up or down. Presto, we seemingly have a strategy that attempts to minimize market risk. But you still retain the company's specific risk.

Small spreads, like the one between Ford and GM, can become large spreads through various strategies that hedge funds employ, like using leverage or borrowing money and the carry trade. Many hedge funds use leverage to increase the risk and expected returns. The amount of leverage varies widely by the type of hedge fund, but it can be as high as 30 to1 or more. Two or three to one is more typical of most hedge funds in the aftermath of the 2008 financial crisis when heavy borrowing and magnified losses destroyed some firms.

You might be thinking, Where does all this leverage, or borrowed money, come from? It comes from a variety of sources, but among the principal ones are investment and commercial banks. The unit of the investment and commercial banks that deal with hedge funds is typically called the prime brokerage unit. The prime brokerage unit basically wires the money and handles the trading back-office functions when a hedge fund makes a trade. Since the prime brokerage unit is a source of funding or source of liquidity for hedge funds, especially during times of market distress, the funds have a strong incentive to maintain good relations with their prime brokers.

Banks are leveraged by their very nature. That's why our banking system is sometimes called a fractional banking system, which means banks don't keep all of their deposits locked up in a vault. Without fractional banking, the amount of lending done in the economy would be greatly restricted. For example, if you deposit $100 in your local bank, it keeps only about

$10 in the vault and lends out the rest. So your local bank is leveraged about 10-to-1. It can loan 9 or 10 dollars for each dollar it has in capital, expanding credit in the economy. Some Wall Street investment banks used to be leveraged at more than 30 to 1 before the financial markets crisis of 2008–2009. After the crisis, Congress passed the Dodd-Frank Act, which took down the leverage of banks by about half to a maximum of 15 to 1.

But well-capitalized banks still have plenty of leverage to offer hedge funds. From the bank's perspective, it if lends money to hedge funds the managers have to pay interest, and they are also more likely to trade more—generating commissions for the bank. These loans are secured by the assets of the fund, so, on balance, they are pretty safe.

So leverage is one arrow in a hedge fund's quiver. Another is the carry trade, a term that I mentioned a few minutes ago. Here, an investor not only seeks to borrow money but to find the cheapest money meaning interest rates in the world. A simple version of the carry trade might be to borrow money in Japan or Switzerland when interest rates were close to zero or even negative for many years. A fund can then take that borrowed money at really low interest rates and invest elsewhere, at higher returns. For instance, one option might be to invest the borrowed Japanese yen in Brazilian bonds giving an 8% return. Even after adjusting for currency hedging, that is, the difference in exchange rate movements between the Yen and Brazilian Real while the trade is still open, it could be a good return. Add leverage on top of this and it could be a really good return.

Of course, no strategy works all of the time. The most obvious problem is if your research is wrong and, in our theoretical stock-picking example, GM outperforms Ford. The worst-case scenario is the stock you expect to go up actually goes down, and the stock you expect to go down actually goes up. I've been there and it is not a good feeling. Now, this risk is partly controlled by having a diversified portfolio. It can also be partly controlled by setting stop-loss limits. For example, you might want to close out the Ford-GM trade in which you were betting on Ford to outperform GM if the trade produced losses of 10% or more on your investment. This loss might occur if shares of GM were to surge 10% ahead of Ford in a bull market, or with GM losing 10% less than Ford in a bear market.

Many hedge fund strategies also engage in a type of trade called arbitrage. Arbitrage is an extension of the Law of one Price. Even if you never heard of the Law of One Price, you might have some intuition on how it works. Take a can of Coca-Cola. You might buy it at Wal-Mart or Costco for 10 cents per can, but if you buy it at your local convenience store, like 7-Eleven, it might cost a dollar. When the same good—a can of Coca-Cola, in this example— trades at different prices at the same instant in time, it is being exchanged outside of the so-called Law of One Price. An arbitrageur, in this example, would be motivated to buy the can of Coca-Cola from Wal-Mart and sell it at 7-Eleven if this were possible. The Law of One Price doesn't work so well in the consumer markets. But it is followed very closely in financial markets. Powerful computers literally scour the investment universe looking for small discrepancies in price.

Let's look at an example to show why the Law of One Price holds up so well in the financial markets. IBM's stock trades in New York, and it also trades around the world in places like London and Tokyo. Suppose IBM is trading for $200 a share in New York and $201 a share in London even after adjusting for currency hedging and other transaction costs. Imagine if you could buy 1 billion shares of IBM in New York and, in the same instance, sell a billion shares in London. Under this simple example, you would make a billion dollars in one second. In reality, that would never happen because the act of buying pushes up the price and the act of selling or more accurately in this example, selling short, pushes the price down. Eventually, the two prices would meet in the middle, and the arbitrage opportunity would disappear. So there are arbitrage opportunities. But they are fleeting in nature, and often exist for only a few seconds—or milliseconds—and typically are worth pennies, or fractions of pennies, and not dollars a share. And that's also why arbitrage strategies are often likened to picking up pennies in front of a steam roller. If a trade goes wrong, it can wipe out the profits of many trades.

Arbitrage extends the Law of One Price to two different securities—and even entire portfolios of securities—where both sides, the longs—the buyers— and shorts—the sellers—have the same general risk characteristics, but different expected returns. Arbitrage strategies always involve buying the cheaper item—be it the 25-cent can of Coca-Cola, or IBM stock in New

York—and selling short the expensive item, the $1 can of Coca Cola, or IBM stock in London, in our examples.

Now, stepping back to the beginning, let's look at how A. W. Jones operated his hedge fund in the middle part of the 20th century. Much like our Ford/GM example, if Jones' investors gave him $10 million in capital, and he had $20 million in long investments, and $5 million in short investments, the difference between his long and short assets would be a positive $15 million. This represents a net exposure ratio of 1.5 when dividing the positive $15 million investment position, against his $10 million in capital provided by investors. So, in this example, Jones would be bullish on the market, and also leveraged on a gross basis of 2.5 to 1, signifying even greater conviction in his position.

In contrast, let's see what happens when the numbers are reversed. If A.W. Jones was short $20 million and long $5 million, this would result in a $15 million net short position. And it signifies a net exposure ratio of minus 1.5—and conviction for the bearish case. And that's just based on the same math that we went through, dividing the $15 million net short position against the $10 million in capital provided by investors. Now keep in mind that an active trader is not necessarily going to just let a position ride, not if it's a winning position, and especially not if it's a losing position. Jones dynamically adjusted his long and short exposure—as well as his use of leverage, or borrowing—on a regular basis. Jones, like most hedge fund managers, tended to be more long than short. Part of the reason is that the market usually trends up. Most equity managers are short about 50 cents for each dollar that they are long.

Fortune magazine's Carol Loomis wrote an article many years ago called "The Jones Nobody Keeps Up With." It was obviously a play on A.W. Jones's name, and the expression "Keeping up with the Joneses." But this profile, published in April 1966, also provided hedge funds with perhaps their first mainstream attention. It noted that Jones's partnership returned a 670% profit to investors in the prior 10 years. And that was after Jones's 20% profit sharing fee. In contrast, the best-performing mutual fund over the same period, The Dreyfus Fund, returned 358%. And Jones's original partnership charged only a profit-sharing fee without any asset-based fee, meaning the firm was paid solely on its investment performance.

Jones's partnership structure—and impressive results—attracted the attention of many other investment managers, some of whom launched their own hedge funds. Among these were a few legendary managers such as George Soros, Michael Steinhardt, and Barton Biggs. A. W. Jones wasn't known for his stock-picking ability per se, but he harvested ideas from a vast network of brokers and other investors. And he offered generous commissions as a way of getting good investment ideas. This flow of ideas was at least one reason for Jones's strong investment performance.

In 34 years under Jones, the partnership had only three down years. By comparison, the S&P 500 had nine annual declines over the same period. Jones stopped running the fund according to its original approach sometime before or around 1984. By that time, the partnership had evolved to what is known as a fund-of-funds structure, which, instead of owning individual security positions, it invests in other, outside hedge funds. Sometimes this is known also as a manager-of-managers approach. The fund-of-fund approach has its pros and cons.

Perhaps the best attribute of a fund-of-funds is you get a diversified portfolio of hedge funds. Today, most hedge funds have a minimum investment of 1 million dollars. Unless you're a really rich person, it would be difficult to own a diversified portfolio of hedge funds. A $1 million investment in 10 funds would cost $10 million. In contrast, most fund-of-funds require a minimum investment of $500,000, or even less. The managers of a fund-of-funds typically also perform substantial research and due diligence on the external hedge fund managers that they select. It would be hard for most individuals to replicate this research on their own. Fund-of-funds sometimes also advertise the ability to get investors into very selected hedge funds of top managers that might be closed to individuals.

The main disadvantage of a fund-of-fund is its second layer of fees. The most common fee structure for a fund-of-funds is 1% of assets and 10% of profits. So adding this to the common fee structure of the underlying hedge fund—that is 2% of assets and 20% of profits—results in a total fee structure 3% of assets and 30% of profits. It takes a very strong investment performance to overcome all these fees. And hedge funds can be tax-inefficient because of the short-term capital gains they usually produce.

Today, more than 12,000 hedge funds manage in excess of $3 trillion dollars. Some managers, such as Carl Icahn, George Soros, and David Tepper have come to be regarded as investment superstars. And hedge funds have become mainstream, at least for high net worth investors and institutions—including pension funds of many rank and file workers, such as teachers, police officers, and civil servants. At the same time, since the financial markets crisis of 2008–2009, the SEC has required greater regulation of hedge funds. U.S. funds that manage more than $100 million must register with the SEC as a Registered Investment Advisor or RIA. Being a registered investment advisor subjects a firm to inspection, and requires periodic reporting of its assets and client base.

However, the SEC does not impose diversification and leverage limits on hedge funds, unlike what it requires for mutual funds and pension funds. In other words, hedge funds can pretty much still do what they want with their investments, as long as it is disclosed in the operating documents sent to investors. Hedge funds would probably not be where they are today without the efforts of A. W. Jones, who, as a middle-aged sociologist launched possibly the first modern hedge fund.

Jones had the foresight to realize that many investors disliked the wild gyrations of the stock market, that are characteristic of a traditional buy-and-hold investment approach. Jones tempered market volatility by offsetting his long purchases with positions in short sale positions. And he realized that he could even profit from a decline in the market if he were net short.

Jones also added leverage to the equation, an aspect that is generally prohibited in mutual funds and pension funds, except in small amounts. Leverage gives managers the ability to increase the amount of their conviction to their ideas, beyond concentration, or putting all of your eggs in one or few baskets. And over more than a 30-year period, Jones's partnership earned positive returns more than 90% of the time.

14

Activist Investors: Icahn, Loeb, Ackman

Carl Icahn made activist investing famous years ago. Daniel Loeb, the founder of Third Point LLC, a hedge fund with $17 billion or so in assets under management, is an activist investor. Bill Ackman is a part of a slightly later generation of activist investors. Activist investors frequently take a large stake in a particular company to get management's ear—or a seat at the board table. They use their stakes to spur changes to increase the company's stock price. Their demands might involve changes to corporate strategy or management; a dividend increase, buyback, or outright sale of the company.

Activist Investing 101

> Activist investors get companies to do what they want, first, by talking to them. As you might guess, this tactic doesn't always generate good results. Other times, the activist may publish a white paper detailing ideas to improve the company. Making these reports public puts pressure on management.

> Sometimes, the activist will issue a takeover offer for a firm that is viewed as mismanaged, or undervalued. As in the corporate raider days, the takeover offer may be financed all or in part with the

target company's borrowing power, sometimes in the form of junk bonds. In other words, an activist investor might offer to buy some or all of a company's shares, to be paid for by borrowing against the company's assets.

> This offer might be at a premium to the current share price, but conditioned on the consent of 50.1% or more of the shareholders. The offer puts pressure on sitting management to improve the stock price, comparable with the offered premium: Many investors would prefer to pocket the short-term in the stock price rather than rely on management's promises of long-term improvements.

> In some instances, the target firm might pay the activist to go away. This tactic is called Greenmail. The payment comes out of the company treasury, usually at a premium to the current market price. Since typically only the raider or activist gets this premium—and other shareholders do not—the SEC largely outlawed the payment of Greenmail in recent years.

> The most contentious and costly way for an activist investor to pursue changes at a company is by mounting a campaign for board seats through a proxy contest, wherein the activist attempts to persuade other shareholders to vote for the activist's slate of board candidates. If successful, the new board will be likelier to implement the activist's strategy. Sometimes, the new board will appoint a CEO handpicked by the activist.

> Some firms defend themselves against hostile takeover bids with a strategy called a poison pill. The firm pledges to issue new shares to existing shareholders at a bargain-basement price with a view toward making the unsolicited takeover more expensive and perhaps less appealing.

> Another defense strategy is to find a different partner—a white knight—friendlier to management. Warren Buffett is often viewed as a white knight because he usually leaves management alone when he buys or invests in a company.

> Shark repellent is a defensive strategy that uses the corporate charter to make a hostile takeover difficult. One approach is to stagger the election of the Board of Directors so that directors come up for election in different years; as a result, corporate raiders have a hard time voting their preferred directors onto the Board all in one year. Another approach is requiring a 2/3 majority vote to remove a director.

Carl Icahn

> Carl Icahn was born February 16, 1936, in New York City and grew up in a middle class family. He went to Princeton and is said to have paid for part of his tuition with poker winnings. In 1961, he found his way to Wall Street. In 1968, he set up his own firm, which focused on options trading and arbitrage, a type of trade in which similar assets sell at different prices. The idea is to buy the cheaper asset and sell or short the more expensive one, profiting by the price difference.

> The seeds of Icahn's activist philosophy may have been planted when he was trying to arbitrage closed-end mutual funds, which usually reflect the net asset value of all securities in which they are invested. But sometimes the fund's quoted price diverges from the collective value of its underlying stocks and bonds, creating an arbitrage opportunity. If a fund's basket of securities exceeded the quoted value of the fund itself, Icahn would urge management to liquidate the securities and distribute the unrealized profit to investors.

> Icahn's reputation as a corporate raider rests in part on his hostile takeover of Trans World Airlines. He reportedly made $469 million on the deal, and the company was saddled with $540 million in debt. TWA couldn't handle the debt load and went bankrupt.

> Another of Icahn's higher profile investments was Apple. At the time Icahn disclosed his stake in April 2013, some investors were concerned that Apple would not be as able to innovate after Steve

Jobs's death. The market also fretted over gains made by some of Apple's large competitors, such as Samsung and Google.

> But Icahn saw value, starting with Apple's $100 billion plus pile of cash and a brand name that could be slapped on many new products. Apple was—and is—one of the most valuable companies in the world. So selling it to somebody else was probably not a realistic possibility. Instead, Icahn demanded that Apple use its cash balance to aggressively repurchase its own shares and increase its dividend.

> Apple eventually followed much of what Icahn proposed. It bought back its stock and increased its share dividend, and it experienced a resurgence in its core business. Resulting in more than $3 billion profit for Icahn and his investors.

Dan Loeb

> Dan Loeb December 18, 1961, in California. His father was a partner at a Los Angeles law firm, and his mother was a historian. Loeb started investing in the stock market when he was in high school. He entered college at the University of California at Berkley in northern California. And, after 2 years, he transferred to Columbia, where he earned a bachelor's degree in economics. After graduating, Loeb worked for several firms, both on and off of Wall Street.

> Loeb began his finance career in 1984 at Warburg Pincus, a well-respected private equity firm. In 1991, he joined the Los Angeles branch of a traditional Wall Street firm, Jefferies—first as a research analyst, and then trading the securities of firms in financial distress. His last position before setting up his own hedge fund was at Citigroup, as a vice president of institutional sales in the high-yield bond area.

> He started his hedge fund, Third Point, in 1995 with only $3.4 million under management. His Third Point fund averaged investment

returns of about 20% a year over a 20-year period. That roughly doubled the S&P 500 return during the same time. Loeb says that most of his investments share the following characteristics:

○ They have talented management teams. Over time, good management increases sales, earnings, profit margins, and stock prices.

○ They are businesses with strong and growing free cash flows. Free cash flow is money remaining after reinvesting in the business.

○ They are firms with a proven track record of capital allocation; that is, the company has invested its money wisely over the long term, whether in new projects or in mergers or acquisitions. Capital allocation also includes returning capital to shareholders in the form of stock buybacks or dividends.

> Loeb calls these firms value compounders. Loeb certainly has talent in identifying these types of companies, but his activist approach also often closes the gap between a stock's lesser, unrealized value, and its higher potential.

Bill Ackman

> Born May 11, 1966, Bill Ackman grew up in an affluent family in Westchester County, New York, and attended Harvard for his undergraduate and M.B.A. degrees. Right after getting his M.B.A., he set up a hedge fund, Gotham Partners, with classmate David Berkowitz.

> On balance, Gotham was successful, but it closed down because of litigation costs related to its trading practices. Ackman was found not to have committed wrongdoing and later resurfaced with his own hedge fund, Pershing Square, partly funded by the conglomerate, Leucadia National.

> When Ackman talks about his investment strategy for common stocks, he sounds like a page from Warren Buffett's book: Buy value stocks that you understand and that have a moat against competitors, and buy companies that can be acquired, especially if prodded by an activist investor.

> Like Loeb, Ackman prefers companies that generate a lot of free cash flow, an important and recurring concept.

  ○ The cash-flow statement has 3 parts: cash flow from operations, generated by a company's core business; cash flow from investing activities, which mainly refers to capital expenditures or long term investments; and cash flow from financing activities, relating to the issuance or repurchase of stock or debt. The net increase (or decrease) in cash is the sum of the 3 parts of the cash-flow statement.

> Ackman is ideally looking for a company that generates a great deal of cash after appropriate reinvestments in the business, giving him the flexibility to make his activist ideas more easily implemented.

Value Investing Philosophy

> These 3 investors' (Icahn, Loeb, and Ackman) addition of activism to the value investing approach is a major contribution to the philosophy of investing. Value investing is the investment strategy that selects stocks based on a belief that they trade for less than their intrinsic value. That is, value investors seek stocks they believe the market has undervalued.

> Sometimes stocks stay cheap for a long time, requiring a catalyst to push the market to revalue the firm. That catalyst could be a new product, new service, new management, or the pro-shareholder strategies recommended by an activist investor.

> A value investor's worst fear is a value trap—a stock that appears to be selling at a discount but that keeps getting cheaper. Think

Kodak, GM, Blockbuster, WorldCom, Enron, Lehman Brothers, and Radio Shack. The presence of an activist investor like Ackman might spur the firm to change its strategy or sell itself before its core business starts to slip away.

Conclusion

> Sometimes, activist investors are likened to corporate raiders, or the Darth Vaders of the investment industry, especially by target boards and management. In some cases, the negative description may be justified. During the initial large wave of activist investing in the 1980s, some raiders even tried to raid company pension funds.

> A more positive assessment of activist investors is that they help keep management on its toes while encouraging more independent boards, and putting firms back in the hands of their shareholders.

Suggested Reading

Ahuja, *The Alpha Masters*.
Stevens, *King Icahn*.

Questions to Consider

1. How would you describe the investment strategies of Carl Icahn, Daniel Loeb, and Bill Ackman?

2. What tactics are used by activist investors to improve stockholder returns?

14

Transcript

Activist Investors: Icahn, Loeb, Ackman

Put yourself in the shoes of Irik Sevin, the CEO of Star Gas Partners. Star Gas is a home heating-oil company in Stamford, Connecticut. And one of its largest shareholders once wrote to the CEO, Sevin, with this blistering evaluation,

> A review of your record reveals years of value destruction and strategic blunders, which have led us to dub you one of the most dangerous and incompetent executives in America. I was amused to learn, in the course of our investigation, that at Cornell University there is an Irik Sevin Scholarship. One can only pity the poor student who suffers the indignity of attaching your name to his academic record.

The correspondence concludes,

> It is time for you to step down from your role as CEO and director so that you can do what you do best, retreat to your waterfront mansion in the Hamptons where you can play tennis and hobnob with your fellow socialites. The matter of repairing the mess you have created should be left to professional management and those that have an economic stake in the outcome.

Who wrote the letter? Well, it was Daniel Loeb, the founder of Third Point LLC, a hedge fund with $17 billion or so under management. Loeb is one of the leading investors of his kind—which is activist investors. Carl Icahn made activist investing famous many years ago. After him, many other fund managers became known after entering the space. Activist investors frequently take a large stake in a particular company in order to get management's ear—or a seat at the board table. And activists use their stakes to spur changes, in an effort to increase the company's stock price. These demands might involve changes to corporate strategy or management; a stock dividend increase, or buyback and sometimes, an outright sale of the company.

In this lecture, we will examine the concept of activist investing, and three of its leading practitioners, Carl Icahn, Dan Loeb, and Bill Ackman. Activist investing has a long history. As early as 1928, Warren Buffet's mentor, Benjamin Graham, waged a successful shareholder-led fight against Northern Pipeline, then an affiliate of the John D. Rockefeller's Standard Oil empire. Graham persuaded the firm to pay a special dividend that was almost equal to its share price. corporate raiders burst onto the scene in mass in the 1980s, as the market developed for below-investment-grade debt. Drexel Burnham Lambert investment banker, Michael Milken, helped turn junk bonds, from a sleepy corner of the bond market, into one of its driving forces.

Let me say a little more about this. Before Milken, junk bonds mainly consisted of fallen angels—that is, former investment-grade bonds that had fallen on hard times, and were relegated to the corporate scrap heap. But Milken used junk bonds as a way for some growing, but less established, firms to raise capital. Corporate raiders also used junk bonds as a source of capital to take runs at established firms, leveraging the companies' own assets to buy them—or threatening to. Milken and some others went too far and were convicted of various securities laws violations. But, they also created a viable, and continuing, market in below-investment-grade bonds.

So, how do activist investors get companies to do what they want? First, they talk to them. As you might guess, this tactic doesn't always generate good results. Other times, the activist may publish a white paper detailing ideas to improve the company. Making these reports public puts pressure on management. Sometimes, the activist will issue a takeover offer for a firm that is viewed as mismanaged or undervalued. As in the corporate raider days, the takeover offer may be financed, all, or in part, with the target company's borrowing power—sometimes in the form of junk bonds. In other words, an activist investor might offer to buy some or all of a company's shares, to be paid for by borrowing against the company's assets.

The offer might be at a premium to the current share price but conditioned on the consent of 50.1%, or more, of shareholders agreeing. The offer puts pressure on sitting management to improve its stock price, comparable with the offered premium—since many investors would prefer to pocket the short-term pop produced in the stock price, rather than management's promises of long-term improvements. In some instances, the target firm may pay for the activist to go away. This is called greenmail. The payment comes right out of the corporate treasury, usually at a premium to the current market price. Since typically only the raider, or activist, gets this premium—and other shareholders do not—the SEC has largely outlawed the payment of greenmail in recent years.

The most contentious—and costly—way for an activist investor to pursue changes at a company is by mounting a campaign for board seats through a proxy contest, in a vote of all shareholders. In a proxy contest, the activist attempts to convince other shareholders to vote for the activist's slate of board candidates. If successful, the new board will be likelier to implement the activists' strategy. And sometimes, the new board will appoint a handpicked CEO by the activist.

The Oliver Stone movie, *Wall Street*, featured a proxy contest in which the star Michael Douglas's character, Gordon Gekko, utters the famous phrase, "Greed … is good." In the movie, Gekko gets investors to vote him on the board of Bluestar Airlines, and he gains a controlling position of the firm. He then ruthlessly wrings out money from the firm, enriching himself, at the expense of other stakeholders. Although the movie is fictional, many of these techniques—proxy contests, layoffs, short-sighted behavior and use of company assets—are sometimes used by real-life activist investors.

Some firms defend themselves against hostile takeover bids with a strategy called a poison pill. In this event, the firm pledges to issue new shares to existing shareholders at a bargain-basement price, with a view toward making the unsolicited takeover more expensive, and perhaps less appealing. Another strategy is to find a different partner—more friendly to management. This strategy is called a white knight strategy, in contrast to the black knight corporate raider. Warren Buffett is often viewed as a white knight since he usually leaves management alone when he buys or invests in a company.

Shark repellent is another defensive strategy, based on using the corporate charter, to make a hostile takeover difficult. One approach is to stagger the election of the Board of Directors. Staggering the board means that directors come up for election in different years, making it difficult, or even impossible, for corporate raiders to vote their preferred directors onto the Board all in one year. Another approach is requiring a supermajority of votes to remove a director. A simple majority is more than 50% while a supermajority typically requires two-thirds or more of shareholder votes to appoint a new director.

The Pac-Man strategy is yet another tactic where you try to take over the company that is trying to acquire you. In one of the most famous cases—dating to the early 1980s—the defense and aerospace firm Martin Marietta tried to take over Bendix, a larger company that was simultaneously was trying to buy it. Yes, they were trying to buy each other. A golden parachute is something else, involving executive compensation, although sometimes it comes into play when an acquiring company wants to make former management go away. Departing executives are rewarded with a large, one-time payment when they leave.

Now let's meet some of the activist investors, beginning with Carl Icahn. Carl Icahn was born on February 16, 1936, in New York, and grew up in a middle-class family in the Far Rockaway section of Queens. He went to Princeton University and is said to have paid for part of his tuition with poker winnings. After Princeton, Icahn entered medical school at New York University. But he was never fully sold on the idea of making a career in medicine. After a patient with tuberculosis sneezed on him, Icahn decided to quit, and join the Army. Eventually, he found his way to Wall Street. That was in 1961. In 1968, he set up his own firm, which focused on options trading and arbitrage.

Arbitrage refers to a type of trade where two similar assets sell at different prices. The idea is to buy the cheaper asset and sell—or short—the more expensive one. You make money on the difference between the two identical, or similar, assets. The seeds of Icahn's activist philosophy may have been planted when he was trying to arbitrage closed-end mutual funds. Closed-end funds usually reflect the net asset value of all the securities they're invested in. However, sometimes the fund's quoted price diverges from the collective value of its underlying stocks and bonds. This creates an arbitrage opportunity. If a fund's basket of securities exceeded the quoted value of the fund itself, Icahn would urge management to liquidate the securities and distribute the unrealized profits to investors.

His activist approach eventually spread outside the arbitrage arena to companies he thought were mismanaged or undervalued. He articulated this approach to investors in a 1976 offering document that the biographer Mark Stevens called The Icahn Manifesto. Icahn said, "It is our contention that sizeable profits can be earned by taking large positions in undervalued stocks, and then, attempting to control the destinies of the companies in question." The Icahn Manifesto calls for doing so by the following: A, convincing management to liquidate or sell the company to a white knight; B, waging a proxy contest; C, making a tender offer; D, selling back its position to the target company that is, greenmail.

Icahn got his reputation as a corporate raider, in part, due to his hostile takeover of the former airline, TWA. He reportedly made $469 MILLION on the deal, and the company was saddled with $540 million in debt. TWA couldn't handle the debt load, though, and eventually went bankrupt. One famous Icahn quote is, "If you want a friend on Wall Street, get a dog."

Another of Icahn's higher profile investments was in Apple. At the time Icahn disclosed his stake in April 2013, some investors were concerned that Apple would not be able to innovate after Steve Jobs' death. The market also fretted over gains made by some of Apple's large competitors, such as Samsung and Google now known as Alphabet. But Icahn saw value, starting with Apple's $100 billion plus pile of cash, and a brand name that could be slapped on many new products. Apple was—and is—one of the most valuable companies in the world. So selling it to somebody else was probably not a realistic possibility. Instead, Icahn demanded that Apple use its cash balance to aggressively repurchase its own shares, and increase its dividend.

Many investors like stocks that pay dividends. Not only is the cash nice to have, but companies can't fake a dividend check in the mail. John D. Rockefeller, who would be worth the equivalent of $340 billion today, once said, "Do you know the only thing that gives me pleasure? It's to see my dividends coming in." Apple eventually followed much of what Icahn proposed. It bought back its stock and increased its share dividend. And it experienced a resurgence in its core business. The end result? A more than $3 billion profit for Icahn and his investors on Apple.

Dan Loeb is quite a bit younger than Icahn. He was born a quarter-century later, on December 18, 1961, and on the opposite coast, in California. His father was a partner at a Los Angeles law firm, and his mother was a historian.

Loeb's great aunt, Ruth Handler, was a co-founder of the Southern California toymaker Mattel, the creator of Barbie dolls and Hot Wheels cars. Loeb started investing in the stock market when he was in high school. He entered college at the University of California at Berkley in northern California. And, after two years, he transferred to Columbia University in New York City, where he earned a bachelor's degree in economics. After graduating, Loeb worked for several firms, both on and off Wall Street.

Loeb began his finance career in 1984 at Warburg Pincus, a well-respected private equity firm. And, after a few years, he left to become director of corporate development at Island Records, a firm best known for once being the record label for the band U2. Then, he returned to the financial services industry, working for the hedge fund Lafer Equity Investors. And, in 1991, he joined the Los Angeles branch of a traditional Wall Street firm,

Jefferies—first as a research analyst, and then trading the securities of firms in financial distress.

His last position, before setting up his own hedge fund was at Citigroup, as a Vice President of Institutional Sales in the high-yield bond area. *Forbes* magazine counts Loeb as a multi-billionaire today, but it is amazing to think that he started his hedge fund, Third Point, in 1995 with only $3.4 million under management. And that amount was gathered from family and friends. The name Third Point is derived from a break in the waves at Malibu's Surfrider Beach. Like many young Californians, Loeb developed an early fascination with surfing. His Third Point fund averaged investment returns of about 20% a year over a 20-year period. That roughly doubled the S&P 500 return during the same time.

Loeb says that many, or most, of his investments, share the following characteristics: First, he likes talented management teams. This is true of all competitive activities, be it in a business or sports. To see the clear importance of management, let's consider a professional football team. I don't know about you, but I would rather have Bill Belicheck coaching my football team rather than almost anyone else. Over time, good management increases sales, earnings, profit margins, and ultimately, stock prices.

Second, Loeb likes business with strong and growing free cash flows. Free cash flow is money the company has left over, after reinvesting in the business. Third, he likes firms that have a proven record of capital allocation. That basically means the company has invested its money wisely over the long-term. The money could be invested in new projects, or in mergers or acquisitions. Capital allocation also includes returning capital to shareholders, in the form of stock buybacks or dividends. Loeb calls firms with these characteristics value compounders.

Loeb certainly has talent in identifying these types of companies, but his activist approach also often closes the gap between a stock's lesser, unrealized value, and its higher potential. Some of Loeb's investments have included Sony, Yahoo!, Sotheby's, and Ligand Pharmaceuticals. Like many activist investors, Loeb is not afraid to take a highly concentrated position. For instance, at one point he put 20% of his firm's assets in a single stock, the healthcare firm Baxter International. Loeb looked to play a role in appointing the new CEO and restructuring the board to be, in his view, more independent and more shareholder friendly. There probably isn't a CEO on earth who looks forward to being on the receiving end of Loeb's poison pen. In most instances, when Loeb takes a new position in a firm, he gives management a bit of time to improve performance—and makes some friendly suggestions—before unleashing his full faith and fury.

Bill Ackman is a part of a slightly later generation of activist investors. He's taken big positions in such well-known companies as Target, J.C. Penney, and Herbalife, among others. Born on May 11, 1966, Ackman grew up in an affluent family in Westchester County, New York. His father, Lawrence, was a successful real estate developer. Bill Ackman attended Harvard University for his undergraduate and MBA degrees. Right after getting his MBA, he set up a hedge fund, Gotham Partners, with classmate David Berkowitz.

Gotham was, on balance, successful. But it closed down due to litigation costs, related to its trading practices. Ackman was not found to have committed any wrongdoing and later resurfaced with his own hedge fund, Pershing Square, partly funded by the conglomerate, Leucadia National. When you hear Ackman talk about his investment strategy for common stocks it sounds like a page right out of Warren Buffett's book. He suggests the following: Understand how the company makes money. Invest at a reasonable price. Invest in a company that can last forever. Make sure the company has limited, or manageable, debt. Look for high barriers to entry. Invest in a company immune to extrinsic factors. Invest in a company with low reinvestment costs. And avoid businesses with controlling shareholders.

In other words, buy value stocks that you understand, and that have a moat against competitors, and buy companies that can be acquired—especially if prodded by an activist investor. Ackman, like Loeb, prefers companies that generate a lot of free cash flow. Free cash flow is the cash flow from operations minus what it costs to run the business. It's an important and recurring concept, so let's drill down a little more.

The cash-flow statement has three parts. The first part is cash flow from operations. This represents the cash generated by a company's core business. For example, Wal-Mart's cash flow from operations mainly represents the cash the firm generates from selling retail goods. The second part of the cash flow statement is cash flow from investing activities. This aspect of the statement mainly refers to capital expenditures or long-term investments. Continuing with our Wal-Mart example, cash flow from investing activities may be related to the cost to open new stores or distribution centers. Or, it may relate to investments in other firms.

The third component of the cash-flow statement is cash flow from financing activities. This section usually relates to the issuance or repurchase of stock or debt. The net increase or decrease in cash is the sum of all three parts of the cash-flow statement. Although it might seem a bit confusing, one way to think of the sum of the three parts of the cash-flow statement is that it is the net of cash coming into the business, versus cash going out of the business. The cash coming in is basically the cash the firm generates from operations, money from its external investments, and new money contributed to the firm by its stockholders or bondholders. The cash coming out of the business includes the part needed to fund its business— making short and long term investments, the payment of dividends, stock repurchases, and the retirement of debt. What Ackman is ideally looking for is a company that generates a great deal of cash, after the appropriate reinvestments in the business. This gives him the flexibility to make his activist ideas more actionable.

The addition of activism to the value investing approach is one of Icahn's, Loeb's, and Ackman's contributions to the philosophy of investing. Value investing is the strategy of selecting stocks based on a belief that they trade for less than their intrinsic value. In other words, value investors seek to buy stocks that they believe the market has undervalued. Value investing legends Benjamin Graham and Warren Buffett also made activist investments at one time. But Icahn, Loeb, and Ackman have made it a core part of their investment philosophies.

Now, sometimes stocks stay cheap for a very long time. A catalyst is often needed to push the market to revalue the firm. That catalyst could be a new product, new service, new management or the pro-shareholder strategies recommended by an activist investor. A value investor's worst fear is a value trap. A value trap is a stock that appears to be selling at a discount but that keeps getting cheaper. Sometimes all the way to zero. Think Kodak, GM, Blockbuster, WorldCom, Enron, Lehman Brothers, and Radio Shack. The presence of an activist investor like Ackman might spur the firm to change its strategy, or sell itself completely before its core business starts to slip away.

One of Bill Ackman's most successful investments was in General Growth Properties—one of the largest mall operators in the United States. The story of General Growth provides a nice illustration of value plus activism. Like many real estate firms, General Growth was in severe financial distress during the financial markets crisis of 2008. Ackman and other investors encouraged the firm to file for protection from its creditors in bankruptcy court, and then provided capital for the reorganized firm, as it worked through the Chapter 11 reorganization process. The fundamentals of the business were in place, General Growth just needed to get out from the crushing $27 billion debt load. Ackman's investment and management counseling enabled it to do so. The net result for Ackman was that a $60 million value investment turned into at least $1.6 billion, a return of more than 25 times his original stake.

But things don't always work out well for him. Ackman's investment in J.C. Penney turned out to be ill-fated. Ackman thought that CEO Ron Johnson, the former head of Apple Stores, would turn around the struggling department store. And Johnson did try to transform the culture of J.C. Penney, in part by moving the retailer away from its history of using big discounts and coupons to lure customers. But traditional customers balked at the new, higher priced and hipper J.C. Penney. And sales plummeted. Plus, J.C. Penney and other retailers had to deal with the substantial and pervasive threat of Amazon.com. Within two years, the stock cratered, and Johnson was fired. Ackman lost almost 50% on his J.C. Penney investment, or 500 million in dollar terms.

Ackman also had an up-an-down experience after taking a short position in vitamin marketer Herbalife. Ackman accused the firm's management of running a pyramid scheme, and the stock initially crashed. But, other investors came to Herbalife's defense, including activists Carl Icahn and Daniel Loeb, who lined up on the buy side of the equation. This became a real battle of wills. So, the activist approach of holding an undiversified portfolio can be risky, if you're not on the right side of the trade.

Sometimes, activist investors are likened to corporate raiders, or the Darth Vaders of the investment industry, especially by target boards and management. In some cases, the negative description may be well justified. During the initial wave of activist investing in the 1980s, some raiders even tried to raid the companies' pension funds. While many companies have underfunded pension plans today, during the bull markets of the 1980s and 1990s many pension funds were overfunded as hard as that might be to remember.

Sometimes, management returned the excess to shareholders in the form of reported profits. At other times, raiders might take a company private, often through a leveraged buyout, or LBO, financed in various ways—including junk bonds and excess pension assets paid out as a dividend to themselves. A more positive assessment of activist investors is they help keep management on its toes while encouraging more independent boards, and putting firms back in the hands of their shareholders.

Activists do help solve what is known in management theory as the principal-agent problem. The principal is the owner, and the agent is the representative, who acts on the owner's behalf. In the case of investing, the owners are the shareholders, and the agents are the managers of a firm. So it helps to have someone independently watching the wheel. The activist investors watch the wheel. The only problem is that sometimes they run the car off the road.

15

The Big Shorts: Livermore, Chanos

Even after the Crash of 1929, Jesse Livermore was said to be worth more than $100 million. This fortune and a smaller one he earned during the Panic of 1907 were built largely by selling short, a technique to profit from falling stock prices. Livermore relied on technical analysis, looking at past changes in price and volume, in an attempt to determine future price trends. By comparison, James Chanos helps us understand fundamental analysis: assessing the business prospects of an enterprise and digging into its financial statements.

Selling Short

> Selling a stock in which you have no current position is called selling short: selling borrowed shares and hoping to buy them back later at a lower price. Brokerage firms often include in their account agreements a provision called a hypothecation agreement, which allows the firm to lend your shares to other investors, usually hedge funds. To help a client sell short, the firm borrows the shares from another client of the firm.

> To engage in this kind of trading means establishing a margin account using borrowed funds. While you have the ability to buy

and sell stocks on margin, custody remains with the brokerage firm until the transaction is complete and you've fulfilled your obligation.

> Margin trading and short selling also can wring out excesses in the economy. An example is a stock that is overvalued: Investors rightly expect to profit by selling it short, pocketing today's price on the expectation the price will fall and completing the purchase after the price has dropped.

> Short selling is often considered a risky strategy. The market as a whole usually goes up over time, so short selling is trading against the long-term tide. But the main risk is that losses theoretically are unlimited. If the stock price keeps rising while you're betting it will go down, you are on the hook to buy it at any price to replace the shares you borrowed.

> Some market observers think short selling is un-American because its practitioners profit from the decline or destruction of a company's stock. Occasionally, short sellers go well over the line

in attacking a firm and its management. But shorts can also serve a useful function, such as rooting out suspected financial frauds and limiting the size of speculative bubbles.

Jesse Livermore

> Jesse Livermore was born July 26, 1877 in Shrewsbury, MA, and started trading at the age of 14. Livermore initially traded in so-called bucket shops. These were a cross between brokerage firm and bookie, and are now illegal. Bucket shops allowed people to bet on stock prices on the side, without the trades actually going to the exchange. They were mostly used by small investors and gamblers.

> Livermore was a speculator—the kind of trader who stands in contrast with the traditional investment approach of a Benjamin Graham or Warren Buffett, who view stock as the ownership of a business. The way Livermore saw things, long-term investing was riskier than trading. At the same time, Livermore wasn't what we think of today as a day trader. Instead, he generally held his positions from weeks to months.

> His views on trading versus investing were shaped in part by the Great Depression, when he saw a nearly 90% drop in the Dow Jones Industrial Average from peak to bottom. Livermore felt that if blue-chip stocks could fall by such a magnitude, then almost any company could go out of business over the long term, and therefore buying to hold it was risky.

> Livermore believed nothing new happened in the stock market. The names might change, but price movements repeat, and we can learn and profit from these patterns. In this view, the Apple and Facebook of today might just as well have been the railroads and automotive companies of yesteryear. Livermore criticized traders who tried to get rich overnight, but he thought it was possible for good traders to make a lot of money relatively quickly. In Livermore's day, an accomplished trader could earn 500% over a 2- to 3-year period, mainly through leverage.

> Livermore didn't trust inside information. He concentrated on the leading stocks of the day and maintained a very concentrated portfolio—typically 8 stocks. That is 4 industries, and 2 stocks per industry. Livermore also traded in commodities such as cotton, wheat, and corn. He felt that while individual stocks could be manipulated, basic commodities were influenced mostly by supply and demand.

> Livermore kept a trading journal in which he kept track of price and volume statistics before making a trade and while invested in it. He would also jot down thoughts and ideas related to his positions, or the market as whole.

> Livermore was a pioneer of the strategy that is today known as trend following or momentum—the trader's equivalent of Newton's First Law of Motion. According to Livermore, if a stock is moving in one direction, it will keep going in that direction until something changes it.

  ○ Some people act on inside information and leave the equivalent of footprints with their trades. Others uncover—or become aware of—news before it is reported. In both cases, other investors try to piggyback on their trades.

  ○ Momentum also works because of market psychology. Investors tend to trade in crowds, getting swept up by greed or fear.

  ○ The biggest risk of momentum trading is a whipsaw: A stock goes up, then down, then up, and so forth. With this type of pattern, you could always be on the wrong side of the trade.

> When Livermore entered a position, he did it in stages. If he lost money on the first trade, he would not put any more money into that stock. The trade either had to turn profitable in the relatively near future, or he would cut his losses: Each succeeding purchase should be at a higher purchase price. If he were short selling,

each succeeding short sale should be at a lower sales price. He believed that if your trades showed a profit, it was proof that your analysis was right.

> Livermore's biggest trading successes occurred during the Panic of 1907 and the Crash of 1929. The Panic of 1907 was set off by a group of investors trying to corner the stock in United Copper Company. This group used a lot of borrowed money, and when the stock fell they couldn't repay the loans, leading to a run on the banks.

  ○ Livermore noticed that credit conditions were getting tight. As the market started to fall, he thought margin calls would result in a wave of forced selling. J. P. Morgan personally implored Livermore to stop shorting during the ensuing panic, when the success of the strategy allowed Livermore to pour his trading profits into selling more stocks short. Stocks fell roughly 40% from March through October of 1907. Eventually he did stop shorting, and went long, after earning a profit of $3 million.

  ○ The Roaring '20s saw the U.S. stock market rise about 400% from 1926 to 1929. One high-profile stock, Radio Corporation of American or RCA, went from $2.50 a share to more than $500. Livermore recognized that excesses were building up, and when the market started to crack, he went short. He knew a panic would ensue. As stock prices kept falling, Livermore—just as he had done in 1907—kept shorting, profitably.

James Chanos

> The most famous short seller of recent times is, perhaps, hedge fund titan James Chanos, who runs a firm called Kynikos Associates. (The Greek translates into English as Cynic Associates). Chanos does not rely on momentum trading but rather looks deeply into the fundamentals of a company: its financials and business model.

> Chanos was born in 1957 and grew up in a Milwaukee. His family operated a chain of dry cleaners. An excellent student, he enrolled at Yale and majored in economics and political science. He began his investment career at a now-defunct Chicago investment bank. A group of partners there split off to start their own firm, and the 24-year-old Chanos went with them as an analyst.

> His first high-profile "short" recommendation identified Cincinnati-based Baldwin-United, a piano maker that had branched out into the insurance business. Chanos thought the company's financial disclosures were confusing and received an anonymous phone call alleging management shenanigans. In the summer of 1982 Chanos issued a Sell recommendation on Baldwin-United's stock. The share price quickly doubled, but the company soon began to unravel and declared bankruptcy in 1983. The Baldwin-United analysis gave Chanos the confidence to set up his own firm in 1985.

> Chanos looks to short 3 types of firms: companies with a fad product, companies with too much debt, and companies with accounting problems.

  ○ Fads are products or behaviors that are the equivalent of bubbles. They become a craze and then die out. For instance, Chanos made money shorting the toy company Coleco, which marketed Cabbage Patch Dolls in the early 1980s. They were initially scarce, but eventually, anyone who wanted a Cabbage Patch doll was able to get one. Coleco ultimately declared bankruptcy.

> Chanos's most famous short is Enron. Enron started out as a traditional utility. In the 1990s, the power sector was deregulated and some traditional utilities began trading energy contracts, which became a huge part of the business at the Northern Natural Gas Company, which changed its name to Enron.

  ○ Enron's stock price soared, and the company was routinely lauded as one of the most-admired companies in America.

When Chanos analyzed Enron's financials, he found that 80% of its reported profits were generated from energy trading. But they were earning only 7% on their trades, while their cost of capital was 10%. In essence, the firm was a house of cards being held up by some strange accounting.

- ○ Further, he discovered that management used hidden off-balance-sheet entities to mask the firm's debt. Enron's accounting misdeeds finally came to light, resulting in one of the biggest bankruptcies ever.

> In 2002, a *Barron's* cover story dubbed Chanos "The Guy Who Called Enron."

Conclusion

> Livermore and Chanos both profited immensely from short selling, albeit by using different approaches. Livermore combined momentum with a keen understanding of the macro environment and investor psychology.

> Chanos believes fundamentals drive prices in the end, and he's willing to wait years to see his bets proved correct. Chanos also views himself as something of a sheriff in the market, rooting out corporate misdeeds and popping bubbles. The Enron example proves that short sellers can act as powerful deterrents to unethical management behavior.

Suggested Reading

Burton, *Hedge Hunters.*
Lefèvre, *Reminiscences of a Stock Operator.*
Rubython, *Plunger.*

Questions to Consider

1. How would you describe the investment strategies of Jesse Livermore and James Chanos?

2. How does short selling differ from traditional long-only investing?

15

The Big Shorts: Livermore, Chanos

On November 28, 1940—at the coat check room of the Sherry Netherland Hotel, in Manhattan—a man shot and killed himself. That man was Jesse Livermore, one of the greatest Wall Street traders who ever lived. Livermore had suffered from clinical depression throughout most of his life. But for many years, he defined living large on the spoils of his unparalleled trading ability. Modern-day hedge fund titans, such as Paul Tudor Jones and John Paulson, credit Livermore as a major influence.

Livermore seemed like a character right out of *The Great Gatsby*. He owned a series of mansions around the world, fully staffed with servants. He owned a fleet of limousines and Rolls Royce, and a 300-foot yacht. Even after the Crash of 1929, Livermore was said to be worth more than $100 million. This fortune—and a smaller one earned during the Panic of 1907—was built largely by selling short, which is a technique to profit from falling stock prices.

In this lecture, we'll discuss the mechanics of selling short, along with the life and times of two of its greatest practitioners, Jesse Livermore, during the first half of the 20th century, and the contemporary hedge fund investor, James Chanos. As we'll see, they took different approaches. Livermore relied on technical analysis, looking at past changes in price and volume, in an attempt to determine future price changes. By comparison, Chanos helps us understand fundamental analysis, which consists of assessing the business prospects of an enterprise and by digging into its financial statements.

The way most investors try to make money is buying low and selling high. But when you sell a stock in which you have no current position—you don't actually own it—that is called selling short. Now, you might be wondering how can you sell something you don't own? Good question. You are literally selling first, with borrowed shares, and hoping to buy them back later, at a lower price. Typically, your brokerage firm borrows the shares from another client of the firm to help you. When you open a brokerage account, the fine print usually contains a provision called a Hypothecation Agreement, which allows the firm to lend your shares to other investors, usually hedge funds, even if you're never aware of it doing so.

To engage in this kind of trading, you have to establish a margin account which means using borrowed funds. So while you have the ability to sell and buy stocks on margin, custody remains with the brokerage firm until the transaction is completed and you've fulfilled your obligation. Sometimes, trading on margin is so extensive that the borrowings, and leverage throughout the economy, become a destabilizing factor. The most famous example of this occurred with the Crash of 1929 when many investors borrowed $10 for each dollar they held in capital. However, margin trading and short selling also can wring out excesses in the economy, as, for example, when a stock is overvalued, and you rightly expect to profit from it by selling it short—pocketing today's price on the expectation that the price will fall. And you can complete the purchase of the underlying security later after the price has dropped.

Let's look at an example. Suppose you think Disney is going to fall in price. And suppose Disney is selling at a price of $100 a share when you make the short sale trade. Assume exactly one year later that Disney is selling for $80 a share, and you now want to close out your trade. To do so, you would buy—or more specifically, buy to cover—Disney at the price of $80. You've now made a gross profit of $20 a share. Selling and then buying, in that specific order, is what short selling is all about. Now, if Disney paid a 2% dividend—or $2—during the holding period, you would also owe the dividend payment to the original holder of Disney that you borrowed the shares from. So your profit would be $18.

There is one catch to making money by selling short. If the stock is considered hard to borrow, the effective interest rate in those cases can be more than 30% a year. What's an example of hard to borrow? Well, after Martha Stewart went to jail for insider trading, a lot of traders tried to sell short her firm, Martha Stewart Living Omnimedia. There is a hard-to-borrow list that brokerage firms update daily. It varies a bit from firm to firm, but most of the names are similar.

How long can you keep a short trade open? It depends. If you are shorting a big company whose stock is not hard to borrow, like Johnson & Johnson, you can keep the short position open for years. However, if you are shorting a stock that is hard to borrow, you might be forced to close out your short trade, even though you are not ready. This is called a short squeeze. In a short squeeze, the broker calls, or emails you, and says they don't have any more shares available for lending. Perhaps the original client who lent the shares has now sold them. A rule of thumb is that if 20% or more of a stock's float—or market-traded shares—is sold short, then that stock may be susceptible to a short squeeze. Brokerage firms have to be able to get the stock from an existing client in order to let another client sell short. This is not always an easy task. Selling short without the shares from another client is called naked short selling. Regulators have cracked down on the practice of naked shorting, so it occurs less often.

Short selling is often considered a risky strategy. And it can be. First, the market as a whole usually goes up over time. So by shorting, you are trading against the long-term tide. But the main risk is that your losses are theoretically unlimited. Because, if the stock price keeps rising while you're betting it will go down, you are on the hook to buy it at any price, to replace the borrowed one that you have. In practice, such risks can be made more manageable with a stop-loss order.

Imagine selling short a young Microsoft after its Initial Public Offering in 1986. If somehow, you maintained your initial position up through today, you would have lost more than 55,000%. Other examples abound. An amateur trader named Joe Campbell shorted a biotech stock that went from roughly $2 to $18.50 a share virtually overnight, and he lost more than $100,000. He advertised his predicament at a crowdfunding site called GoFundMe.com and asked for the public's help in settling his debt. He ended up raising a little over $5,000 and said, "For the record—I will not be shorting low float stocks ever again." These examples bring to mind something the economist, John Maynard Keynes once said, "The market can remain irrational longer than you can remain solvent."

Some market observers deem short selling as un-American, since its practitioners profit from the decline, or destruction, of a company's stock. Occasionally, short sellers go well over the line in attacking a firm and its management. But shorts can also serve a useful function, such as rooting out suspected financial frauds and limiting the size of speculative bubbles. And shorting can also be used as a hedge to offset long, or buy, positions. This was the original goal of many hedge funds, starting with Alfred Winslow Jones in the 1940s. And there are many inverse Exchange Traded Funds that use this approach to move in the opposite direction of the market.

Jesse Livermore was born on July 26, 1877, in Shrewsbury, Massachusetts, and started trading at the age of 14. He made about $1,000 trading in his first year—about $26,000 in today's dollars—and pretty good money for a teenager. Livermore initially traded in so-called bucket shops. These were a cross between a brokerage firm and bookie, and are now illegal. But, bucket shots allowed people to bet on stock prices, on the side, without the trades actually going to the exchange. They were mostly used by small investors and gamblers.

Livermore was an extremely successful bucket shop trader and earned the name Boy Plunger, due to his youth and the growing size of his trades at the time. He was so successful that he was banned from several bucket shops. That's like a card shark being banned from a casino. A somewhat fictionalized biography of Livermore's early days can be found in the Wall Street classic book, *Reminiscences of a Stock Operator* by Edwin Lefèvre. It's on the shelves of many serious traders.

Livermore was a speculator—the kind of trader who stands in contrast with the traditional investment approach of a Benjamin Graham or Warren Buffett, who view stock as the ownership of a business. The way Livermore saw things, long-term investing was riskier than trading. He said, "The money lost by speculation alone is small compared with the gigantic sums lost by so-called investors who have let their investments ride." At the same time, Livermore wasn't what we think of today as a day trader. Instead, he generally held his positions from weeks to months. He said, "No real move of importance ends in one day or week." His views on trading versus investing were shaped in part by the Great Depression, by which time he was no longer a boy, but rather a man in his early 50s, and confronting a nearly 90% drop in the Dow Jones Industrial Average from peak to bottom. Livermore felt that if blue-chip stocks could fall by such a magnitude, then almost any company can go out of business over the long-term, and therefore buying it and holding it was risky.

So what can we learn from a trader who was born when the West was still wild, and who lived through the Jazz Age? The answer is a lot. Livermore said nothing new happened in the stock market. The names might change, but price movements repeat, and that we can learn and profit from these patterns. In this view, the Apple and Facebook of today might just as well have been the railroads and automotive companies of yesteryear. Livermore said, "There will always be change in market leadership. In the course of time, new leaders will come to the front; some of the old leaders will be dropped. It will always be that way as long as there is a stock market." Livermore criticized traders who tried to get rich overnight. But he thought it was possible for good traders to make a lot of money relatively quickly. In Livermore's day, an accomplished trader could earn 500% over a two- to three-year period, mainly through leverage, or borrowing. You still might, but there are tighter limits today on margin trading.

Let's talk about some of the trading strategies that Livermore did not like. He hated stock tips, or touts, which were commonplace during his time. He thought there was no consistent value in the whispers, and that they lacked rigor. Livermore also didn't trust inside information. Beware of inside information, he cautioned—all inside information. Success only comes to those that work for it. No one is going to hand you a lot of easy money.

So, what did Livermore focus on? Well, he concentrated on the leading stocks of the day. He said, "If you cannot make money out of the leading active issues, you are not going to make money out of the stock market as a whole." And he maintained a very concentrated portfolio—typically eight stocks. That is four industries, and two stocks per industry. He said, "It is much easier to watch few than many." Livermore also traded in commodities, like cotton, wheat, and corn. He felt that while individual stocks could be manipulated, that basic commodities were influenced mostly by supply and demand.

Livermore kept meticulous trading records, a trading journal, in which he kept track of the price and volume statistics before making a trade, and while invested in it. He would also jot down thoughts and ideas related to his positions, or the market as a whole. Livermore practiced many of the rules that some professional traders follow today, such as letting your winners run and cutting your losers. Back then, trades were often based on prices that were streaming out from a ticker tape machine. The trend in the price was perhaps the most important output from the ticker tape.

Livermore was a pioneer of the strategy that is today known as trend following, or momentum. Momentum is like the trader's equivalent of Newton's First Law of Motion, which states that, "A body at rest will remain at rest unless an outside force acts on it, and a body in motion, at a constant velocity, will remain in motion in a straight line, unless acted upon by an outside force." So, according to Livermore, if a stock is moving in one direction, it will keep going in that direction until something changes it.

Why does momentum often work? Some people act on inside information and leave the equivalent of footprints with their trades. Other times, due to original research, or being in the right place at the right time, sometimes people uncover—or become aware of—news before it is reported. In both cases, other investors try to piggyback on the trades of the so-called smart money investors. Momentum also works because of market psychology. Investors tend to trade in crowds, getting swept up by fear or greed. You might have heard the expression "It is warm in the herd."

The biggest risk of momentum trading is something called a whipsaw. Picture a saw-tooth pattern where a stock goes up and down and up and down, and so forth. With this type of pattern, you could always be on the wrong side of the trade. When Livermore entered a position, he would do it in stages. He called it putting in a line, like a fishing line. Today we might call this dollar-cost averaging. So, if you wanted to invest $10,000 in a stock you might do five trades of $2000 each. But there's one important difference between dollar-cost averaging and Livermore's approach. Unlike dollar cost averaging, if Livermore lost money on the first trade, he would not put any more money into that stock. The trade either had to turn profitable in the relatively near future, or he would cut his losses. He said "It is foolhardy to make a second trade if the first one shows you a loss. never average losses." Each succeeding purchase should be at a higher purchase price. Or, if he were short selling, each succeeding short sale should be at a lower sales price. He believed that if your trades show a profit, it is proof that you are right in your analysis. He said, Markets are never wrong – opinions often are. Don't be too anxious to get in. Wait and watch the action of that stock.

Here's an example he discussed. He would prefer to buy a stock that went up sharply on big volume, say at least twice the average daily volume of a stock. Some people today call this a breakout. Suppose the stock went from 50 to 54. He would then start his long position in the stock. He thought it would be natural for the stock to pull back a bit, say to 51 and one-half. If the stock continued to move upward to 59 or so, he would invest more in the stock. He would view a pullback to say 57 as normal. If the stock went back up to the mid-60s, he would take another position. In this idealized pattern, the stock makes higher highs and higher lows. He recommends selling shortly after a position shows a loss. If his portfolio doubled in value, he suggested taking half the profits and putting it in a safe place. Although Livermore did not strictly follow a formula for trading, he tried to codify his strategy in something known as the Livermore Key in his 1940 book, *How To Trade In Stocks*. It's basically a trend-following system that filters out small movements—which Livermore viewed as noise.

Livermore's biggest trading successes occurred during the Panic of 1907 and the Crash of 1929. The Panic of 1907 was set off by a group of investors trying to corner, or artificially control, the stock in United Copper Company. This group used a lot of borrowed money, and then when the stock fell they couldn't repay the loans. This led to a run on the banks. Livermore noticed credit conditions were getting tight. As the market started to fall, he thought margin calls would result in a wave of forced selling. The Federal Reserve did not yet exist so there was no government lender of the last resort. And there was no federal deposit insurance. The financier, J.P, Morgan, personally implored Livermore to stop shorting during the ensuing panic when the success of the strategy allowed Livermore to pour his trading profits into selling more stocks short.

Stocks fell roughly 40% from March through October of 1907. But eventually, he did stop shorting, and went long, after earning a profit of $3 million, or $75 million in today's dollars. Later, at the end of World War I, the Roaring '20s saw the U.S. stock market rise about 400% from 1926 to 1929 alone. One high-profile stock, Radio Corporation of American or RCA, went from $2.50 a share to more than $500. Livermore recognized that excesses were building up, and, when the market started to crack, he went short. He knew that a panic would ensue. As stock prices kept falling, Livermore—just as he did in 1907—kept shorting profitably. Livermore married three times, made and lost four fortunes, and declared bankruptcy twice. How did Livermore lose his money? Well, he said he didn't follow his own rules rigorously enough. Like all speculators, he said, I permitted impatience to outmaneuver good judgment.

The most famous short seller of recent times is, perhaps, hedge fund titan James Chanos, who runs a firm called Kynikos Associates. The Greek translates into English as Cynic Associates. Chanos does not rely on momentum trading but rather looks deeply into the fundamentals of a company, its financials and business model. James Chanos was born in 1957 and grew up in a Milwaukee, Wisconsin. His family operated a chain of dry cleaners. An excellent student, he enrolled at Yale University and majored in Economics and Political Science.

Chanos began his investment career at a now-defunct Chicago investment bank. A group of partners there split off to start their own firm, and the 24-year-old Chanos went with them as an analyst. His first high-profile short recommendation identified Cincinnati-based Baldwin-United, a piano maker that had branched out into the insurance business. Chanos thought the company's financial disclosures were confusing and received an anonymous phone call alleging management shenanigans.

In the summer of 1982—at the beginning of a bull market—Chanos issued a sell recommendation on Baldwin-United's stock. The share price quickly doubled. Chanos felt like a fool and was almost fired. But the company soon began to unravel and declared bankruptcy in 1983—a short seller's best-case scenario. The Baldwin-United analysis gave Chanos the confidence to set up his own firm in 1985.

He looks to short three types of firms. The first is companies with a fad product. The second is companies with too much debt. And the third is companies with accounting problems. Fads are products, or behaviors, that are the equivalent of bubbles. They become a craze, and then die out. For instance, Chanos made money shorting the toy company Coleco, which marketed Cabbage Patch dolls in the early 1980s. Each doll had a unique name and features. But, eventually, anyone who wanted a Cabbage Patch doll was able to get one. And competitors sprang up. Coleco ultimately declared bankruptcy.

Chanos also made money shorting a firm called Salton, that made the popular George Foreman Grill, named for a former heavyweight boxer who was a champion of the world. Foreman was a gregarious man who loved to eat. And he had a deal with Salton to put his name on the grill. But eventually, everyone who wanted a grill had one. And Salton declared bankruptcy.

Chanos's most famous short is Enron—the one-time wonder of the Houston energy patch, that came to be loved on Wall Street and emulated around the world, at least for a time. Enron started out as a traditional utility. But in the 1990s, the power sector was deregulated, and some traditional utilities began trading energy contracts. This became a huge part of the business at the Northern Natural Gas Company, which changed its name to Enron. Enron's stock price soared, and the company routinely was lauded as one of the most-admired companies in America. When Chanos analyzed Enron's financials, he found that 80% of its reported profits were generated from energy trading. But he also found they were earning only 7% on their trades, while their cost of capital was 10%. In essence, the firm was a house of cards being held up by some strange accounting.

Further, he discovered that management used hidden off-balance sheet entities to mask the firm's debt. Enron's accounting misdeeds finally came to light, resulting in one of the biggest bankruptcies ever. In 2002, a *Barron's* cover story dubbed Chanos "The Guy Who Called Enron." But Chanos doesn't always get it right. He shorted America Online, or AOL, in 1996, well before the Internet Bubble came to a head. And for a time, he watched his losses pile up as the stock skyrocketed. Two years later, he exited the position at a big loss, even though the stock ultimately fell more than 90% from its peak.

Livermore and Chanos both profited immensely from short selling, albeit by using different approaches. Livermore combined momentum with a keen understanding of the macro environment and investor psychology. He said, The human side of every person is the greatest enemy of the average speculator. Chanos believes fundamentals drive prices. In the end, he's willing to wait years to see his bets proven correct. Chanos also views himself as something of a sheriff in the market, rooting out corporate misdeeds and popping bubbles. The Enron examples prove that short sellers can act as powerful deterrents on management from behaving unethically.

There are many other successful practitioners of the art of short selling, as well. George Soros made a fortune shorting the overvalued British Pound in 1992 and broke the Bank of England's will to prop up the currency. John Paulson used credit derivatives to short overvalued subprime-mortgage securities at the outset of the Credit Crisis in 2008—a trade that some called the greatest trade ever. Some countries prohibit selling short, arguing that their markets are too fragile and that the practice might aid in the destruction of small companies. During the Credit Crisis of 2008–2009, the U.S. government prohibited the short-selling of most financial firms in the country.

So, selling short is another way to find value in the market and make money. It's risky business, and not for the fainthearted. But, it can provide investors with a sense of control and empowerment. It can be used to hedge—or outright speculate. And so, it is a weapon to fight with when the market is falling.

16

George Soros's $10 Billion Currency Play

Investment managers, primarily in the hedge-fund space, search for opportunities on a global basis. Global macro managers are just as happy to sell short as they are to go long, a bet that the asset price will rise. They might pick individual securities, but these are usually secondary to big-picture themes: which market to invest in; which currency to trade; where to borrow money at its cheapest cost; and how much leverage to use.

George Soros

> George Soros didn't aspire to be a financier. He wanted to be a philosopher, and to be recognized as a great thinker. He calls himself a failed philosopher. As it turns out, Soros did develop his own vision, which focuses on global macro investing.

> George Soros was born George Schwartz August 12, 1930, in Budapest, His father was a lawyer and his mother's family owned a prosperous silk shop. The family changed its name in 1936 to avoid rising discrimination against Jewish people at the time. When Germany occupied Hungary in March 1944, Soros very possibly saved his life by posing as the godson of an employee of the Hungarian Ministry of Agriculture.

> Three years later, he left the country to live with some cousins in London, and enrolled at the London School of Economics. There, he met the person who would have the greatest intellectual influence on his life: Karl Popper. Soros was chiefly intrigued by Popper's application of the scientific method to the social sciences.

> In 1956, Soros found his way to New York, joining the investment firm of F. M. Mayer and in 1959 joined Wertheim & Co. as a European securities analyst. After about 4 years of seasoning at this well-regarded bank, he moved again to begin a 10-year stint at Arnhold and S. Bleichroeder, today known as First Eagle Investment Management. It was here that he entered the hedge fund business through a fund called Double Eagle. In 1970, near the end of his time at Arnhold, he set up Soros Fund Management.

The Theory of Reflexivity

> In 1987, he wrote a book titled *The Alchemy of Finance*, which discusses some of his theories about the social sciences in the context of financial markets. Soros's main concept is the Theory of Reflexivity.

> His first insight was that applying the scientific method to the social sciences is problematic because, unlike a scientific experiment that replicates results, you might get a different result each time.

  ○ Soros posits a feedback loop between prices and fundamentals—earnings, dividends, and interest rates—wherein the price itself impacts the fundamentals.

  ○ Soros's investment thoughts were influenced in part by Werner Heisenberg, one of the pioneers of quantum mechanics, best known for the Heisenberg Uncertainty Principle, which says that that the act of measuring influences the measurement.

> Soros's theory of reflexivity states that the connection between participants' thinking and the situation in which they participate reflects two functional relationships: cognitive and participating.

  ○ The cognitive function is the participants' efforts to understand the situation.

  ○ The participating function is the impact of their thinking on the real world.

> Because these two functions interact with one another in a recursive process, markets are rarely in equilibrium, or balance. And yet, equilibrium is one of the central concepts of economics. The market is prone to boom-and-bust cycles.

Boom and Bust

> Soros has been able to capitalize on identifying these cycles and turning points, perhaps better than any other investor in history. Although no two markets are ever the same, Soros provides some guidance on how a boom-bust cycle usually plays out. He says it consists of 7 stages.

- ○ Start with a trend that is not yet recognized by the public as a whole, such as the great returns realized by the early purchasers of Internet stocks.

- ○ When the trend becomes broadly recognized, that recognition reinforces it; other people act on news and make the same trades. Soros calls this the initial phase.

- ○ Sometimes a surge in prices peters out. Price increases don't always result in more increases. However, if the stocks that attracted attention survive this initial phase, they emerge strengthened. Soros calls this a period of acceleration.

- ○ At some point, a large gap emerges between public perceptions and a company's fundamentals, and the market also recognizes this reality. For example, investors might realize the company cannot grow profitably or that its market value is out of sync with its potential profits. Soros calls this the moment of truth.

- ○ Stocks can stay inflated for a long time. They might not immediately plunge in price just because they are overvalued. Soros calls this the period of stagnation, or twilight period.

- ○ Eventually, something causes a broad loss of belief in the stock. Perhaps the company announced an earnings warning or is met with increased competition. This widespread loss of belief causes a reversal in the popular buying trend. Soros calls this the crossover point.

- ○ Selling results in more selling, causing an accelerating downward trend. Soros calls this phase a crash. Stock prices fell about 50% between 2000 and 2002, and many Internet stocks fell more than 90% from top to bottom.

> In his book, Soros discusses one boom-and-bust cycle specifically—the conglomerate boom Shorting the Pound.

> Great Britain is not a member of the euro currency bloc; its currency is based on the pound sterling, not the euro. However, there was a time when it was on the path to joining the European Exchange Rate Mechanism, or ERM, created 2 decades before the formal launch of the euro.

> The vision behind the creation of the euro was to coordinate fiscal, trade, and border policies. The idea was to have a currency bloc whose members would have a combined GDP roughly the size of the U.S. economy and to reduce the risk of another world war by linking member's pocketbooks.

> As a condition of participating in the ERM, members agreed to fix their currency exchange rates within a band relative to the value of other participants' national currencies. At the time, Germany had the strongest currency, so ERM members agreed to tie their currency to the Deutsche Mark within a plus or minus 6% band.

> Britain entered the ERM in October of 1990 at a rate of 2.95 Deutsche Marks for each British pound. Using this ratio, Britain was obligated to keep the pound in a range between 2.78 and 3.13 Deutsche Marks.

> For the first couple of years, the British economy performed pretty well. But by 1992, Britain was mired in a recession. Unemployment hit almost 13%. The typical remedy for unemployment is lowering interest rates, but lowering interest rates would have pushed the British pound lower, and the government had to stay within that 6% ERM band.

> Market participants knew Britain was caught between a rock and a hard place, and traders began to short the British pound. At first, the Bank of England tried to defend the nation's currency, buying pound sterling on the open market, and increasing its bank interest rate—the rate the Bank of England charges other banks for overnight lending—from 10% to 12%.

> On the surface, increasing interest rates would attract foreign capital, helping to support the price of the British pound, but raising interest rates was also likely to make the domestic economy worse. It would be more expensive for British companies to raise capital, and approval for projects for individual companies would depend on higher projected returns; rising interest rates usually put the brakes on an economy.

> Hedge fund sharks believed that Britain couldn't afford to prop up the pound indefinitely, so betting against the British pound had almost no downside: The British currency would remain pinned to the lower end of its range with the Deutsche Mark. But the upside was large if the pound were revalued or if it exited the ERM entirely.

> An article published in the *Wall Street Journal* on September 16, 1992, acted as a catalyst. Because Germany was financially the strongest country in Europe, its Bundesbank was Europe's most important central bank. The *Journal* article paraphrased the Bundesbank's president as saying that 1 or 2 currencies in the ERM could come under pressure, a move that signals a devaluation. All eyes turned to England.

> Soros's chief investment officer, Stanley Druckenmiller, initially put a short position on the pound equal to $1.5 billion. But after Druckenmiller explained the logic of the trade, Soros told him to bet big, to the tune of $10 billion. Soros is known for saying, "There is no point in being confident and having a small position."

> On the same day that the *Journal* article appeared, Britain withdrew from the ERM, abandoning the commitment to keep the British pound within a narrow range. Market forces drove the pound sharply lower against most other currencies, especially the German currency. The British government lost more than £3 billion because it had been purchasing the pound, which now plummeted.

Conclusion

> George Soros's Quantum Fund, from its inception in 1973, provided investors with compound returns of about 20% a year. George Soros's unique life experiences helped him to become a very successful global macro trader. His theory of reflexivity also provided him with a framework to identify boom-and-bust cycles ahead of the crowd.

> Soros came to believe that modern economic theory has a fundamental problem: that it is based on the assumption of a market usually in equilibrium, where fundamentals almost always drive prices. Soros believed the market is rarely in equilibrium, and he added an element of thinking previously all but unaccounted for in market dynamics. And that is that investors impact market fundamentals through the feedback loop of their own thinking and trading in the market.

> We can learn several lessons from Soros and his theories:

   ○ First, have a global outlook.

   ○ Second, try to understand how our own investing decisions are based on market movements and the actions of others and not simply on the market fundamentals.

   ○ Third, be cognizant of the market's tendency to gravitate toward boom-and-bust-cycles and the opportunities that these movements might afford.

   ○ Fourth, if you are a trader, as opposed to being a long-term investor, be as willing to go short as you are willing to go long.

   ○ And lastly—for the more adventurous and less risk averse—if you have high conviction in an idea, be willing to bet big.

Suggested Reading

Soros, *The Alchemy of Finance*.
Train, *Money Masters of Our Time*.

Questions to Consider

1. How would you describe the investment strategy of George Soros?

2. How would you define global macro investing?

16

George Soros's $10 Billion Currency Play

George Soros didn't aspire to be a financier. He wanted to be a philosopher and to be recognized as a great thinker. He calls himself a failed philosopher. But, it's lucky for Soros—and his investors—that his philosophy career didn't exactly pan out. In this lecture, we'll examine the remarkable life of George Soros, the man who broke the Bank of England when his hedge fund, The Quantum Fund, made $1 billion in one day by shorting the British Pound.

As it turns out, Soros did develop his own ideas, and vision, which focuses on global macro investing. And this is exactly what it sounds like. Investment managers—primarily in the hedge fund space—search for investment opportunities on a global basis. Their main focus is not on individual stocks, but rather on big picture ideas, such as currency changes, and on aggregate stock and bond movements. So, they might bet that the U.S. dollar will surge against the Euro. Or that U.S. stocks will tank, and that Japanese stocks will rise. Or that U.S. bonds are headed down, while Canadian bonds are headed up. Global macro managers stake out ground neither as permabulls nor permabears. They are just as happy to sell short—which is a bet that an asset will go down in value—as they are to go long, a bet that the asset will rise in value.

Yes, global macro managers might pick individual securities, like AT&T. But these company-specific securities are usually secondary In importance to big-picture themes, like which market to invest in, and which currency to trade, where to borrow at the cheapest cost, and how much leverage, or borrowed money, to use. Borrowing makes the good times better and bad times worse. One study found that the average global macro fund uses leverage of about 6 to 1. That is, they borrow $6 for every $1 already in their wallet. Not only do they borrow money, but they often do something through what's called a carry trade. In a carry trade, the manager borrows money where it is cheapest anywhere around the world and tries to invest it in a higher-return investment.

For example, suppose you could borrow money in Japan at 1% and invest it in a Brazilian government bond yielding 10%. On its face, that's a 9% spread.

But this trade might be somewhat riskier than that, as the Brazilian Real may go down, or depreciate, against the Japanese Yen. So, let's suppose it costs 5% to hedge the currency risk. Now, you would be left with a return of 4%, which represents the 9% spread less the 5% cost of hedging the currency movements. So, that's a 4% return. However, if we're leveraged— let's say we've borrowed at a rate of 5-to-1, then our 4% return becomes 20%.

George Soros was born as George Schwartz in Budapest, Hungary, on August 12th, 1930. His father was a lawyer, and his mother's family owned a prosperous silk shop. The family changed its name in 1936 from Schwartz to Soros—which means successor in Hungarian—in an effort to avoid rising discrimination against Jewish people at the time. In Esperanto, a sort of trans-European Language that was created in the late 19th century, soros also means soar. Nazi Germany occupied Hungary, beginning in March 1944. George Soros very possibly saved his life by posing as the godson of an employee of the Hungarian Ministry of Agriculture.

Three years later, he left the country to live with some cousins in London and enrolled at the London School of Economics. There, he met the man who would have the greatest intellectual influence on his life, Karl Popper. The Austrian-British philosopher Popper was one of the most accomplished thinkers of the 20th century. He made many contributions to the field of philosophy. Soros was chiefly intrigued by Popper's application of something called the scientific method to the social sciences—fields, such as Economics, Sociology, and Psychology.

The scientific method provides a rigorous way for testing a theory. The number of steps in the scientific method varies by source, but it usually includes the following. First, start with a question, such as, "What causes the tides of the ocean?" Then, research the question and form a hypothesis. For example, your hypothesis might be, "The tides of the ocean are caused by the gravitational attraction of the moon." You would then test your hypothesis with experimentation or observation. These experiments and observations would give you data that help you draw a conclusion.

Soros completed his bachelor's degree in Philosophy at the London School of Economics in 1951 and went on to earn a master's of Science in Philosophy there in 1954. Soros didn't find work as a philosopher. At first, he was employed as a traveling salesman. But soon, he landed with the London merchant bank, Singer & Friedlander. He believes the main reason he got the job was because one of the managing director's there was also Hungarian.

Soros started out as a clerk, processing the trades, and made his way to a niche area of the trading department called arbitrage. Arbitrage involves trading two similar securities that have temporary price discrepancies. For example, the price of IBM in New York might be trading at $100 and its price in London adjusted for currency and transaction costs might be $100.25. The 25 cent spread is the equivalent of free money lying on the ground, though buying pressure in New York, and selling pressure in London, will quickly make the prices converge.

In 1956, Soros found his way to New York City, joining the investment firm of F.M. Mayer, which was owned by the father of one of Soros's colleagues at Singer. And in 1959, Soros joined the investment bank Wertheim & Co. as a European securities analyst. After about four years of seasoning at this well-regarded bank, he moved again to begin a 10-year stint at Arnhold and S. Bleichroeder, today known as First Eagle Investment Management. It was here that he entered the hedge fund business, through a fund called Double Eagle. And in 1970, near the end of his time at Arnhold, he set up Soros Fund Management.

Meanwhile, Soros had spent three years during the 1960s developing his own philosophy on the self and social sciences. He wrote a book that he planned to call *The Burden of Consciousness* but left it unpublished when he found his own ideas confusing. Much later, in 1987, he wrote a book called *The Alchemy of Finance*, which discusses some of his theories about social sciences, in the context of the financial markets.

Soros calls his main concept the theory of reflexivity. And it's not a coincidence that reflexivity sounds a lot like relativity since Soros always longed to be recognized in the same breath as intellectual giants like Albert Einstein. The term reflexivity also comes from something known as a reflexive verb, a grammatical concept in which the direct object is the same as the subject of the verb; like in the phrase I teach myself. Keeping in mind that Soros wanted to be a philosopher, his thoughts on reflexivity are theoretical—and a bit hard to follow. But I'll try to explain them in a straightforward manner.

The first insight that Soros had is that applying the scientific method to the social sciences is problematic. If you conduct a scientific experiment, like Galileo dropping weights from the Leaning Tower of Pisa to test the Law of Gravity, it will give the same result virtually 100% of the time. But, if you conduct an experiment in the social sciences, like how the stock market moves when the Federal Reserve increases interest rates, you might get a different response each time. People know that you never get 100% accuracy in social science models. But Soros goes one step further by saying that there is a feedback loop between prices and fundamentals. What does this mean? Well, most traditional courses in economics and finance teach that the price of an asset is related to its fundamentals, such as earnings, dividends, and interest rates. The feedback loop means that sometimes the price itself impacts the fundamentals.

Let's look at a couple of examples. Imagine that you were a bank loan officer, and you saw your client's stock crashing, and heard rumors of a potential bankruptcy. If this were the case, you'd be more cautious about lending to the firm. Or, perhaps you would demand more collateral, or charge a higher interest rate. Employees might leave the firm since their stock holdings would be worth less, removing an important incentive to stick around. In this case, the price drop would have impacted the fundamentals. On the positive side, if you were the CEO of a company whose stock sharply increased, you could improve your fundamentals by purchasing other firms with your inflated stock price—or by extracting better terms on borrowings, and possibly by attracting better employees who want to work for a winner.

There is an analog to this behavior in the physical sciences. The name Quantum Fund comes from quantum mechanics in physics. Soros's investment thoughts were influenced in part by Werner Heisenberg, one of the pioneers of quantum mechanics. Heisenberg is perhaps best known for his Heisenberg Uncertainty Principle, which says that that the act of measuring influences the measurement. So, here, Soros says that the thinking and behavior of investors impacts the fundamentals. The changes in thinking and behavior could be due to the emotions of fear and greed, or perhaps by learning new information. This line of thought helps explain the alchemy part of his book's title. Chemists can't turn just any kind of metal into gold since that would violate the laws of nature.

However, investors and policymakers might be able to impact the direction of prices by their actions. Soros's theory of reflexivity states that the connection between participants thinking, and the situation in which they participate—such as investing in the stock market—can be broken up into two functional relationships, the cognitive function, and the participating function. The cognitive function is the participants' efforts to understand the situation, in our example, that's stock market prices. The participating function is the impact of their thinking on the real world, such as how trading behavior impacts stock prices. Because these two functions interact with one another in a recursive or repeating process, Soros says that markets are rarely in equilibrium or balance. And yet, equilibrium is one of the central concepts of economics.

If all of this sounds too theoretical for you, don't worry. There's an important practical takeaway for investors. It's that the market is prone to boom-and-bust cycles. And Soros has been able to capitalize on identifying these cycles and turning points, perhaps better than any other investor In history. Although no two markets are ever the same, Soros provides some guidance on how a boom-and-bust cycle usually plays out. He says it consists of seven stages. So, let's discuss each stage in the context of a stock that was around during the Internet bubble—and eventual crash. The example I'll offer you is JDS Uniphase, a company that made fiber-optic networking equipment. Today, the company is known as Lumentum Holdings.

Under Soros's seven stages of boom-and-bust, first, we start with a trend that is not yet recognized, by the public as a whole, such as the great returns realized by the early purchasers of Internet stocks. Two, when the trend becomes broadly recognized, that recognition reinforces it because other people act on news, and make the same trades. Soros calls this the initial phase. Three, sometimes a surge in prices peters out. Price increases don't always result in more increases and bubbles. However, if the Internet stocks that attracted this attention survive this initial phase, they emerge strengthened. Soros calls this a period of acceleration. Four, at some point, a large gap emerges between public perceptions and a company's fundamentals, and this reality is also recognized by the market. For example, investors might realize that the company cannot grow profitably, or that its market value is out of whack with its potential profits. Soros calls this the moment of truth.

Five, stocks can stay inflated for a long period of time. They might not be immediately plunging in price just because they are overvalued. Kind of like Wile E. Coyote going over a cliff, but he doesn't fall until he looks down. Soros calls this the period of stagnation, or twilight period. Six, eventually, something causes a loss of belief in the stock. Perhaps the company announced an earnings warning or is met with increased competition. This widespread loss of belief causes a reversal in the popular buying trend. For Internet stocks like JDSU, this point for many of them occurred in March of 2000. Soros calls this the crossover point. Seven, selling results in more selling, causing an accelerating trend, in a downward direction. Soros calls this phase a crash. Stock prices fell about 50% over the 2000 to 2002 time period, and many Internet stocks, like JDSU, fell more than 90% from top to bottom.

Soros discusses several boom-and-bust cycles, and how his theory applies to them. For example, he notes the conglomerate boom in the 1960s; the nifty 50 stock boom of the 1960s and 1970s; the real estate investment trust boom of 1970; and the leveraged buyout and mergers and acquisitions booms of the 1980s. There hasn't been a shortage of boom-and-bust cycles since Soros wrote *The Alchemy of Finance*.

Now, let's look at one example specifically that Soros discusses—the conglomerate boom—and how this bubble became unsustainable. A conglomerate is a company that owns a number of unrelated businesses. General Electric was a successful industrial and financial conglomerate until it decided to sell off many of its non-industrial businesses. At one point, GE owned NBC TV, Universal Pictures, a huge financial services division, a power plant business, a jet aircraft engine business, an appliance unit, and an oil and gas unit, along with several other divisions.

Another example is Warren Buffett's firm, Berkshire Hathaway. This is probably one of the best-known conglomerates today. Typically, a company with a higher stock valuation would merge with a company with a lower valuation, capturing its earnings, and increasing the earnings of the combined firm. But the earnings gains were often not sustainable going forward, as the supposed efficiencies usually didn't materialize.

As an example, let's use the price-to-earnings ratio, or P/E, as the metric for an expensive company, and for a cheap company. P/E is computed by taking the price per share of a stock and dividing it by its earnings per share. Suppose a company with a P/E ratio of 50—let's call it Bidder Co— buys a company with a P/E of 10, which we'll call Target Co. Let's make the math simple and assume each company has earnings of $1 a share. The combined firm, the new and improved Bidder Co, will now have earnings of $2 a share. If investors think Bidder Co, deserves the same P/E multiple of 50, its stock price will increase 100%. In reality, it wouldn't increase quite that much since the Bidder Company would have to give some shares to Target Co shareholders, resulting in some dilution. But, it would almost certainly get a pop in price, assuming investors thought Bidder Co deserved a similar multiple after the deal.

What's the problem with this merger approach? Well, for starters, most mergers don't work. About 70% of all mergers aren't worth what the bidding firm offers, according to various academic studies. A more significant flaw with the conglomerate approach is that there aren't many synergies in unrelated companies. Few people can manage disparate businesses well. For that reason, many conglomerates in the 1960s and 1970s—such as ITT and LTV—ultimately crashed and burned.

Soros's most famous trade—which I alluded to earlier—was shorting the British Pound. Now, Great Britain is not a member of the Euro currency bloc, and its currency is based on the Pound Sterling, and not the Euro. However, there was a time when it was on the path to being part of the Euro. Specifically, there was a precursor to the Euro called the Exchange Rate Mechanism, or ERM, which was created in 1979, two decades before the formal launch of the Euro. Europe's vision for the Euro was to have a currency bloc, whose members would have a combined GDP roughly the size of the U.S. economy, and also to reduce the risk of having another World War by having member's pocketbooks tied together.

The vision behind the creation of the Euro was to coordinate fiscal, trade, and border policies. It was and is a noble vision. As a condition of participating in the Exchange Rate Mechanism, or ERM, members agreed to fix their currency exchange rates within a band relative to the value of other participants' national currencies. It did this rather than let the market freely determine relative currency rates. At the time, Germany had the strongest currency, so the Exchange Rate Mechanism members agreed to keep their currency tied to the Deutsche Mark, within a plus or minus 6% band.

Britain entered the Exchange Rate Mechanism in October of 1990 at a rate of 2.95 Deutsche Mark for each British Pound. Using this ratio, Britain was obligated to keep the pound in a range of 2.78 Deutsche Mark to 3.13 Deutsche Mark. For the first couple of years, the British economy performed pretty well. But by 1992, Britain was mired in a recession. Unemployment hit almost 13%.

The typical medicine for unemployment is lowering interest rates. But lowering interest rates would have pushed the British Pound lower since capital might leave the country in search of higher returns. And the government needed to stay within that 6% Exchange Rate Mechanism band.

Market participants knew that Britain was caught between a rock and a hard place, and traders began to short the British Pound. Shorting, or selling short, is a technique designed to profit from a decline in price. It involves first selling an asset and then buying the same, or comparable, asset back later, hopefully at a lower price. Your profit, or loss, is the difference between the buy price, or more accurately, buy to cover price and the short sale price.

At first, the Bank of England—Britain's central bank—tried to defend the nation's currency, buying pound sterling on the open market, and increasing its bank interest rate,—the rate the Bank of England charges other banks for overnight lending—from 10% to 12%. On the surface, increasing interest rates would attract foreign capital, helping support the price of the British Pound. But, raising interest rates was also likely to make the domestic economy worse. It would be more expensive for domestic British companies to raise capital. Projects for individual companies would also need to have a higher projected return in order to be approved. Basically, rising interest rates usually puts the brakes on an economy. The move to increase interest rates also spilled a bit of blood in the water around hedge fund sharks who believed that Britain couldn't afford to prop up the pound indefinitely.

The trade of shorting, or betting against, the British pound had almost no downside since the British currency would remain pinned to the lower end of its range with the Deutsche Mark. But the upside was large if the Pound were revalued against the Deutsche Mark, or if it exited the Exchange Rate Mechanism entirely. The trade of shorting the British Pound was brought to Soros's attention by his chief investment officer, Stanley Druckenmiller, who had served him for many years, and who would become known as a billionaire investor in his own right.

An article published in *The Wall Street Journal* on September 16, 1992, acted as a catalyst for the trade to work in spectacular fashion. Since Germany was financially the strongest country in Europe, at the time, its Bundesbank was Europe's most important central bank. The *Journal* article paraphrased Bundesbank President, Helmut Schlesinger, as saying that one or two currencies in the Exchange Rate Mechanism could come under pressure, which basically signals a devaluation. All eyes zeroed in on England. Druckenmiller initially put a short position on the British Pound equal to $1.5 billion. But after Druckenmiller explained the logic of the trade, Soros told him to go for the jugular and bet big to the tune of $10 billion. As Soros is known for saying, There is no point in being confident and having a small position.

On, September 16, 1992—which became known as Black Wednesday—Britain withdrew from the European Exchange Rate Mechanism, abandoning the commitment to keep the British Pound within a narrow range. Market forces drove the Pound sharply lower against most other currencies, and especially the Deutsche Mark. The British government lost more than 3 billion pounds because it had been purchasing the national currency, which now plummeted. And this is how Soros's fund's short position made $1 billion in that single day.

It was more than simply a financial blow for the United Kingdom. It was a loss of political face for the nation and its prime minister, John Major. Before becoming the PM, Major had been chancellor of the Exchequer in Prime Minister Margaret Thatcher's cabinet. This is akin to the U.S. Secretary of the Treasury. Major was one of the strongest proponents in the U.K. for entering the Exchange Rate Mechanism. So withdrawing from it must have been a bitter pill for him to swallow. By leaving the ERM, the U.K. also lost power and prestige of being one of the leading countries in Europe. It was now outside the circle of a new and powerful currency bloc.

George Soros's Quantum Fund, from its inception in 1973 to its conversion into a family office nearly 30 years later, in 2011, provided investors with compound returns of about 20% a year. George Soros's unique life experiences of evading the Nazis in Hungary during World War II, and then being educated as a philosopher at the London School of Economics—and later trading securities around the world—provided him with experiences that helped him to become a very successful global macro trader. His theory of reflexivity also provided him with a framework to identify boom-and-bust cycles ahead of the crowd.

But Soros was willing to take huge risks, too. He came to believe that modern economic theory has a fundamental problem; and that is modern economic theory is based on the assumption of a market usually in equilibrium, where fundamentals almost always drive prices. Soros believed that the market is rarely in equilibrium, and he added an element of thinking previously all but unaccounted for in market dynamics. And that is that investors impact market fundamentals through the feedback loop of their own thinking and trading in the market. This feedback loop can sometimes result in momentum to the upside—causing booms—and to the downside, causing busts.

These days, it seems like we have a 100-year flood every five to ten years. And I think we can learn several things from Soros and his theories. First, have a global outlook. Second, try to understand how our own investment decisions are based on market movements—and the actions of others—and not simply on the market fundamentals. Third, be cognizant of the market's tendency to gravitate towards boom-and-bust-cycles, and the opportunities these movements might afford. Fourth, if you are a trader, as opposed to being a long-term investor, be as willing to go short as you are willing to go long. And lastly—for the more adventurous and less risk-averse—if you have high conviction in an idea, be willing to bet big.

17

Bridgewater's Multi-Strategy Investing

Ray Dalio has always worked for what he wants and not what others want of him. This principle left Dalio feeling that he isn't forced to do anything—he is doing what is naturally in his self-interest. But part of his having confidence in an investment decision is to see it criticized by others, so he solicits the best independent opinions he can muster. If his argument still holds water afterward, he can have greater confidence in his choice. He calls this approach "stress testing" his opinions. Dalio remains wary about being overconfident, recognizing that all investments engender some uncertainty

Ray Dalio

> Ray Dalio was born August 1, 1949, in Jackson Heights, Queens. He was an only child, raised by a stay-at-home mother and a jazz-musician father who played the clarinet, piccolo, flute, and saxophone. When Ray was 8, the Dalio family moved to Manhasset, Long Island.

> Like many boys, Dalio shoveled snow and mowed lawns to earn extra money. At the age of 12, he used some of his earnings to buy his first stock, Northeast Airlines through his father's broker.

He got lucky when the company was acquired in short order, and he tripled his money.

> Dalio kept investing, and by the time he graduated from high school he had a portfolio worth several thousand dollars. But he wasn't a great student, so when it came time to pick a college, he stayed close to home, attending Long Island University. There, Dalio branched out from stocks to trade futures contracts on commodities. Futures contracts offer investors the opportunity to trade with a lot of leverage.

> Dalio managed to become a strong and focused student at Long Island University, which helped gain him admission to Harvard Business School. During the summer after his first year at Harvard, Dalio interned as a commodities trader at Merrill Lynch, and while finishing his M.B.A. program, Dalio and some friends set up a commodities trading shop called Bridgewater Associates. That venture never took off, but Dalio held onto the Bridgewater name.

> After getting his degree, Dalio worked as a trader, first at a small, well-regarded, investment bank and then at Shearson Hayden Stone. Dalio didn't like the corporate culture at Shearson and reportedly came to blows with his department head at a New Year's Eve party. He left Shearson with some of his commodities trading clients in tow and launched Bridgewater Associates. He was 26 years old. Today, Dalio runs the largest hedge fund in the world.

Bridgewater Strategies

> Bridgewater's focus is global macro- and multi-strategy. That is, the firm searches the world for investment opportunities and uses a range of strategies, both long and short, with a variety of financial instruments.

> Dalio attributes at least part of his success to Transcendental Meditation, a discipline he claims to have practiced daily since

1968. He believes that meditation frees the mind and allows it to detach from emotion and perceive the environment more clearly.

> Dalio's philosophy is spelled out in a self-published 100-plus page handbook called Principles, given to all new employees and available for download on the Internet. Bridgewater employees must be prepared to follow these more than 200 principles closely and be open to scab-picking reviews of themselves and their peers.

> Bridgewater has two main funds: Pure Alpha and All-Weather. Alpha signifies superior performance on a market risk-adjusted basis or relative to a certain benchmark. All-Weather is designed to withstand any market environment.

  ○ Pure Alpha fund historically has provided a return of about 13% per year after fees as compared to the S&P 500, which returned about 10% a year over a comparable period, with less risk compared to the market.

  ○ All-Weather strategy is divided into 4 quadrants, driven by growth and inflation. It is managed by using trading models that historically have worked in each of the 4 quadrants. Thus, regardless of the general state of the economy and financial markets, usually at least something is working well in this portfolio.

> Another unique factor at Bridgewater is that the firm lets its clients combine the Pure Alpha and All-Weather portfolios in custom-tailored ways. Academics call the combination of alpha and beta strategies portable alpha, and it combines the best features of both efficient and inefficient markets. Clients can pick the beta exposure they want through the All-Weather strategy and combine it with the Pure Alpha strategy.

> Bridgewater is a leader in an area of portfolio management known as risk parity. The standard institutional portfolio is about 60% stocks and 40% bonds. But more than 80% of the risk is tied up in

stocks. Risk parity aims to level the risk of each asset class and can be applied to other asset classes on a global basis. The end result is a more risk-balanced portfolio.

- ○ Giving stocks a smaller weight or hedging some of the equity exposure—either through derivatives or short sales—can lower equity risk.

- ○ Borrowing or taking on more credit exposure could increase the bond-related risk.

Dalio's Principles

> Employees are encouraged to engage in constructive criticism. Even a first-year analyst has the ability to constructively criticize Dalio—supposedly without fear of retribution. And virtually all meetings at Bridgewater are recorded, and freely available to all employees. Although the culture might work for Dalio and many

Bridgewater employees, it doesn't work for everyone. About A quarter of Bridgewater's new employees are reported not to make it to the 1-1/2 year point with the firm.

> Dalio's handbook, Principles, was originally meant for Bridgewater's employees, but when the financial press heard about it and some stories started depicting Bridgewater as a hedge fund cult, Dalio responded by making Principles available to anyone via the Internet. He stresses that a fundamental principle of the firm's culture is thinking for oneself—the opposite of cult-like behavior.

> Dalio's management principles revolve around a culture where it is acceptable to make mistakes but unacceptable to not identify, analyze, and learn from them, where opinions are stress-tested, and where reality is faced head-on.

> Bridgewater trades a large number of models across many different types of products and global markets, and some important information about investing can be gleaned from the way Dalio and his colleagues look at the markets. According to Dalio, Bridgewater's trading system is 99% systematized, or model based.

> Neither Dalio nor his employees follow a discretionary approach, but he is a big believer in the idea of evolution. In the context of investing, his systems evolve as they gain experience, enabling Bridgewater to add or change rules.

  ○ For example, Dalio looks at how changes in oil prices affect countries. Between the first and second oil shocks during the 1970s, crude oil was discovered in the North Sea. Dalio noted that this oil find enabled the United Kingdom to go from being a net importer of oil to a net exporter. So his models would be updated when the facts change.

> In Bridgewater's early years, Dalio kept a journal of his trades, writing down his reasons for entering or exiting a position on a

pad of paper. When he closed a transaction, he would look at what actually happened, and compare it with his reasoning and expectations when he put on the trade—an early approach he took to learning from his mistakes—but it is inefficient compared to what a computer can do with a process known as back testing.

> Back testing is testing an investment strategy against historical data on how it would have performed in the past. There are two potential problems with back testing.

  ○ One is that when something new occurs, no historical data are available to use as a reference point.

  ○ The second is finding patterns or rules that appear to work but are simply due to chance. Statisticians call this spurious correlation. Some techniques can reduce spurious correlation, but it can never be eliminated.

> In creating the Bridgewater system, Dalio and his team focus on models that they believe are universal and timeless. The firm tests these models over long periods—hundreds of years if the data are available—and across many countries, emerging and industrialized alike.

> Bridgewater's computer models focus on fundamental analysis, rather than technical analysis. Fundamental analysis looks at financial ratios, valuation levels, credit spreads, inflation, central bank policy, and the like, while technical analysis looks at changes in price and volume data.

> His Bridgewater strategies now have about 15 uncorrelated return streams Dalio believes that these streams can turn a profit no matter what happens to the overall market. Dalio focuses on the return streams, or drivers, first. He says that drivers are the cause, and that correlations are the consequence of observed actions.

> Two randomly selected U.S. stocks will correlate historically at about 60%, since both are probably tied to the performance of the U.S. economy. Dalio finds that a portfolio of about 15 strategies with close to zero correlation reduces portfolio risk by about 80% against a basket of U.S. stocks like the S&P 500.

> Dalio and his team trade in about 150 different markets around the world. Markets to Dalio mean not only different asset classes—like stocks, bonds, currencies, and derivative exchanges—but also spread positions, long in one security and short in another.

> The firm wants to be sure it's not overweighted in any market. Therefore, it trades in virtually every liquid market available, and the amount it trades in each market tends to be small in relation to the total size of the market. Bridgewater generally holds its positions for a year to a year and a half, so that the firm can gradually enter and exit positions.

Conclusion

> One of the unique things about Ray Dalio is his intense focus on learning from his mistakes. He thinks that anyone who has made money in the markets has also experienced the tremendous pain of a terrible mistake and that pain can be a catalyst for growth: The same mistakes are then less likely to be repeated.

> Dalio's focus on the macro helped him avoid losses during the Great Recession, and his focus on uncorrelated return streams is an important part of his funds' risk-control process. Until recently, his Pure Alpha Fund had experienced only 2 down years in its 20-plus years of existence.

> Bridgewater's culture very likely contributes to the firm's stellar results. Dalio says the culture of the firm is to seek truth by encouraging independent thinking and innovation in an environment of radical transparency, meaning that people hold

each other to high standards and are completely honest with each other while still being extremely considerate.

Suggested Reading

Dalio, *Principles.*
Schwager, *Hedge Fund Market Wizards.*

Questions to Consider

1. How would you describe the investment strategy of Ray Dalio?

2. What role does culture play in the success of Bridgewater Associates, according to Ray Dalio?

17

Transcript

Bridgewater's Multi-Strategy Investing

Ray Dalio was born on August 1, 1949, in the Jackson Heights section of Queens, New York. He was an only child, raised by a stay-at-home mom, and a jazz musician father who played the clarinet, piccolo, flute, and saxophone. When Ray was eight, the Dalio family moved to the Manhasset section of Long Island—about 20 miles from midtown Manhattan. His father's talent for music was influential on Ray. And finance and music—jazz, blues, and rock and roll—became his greatest passions. Ray once said, "The markets are my instrument."

Like many boys, Ray Dalio shoveled snow and mowed lawns to earn extra money. And at the age of 12—when he was a caddy at an exclusive Long Island golf club—Dalio used some of his earnings to buy his first stock, Northeast Airlines. He did this through his father's broker. Dalio says he bought the airline stock because it was the only one he'd heard of that was selling for less $5 a share on the New York Stock Exchange. He got lucky when the company was acquired in short order, and he tripled his money.

Behavioral scientists who specialize in finance describe the experience of succeeding early in a risky, or uncertain, field as the house-money effect. If your early experience is good, you're more likely to stick with it, and take on the associated risks. Investment success, to a great extent, depends on the ability to deal with risks in the face of uncertainty. The opposite case is called the snakebite effect. If your early experience is bad, you're less likely to continue and less willing to take on the associated risks.

Dalio kept investing, and by the time he graduated from high school he had a portfolio worth several thousand dollars. That was pretty good money for a teenager. But he wasn't a great student. So, when it came time to pick a college, he stayed close to home, attending Long Island University. There, Dalio branched out from stocks to trade futures contracts on commodities. Futures contracts offer investors the opportunity to trade with a lot of leverage—or borrowed money. Dalio managed to become a strong and focused student at Long Island University, which helped him gain admission to Harvard Business School to pursue an MBA. During the summer after his first year at Harvard, Dalio interned as a commodities trader at Merrill Lynch. And, while finishing his master's program, Dalio and some friends set up a commodities trading shop by the name of Bridgewater Associates. That venture never took off. But Dalio held onto the Bridgewater name.

After getting his MBA, Dalio worked as a trader, first at a small, but well-regarded, investment bank known as Dominick and Dominick, with a history dating back to 1870; and then at Shearson Hayden Stone, which was headed by future Citigroup CEO Sandy Weil. Dalio didn't like the corporate culture at Shearson and reportedly came to blows with his department head at a New Year's Eve party. He left Shearson, with some of his commodities trading clients in tow, and launched Bridgewater Associates out of the spare bedroom in his Manhattan apartment. He was 26 years old, at the time. Today, Dalio runs the largest hedge fund in the world.

Bridgewater, with offices in Westport, Connecticut, has a unique—and almost cult-like—culture. But regardless of how you characterize the firm, it works for Dalio and Bridgewater investors. Today, Dalio is among the richest people in the world, with a net worth in excess of $15 billion. And he and his team manage more than $150 billion in assets. In this lecture, we'll examine the academic foundation of some of Ray Dalio's investment strategies, along with Bridgewater's unique hedge fund culture; and how these qualities have played an important role in Bridgewater's investment success over the years. Bridgewater's focus falls under the umbrella known as global macro and multi-strategy. Global macro means the firm searches around the world for investment opportunities. Multi-strategy means it doesn't follow a single strategy—such as stock picking—but instead a range of strategies, both long and short, with a variety of financial instruments.

Dalio attributes at least part of his success to transcendental meditation, a discipline he claims to have practiced daily since 1968. Dalio was a huge fan of The Beatles. So, after they studied with the Maharishi Mahesh Yogi in India in 1967, he thought there might be some value in transcendental meditation for him, too. "Meditation," says Dalio, "leads to openness, to freedom, where a kind of intuition just comes through." He says, "The emotions are the same, but you can step back and say, I'm not going to be controlled by that emotion, and I think it then helps to see things at a higher level." Dalio's philosophy is spelled out in a self-published, 100-plus page handbook called Principles, which is given to all new employees. It's freely available for download on the Internet. And if you work at Bridgewater, you must be prepared to follow these more than 200 principles closely—and also be open to scab-picking reviews of yourself and your peers.

Bridgewater has two main funds, Pure Alpha and All Weather. Alpha is a term professional investors and academics use to mean outperformance, that is, superior performance relative to a certain benchmark, or, on a market risk-adjusted basis. For example, if you're managing a U.S. equity portfolio that returns 12% from the large companies that you invest in, and the Standard & Poor's 500 index of large companies returns 10%, your alpha would be 2%. The higher the alpha, the better. Often, you hear the terms alpha and beta hand in hand. Beta is the measure of the amount of market risk of a stock or portfolio. The higher the beta, the greater the upside when the market goes up, as well as the greater the downside when the market goes down.

Bridgewater's Pure Alpha fund historically has provided a return of about 13% per year, after fees. This compares to the S&P 500, which returned about 10% a year over a comparable period. And the Pure Alpha Fund did it with less risk, or a low beta, compared to the market. Bridgewater's All Weather fund is a different product designed to withstand any market environment. Dalio breaks his All Weather strategy into four quadrants, driven by two factors, growth and inflation. Perhaps the best quadrant for the financial markets is high growth and low inflation. The worst is probably low growth and high inflation. The other quadrants are high growth and high inflation, and low growth and low inflation.

But the All Weather fund is managed by using trading models that historically have worked in each of the four quadrants. So, regardless of the general state of the economy and financial markets, usually at least something is working well in this portfolio. For example, when stocks are down, gold and U.S. Treasuries are often up. Another unique factor at Bridgewater is that the firm lets its clients combine Pure Alpha and All Weather portfolios in custom-tailored ways. Academics call the combination of alpha and beta strategies portable alpha. Here's how it works.

Let's say there are two markets out there, one that is hard to beat and one that is easy to beat. Academics call the hard-to-beat market efficient, and the easy-to-beat market inefficient. For the sake of argument, let's call the U.S. large-cap equity market efficient, and the Australian stock market as inefficient. Suppose you are a U.S. pension fund manager, and your equity benchmark is the S&P 500. You can throw your hands up and say that consistently beating the S&P 500 is impossible, and so put your money in an index fund. Or, you could pull out your portable alpha card and do the following.

First, you can get exposure to the S&P 500 through a futures contract that basically tracks the market. All you need to do is pay a small fee, on a percentage of assets basis, and keep your portfolio of securities as collateral, in order to buy the futures contract. The collateral could consist of any marketable securities, including the Australian stocks. Since the Australian stock market, in our example, is inefficient, let's assume our portfolio of Australian stocks outperforms the Australian stock market index, the ASX, by 5% over the course of the year. Just buying Australian stocks is too risky since there could be a crash in this smaller market. So we need to hedge our exposure to Australian stocks. This hedging is usually accomplished by selling a futures contract on the ASX.

Once again, the Australian securities you bought, your long position, can act as collateral for the futures contract. Your alpha from your Australian portfolio is the return of the Australian stocks minus the return of the ASX, again 5%. The net result of this series of trades is to have the return of the S&P 500—the beta—from the futures contract plus the alpha from the Australian market. So, you have ported the Alpha from Australia over to the U.S Market. Hence the term portable alpha.

Bridgewater is a leader in another area of portfolio, or risk, management, as well, known as risk parity. The standard institutional portfolio is about 60% stocks and 40% bonds. But more than 80% of the risk in this 60/40 portfolio is tied up in stocks. Risk parity aims to level the risk of each asset class. So, in the stock/bond example, you can lower your equity risk by giving stocks a smaller weight, or by hedging some of the equity exposure—either through derivatives or short sales that is, a bet on declining prices. You could also increase the bond-related risk with borrowings, or by taking on more credit exposure. The concept of risk parity can be applied to other asset classes on a global basis. The end result is a more risk-balanced portfolio.

Dalio's thoughts on risk are rooted in personal experience. In Jack Schwager's book, *The Hedge Fund Market Wizards: How Winning Traders Win*, Dalio recounts a harrowing story that helped shape his risk management philosophy. It was the early 1970s, and he was long futures contracts in pork bellies, which are used in making bacon. Going long means you are a buyer, and an owner, rather than a seller. In the futures market, given the leverage involved, prices generally can't fall 50% overnight. There are price limits for each futures contract, generally about 10% a day. After this limit is hit, the contracts stop trading until the next day. This kind of market time out is done to try to limit investor panic as well as to help protect the solvency of the exchange.

Dalio's pork bellies trade went limit down several days in a row, leaving him with the fear of being wiped out. This brush with bankruptcy taught him more about risk and the importance of diversification than he believes a Ph.D. in Finance could. He said

> The pork bellies trade taught me the importance of risk controls because I never wanted to experience that pain again. It enhanced my fear of being wrong and taught me to make sure that no single

bet, or even multiple bets, could cause me to lose more than an acceptable amount.

In Schwager's *Hedge Fund Market Wizards* book, he titled the chapter on Dalio "The Man Who Loves Mistakes." Employees are encouraged to engage in constructive criticism. Even a first-year analyst has the ability to constructively criticize Dalio—supposedly without fear of retribution. And virtually all meetings at Bridgewater are recorded, and freely available to all employees. Although the culture might work for Dalio and many Bridgewater employees, it doesn't work for everyone. About a quarter of Bridgewater's new employees are reported not to make it to the 1-1/2 year point with the firm.

Dalio's Handbook on Principles was originally meant for Bridgewater's employees. But when the financial press heard about it—and some stories started to depict Bridgewater as a hedge fund cult—Dalio responded by making Principles available to anyone. He stresses that a fundamental principle of the firm's culture is thinking for one's self—the opposite of cult-like behavior. The handbook has three parts. The first is on the purpose and importance of principles.

The second explains Dalio's most fundamental life principles, applying to everything he does. And the third part explains his management principles as they are practiced at Bridgewater. Here's a sampling, Dalio says that he has always worked for what he wanted, and not what others wanted of him. The principle left Dalio with the feeling that he wasn't forced to do anything. He was doing what was naturally in his self-interest. But, part of having confidence in an investment decision was to see it criticized by others. So Dalio would solicit the best independent opinions he could muster. If his argument still held water afterward, he would have greater confidence in his choice. He calls this approach stress testing his opinions.

Dalio also remains wary about being overconfident and recognizes that all investments engender some uncertainty. So he decided that he would gather information until most of his uncertainty went away. And if the uncertainty didn't go away, he would try to eliminate his exposure to the investment. Dalio calls his most fundamental principle "Truth—or more precisely, an accurate understanding of reality as essential for producing good outcomes."

And Dalio has a basic equation for happiness. He says, Reality + Dreams + Determination = A successful life. Dalio says there are five major choices that individuals have to make, and they can be summarized in two words, I believe. He says,

> You can probably get what you want out of life if you suspend your ego and take a no-excuses approach to achieving your goals with open-mindedness, determination, and courage, especially if you rely on the help of people who are strong in areas that you are weak.

So Dalio's management principles revolve around a culture where it is acceptable to make mistakes, but unacceptable to not identify, analyze, and learn from them.

Some of Dalio's best investment decisions were learned in practice, during times of market crisis. He says, "You can read about what happened after Mexico defaulted on its debt, but it is not the same thing as being in the market and actually experiencing it." If you're managing a huge amount of money like Bridgewater does, you can't put everything in one model or product. Bridgewater trades a large number of models across many different types of products and global markets. But, some important information about investing can be gleaned from the way that Dalio and his colleagues look at the markets. He says that his trading system is 99% systematized, or model based. So neither Dalio nor his employees follow a discretionary approach, with the proverbial genius trader shooting from the hip. That said—and as noted in Dalio's discussion of Principles—he is a big believer in the idea of evolution.

In the context of investing, his systems evolve as they gain experience, enabling Bridgewater to add or change rules. For example, Dalio looks at how changes in oil prices affect countries. Between the first and second oil shocks during the 1970s, crude oil was discovered in the North Sea. Dalio noted that this oil find enabled the United Kingdom to go from being a net importer of oil to a net exporter. So his models would be updated when the facts change. Where human discretion may play a role in trading is when something happens that has never, or rarely, happened before—like the market shutting down for a week after the 9/11 terror attacks in Manhattan. And in those rare instances, the decision typically is to reduce portfolio risk, rather than making an off-the-cuff investment decision.

In Bridgewater's early years, Dalio kept a journal of his trades, writing down his reasons for entering or exiting a position on a pad of paper. When he closed a transaction, he would look at what actually happened, and compare it with his reasoning and expectations when he put on the trade. This was an early approach that he took to learning from his mistakes. A trading journal provides important insight to one man's thinking, but it is inefficient compared to what a computer can do with a process known as backtesting. Backtesting is pretty much what it sounds like. You come up with an investment strategy, and then test how it would have performed in the past, based on historical data. There are two potential problems with backtesting. One is that when something new occurs, there is no historical data to use as a reference point.

The second problem is finding patterns or rules that appear to work, but that are simply due to chance. Statisticians call this spurious correlation. For example, a lot of sports players have superstitions, such as a baseball pitcher being careful to not step on the foul line on his way to and from the dugout. There's probably no relationship between stepping on a line of chalk dusk and pitching performance, but you can't convince some people of this point. There are some techniques that can be used to reduce spurious correlation, but it can never be completely eliminated. For example, you should be able to logically explain the relationship between two variables before testing it. The logical relationship may be based on widely accepted theories or personal experience.

It's easy to see how this approach might work when valuing a bond. Bond prices move in an inverse relationship to interest rates. That is, when interest rates go up, bonds fall in price. The logic is that when interest rates go up, the bond is riskier, and therefore the price should fall. In creating the Bridgewater system, Dalio and his team focus on models that they believe are universal and timeless. The firm tests these models over long periods of time, and across many countries, emerging and industrialized, alike. And by long periods of time, Dalio means hundreds of years—if the data are available.

His computer models focus on fundamental analysis, rather than technical analysis. Fundamental analysis looks at financial ratios, valuation levels, credit spreads, inflation, central bank policy, and the like, while technical analysis looks at changes in price and volume data. Dalio believes there is an art to constructing a portfolio. Perfecting this art is something he calls the holy grail of investing. His Bridgewater strategies now have about 15 uncorrelated return streams.

Correlation is a statistical measure of how two things move together. It is a number between positive one and negative one. Things that always move in lockstep are positive one. Things that move in the exact opposite direction have a correlation of negative one. Things that move in a totally random fashion have a correlation of zero.

Getting back to Dalio's 15 uncorrelated return streams, he thinks his strategy can turn a profit no matter what happens to the overall market. That's why he calls it the holy grail of investing. Dalio focuses on return streams, or drivers, first. He says that drivers are the cause and the correlations are the consequence of observed actions. By return streams, Dalio can be referring to any of many different investment indices, including the returns of the stock market, the returns of the bond market, or the spread between various financial instruments, such as U.S. Treasury Bond yields and Corporate Bond yields.

If you take two randomly selected U.S. stocks, their correlation historically averages out to about 50 or 60%. They have a high positive correlation since both are probably tied to the performance of the U.S. economy. Dalio finds that a portfolio of about 15 strategies with close to zero correlation reduces portfolio risk by about 80% against a basket of U.S. stocks like the S&P 500.

Now, you might think it would be hard to find 15 or so strategies that are uncorrelated. But Dalio and his team trade in about 150 markets around the world. Markets to Dalio mean not only different asset classes—like stocks, bonds, currencies, and derivative exchanges—but also spread positions, where you take a long position in one security and a short position in another. Given Bridgewater's size, the firm wants to be sure it's not too big, or overweighted, in any one market. So they trade in virtually every liquid market available to them. And the amount they trade in each market tends to be small in relation to total equity, or size, of the market. They also aren't a rapid-trading firm. Bridgewater generally holds its positions for a year to a year and a half, so that the firm can gradually enter and exit positions.

Dalio's background in global macro paid off during the 2008 global market meltdown. Sometime in 2006, Bridgewater analysts estimated that personal, corporate, and government debt was running out of control and that the global economy was heading towards a major economic contraction driven by a credit crunch, or a cutback in lending. Dalio's team looked at prior debt reduction or deleveraging episodes, including those in Germany in 1920s, the Great Depression during the 1930s, Latin America in 1980s, and Japan in the 1990s. This analysis led Bridgewater to overweight its positions in U.S. Treasuries, gold, and the Japanese Yen— traditional safe-haven trades. Bridgewater's Pure Alpha Fund gained 9 ½ percent in 2008, while U.S. and global stock markets fell by 35% or more. Dalio shared his perspective on the global economy in a 30-minute video he narrated and is posted on YouTube. It's called, "How the Economic Machine Works: A Template for Understanding What is Happening Now." It's been viewed more than 2.7 million times.

Ray Dalio and his colleagues at Bridgewater made more money for investors than any other hedge fund on the planet in recent decades. But if you're thinking about being a Bridgewater client, you can probably forget about it. The firm is essentially closed to outside investors. Instead, it serves institutions—like pension funds and sovereign wealth funds— almost exclusively. Even when its funds were open to the public, the firm focused on institutional investors with at least $5 billion in assets.

Even so, we might all be able to learn something from Ray Dalio's successes. One of the most unique things about him is his intense focus on learning from his mistakes. He thinks that anyone who has made money in the market has also experienced tremendous pain at some point in their lives and that this pain can be used as a catalyst for growth since the same mistakes are less likely to be repeated. Dalio also says the biggest mistake investors make is that something that happened in the recent past is likely to persist. They assume that something was a good investment in the recent past is still a good investment.

Dalio's focus on the macro the forest rather than the trees, so to speak, is important. It helped him avoid losses during The Great Recession. And his focus on non-correlated return streams, or investment factors, is also an important part of his funds' risk-control process. Until recently, his Pure Alpha Fund had experienced only two down years in its 20 years of existence.

And Bridgewater's culture, despite its quirkiness, very likely contributed to the firm's stellar results. Dalio says that the culture of the firm is to seek truth by encouraging independent thinking and innovation in an environment of radical transparency. He says this means that "People hold each other to high standards and are completely honest with each other while still being extremely considerate." In other words, Dalio believes that ideas that are poked, prodded, and stress tested improves the chance they will really work.

18

Paul Tudor Jones,
Futures Market Seer

A way to think about futures contracts is the hedging principle. If you own something—in the way that Exxon owns oil—you can hedge your ownership of the physical commodity by selling futures contracts against the same product, essentially locking in today's value and protecting against any decline. Conversely, if you need something in your supply chain—like Starbucks needs coffee—you can hedge against a future price increase in the commodity, and therefore your cost of restocking, by buying coffee futures today.

Futures Fundamentals

> In the United States, futures markets emerged in the mid-1800s, mainly as a way to help farmers hedge their risks against the uncertainty of prices. A futures contract during the spring could lock in the price a farmer would get after selling his crops in the fall. Most futures contracts expire within 9 months. This is not a coincidence, as the agreements originally were closely tied to the farming cycle.

> Futures contracts tend to be very large; futures contracts on the S&P 500 are for 250 times the value of the index. Thus, if the

S&P 500 is trading at a level of 2000, the face value of the futures contract is $500,000. Investors typically must put down a deposit, called margin, of between 10% and 25% of the face, or notional, value. The less volatile contracts, like Treasury bills, require a lower margin. The more volatile contacts, like oil and gas, require larger margins.

> Every day, the exchange and your broker update the market price of your investment and compare it to the margin, a practice called marking to market, to ensure that you have enough equity to maintain the contract. If the market goes against you, you receive a margin call, which requires additional contribution of capital to maintain the contracted margin. Otherwise, your position will automatically be closed.

> The intermediary in the commodities exchange that makes sure the trading goes smoothly from start to finish is the clearinghouse. It guarantees that the contracts will be honored should an investor default.

- Suppose you bought a futures contract for 1000 barrels of oil, and have no interest in taking physical delivery of the petroleum product. You could enter into another contract to sell 1000 barrels of oil on the same expiration date. Since your net purchase—or delivery—of oil is zero, the trade is settled according to the exchange.

> When you enter into a futures contract, the price is locked in for the life of that contract. But the market price changes every day, so the potential profit on a long (or purchase) contract in the futures market equals the today's price less the contracted price. If there are differences in the value of the contacts, they must settled in cash.

> Futures contracts, in aggregate, are informative about what the market thinks the price of commodities will be in the future. Mapping out the prices of all these different contracts on a graph produces the futures curve. Some other factors go into futures pricing, but the futures curve provides a good indication of the market's expectations of prices in the future.

Paul Tudor Jones

> Paul Tudor Jones was born September 28, 1954, in Memphis. His father was a lawyer who attended the University of Virginia Law School and encouraged his son to attend UVA as well. He majored in economics. Two weeks after he graduated, an uncle introduced Jones to a legendary commodities trader named Eli Tullis, who had a special talent for the cotton futures market.

> Jones went to work for Tullis as a trading clerk in New Orleans. One lesson he learned under the older master was to stay calm. But New Orleans is, of course, also home to Mardi Gras, the New Orleans Jazz Fest, the Sugar Bowl, the New Orleans Saints, and the French Quarter of bars and restaurants.

> Jones enjoyed the nightlife of New Orleans a little too much. His job was to man the phones during trading hours and call in

the cotton quotes he got from New York to Tullis's office in New Orleans. But, after partying with his friends late one night, Jones said he fell asleep at work the next day. He recalls Tullis using a ruler to pry his chin off his chest, and when he woke up, Tullis said, "Son, you are fired."

> Though getting fired was a painful experience, Jones learned from it and developed a legendary work ethic. He routinely worked 80 hours a week early in his career. He landed a job as a floor trader at the New York Cotton Exchange and then became a commodities broker for the Wall Street brokerage, E. F. Hutton. At age 25, he became the firm's youngest vice president.

> He decided to begin trading full-time for his own account in 1980, when he formed Tudor Investment. Jones says he enjoyed 2.5 very profitable years but got bored. He decided to build up his own firm, instead and, in 1983, he started managing other people's money at Tudor.

Jones's Trading Strategies

> Jones made most of his money with technical analysis, which relies on historical patterns in price and volume data in the belief they have some predictive value. A simple technique that Jones uses is called a moving average, which averages a stock's data over different time periods and has the benefit of smoothing out erratic data. A stock trading above its moving average is considered bullish, while a stock trading below its moving average is considered bearish.

> Jones uses the 200-day moving average of closing prices. By keeping an eye on the 200-day moving average, an investor can sell quickly if the trend is down. Jones advises never averaging losers. In other words, if a position starts losing money, either sell or wait for the trade to be profitable before adding more capital.

> In addition to technical analysis and his own personal investing principles, Jones also employs fundamental analysis: examining such factors as earnings, interest rates, and industry gossip. Keeping up with price and volume data helped Jones developed a keen understanding of his own personal psychology as well as a broader sense of market psychology. Jones also attributes a good part of his success to strong risk management. He says, "Every day I assume every position I have is wrong."

> Jones says that a target investment's low valuation (or price) is not, by itself, a sufficient risk-management technique to guard against losses. He uses a number of techniques to reduce risk. One is to make use of stop-loss orders. Rather than enter formal stop loss orders into a brokerage's trading system—where they might be viewed by other investors—Jones uses mental stop-loss. If that number is hit, he gets out no matter what.

> Jones also decreases trading volume when things are going poorly and advises others never to trade in situations where they have no control, such as trading in advance of a company's earnings report or a Federal Reserve announcement.

> As his hedge fund got bigger, Jones also came to look closely at the liquidity of his positions. Large investors can move the market on their own with their buying and selling behavior, a dynamic called market impact.

Conclusion

> Jones's trade right before the stock market crash of 1987, when he shorted stock futures tied to the S&P 500 index, actually went against his main approach of following the trend, and it's interesting from several perspectives.

> The stock market had traded sideways from 1968 to 1981 before moving into a long bull market for much of the 1980s. Then, in late 1986, one of Jones's colleagues—Peter Borash—superimposed

a graph of the 1929 market atop recent market behavior. The patterns looked eerily similar. Jones was convinced that stocks were substantially overvalued.

> The market had more recently experienced a near-term peak in August 1987. Stocks were up 44% over the previous 12 months, and the price-to-earnings ratio of the S&P 500 index was a pricey 23 to 1—well above its long-term average of 15.

> Then, on October 13, 1987, at the end of a long wave of mergers and acquisitions funded by low-grade corporate debt, known as junk bonds, the House Ways and Means Committee took up a major piece of financial legislation. The legislation proposed to limit interest deductions on debt that financed corporate takeovers, as well as other financial engineering, such as leveraged buyouts.

> Although potential explanations for the turn that the stock market was about to take were many, major stock indexes fell 10% over the next 3 days: Wednesday, October 14, through Friday, October 16. That was the biggest 3-day decline since May 1940, when German forces broke through French lines.

> Jones was particularly worried about an investment strategy called portfolio insurance, which was in wide use at the time. This strategy uses derivatives to help hedge the risk of a portfolio and includes a trend-following component.

> No news story or rumor had circulated on Friday, October 19— or over the weekend—sufficient to rattle the markets. Even so, a great deal of anxiety permeated the markets, and while buyers and sellers alike believed the market was overvalued, they also were confident that they could predict—or stay ahead—of the market.

> On Monday, October 19, 1987, the Dow Jones Industrial Average plunged a record 508 points, or 22.6%, on the largest trading volume in history. (The Dow's biggest drop previously had been

the 12.8% decline on October 28, 1929, known famously as Black Tuesday.)

> Jones made special efforts to safeguard, or conceal, his positions, but it doesn't cost much to trade, and Jones would pay the transaction costs to safeguard the confidentiality of key trades. It's been reported that he was up 62% in the month of October 1987.

Suggested Reading

Jones, "Perfect Failure."
Schwager, *The Market Wizards*.

Questions to Consider

1. How would you describe the investment strategy of Paul Tudor Jones?

2. How does investing in futures differ from stock or bond investing?

18

Transcript

Paul Tudor Jones, Futures Market Seer

Paul Tudor Jones manages more than $30 billion through his hedge fund firm, Tudor Investment Corporation, in Greenwich, Connecticut. More than $4 billion of it is Jones's own money, making him one of the richest investors in the world. Jones made his reputation as a futures trader. Futures stake a financial claim today on what you think is going to happen tomorrow. It's fairly easy to lose a lot of money predicting the future. And Jones hates losing money. So he looks for trades with tremendously skewed risk-to-reward opportunities, specifically, five-to-one. He says, "Five-to-one means I'm risking one dollar to make five. What five-to-one does is allow you to have a hit ratio of 20%. I can be actually a complete imbecile. I can be wrong 80% of the time, and I'm still not going to lose."

Of course, finding those returns is extremely difficult. But one illustration is Jones's trade right before the stock market crash of 1987, when he shorted stock futures tied to the Standard & Poor's 500 index of large corporations. Shorting allows you to profit from the decline of a security. It involves selling first and buying back later—hopefully at a lower price. The 1987 trade that made Jones famous actually went against his main approach of following or trading with the trend. And it's interesting from several perspectives.

You see, the stock market basically traded sideways from 1968–1981 before moving into a long bull market for much of the 1980s. And then, in late 1986, one of Jones's colleagues—Peter Borash—superimposed a graph of the 1929 market atop recent market behavior. And the patterns looked eerily similar. Jones was convinced that stocks were substantially overvalued. In this session, we'll examine Jones's background and his investment strategy. Along the way, we'll also learn something about the futures markets, technical analysis, and market psychology. And we'll return to finish the story about October 1987.

In the United States, futures markets emerged in the mid-1800s mainly as a way to help farmers hedge their risks against the uncertainty of prices. In this example, a futures contract during the spring could lock in the price a farmer would get after selling his crops in the fall. Here's another way to think about futures contracts. I call it the hedging principle. If you own something—in the way that Exxon owns oil—you can hedge your ownership of the physical commodity by selling futures contracts against the same product, essentially locking in today's value and protecting against any decline.

Conversely, if you need something in your supply chain—like Starbucks needs coffee—you can hedge against a future price increase in the commodity, and therefore your cost of restocking, by buying coffee futures today. Most futures contracts expire within nine months. This is not a coincidence, as the agreements originally were closely tied to the farming cycle. And futures contracts tend to be very large. So, you may end up borrowing to take a much larger position—one of those five-to-one reward-to-risk opportunities that Paul Tudor Jones likes so much.

For example, each oil future contract is for a thousand barrels. Wheat and corn futures contracts are for 5000 bushels. Treasury futures have a face or notional value of $1 million. Futures contracts on the S&P 500 are for 250 times the value of the index. So, if the S&P 500 is trading at a level of 2000, the notional value of the futures contract is $500,000. Investors typically have to put down a deposit, called margin, of anywhere from 10% to 25% of the face, or notional, value of the contract. A 10% deposit on a $1 commitment puts the trader's leverage at 10-to-1. A 25% margin gives the trader a potential return of 4-to-1. By way of comparison, most brokerage accounts enable investors to trade stocks with leverage of only two-to-one. So, in futures contracts, the large amount of leverage available makes it a relatively cheap way to hedge—or speculate. The less-volatile contracts—like Treasury bills—require a lower margin. The more volatile contacts—like oil and gas—require larger margins.

Every day, the exchange and your broker look at your account. This is something known as marking to market, that is, updating the market price of your investment, and comparing it to the margin. And, it is part of the process of making sure you have enough equity to maintain the contract without additional margin. If the trade goes against you, you will get hit with what's known as a margin call. That means you will be asked to make an additional contribution of capital to maintain the contracted margin, whatever that is. Today, most margin calls are done via email. And when they occur, you typically have until the end of the day to deposit more money—or securities—as collateral. Otherwise, your position automatically will be closed. If you believe the market will turn back in your favor, you'll want to put up the additional capital—if you can—to avoid losing the margin that you've already posted.

The intermediary in the commodities exchange that makes sure the trading goes smoothly from start to finish is called the Clearing House. It guarantees the contracts will be honored in the event of an investor's default. The commodities exchange runs the equivalent of a racetrack, for a small fee, a tiny fraction of 1% per transaction. But the fees add up.

Suppose you bought a futures contract for 1000 barrels of oil, and have no interest in taking physical delivery of the petroleum product. Roughly 95% of futures contracts are settled without making or taking delivery, but rather by what is called reversing a trade. Using our oil-contract example, if you agreed to buy 1000 barrels of oil on a certain date, you could enter into another contract to sell 1000 barrels of oil on the same expiration date. Since your net purchase—or delivery—of oil is zero, the trade is settled according to the exchange.

Now, when you enter into a futures contract—let's say buying oil at $50 a barrel—the price of the contract is locked in for the life of that contract. But, keep in mind, the spot, or market price changes every day. So, the potential profit on a long or purchase contract in the futures market equals the spot price—today's price—less the futures price, the contracted price. If there are any differences in the value of the contracts, they have to be settled in cash. And then, you're off the hook.

So, if the spot price of oil today is $60 a barrel, and the futures price on the contract you purchased is $50 a barrel, then you could recognize a profit of $10 a barrel. And you'd multiply this $10 by the 1000 barrels stipulated in your contract, yielding a gross profit of $10,000. Conversely, the profit on a short position on a futures contract is exactly the opposite. You take the original futures price and subtract the spot price. The difference is multiplied by the contract multiplier—the 1000 barrels—to determine your gross profit or loss per contract. That's the gross. Your net position also takes into account commissions and the time value of money.

Futures contracts, in aggregate, tell us a lot about what the market thinks the price of such things, such as gold and wheat, will be in the future. There are usually futures contracts that start each month. For example, oil to be delivered or picked up in January, February, March and so forth. If you map out the prices of all these different contracts on a graph, it's called the futures curve. So, if the futures curve says that oil will be $60 a barrel six months from now, and if today oil was trading at $50 a barrel, then you can say the market thinks oil prices are going up. There are some other factors that go into futures pricing. But the futures curve provides a good rule of thumb on the market's expectations of prices in the future.

Paul Tudor Jones was born on September 28, 1954, in Memphis, Tennessee. His father, John Jones, was a lawyer who attended the University of Virginia Law School. And John encouraged his son to attend the University of Virginia as well. Paul majored in economics. He also boxed as a welterweight. Yes, boxing. With this background, he was well prepared to end up trading futures. Although the vast majority of trading is electronic these days, back then floor traders in the futures market worked in what were known as trading pits. There was a lot of screaming and pushing and shoving going on. It's no coincidence that a lot of pit traders were former football, lacrosse, or rugby players. Or in Jones's case, a boxer.

Two weeks after he graduated from the University of Virginia, an uncle introduced Jones to a legendary commodities trader named Eli Tullis, who had a special talent for trading cotton futures. Tullis also happened to be a graduate of the same university. So, Jones went to work for Tullis as a trading clerk in New Orleans. One lesson he learned under the older master was to stay calm. Jones says,

> Eli was the largest cotton speculator in the world when I went to work for him, and he was a magnificent trader. I got to watch his financial ups and downs and how he dealt with them. His fortitude and temperament in the face of great adversity were great examples of how to remain cool under fire.

But New Orleans is, of course, home to Mardis Gras, and the New Orleans Jazz Fest, the Sugar Bowl, The New Orleans Saints, and the French Quarter of bars and restaurants. Jones said his mentality at the time was still set on fraternity row, and that he enjoyed the nightlife of New Orleans a little too much. Now, Jones's job was to man the phones during trading hours and call the cotton quotes he got from New York into Tullis' office in New Orleans. But, after partying with his friends late one night, Jones said he fell asleep at work the next day. He recalls Tullis using a ruler to pry his chin off his chest. And when he woke up, Tullis said, "Son, you are fired."

The year was 1978. And Jones says,

> I've never been so shocked or hurt in my life. I literally thought I was going to die, for I had just been sacked by an iconic figure in my business. My shame turned into anger. I was angry at myself. But I knew I was not a failure and I swore that I was going to prove to myself that I could be a success.

Though getting fired was a painful experience, Jones learned from it and developed a legendary work ethic. He says he routinely worked 80 hours a week early in his career.

He also landed a job as a floor trader at the New York Cotton Exchange and then became a commodities broker for the Wall Street brokerage, E.F.

Hutton. At age 25, he became the firm's youngest vice president. But, he didn't stay for long. He says

> I got out of the brokerage business because I felt there was a gross conflict of interest, If you are charging a client commissions and he loses money, you aren't penalized. I went into the money-management business because if I lost money, I wanted to be able to say that I had not gotten compensated for it.

He decided to begin trading full-time for his own account in 1980 when he formed Tudor Investment Corporation. Jones said that he enjoyed two and a half very profitable years but got bored. He then applied to Harvard Business School and was accepted. But Jones thought that Harvard couldn't teach him anything about trading. So he decided to build up his own firm, instead. And, in 1983, he started managing other people's money at Tudor.

Some of Jones's investment philosophy is detailed in Jack Schwager's book, *The Market Wizards: Interviews With Top Traders*. Jones made most of his money with technical analysis, which relies on historical patterns in price and volume data, in the belief they have some predictive value. Many traders love technical analysis because it gives them a clear path to action, while most academics think it is worthless. Now, most technicians use trend following or momentum techniques. That is, if the recent trend has been up, they are usually buying. If the recent trend has been down, they are selling or shorting. Another less common trading strategy is betting on a reversal or mean reversion.

You can think of the concept of mean reversion as the forces behind a pendulum. When prices overshoot on the upside—due to greed, euphoria, or some other reason—they tend to fall back to earth. On the flip side, when prices overshoot on the downside, due to fear, overreaction, or some other reason, they tend to bounce back. A simple technique that Jones uses is called a moving average. It's exactly what it sounds like. You take an average of prices, but the window moves.

For example, if the price of a security three days ago was $10, and two days ago it was $12—and yesterday it was $14—then the moving average is the sum of the three numbers, 36 divided by 3, which equals 12. A moving average has the benefit of taking erratic—or jagged—data and smoothing it out. This way you don't have to flip flop on your trading decisions all the time. A stock trading above its moving average is considered bullish, while a stock trading below its moving average is considered bearish. Jones says, "My metric for everything I look at is the 200-day moving average of closing prices." He says, "You always want to be with whatever the predominant trend is." While saying that he is aware that too many things go to zero in stocks and commodities he also says that by keeping an eye on the 200-day moving average rule, then if the trend is down, you play defense, and you get out.

One more thing, like the great early 20th-century trader Jesse Livermore, Jones advises, "Don't ever average losers." In other words, if you establish a position, and it starts losing money, don't add to it. Either cut your losses or wait for the trade to be profitable, before adding more capital. Traders of Jones's ability do more than follow simple trading rules. They often have a knack for trading, a sort of sixth sense that may be derived from experience and innate skill.

In addition to technical analysis and using his own personal investing principals, Jones also employs fundamental analysis. Fundamental analysis involves looking at factors like earnings, interest rates, and talking to people in the industry. Or as Jones says, "While I spend a significant amount of my time on analytics and collecting fundamental information, at the end of the day I am a slave to the tape and proud of it."

By tape, he means ticker tape, which is how stock prices used to be disseminated to the public, before the advent of the computer. Many traders closely read the price and volume data that these machines spewed out on paper tape in order to discern trends and trading strategies. Reading the ticker tape helped Jones developed a keen understanding of his own personal psychology, as well as a broader sense of market psychology. Part of being comfortable with yourself, he says, is having no ego about past trades—especially losing ones. Jones says he is willing to make a 180-degree shift at any time.

Jones attributes a good part of his success to strong risk management. He says, "Every day I assume every position I have is wrong." He has to re-convince himself a trade is right in order to stay in it. If not, he is willing to take the opposite position. In this regard, Jones follows the famous advice of the early 20th-century financier J.P. Morgan. He said, "If you have a losing position that is making you uncomfortable, that solution is very simple, get out because you can always get back in. There is nothing better than a fresh start".

Paul Tudor Jones says that a target investment's low valuation or price is not, by itself, a sufficient risk-management technique to guard against losses. He says "Everything gets destroyed a hundred times faster than it gets built up." So, he explains,

> If something's going down, I want to be short it, and if something's going up, I want to be long it. The sweet spot is when you find something with a compelling valuation that is also just beginning to move up. That's every investor's dream.

Jones uses a number of techniques to reduce risk. One is to make use of stop-loss orders. A stop-loss order exits a position when the trade goes against you. Rather than enter formal stop loss orders into a brokerage's trading system—where they might be viewed by other investors—Jones uses mental stop-loss. If that number is hit, he gets out no matter what. Jones also decreases trading volume when things are going poorly. He increases trading volume when things are going well. And he advises others never trade in situations where you have no control. For example, trading in advance of a company's earnings report, or a Federal Reserve announcement, might illustrate an example where you have no control over what the earnings release might reveal, or what a Fed interest-rate decision might be. Jones would call that gambling, not trading.

As his hedge fund got bigger, Jones also came to look closely at the liquidity of his positions. Large investors can move the market on their own when buying or selling, a dynamic known as market impact. Jones says, "When you are trading size you have to get out when the market lets you out, not when you want to get out." For, example, it might be easier to get out on high volume trading days, like right after an earnings announcement.

Now, although Paul Tudor Jones and his partners had a graph of the 1929 stock market overlaid on the 1986 stock market, the market had more recently experienced a near-term peak in August 1987. Stocks were up 44% over the prior 12 months. And the price to earnings ratio, or P/E, of the S&P 500 index was a pricey 23-to-1—well above its long-term average of 15. P/E is measured as the price of a stock or index, divided by its earnings per share. Until then, the U.S. stock market had been valued higher only prior to the Crash of 1929, when it was at 26.

Then, on Oct. 13, 1987, the U.S. House Ways and Means Committee in Congress took up a major piece of financial legislation. This was at the end of a long wave of mergers and acquisitions, funded by low-grade corporate debt, known as junk bonds. The legislation proposed to limit interest deductions on debt that financed corporate takeovers, and other financial engineering, such as leveraged buyouts. The bill also contained explicit antitakeover provisions—which didn't survive.

Although there were many potential explanations for the turn that the stock market was about to take, and not everyone agrees with this one, as outlined in more than one academic paper, major stock indexes fell 10% over the next three days, from Wednesday, October 14, through Friday, October 16. That was the biggest three-day decline since early in World War II—in May 1940—when German forces broke through French lines. Jones took note of the record volume day on the downside on Friday, October 16, he said in a later interview "The exact same thing happened in 1929, two days before the crash."

One reason we don't know exactly what Jones did next is because he made special efforts to safeguard, or conceal, his positions. For instance, he might station several traders in each of several futures pits. Some would be buying, and some would be selling, to disguise his hand. It doesn't cost much to trade, and Jones would pay the transaction costs to safeguard the confidentiality of key trades. But, we also know that Jones was particularly worried about an investment portfolio strategy called portfolio insurance, which was widely used at the time.

This strategy uses derivatives to help hedge the risk of a portfolio. Now, portfolio insurance has a trend-following—or momentum—component to it. The strategy involves selling as stock prices fall, to preserve the equity that you have. It also advises buying as prices rise, since you can then afford to lose more. Jones says, It was a situation where you knew that if you ever got to a point where the market started to go down, that the selling would actually cascade instead of drying up. Taking the sell side of S&P 500 futures was one possible defensive position.

Robert Shiller, the Nobel Laureate Economist at Yale University, authored a working paper for the National Bureau of Economic Research that identified some of the curious trends bottled up in this overvalued market. But, he couldn't put his finger on any one market-changing behavior. Based on responses to a survey questionnaire he circulated at the time, he wrote, one, no news story or rumor had circulated on Friday, October 16—or over the weekend—sufficient to rattle the markets. Two, even so, a great deal of anxiety permeated the markets. Three, and while buyers and sellers alike believed the market was overvalued, they also were confident that they could predict—or stay ahead—of the market.

On Monday, Oct. 19, 1987, the Dow Jones Industrial Average plunged a record 508 points, or 22.6%, on the largest trading volume in history. The Dow's biggest drop previously had been a 12.8% decline on Oct. 28, 1929, known famously as Black Tuesday. At the end of the trading day, Paul Tudor Jones, looking much younger than he does today—and not altogether unhappy, all things considered—stood at the floor of the American Stock Exchange to give a rare television interview. He said, "I think that we've got a market that has been seriously overvalued for some time. I think that what we've witnessed the past couple of days has been obviously the piercing of this bubble." When asked what position he had taken in the market, Jones replied, "We've traded it heavily for the past two weeks, and that's the only comment I'll make." But he did say, "One of my favorite trades right now is going long on fear."

Jones summarizes his investment approach this way. He advises,

> It doesn't make any difference whether it's pork bellies or Yahoo!. You need to understand what factors to have at your disposal to develop a core competency to make a legitimate investment decision in that particular asset class. And then, at the end of the day, the most important thing is how good are you at risk control.

Ninety percent of any great trader is going to be the risk control. Yes, Jones has a great focus on risk control. But he's mostly known for his tremendous returns, It's been reported that he was up 62% in the month of October 1987 alone.

There was a time when the portfolio Paul Tudor Jones managed at least doubled in value for five consecutive years. And he not only for called the Crash of 1987 but also for took his firm from a startup business and turned it into a $30 billion-plus investment firm, making himself one of the richest investors in the world.

19

James Simons: Money, Math, and Computers

Quantitative analysts build financial models to estimate the value of security prices. This approach differs from fundamental analysis, which focuses on looking at a company's financials, along with its management, and factors affecting the industry, and from technical analysis, which focuses on changes in security prices and their corresponding trading volume. Quants might look at price and volume data, but also at a host of other data—including interest rates, currency values, financial statement data, and much more—to create their own quantitative models.

James Simons

> James Simons was born in 1938 in Newton, MA, a Boston suburb, and grew up in nearby Brookline. Simons demonstrated an aptitude for math at an early age, and he was drawn to the Massachusetts Institute of Technology, which he entered in 1955. Simons graduated 3 years later, with a bachelor's degree in mathematics. He went on to get a Ph.D., also in math, at the University of California, at Berkeley. He was 23 years old.

> He was recruited to be a cryptographer by the Institute for Defense Analyses, a research group affiliated with the Department of Defense; the next year, the math department at the State University of New York in Stony Brook recruited Simons to be its chair.

> But soon, the urge to apply his math skills to the financial markets began to take hold. He departed Stony Brook to form an investment company, which evolved into Renaissance Technologies.

> Its research and investment staff consists almost exclusively of mathematicians and scientists. By design, very few Renaissance employees have academic backgrounds in finance. Simons didn't want his quantitative analysts—or quants, as they are known on Wall Street—to be biased by conventional financial theories.

Quant Basics

> Almost all investment managers use some sort of quantitative analysis. Traditional fundamental managers use an investment screen to find fast-growing companies trading at reasonable valuations and with high profit margins. They might then look at the financial statements of these firms and try to meet with the management of the firms they like best before ultimately buying a stock.

> No model for quantitative analysis is perfect, especially one that is based on historical data. Sometimes something new happens that has never occurred before. Nassim Taleb, the distinguished professor of risk engineering at New York University and a former derivatives trader, coined the term black swan to describe an unforeseen and perhaps unpredictable event. A Black Swan event occurred after the terrorist attacks on the United States in September 2011: When financial markets re opened several days later, stock prices plunged. So quant models may work, but they will never be perfect.

> One widely used technique is called a factor model, which estimates the relationship between two variables. Independent variables are used to help predict dependent variables, and it's not uncommon for quant models to contain dozens of independent variables.

> Stocks go up or down for a variety of reasons, including for no reason other than general market movements. But stocks are also often impacted by specific actions, such as movements in interest rates. Rising rates, especially when they are unexpected, usually cause stock prices to fall.

> Quants often use dozens of factors in their models. Not only that, but when investing in stocks, the models may weigh these various factors differently, depending on the circumstances. Quants are also constantly updating their models with the latest data. The models make adjustments as they go along, changing to reflect this new information.

19300	19.3	8500/T	8642/T	8661/T	8730/T	8765/T	8783/T	8798/T
4055	-43.50	HK	HK	HK	HK	HK	HK	HK
2621	2571	1186	1462	1446	2514	1029	8227	2415
143.89	1041	-13	+18	-21	+18	-97	-08	+74
95.37	-181	2492/T	2514/T	2528/T	2534/T	2541/T	2553/T	2567/T
865.20	-51.50	TKY	TKY	TKY	TKY	TKY	TKY	TKY
142.30	136.89	2312	1651	1067	1929	27112	1721	1030
1991	-9.67	-09	-13	-32	-98	+65	-34	-87
37280	+1.89	4519/T	4542/T	4598/T	4602/T	4630/T	4698/T	4708/T
897.56	892.16	NY	NY	NY	NY	NY	NY	NY
351.79	326.51	1891	2019	1678	1254	1008	5761	1253
2312	-20.14	-25	-42	+16	-54	-12	-34	+46
1.25-29	29.45	1834/T	1865/T	1887/T	1899/T	1928/T	1945/T	1972/T
981.43	902.98	UK	UK	UK	UK	UK	UK	UK
103		10879	10605	1762	27.1	1933	1535	1195
5318		-1	+07	-24		-46	+24	
902	86	2519/T	256/T	2589/T		26	2698/T	27
21	19		CN	CN			CN	
72				1987			3421	
639							-43	
2534								
9716				RTS			RTS	

> Sometimes quants look for signals before making a trade, such as a spike in stock volatility, which might be indicative of market fear.

  ○ The term risk off refers to an environment in which fear pervades the market, and investors are selling assets that are traditionally risky: such as stocks, high yield bonds, and emerging market securities. In a risk off trade, safe haven assets like U.S. Treasury notes or gold often outperform.

  ○ A positive signal might be triggered by a Federal Reserve announcement that is more welcome than expected. In that case, stock prices might rise as part of the risk on trade.

> The term risk on indicates that investors are willing to increase the risk of their portfolio by purchasing more volatile securities, which they deem to have significant upside. High yield bonds and the stocks of smaller or speculative firms may also do well in a risk on environment.

> Some quants engage in high-frequency trading, a computer-driven investment strategy that emphasizes high transaction volume along with extremely short-duration positions and automated algorithms that do the buying and selling. High frequency trading programs often transact on an electronic communication network, or ECN. ECNs are basically an electronic stock exchange.

> The big fear with the quants' automated trading models is that the computer might act unpredictably and blow up the firm. And there have been instances when quant models wreaked havoc.

  ○ On August 1, 2012, Knight Trading Group fired up a new, untested computer-trading program. While attempting to fill the orders of just 212 customers, it was unable to recognize that orders had been filled. And, in some cases, it entered orders more than 1000 times their intended amounts.

- The result was 4 million unintended trades across 154 stocks totaling 397 million shares. The firm lost $460 million in 45 minutes. Knight's stock crashed, and the company was sold to another high frequency trading firm at a bargain price.

A Cautionary Tale

> Long Term Capital Management focused on arbitrage trades. The bulk of its assets were in 4 different types of trades:

   - Convergence among U.S., Japan, and European sovereign bonds.

   - Convergence among European sovereign bonds.

   - Convergence between newly issued and previously existing U.S. government bonds.

   - Long positions in emerging markets sovereign bonds, hedged back to dollars.

> The differences in the expected returns between the two baskets for each of these trades was small, usually less than 1%. Thus, in order to get an attractive return, the firm had to use leverage. Long Term Capital began trading in 1994, and, for the first few years of operations its strategy worked like clockwork. Then, in August 1998, Russia defaulted on its debt, resulting in a worldwide financial panic.

> During times of market distress, the most liquid and highest-quality assets usually perform the best. Unfortunately, Long Term Capital was short those assets that investors demanded most. The combination of illiquid assets and excessive leverage proved to be the downfall for Long Term Capital. On the hook for $30 for every $1 it had bet, a roughly 3% loss could have wiped out virtually all of the firm's capital.

> The Federal Reserve, fearing that a forced liquidation of Long Term Capital's portfolio would cause a meltdown in the global financial markets, orchestrated a meeting with some of the largest firms on Wall Street and the French banks Paribas, Credit Agricole, and the Société Generale. The Wall Street firms and the French banks collectively agreed to pool $3.625 billion in bailout funds to help Long Term Capital slowly unwind its portfolio and thereby limit broader damage to the financial markets.

> The enduring lesson of Long Term Capital is this: The smartest people on earth can lose all of their money—and their investors' money, too—when greed, overconfidence, and excessive leverage collide.

James Simons Strategy

> James Simon's strategy at Renaissance Technologies managed to steer clear of calamities on the order of Long Term Capital. Simon's Medallion Fund began trading in 1988. It did not immediately set the world on fire. Instead, it generated a peak-to-trough loss of 30% by April of 1989. Simons shuffled the fund's management team and made changes to its computer models to shorten the firm's horizons. The average holding period switched from weeks or days to intraday.

> The changes worked. Incredibly, Medallion returned 98.2% in the peak financial crisis year of 2008, when the S&P 500 fell 37%, and these returns were net of Medallion's hefty fees, which ranged as high as 5% of assets and 44% of profits.

> Medallion uses lots of models, and it trades across all asset classes, including stocks, bonds, currencies, commodities, and more. Diversification across models and asset classes is likely one reason for Medallion's success. No other fund of has been able to replicate its performance.

> When Simons stepped down as CEO in 2009, he named two super quants to succeed him: the co-CEOs Peter Brown and Robert Mercer. Back in 1993, Simons himself had hired Brown and Mercer away from IBM, where they were in charge IBM's speech-recognition group.

> It turns out that speech-recognition software has a lot in common with quantitative stock analysis. Both tasks require getting signals out of noisy data. Speech-recognition software also tries to predict what will come next, using techniques from probability theory. This type of logic can be extended to predicting security prices, though with less precision.

> Besides the raw brainpower of the quants working at Renaissance—and the terabytes of daily data that the firm collects—Simons attributes much of the organization's success to its work culture. When asked about the secret of his organization's success, he once said, "Have an open atmosphere. The best way to conduct research on a larger scale is to make sure everyone knows what everyone else is doing.

> Quants make a living exploiting market inefficiencies, or strategies that appear to consistently offer superior profits. But those who benefit from exploiting market inefficiencies often become victims of their own success.

> Since trends seem not to last, quant firms are constantly trying to update their models and replacing models that have lost their effectiveness. These models may no longer work either because they never found a true anomaly or because they worked so well as to have arbitraged away their value.

> As the Medallion fund got larger and better established, it became too big to produce the returns its investors were accustomed to. Management closed the fund to new investors, and today

manages it mostly for insiders. However, Renaissance has developed a number of new funds for investors.

> These newer funds generally have a longer time horizon and can accommodate more investor capital. For example, the Renaissance Institutional Equities Fund, or RIEF, reportedly has the capacity to handle up to $100 billion in capital.

> From RIEF's launch in September 2005, though September 2015, it returned 9.8% per year. This was better than the S&P 500 return of 6.7% per year over the same period, as well as the performance of most hedge fund indexes.

Suggested Reading

Lowenstein, *When Genius Failed.*
Patterson, *The Quants.*

Questions to Consider

1. How would you describe the investment strategy of James Simons?

2. Why might quantitative investment strategies have an advantage over more traditional stock picking strategies?

19

Transcript

James Simons: Money, Math, and Computers

James Simons was born in 1938 in Newton, Massachusetts—a Boston suburb—and he grew up in nearby Brookline. Simons demonstrated an aptitude for math at an early age. And he was drawn to the Massachusetts Institute of Technology, which he entered in 1955. Simons graduated three years later, with a bachelor's degree in mathematics. And he went on to get a Ph.D.—also in math—at the University of California, at Berkeley. He was 23 years old, at the time.

During Simons's years at Cal Berkeley, he started trading in the financial markets, mostly in commodities. He launched a career in academia, with teaching stints at MIT and Harvard. Then, he was recruited to be a cryptographer, or code breaker, by a research group affiliated with the Department of Defense. This employer is called the Institute for Defense Analysis. And the job paid better than academia while allowing Simons to work half the time on math, and half on code breaking. In case you're wondering, Simons once said that beating the market consistently was harder than code breaking.

Maxwell Taylor, who was the president of the Institute for Defense Analysis in those years, wrote an article in October 1967, in the Sunday *New York Times Magazine*, that was supportive of the Vietnam War. Simons, the young cryptographer working for him, wrote his own letter to the editor of *The New York Times* suggesting the very opposite, that U.S. withdrawal from Vietnam was probably the best policy. Criticizing your boss on the issue might not have been the best career move, especially when you worked for a Defense Department-funded think tank. Not surprisingly, the institute fired him.

The next year, the Math Department, at the State University of New York in Stony Brook, recruited Simons to be its chair. Stony Brook is located in East Setauket, Long Island—a pleasant place. And Simons liked the idea that—as department chair—he couldn't get fired again. At the university, Simons specialized in theoretical geometry, and he was already recognized as one of the top mathematicians in the country. He won geometry's top honor, the Veblen Prize, in 1975 at the age of 37. But soon after, the urge to apply his math skills to the financial markets began to take hold. He was also frustrated with a math problem he was working on. And that frustration provided further impetus for him to leave academia.

So he departed Stony Brook to form an investment company called Monemetrics, which evolved into the much better-known Renaissance Technologies. Today, Renaissance is based in Long Island, New York—with offices in San Francisco, London, and Milan. Its research and investment staff consist almost exclusively of mathematicians and scientists. And some think Renaissance has the best math and physics department in the world. On the other hand, very few Renaissance employees have academic backgrounds in finance. This is by design since Simons didn't want his quantitative analysts—or quants, as they are known on Wall Street—to be biased by conventional financial theories.

Quantitative analysts build financial models to estimate the value of security prices. This approach differs from fundamental analysis, which focuses on looking at a company's financials, along with its management, and factors affecting the industry. It also differs from technical analysis, which focuses on changes in security prices and their corresponding trading volume. Quants might look at price and volume data, but also a host of other data—including interest rates, currency values, financial statement data, and much more—to create their own quantitative models. At the same time, the modelers might not even be able to tell you what the company does, or who runs it. And they probably don't care. They are mainly interested in finding patterns that repeat themselves, patterns they can profit from.

Let's talk a little more about how quants go about their business. Almost all investment managers use some sort of quantitative analysis. Some screening process is needed to reduce the universe of about 5000 stocks, that trade on U.S. exchanges, alone. So, traditional fundamental managers use an investment screen to find maybe fast-growing companies, trading at reasonable valuations, and with high profit margins. They might then look at the financial statements of these firms, and try to meet with the management of the firms they like best, before ultimately buying a stock. The typical quant approach is different and I'll get to it in more detail in a moment. No model for quantitative analysis is perfect, especially one that is based on historical data. Sometimes something new happens that has never occurred before.

Nassim Taleb, the distinguished professor of risk engineering at New York University, and a former derivatives trader coined the term Black Swan to describe an unforeseen and perhaps unpredictable event. And he wrote a book about it called, *The Black Swan: The Impact of the Highly Improbable*. The story behind the title is this. For many years, people thought swans that were only white. Then, people noticed black-colored swans in a remote area of Australia. Taleb drew on the example to explain a Black Swan event as risky, unexpected—and in financial markets—resulting in huge losses.

A Black Swan event occurred after the terrorist attacks on the United States in September 2001. When financial markets re-opened several days later, on September 17, stock prices plunged. Airline stocks, for instance, fell by about half. Another example of a Black Swan event is related to the Housing and Credit Crisis of 2008. Other than during the Great Depression, perhaps, home prices had never previously fallen at the national level. Local and regional real estate markets were correlated very little. So, if you had an asset that never falls, it could support an almost unlimited amount of leverage or borrowing.

Well, we know what happened. Home prices plummeted, financial firms collapsed, and the government put the American taxpayer on the hook to help bail out others. So quant models may work, but they will never be perfect. They will always have flaws. Now that notwithstanding, quants do have a lot of tools in their toolboxes.

One widely used technique is called a factor model. A factor model estimates the relationship between two variables. Independent variables—like the recent changes in interest rates and stock prices, inflation, and government trade data and so forth—are used to help predict dependent variables, such as the value of a stock, the level of interest rates, and the 10-year U.S. Treasury Note, or the exchange rate between U.S. Dollars and Euro. It's not uncommon for quant models to contain dozens of variables. So, let's begin by looking at factor models in the context of stocks, although they can apply to any type of investment.

Sometimes stocks go up—or down—for a variety of reasons, including no reason other than due to general market movements. In a bull market, most stocks go up, and, in a bear market, most stocks go down. Then again, stocks are also often impacted by specific actions, such as movements in interest rates. rising rates, especially when they are unexpected, usually cause stock prices to fall. In the same way, stocks are sometimes affected by changes of oil prices, since oil is used as an input to many products and industries, such as plastics and airlines. The price of oil also impacts consumer spending, since it relates to the cost of filling up your gas tank, as well as home heating costs. Quants often use dozens of factors in their models. Not only that but when investing in stocks, these models may weigh these various factors differently, depending upon the circumstances. For example, interest rates may greatly impact the prices of financial stocks or homebuilding stocks but have little impact on supermarket stocks or healthcare stocks.

Quants are also constantly updating their models with the latest data. The models make adjustments as they go along, changing to reflect this new information. Sometimes quants look for signals before making a trade. One signal could be a spike in stock volatility, which might be indicative of market fear. In a fear or risk-off trade, safe haven assets like U.S. Treasuries or gold often outperform. The term risk-off refers to an environment where fear usually pervades the market, and investors are selling assets that are traditionally risky, such as stocks, high-yield bonds, and emerging market securities.

A positive signal might be triggered by a Federal Reserve announcement that is more welcome than expected. In that case, stock prices might rise as part of the risk-on trade. The term risk on indicates that investors are willing to increase the risk of their portfolio by purchasing more volatile securities, which they deem to have significant upside. High-yield bonds and stocks of smaller or speculative firms may also do well in this risk-on environment.

Here's one way to think about a signal. You don't know when someone is going to throw a rock in a pond. But after it happens, you can anticipate the ripples. You are looking for a tipping point that is needed to push some strategies into action. Some quants engage in high-frequency trading or HFT for short. High-frequency trading is a computer-driven investment strategy, that emphasizes high transaction volume—along with extremely short-duration positions—and automated algorithms that do the buying and selling. High-frequency trading programs do several things but let's consider one example with a globally traded stock like Microsoft. Microsoft trades on Nasdaq in New York. It also trades in London. And it trades in Germany, Hong Kong, Japan, and on several other exchanges around the world.

The country where a security trades is important, but also what type of exchange it trades on. High-frequency trading programs often transact on an electronic communication network or ECNs for short. ECNs are basically an electronic stock exchange. There is no exchange floor but rather a bunch of computer servers in a room.

What if, after adjusting for currency prices and transaction costs, the price of Microsoft's stock sold at two different prices on two different exchanges at the same time? A high-frequency trading computer program would basically swoop in and buy on the exchange with the low price, and sell on the exchange with the high price. This strategy is known as arbitrage. Even if the difference were only a tiny fraction of a penny, it would make sense for computers to make this trade all day long. Many of these trades are so fleeting that they take place within a millisecond.

The big fear with the quants' automated trading models is that the computer might unpredictably act and cause the firm to blow up. Sort of like the trading equivalent of the computer HAL, in Stanley Kubrick's classic film, *2001: A Space Odyssey*. And there have been instances when quant models wreaked havoc. On August 1, 2012, Knight Trading Group fired up a new, untested, computer trading program. While attempting to fill the orders of just 212 customers, it was unable to recognize that orders had been filled. And, in some cases, it entered orders more than 1000 times their intended amounts. The result, four million unintended trades across 154 stocks totaling 397 million shares. The firm lost $460 million in 45 minutes. Knight's stock crashed, and the company was sold to another high-frequency trading firm, called Getco, at a bargain price.

The most often-cited tale of a computer-based trading model gone wrong is that of Long Term Capital Management. It was a curious name, to begin with, for a fund that focused mostly on short-term trading strategies. Long Term Capital formed something of a dream team. It had perhaps the best trader on Wall Street in John Meriwether, formerly of Salomon Brothers a top Wall Street bank that was eventually purchased by Citibank. Long Term Capital also had two Nobel Prize-winning economists on staff in Myron Scholes and Robert Merton. Scholes and Merton are two of the most widely respected and cited finance professors in the world. And they are especially known for their pioneering work in valuing stock options. And Long Term Capital had David Mullins, a former Vice Chairman of the Federal Reserve.

Long Term Capital focused on arbitrage, or convergence, trades. These involve two baskets of securities with similar risk, but different expected returns. A long position is taken in the undervalued basket of securities and a short position is taken in the expensive basket of securities. Being short, or selling short, is a technique to profit from a decline in price. It involves selling first and buying back later, hopefully at a lower price. When you sell an asset without having any prior position in it, we call it selling short, rather than simply selling.

The bulk of Long Term Capital's assets were in four different types of trades. First were convergence among U.S., Japan, and European sovereign bonds. Second, convergence among European sovereign bonds. Third, convergence between newly issued and previously existing U.S. government bonds. And fourth, long positions in emerging markets sovereign bonds hedged back to dollars. The differences in the expected returns between the two baskets for each of these trades was small, usually less than 1%. So, in order to get an attractive return, Long Term Capital had to use leverage or borrowed money. In some cases, the firm borrowed $30 for each $1 held in capital.

Now, Long Term Capital began trading in 1994, and, for the first few years of operations its strategy worked like clockwork, returning profits of 20% in 1994, 43% in 1995, 41% in 1996, and 17% in 1997. Then, in August 1998, Russia defaulted on its debt, resulting in a worldwide financial panic. During times of market distress, the most liquid and highest-quality assets usually perform the best. Unfortunately, Long Term Capital was short these assets that investors demanded the most. The combination of illiquid assets and excessive leverage proved to be the downfall for Long Term Capital. On the hook for $30 for every $1 it had bet, a roughly 3% loss could have wiped out virtually all of the firm's capital. And with about $4 billion in net assets under management, it controlled more than $125 billion in securities.

The Federal Reserve feared that a forced liquidation of Long Term Capital's portfolio would cause a meltdown in the global financial markets. And that is basically what began to happen, from Asia to Russia to Europe and the United States. Long Term Capital lost 44% of its capital during that one month alone, in August 1998. Wall Street sharks smelled blood and traded against Long Term Capital's positions. And, as the market swam in the opposite direction of the firm's leveraged bets, Long Term Capital continued to lose massively in September, resulting in a huge 90% loss for the year.

Now, the Federal Reserve orchestrated a meeting of some of the largest firms on Wall Street—Bankers Trust, Barclays, Chase, Credit Suisse First Boston, Deutsche Bank, Goldman Sachs, Merrill Lynch, J.P. Morgan, Morgan Stanley, Salomon Smith Barney, and UBS. Each of them anted up $300 million in a pool that they agreed to put toward a potential solution. In addition, French banks Paribas and Credit Agricole each put in $100 million. And the French Bank Société Générale put in $125 million. Bear Stearns and Lehman Brothers, among others, declined to participate. Bear and Lehman claimed they were already on the hook for a lot of money since they were two of Long Term Capital's primary brokers.

As an aside, some say that Bear Stearns and Lehman were permitted to go under during the financial markets crisis of 2007– 2009, in retaliation for not participating in the Long Term Capital bailout. Bear Stearns was forced to sell itself to J.P. Morgan for $2 a share—and that's quite a drop since Bear's stock price was almost $160 a share about a year earlier—and Lehman Brothers ended up being the biggest bankruptcy in the history of the world. But, it's unlikely that Wall Street, the Fed, and the Treasury all conspired to take revenge on Lehman and Bear, which had their own problems with leverage. Besides, the survivors had too much else on their minds, at the time, like saving the U.S. and global economies.

So, the Wall Street firms and the French banks collectively agreed to pool $3.625 billion in bailout funds to help Long Term Capital slowly unwind its portfolio, and thereby limit damage to the broader financial markets. The enduring lesson of Long Term Capital is this, The smartest people on earth can lose all of their money—and their investors' money, too—when greed, overconfidence, and excessive leverage collide.

Now let's go back to talking about James Simons's strategy at Renaissance Technologies, which managed to steer clear of the calamities on the order of Long Term Capital's. Simons's Medallion Fund began trading in 1988. And it did not immediately set the world on fire. Instead, it generated a peak-to-trough loss of 30% by April of 1989. So, Simons shuffled the fund's management team and made changes to its computer models to make their horizons more short-term oriented. The average holding period switched from weeks or days to intraday.

The changes worked, with Medallion up, 55.9% in 1990, 39.4% in 1991, 34% in 1992, 39.1% in 1993, and 74% in 1994, along with further successes in later years.

Incredibly, Medallion returned 98.2% in the peak financial crisis year of 2008—when the S&P 500 FELL 37%. And these returns were net of Medallion's hefty fees, which ranged as high as 5% of assets and 44%

of profits. These fees were enormous compared with the hedge fund industry's standard fee of 2% of assets plus 20% of profits. By comparison, index funds charge almost nothing, usually about 1/10th of 1% per year.

Medallion uses lots of models, and it trades across all asset classes, including stocks, bonds, currencies, commodities, and more. Diversification across models and asset classes is likely one reason for Medallion's success. No other fund that I'm aware of has been able to replicate its performance. When Simons stepped down as CEO in 2009, he named two super quants to succeed him, the co-CEOs Peter Brown and Robert Mercer. Back in 1993, Simons himself had hired Brown and Mercer away from IBM, where they were in charge IBM's speech recognition group.

It turns out that speech-recognition software has a lot in common with quantitative stock analysis. Both tasks require getting signals out of noisy data. Speech-recognition software also tries to predict what will come next, using techniques from probability theory. Perhaps the easiest way to see the connection is through the texting function on your cell phone. If you type the letters A and then N, your text program probably guesses the next letter is D—to make the word and. This type of logic can be extended to predicting security prices, though with less precision. Keep in mind that stock predictions are never going to be 100% right. But if you go to Las Vegas, and are correct at predicting Red or Black on a roulette wheel about 60% of the time, you could make a fortune.

Renaissance, no doubt, has countless mathematical techniques in its models. And Renaissance even has staff cryptographers—like Simons once was. Wall Street has also taken to hiring meteorologists, since predicting the weather can provide an edge in estimating the price of heating oil futures, orange juice prices, and a host of other commodity prices.

Besides the raw brainpower of the quants working at Renaissance—and the terabytes of daily data that the firm collects—Simons attributes much of the organization's success to its work culture. When asked about the secret of his organization's success, he once said,

Have an open atmosphere. The best way to conduct research on a larger scale is to make sure everyone knows what everyone else is doing. The sooner the better—start talking to other people about what you're doing. Because that's what will stimulate things the fastest. No compartmentalization. We don't have any little groups that say, "This is our system and we run it, we get paid because of it."

Simons further explained,

> We meet once a week—all the researchers meet once a week, any new idea gets brought up, discussed, vetted, and hopefully put into production. And people get paid based on the profits of the entire firm. You don't get paid just on your work. You get paid based on the profits of the firm. So everyone gets paid based on the firm's success.

Quants make a living exploiting market inefficiencies, or strategies that appear to consistently offer superior profits. But the thing about exploiting market inefficiencies is that those who benefit from exploiting them, often become victims of their own success. To use a simple example, the so-called January Effect seemed to work very well for many years. The January Effect held that almost half of the stock market returns for a given year occurred in the month of January, especially among small-cap firms.

As the pattern became widely known, people started buying stocks in December, and then even earlier, around Thanksgiving. Today, the January Effect seems to work sporadically, if at all. For example, the S&P 500 lost 6.1% in January of 2008; it lost 8.6% in January 2009 and lost 5.1% in January 2016. So, since trends seem not to last—and yesterday's certainty becomes today's uncertainty—quant firms are constantly trying to update their models, and they're replacing models that have lost their effectiveness. These models may no longer work because they never found a true anomaly, or because they worked so well as to have arbitraged away by other traders.

Now, Simons and his successors don't have the Midas touch with everything at Renaissance. As the Medallion fund got larger and better established, it became too big to produce the returns its investors were accustomed to. So, management closed the fund to new investors, and today manages it mostly for insiders. However, Renaissance developed a number of new funds for investors. These newer funds generally have a longer time horizon, and, as such, can accommodate more investor capital. For example, the Renaissance Institutional Equities Fund, or RIEF, reportedly has the capacity to handle up to $100 billion in capital.

The institutional equities fund's performance was good, but it couldn't seem to hold a candle to the Medallion Fund. From RIEF's launch in September 2005, through September 2015, it returned 9.8% per year. This was better than the S&P 500 return of 6.7% per year over the same period, as well as the performance of most hedge fund indexes. Solid performance, but hardly the type of returns that have earned Simons the admiration of many quants around the world.

As he eased into retirement, Simons—like many other wealthy benefactors—came to be known for donating huge sums of money to support a variety of causes that were meaningful to him. These include mathematics education in United States schools, and, more broadly, research on autism. He has a daughter that was diagnosed with a mild form of autism. So Simons has heavily funded research to decode the relationship between genes and autism. As for Renaissance Technologies, it manages something on the order of $65 billion or more today.

20

Distressed-Asset Investors: Tepper, Klarman

The notion of investing in distressed stocks and bonds gives some investors the shivers. They would rather sell than buy, and move onto healthier firms. But therein lies the opportunity. Buying what others don't want—and what they might indiscriminately sell—creates opportunity. That is, if you have the temperament to tread there and the ability to perform detailed analysis that differentiates a zero investment from a hero investment. Two of the best investors ever to set foot in the distressed-investing space are David Tepper and Seth Klarman.

David Tepper

> David Tepper was born in Pittsburgh September 11, 1957. His father was an accountant and his mother taught at a public elementary school. He bought his first stock, Career Academies, while still in high school. The stock traded at $2 a share, and Tepper bought one lot, or 100 shares. The company went bankrupt and Tepper lost all his money. It was a good reminder that just because an asset is cheap doesn't mean it can't go lower. That was a lesson Tepper never forgot.

> Tepper attended the University of Pittsburgh, paying for his undergraduate degree with a combination of student loans and the meager pay he made working at the school's library. He also hit his stride, academically speaking, graduating with high honors and a degree in economics in 1978. Tepper was hired as a credit and securities analyst in the trust department of a local bank, which has since disappeared in a series of mergers.

> He left 2 years later to pursue his graduate degree in finance at Carnegie Mellon University and worked for 2 years in the treasury department at Republic Steel in Youngstown, Ohio. By this time, Tepper already had a lot of experience in evolving and distressed industries.

> In 1984, he joined the former Keystone Investments in Boston as a junk-bond analyst. Keystone was one of the nation's first mutual fund companies until it, too, was merged out of existence. About a year after joining keystone, Goldman Sachs recruited him to work as part of its newly formed junk bond group. And, in short order, he became the head of Goldman's junk bond trading desk.

> He considered himself one of the best traders at the firm, but repeatedly was passed over for partner; reportedly, he didn't get along well with Jon Corzine, who was then head of fixed income trading at Goldman, and would go on to become CEO and then a U.S. senator and governor of New Jersey.

> Frustrated, he left Goldman in 1993 to set up his own hedge fund, Appaloosa Management. He was 35, and he started with $7 million of his own money and $50 million from investors. In the years since, Appaloosa Management became one of the most successful hedge funds of all time, averaging about 27%, net of fees, a year over a period of more than 20 years.

> Although Tepper specializes in distressed assets—meaning damaged firms that are on the brink of, in, or recently emerged from bankruptcy—he starts with a global or macro view of the

world, and then drills down to the micro to identify specific securities to trade.

Distressed Investing Background

> Any list of once-distinguished firms that have gone bankrupt would be quite long: General Motors, Kodak, Texaco. Some never come back. Others, like GM and Texaco, reorganize and continue to operate.

> o The billionaire investor, Bill Ackman, made one of his most famous bets on the firm, General Growth Properties, when it was severely distressed. General Growth is one of the largest mall owners in the United States. it went bust during the financial markets crisis of 2007–2009. Ackman helped steer the firm through the bankruptcy process and turned a $60 million investment into $1.6 billion 2 years later.

> The two types of bankruptcies for U.S. corporations are chapter 7 and chapter 11. In a chapter 7 bankruptcy, the firm liquidates and shuts its doors. In a chapter 11 bankruptcy, the firm continues to operate while taking at least temporary protection from its creditors.

> One potential resolution may be for the reorganizing firm to issue new stock to its bondholders and thereby retire or defray its debt. In this case, the original shareholders might lose some or all of their equity investment in the company.

> Who gets paid—and in what order—can be complex, in bankruptcy court. Employees, attorneys and firms that extend trade credit typically are paid first. If a fund or investor group controls more than a third of the debt, the entity can petition the court with its own restructuring proposal. Two-thirds of the creditors must approve any restructuring plan before it goes to the bankruptcy judge for final approval.

> For the firm's security holders, the absolute priority rule determines the subsequent sequence. Debt holders are first, ranked by seniority. Then preferred stockholders are paid, followed by the original common stockholders of the firm.

> If the firm was considered investment grade before the bankruptcy filing, its bondholders can expect to get about 60 cents to 90 cents on the dollar. If the bonds were rated as noninvestment grade, or junk, before the filing, the recovery rate is usually much lower: typically, about 20 to 30 cents on the dollar. This payment is called the recovery rate.

> Being a successful distressed-assets investor requires a unique combination of skills. The first is the temperament to invest in this

risky area. Second is the ability to estimate the investors' recovery rates and envision what a firm will look like post-bankruptcy. Large investors in this space also need the ability to create alliances with other interested parties in the bankruptcy proceedings to develop a reorganization plan that will be accepted by fellow creditors and the bankruptcy judge.

> David Tepper made a fortune by buying the debt and equity of bank stocks like Citigroup and Bank of America during the financial markets crisis. He correctly reasoned that these banks were too big to fail and would be bailed out by the U.S. government. Tepper's funds netted $7 billion in 2009 alone. The example of distressed-bank securities makes clear that Tepper is not afraid to go where other investors fear to tread.

Seth Klarman

> Seth Klarman, the other distressed-assets investor, was born May 21, 1957, in New York. His family moved to Baltimore when he was 6. His father was an economist at Johns Hopkins University, and his mother taught English at a local high school.

> Klarman bought his first stock at the age of 10. It was a good one: Johnson & Johnson. Finding himself in regular need of Johnson & Johnson Band-Aids, Klarman was following what would become known as the Peter Lynch theory of investing in what you know.

> Klarman majored in economics at Cornell. After his junior year, an uncle helped him land a summer internship at the New York-based investment firm, Mutual Shares, which specialized in distressed and deep-value investing. It was run by two investing legends: Max Heine and Michael Price. Klarman said, "I learned the business from two of the best, which was better than anything you could ever get from a textbook or a classroom." After graduating from Cornell with honors in 1979, Klarman joined Mutual Shares full-time as an analyst.

> While he was earning his M.B.A. at Harvard, one of his professors there, William Poorvu, recognized Klarman's potential and asked him to manage some money for him and friends. Thus, in 1982, Klarman launched his own firm, Baupost Group, right out of the classroom. Baupost is an acronym of the names of the 4 investors who seeded Klarman with $27 million. It now manages about $30 billion and provided investors with a return of about 20% a year for more than 30 years.

Klarman Strategy

> Klarman typically begins his investment analysis by looking for a margin of safety before entering a position. With bonds, it involves an assessment of the likelihood that a company can repay its debt. If the company is distressed, or bankrupt, the analysis will include detailed estimates of recovery rates. When looking at stocks, Klarman assesses various valuation metrics, including financial measures such as price to book, price to earnings, price to cash flow, dividend yield, and price to replacement cost.

> One example is Klarman's investment in the debt of the former Enron Corporation while the disgraced company was in bankruptcy proceedings. Most investors wouldn't touch Enron with a 10-foot pole, but Klarman analyzed Enron's assets and liabilities and bought some of its debt for 10 to 15 cents on the dollar.

   o Klarman's analysis suggested the company's debt was worth 30 to 40 cents on the dollar. It took a few years to sort out, but Enron's debt eventually traded at about 50 cents on the dollar.

> A way of finding value is to seek for motivated sellers. Klarman cites several examples: One is buying a stock after it is removed from a leading market index. Index funds typically can't own things outside the index they are formed to replicate: They have to sell non-index assets. This type of behavior may temporarily depress the because of the selling pressure, but it will eventually revert to its fair value.

> Klarman also likes to invest in spinoff companies. Many investors will sell a spinoff, or divested asset, either because they don't want it or because it constitutes too small a share of their portfolio to be worth monitoring. This selling pressure—independent of the fundamental value of the stock—may create opportunities.

> Klarman also sees opportunities in an absence of buyers for otherwise attractive investments. The major Wall Street firms might see little advantage in making a market trading in a company's stock. This lack of competition creates opportunities for investors like Klarman who are willing to value stocks independently and do original research.

> Klarman also looks for investing catalysts that are independent of the market, such as a company increasing its dividend payments or resuming dividend payments after having stopped them at some point in the past. The same thinking holds for investing in a distressed firm that resumes the payment of interest on its bonds.

> Klarman is a bottom-up investor who looks at the fundamentals of a stock and what it is worth. Macro issues are of far less importance to him. Klarman thinks it is easier to be correct about a single company than it is to forecast what is going to happen in a large and diverse economy.

> Finally, patience is an important factor in Klarman's success and that of most value and distressed investors. He is willing to hold onto investments for several years in order to achieve their full value.

Suggested Reading

Ahuja, *The Alpha Masters*.
Greenwald, Kahn, Sonkin, and van Biema, *Value Investing*.
Klarman, *Margin of Safety*.

Questions to Consider

1. How would you describe the investment strategies of David Tepper and Seth Klarman?

2. How would you define distressed investing?

20

Transcript

Distressed-Asset Investors: Tepper, Klarman

B e forewarned. We are about to enter an area that's not for the faint of heart, distressed investing. The notion of investing in distressed stocks and bonds gives some investors the shivers. They would rather sell than buy and move onto healthier firms.

But therein lies the opportunity. Buying what others don't want—and what they might indiscriminately sell—creates opportunity. That is if you have the temperament to tread there; and the ability to perform detailed analysis, that differentiates a zero investment from a hero investment.

Two of the best investors ever to set foot in the distressed-investing space are David Tepper and Seth Klarman. In this lecture, we'll explore the field of distressed investing; discuss potential opportunities in this market; and learn something about two of its greatest practitioners in Tepper and Klarman.

David Tepper was born in Pittsburgh on September 11, 1957. He grew up in Stanton Heights, a middle-class section of Steel City—as Pittsburgh once was known. His father was an accountant, and his mother taught at a public elementary school. Tepper played football in high school and was, naturally, a Pittsburgh Steelers fan. Things would come full circle decades later when Tepper became a minority owner of the pro football team.

Tepper considered himself a good—but not great—student in school. He doesn't recall getting any As, but he was in the honors program. Maybe he was destined to make his fortune in distressed assets. He bought his first stock, Career Academies, while still in high school. The stock traded at $2 a share, and Tepper bought one lot or 100 shares. The company went bankrupt, and Tepper lost all of his money. It was a good reminder that just because an asset is cheap doesn't mean it can't go lower. And that was a lesson Tepper never forgot.

After high school, Tepper attended the University of Pittsburgh and paid for his undergraduate degree with a combination of student loans, and the meager pay he made working at the school's library. He also hit his stride, academically speaking, by graduating with high honors and a degree in Economics in 1978. Tepper then got hired as a credit and securities analyst in the trust department of a local bank, Equibank, which has since disappeared in a series of mergers. Tepper left two years later to pursue his graduate degree in finance at Carnegie Mellon University, also in Pittsburgh. And then he worked for two years in the treasury department at Republic Steel, which is based in Youngstown, Ohio. By this time, Tepper already had a lot of experience in evolving and distressed industries.

In 1984, he joined the former Keystone Investments in Boston as a junk-bond analyst. Keystone was one of the nation's first mutual fund companies until it, too, was merged out of existence. About a year later after joining Keystone, Goldman Sachs recruited him to work as part of its newly formed junk bond group. And, in short order, he became the head of Goldman's junk bond trading desk. He considered himself one of the best traders at the firm but repeatedly was passed over for partner. Reportedly, he didn't get along well with Jon Corzine—who was then head of fixed income trading at Goldman, and would go on to become CEO of Goldman—and then a U.S. senator and governor of the State of New Jersey.

Tepper later bought the Hamptons, Long Island, mansion of Corzine's ex-wife, which he set about demolishing to build a mansion about twice the size of the original in its place. Frustrated that he didn't make partner at Goldman, Tepper left in 1993 to set up his own hedge fund, Appaloosa Management. He was 35, and started with $7 million of his own money, along with another $50 million from investors. Tepper originally wanted to name the firm after something related to Greek mythology. He and his business partner, Jack Walton, considered the term Pegasus, after the flying horse, but that was taken. So, he and Walton found a book on horses and searched for names with the letter A. At the time, a lot of the research reports from brokerage firms were distributed to investors on an alphabetical basis, via fax. That meant that firms whose name began with the letter A enjoyed a small advantage. In this way, Tepper settled on the Appaloosa breed of horses as the name for his firm.

In the years since, Appaloosa Management became one of the most successful hedge funds of all time, averaging about 27% a year net of fees over a more than 20 year period. Although Tepper specializes in distressed assets—meaning damaged firms that are on the brink of bankruptcy, or that are in bankruptcy, or have recently emerged from bankruptcy—he starts with a global—or macro—view of the world, and then drills down to the micro, to identify specific securities to trade.

Any list of once-distinguished firms that have gone bankrupt would be quite long. Mine includes such blue-chip names as General Motors, Kodak, and Texaco. Some never come back. Others, like GM and Texaco—now a part of Chevron—reorganize, and continue to operate. The billionaire investor, Bill Ackman, made one of his most famous bets on the firm, General Growth Properties when it was severely distressed. General Growth is one of the largest mall owners in the United States. It went bust during the financial markets Crisis of 2008 and 2009. Ackman helped steer the firm through the bankruptcy process and turned a $60 million investment into $1.6 billion two years later.

Almost forgotten now, Microsoft Corporation gave its one-time archrival, Apple, a $150 million cash infusion in August of 1997. That stabilized the company's financial condition and allowed it to invest in new products. After a brush with insolvency and oblivion, Apple's stock rose more than 200-fold over the next two decades.

There are basically two types of bankruptcies for U.S. corporations, Chapter 7 and Chapter 11. In a Chapter 7 bankruptcy, the firm liquidates and shuts its doors. The Borders bookstore chain and the music-download service Napster were two highly publicized Chapter 7 cases. In a Chapter 11 bankruptcy, the firm continues to operate while taking, at least temporary protection, from its creditors. One potential resolution might be for the reorganizing firm to issue new stock to its bondholders and thereby retire or defray its debt. In this case, the original shareholders might lose some or all of their equity in the company.

Who gets paid—and in what order—can be complex in bankruptcy court. Employees, attorneys, and firms that extend trade credit typically are paid first. Then, in terms of the firm's security holders, there is something called absolute priority rule that determines the subsequent sequence. Debt holders are next in line, ranked by seniority. Then preferred stockholders are paid. Preferred stock is a cross between a stock and a bond. It pays a dividend rather than an interest payment. Preferred stock is somewhat of a rare bird. About 10% or so of companies have it. Lastly, any money left over goes to the original common stockholders of the firm. So, bondholders may get a fraction of what they are owed. That's called a haircut.

Preferred and common stockholders often get little to nothing. But the amount investors get back is called the recovery rate. If a fund or investor group controls more than one-third of the debt, the entity can petition the court with its own restructuring proposal. Two-thirds of the creditors must approve any restructuring plan before it goes to the bankruptcy judge for final approval.

So, you might be asking, When a company reorganizes in bankruptcy court and issues new equity, how is this stock distributed? Well, there is a term called the Fulcrum Security, which refers to the debt issue that is converted to equity ownership. For example, let's say a firm has assets of $150 million and liabilities of $200 million. And we'll say that the $200 million increase in liabilities includes $100 million in secured debt and $100 million in unsecured debt. In this example, the secured debt holders with a $100 million stake in the bankrupt firm would be paid in full, while the unsecured debt holders would be paid with the remaining $50 million of assets, and then receive equity in the newly reorganized firm. The equity that existed before the bankruptcy would typically be wiped out, as I mentioned earlier.

Being a successful distressed-assets investor requires a unique combination of skills. The first is the temperament to invest in this risky area. Second is the ability to estimate the investors' recovery rates, and envision what a firm will look like post-bankruptcy. Large investors in this space also typically need to create alliances with other interested parties in the bankruptcy proceedings, to develop a reorganization plan that will be accepted by fellow creditors, and the bankruptcy judge. It might make a big difference to your return if the court proceedings are tied up for a few months or a few years.

David Tepper made a fortune by buying the debt and equity of bank stocks like Citigroup and Bank of America during the financial markets crisis. He correctly reasoned that these banks were too big to fail, and would be bailed out by the U.S. government. In doing so, Tepper's funds netted $7 billion in 2009 alone, and he personally took home about $3 billion that year. The example of distressed bank securities makes clear that Tepper is not afraid to tread where other investors are afraid to go. Appaloosa was one of the first hedge funds to invest in Soviet-era Russia, entering the market shortly after an attempted coup there in 1991.

Tepper returned to distressed Russian debt in 1998, in the midst of the Asian currency crisis. He didn't think Russia would default on its debt. But, it did, and Tepper's fund was down more than 20% for a while. Rather than panic, Tepper bought more Russian debt and turned a net profit on the trade. He says, "We won't stop if we're down a little bit. We don't freeze. We keep investing with a disciplined, logical approach."

Tepper also had winning trades with a couple of big utilities in California— Pacific Gas & Electric and Edison International—some years ago. In the late 1990s, the state of California began to deregulate the prices of electricity. Its thinking was that deregulation would encourage competition and lower prices for consumers. But the opposite happened, as prices surged—in extreme cases by a factor of 20 times.

Years later, it was determined that the infamous Enron Corporation was one of the companies that manipulated the state's supply of energy, thus playing a role in its price increase. Meanwhile, Pacific Gas & Electric declared bankruptcy, and Edison International was on the verge of bankruptcy. That's when Tepper stepped in. He correctly reasoned that the state would provide some financial support to the utilities, in the form of price increases. Much later, Tepper recommended investments in the distressed insurer, AIG, which the United States Treasury ended up supporting, as well as in the troubled debts of the sovereign [?] nations Portugal, Ireland, Italy, Greece, and Spain. As for the latter, he correctly reasoned that the European Central Bank would help its member nations avoid default. As it turns out, neither AIG nor the distressed sovereigns defaulted, earning Tepper another multibillion-dollar payday.

Tepper generally keeps a low profile. But he made a rare appearance on the business TV channel CNBC in September 2010, when he argued that the Federal Reserve's multitrillion-dollar injection of funds into the economy—through its quantitative easing program—would be bullish for stocks. In what is known as the Tepper Rally, stocks went up 2% on the day of the interview. And a lot more, in the months that followed. Tepper says, "We keep our cool when others don't. The point is, markets adapt. People adapt."

Seth Klarman, the other distressed-assets investor I want to highlight for you, was born on May 21, 1957, in New York City. His family moved to Baltimore, Maryland, when he was six years old. His father was an economist at Johns Hopkins University. His mother taught English at a local high school. And Klarman grew up as a fan of horse racing. Pimlico Race Course is located in Baltimore and hosts the Preakness Stakes, one of the events in horse racing's Triple Crown. Klarman would go on to own a number of thoroughbred horses in later years.

As a boy, he kept track of baseball statistics and stock tables in the newspaper. And he bought his first stock at the age of 10. It was a good one, Johnson & Johnson. Finding himself in regular need of Johnson & Johnson Band-Aids, Klarman would be following what became known as The Peter Lynch Theory of investing in what you know. Peter Lynch, of course, is the famed former Fidelity Investments mutual fund manager.

After high school, Klarman majored in economics at Cornell University. After his junior year, an uncle helped him land a summer internship at the New York-based investment firm Mutual Shares. The firm specialized in distressed and deep-value investing. And it was run by two investing legends, Max Heine and Michael Price. Klarman said, "I learned the business from two of the best, which was better than anything you could ever get from a textbook or a classroom." Michael Price, by the way, also mentored David Tepper after he left Goldman Sachs.

After graduating from Cornell, with honors, in 1979, Klarman joined Mutual Shares full-time as an analyst. A year and a half later, he entered Harvard to get his MBA. One class he took was in real estate. The professor, William Poorvu, recognized Klarman's potential and asked him to manage some money for him and friends. So, in 1982, Klarman launched his own firm, Baupost Group, right out of the classroom. Baupost is an acronym of the names of the four investors who seeded Klarman with $27 million. It now manages about $30 billion and provided investors with a return of about 20% a year for more than 30 years.

Klarman once wrote a book called *Margin of Safety*, whose name comes from value investing pioneer Benjamin Graham. It means you should try to buy investments at a discount, thereby providing yourself with a margin of safety if things go wrong. Klarman's book is out of print but is so highly revered that used copies go for about $1000 a piece. Klarman typically begins his investment analysis by looking for a margin of safety before entering a position. With bonds, it involves an assessment of the likelihood that a company can repay its debt.

If a company is distressed, or bankrupt, it will include detailed estimates of recovery rates. One example is Klarman's investment in the debt of the former Enron Corporation while the disgraced company was in bankruptcy proceedings. Most investors wouldn't wanna touch Enron with a 10-foot pole. However, Klarman analyzed Enron's assets and liabilities and bought some its debt for 10 to 15 cents on the dollar. His analysis suggested the company's debt was worth 30 to 40 cents on the dollar. It took a few years to sort out, but Enron's debt eventually traded at about 50 cents on the dollar.

When looking at stocks, Klarman looks at various valuation metrics, including financial measures such as price to book, price to earnings, price to cash flow, dividend yield, and price to replacement cost. Bruce Greenwald's book, *Value Investing: From Graham to Buffett and Beyond*, contains a chapter on Klarman and provides some further insight into his strategy. One way of finding value is to look for motivated sellers. Klarman cites several examples.

One is buying a stock after it is removed from a leading market index. Index funds typically can't own things outside the index they are formed to replicate. So, they have to sell non-index assets. This type of behavior may temporarily depress the stock due to the selling pressure, but it will eventually revert to its fair value. Klarman also likes to invest in spinoff companies. Many investors will sell a spinoff or divested asset, either because they don't want it as it may not fit their investment profile, or because it constitutes too small a share of their portfolio to be worth monitoring. This selling pressure—independent of the fundamental value of the stock—may create opportunities.

Another example of a motivated seller is when real estate is in the wrong hands. For example, banks generally don't want to hold foreclosed real estate for a long period of time after a borrower defaults. Klarman helped to make a name for himself by buying assets from the former Resolution Trust Corporation, or RTC, in the early 1990s. He previously bought real estate that previously belonged to insolvent savings and loan institutions that the government had seized. The government formed the RTC as a liquidating agency to dispose of these troubled assets. And Klarman wasn't afraid to perform a lot of the grunt work to calculate how much the real estate was really worth, and what was the likelihood that it could be profitably sold.

Klarman also made money on an unrelated opportunity known as thrift conversions. This occurred when a private, or mutual, bank was converted to a profit-making entity that traded on a stock exchange. Thrift customers usually had the option to obtain stock in the new, publicly traded entity. And when the stock started trading, it often benefited from a price bump of 10% or more, since the investment was now liquid—and enjoyed what analysts refer to as a liquidity premium.

If a stock is public and trades on an exchange, then it is relatively easy to sell and therefore, theoretically should be worth more. If a bank is public, it also becomes easier to be acquired by another institution, providing yet another potential source of a seller's premium. Conversely, if you own stock in a privately held bank, it may be hard to sell. Klarman's investment vehicle, Baupost, is said to have engaged in more than 1000 thrift conversions, most of which involved Klarman, or a representative, going down to the branch office and opening an account before the conversion took place.

Klarman also sees opportunities when there is an absence of buyers for otherwise attractive investments. For example, there are thousands of small stocks out there will little to no research coverage. The major Wall Street firms might not cover a stock on the expectation that they won't be able to do much investment-banking business with the firm - or won't earn much in the way of brokerage commissions by making a market trading in the company's stock. This lack of competition creates opportunities for investors like Klarman who are willing to value stocks independently and do original research.

Wall Street firms also drop coverage on firms once they become distressed. Further, many institutional investment managers will sell stocks or bonds when there is little to no research coverage since they don't like losing visibility to the thinking of the company. When more buyers show up—or the stock starts getting more analyst coverage, or when firms with distressed bonds start making payments—it could be a sign that the party is over and that for Klarman it's time to get out.

Klarman also looks for investing-catalysts that are independent of the market. One example is when a company Increases its dividend payments or resumes dividend payments after having stopped them at some point in the past. The same thinking holds for investing in a distressed firm that resumes the payment of interest on its bonds. The closing of spreads in a merger transaction is yet another catalyst that is independent of the market. After a merger or acquisition is announced, the price of the target firm usually falls a bit short of that stated purchase price, resulting in a difference, or spread.

The reason for the spread is that there is a chance that the deal might fall apart. As the closing date of the merger approaches, these spreads usually close, and Klarman collects the small profit between the traded discount and deal price. Although not the firm's main strategy, Klarman and Baupost will occasionally engage in these merger-arbitrage type transactions.

Klarman is a bottom-up investor who looks at the fundamentals of a stock, and what it is worth. Macro—or big picture—issues are of far less importance to him. Klarman also thinks it's easier to be correct about a single company than it is to correctly forecast what's going to happen in a large and diverse economy. Finally, the ability to be patient is an important factor in Klarman's success—and that of most value and distressed investors. He is willing to hold onto investments for several years in order to achieve their full value. One of Klarman's most controversial investments illustrates this point.

Between 2006 and 2010, Klarman and an associate of his, named John Lowndes, purchased about 7,000 of acres of potato farms for $80 million from a variety of farmers near Ontario, Canada. Lowndes grew up in the area and enjoyed the trust of some of the farmers prior to the sale. But, then it became known that Klarman and Lowndes wanted to turn the potato farms into a giant rock quarry. One estimate holds that there are 6 billion tons of limestone and other rocks beneath the surface. At a price of $20 a ton, a massive quarry on the site could be worth $120 billion. Ontario residents protested the quarry concept on environmental and other grounds. But, Klarman could afford to be patient. He knows that there is a margin of safety in the value of the assets in the ground. And he realizes that Canada may someday need the building materials and the jobs that his massive quarry could provide.

One of the opening lines in the original Star Trek TV show in the 1960s was "To boldly go where no man has gone before." Well, distressed investing is one such place. I wouldn't say nobody is there, but few want to go there. It requires hard work. Usually, you have less information available to you than in a more conventional investment. Stocks and bonds in the distressed sector are typically tarred with poor performance or poor future prospects. And sometimes you can get crushed. That's a lot less likely to happen when investing in a regulated utility, or a well-known name, such as Johnson & Johnson or Berkshire Hathaway.

David Tepper and Seth Klarman never sought to avoid the distressed space. They boldly seized opportunities. And it made them—and their investors—very rich. Tepper today is one of the richest investors in the country with an estimated net worth of more than $10 billion. When he relocated from New Jersey to Florida a few years ago, the move was of such significance from a tax perspective, that it created a hole in New Jersey's state budget.

Tepper keeps a pair of brass testicles on his desk. It was a gag gift from one of his employees. But, he often rubs them for luck—and for a laugh to start the trading day. Brass testicles aside, Tepper and Klarman both maintain great confidence in what they do for a living. When a reporter once asked Tepper where such certainty came from, he replied, "I was never afraid to go back to Pittsburgh and work in the steel mills."

21

Motorcycles, Gold, and Global Commodities

Commodities trading in the United States began to take shape in the mid-1800s as railroads started to crisscross the country. Centrally located Chicago thus became home to many of the largest commodity exchanges. A farmer who plans to harvest a crop in the fall probably has no idea of what the market price will be several months out. Locking in the price before the fall harvest reduces downside risks, and this certainty improves expense planning. Commodities can be defined broadly to include metals, oil, gas, and food. Over the years, a large number of commodities came to be traded on organized exchanges.

Commodities

> Time magazine once called Jim Rogers the "Indiana Jones of finance." He is best known for bringing commodities such as precious metals and agricultural products to the broad investing public. Along with the billionaire George Soros, Jim Rogers was a cofounder of the hedge fund, The Quantum Fund. Over the decade he worked there, The Quantum Fund returned an incredible 42,000% to investors.

> Today, commodities trading can include livestock, energy (oil, natural gas), and metals (copper, aluminum, silver, and gold). Jim Rogers suggests 4 ways that commodities investing works:

  o Buy shares in companies that produce commodities or that provide services to those companies: mining companies, for example, or heavy-equipment manufacturers that support mines.

  o Invest in countries that produce commodities. Commodity-rich countries include Canada, Argentina, Australia, and New Zealand.

  o Invest in real estate in areas rich in commodities. Wealth is created in a particular country is often spent on real estate.

  o Invest in index funds, mutual funds, and futures contracts tied directly to commodities, though if you do trade futures, Rogers suggests exercising caution when borrowing to execute the transaction because there is no limit to your potential losses.

> Jim Rogers himself created one of the first commodity indexes in 1998, the Rogers International Commodity Index, which tracks a basket of global commodities. Rogers also set up a number of commodity-index investment funds. Today, most large money-management firms offer their own commodity funds.

> One of Rogers's earliest experiences with the commodities market was his bullish call on oil in the early 1970s. Oil was trading for less than $4 a barrel. Rogers realized that oil and gas supplies were being depleted, and his research showed that gas pipelines had little in the way of reserves. In the early 1970s, the supply-demand balance tilted in favor of the oil producers. the Arab oil embargo specifically and the lack of readily available alternatives, generally no doubt played a role in oil's massive price acceleration.

Jim Rogers

> James "Jim" Rogers was born October 19, 1942, in the small town of Demopolis, AL. His father managed a plant for Borden Chemical, which made Elmer's Glue, among other things. Rogers went to Yale for his undergraduate degree and majored in history. While at school, Rogers landed a summer internship at the Wall Street wealth-management and investing firm of Dominick & Dominick, and by the end of that summer, he knew he wanted to try his hand at making his fortune on Wall Street.

> Upon graduating from Yale, Rogers received a scholarship to study philosophy, politics, and economics at Oxford. As a young man, he was influenced to travel in search of adventure by Charles Dickens's novel, *The Pickwick Papers*. The fictional Pickwick Club of London forms a traveling society, in which 4 members journey about England, and report on their adventures.

> The two 6-week breaks a year Oxford offered gave Rogers the opportunity to travel throughout much of Europe, and these excursions planted the seeds for his future as a world traveler and global investor. After graduating from Oxford, Rogers served a 2-year stint in the Army during the Vietnam War. His posting was to an Officer's Club in Brooklyn, which he helped manage. He also began managing the investment portfolio of his superior officer—which, during a bull market, did well.

> In 1970, Rogers went to work for a well-regarded Wall Street investment bank known as Arnhold and S. Bleichroeder, which was known for its international brokerage operation. Today, the firm is known as First Eagle Investment Management. While at Bleichroeder, Rogers met his future business partner, George Soros, and the two men set up a hedge fund: The Double Eagle Fund.

> In time, Rogers and Soros left Bleichroeder to form the legendary Quantum investment fund, one of the best-performing hedge

funds ever. At Quantum, Rogers was known for his rigorous and original research, while Soros was known for his trading ability and his willingness to use a lot of leverage.

> An early win for the pair at Quantum was seeing the changes underway in the trash-collection. Waste services were moving away from a municipal-collection model, often dominated by organized crime, and toward a more mainstream business run by publicly traded companies, like Waste Management.

> The Quantum Fund was so successful that it afforded Rogers the luxury of retiring 3 years before he turned 40. He took to traveling extensively, taught security analysis for several years at Columbia, and wrote magazine articles and 6 books. All the while, Rogers expanded his interest in investing globally, with a particular emphasis on what he saw firsthand during his travels: emerging markets and commodities.

> Fairly early on—and long before the idea registered broadly around the world—Rogers became convinced that the 21st century belonged to Asia generally and to China in particular. He saw a geopolitical reordering of countries and economies.

Investment Strategy

> Jim Rogers's investment performance—including that incredible 42,000% gain over the decade he was at Quantum—did not happen by accident or dumb luck. It is the result of enormous hard work. It's said that he didn't take a vacation for 10 years while he worked at the Quantum Fund. He regularly read 40 periodicals and 8 trade journals. He also devoured hundreds of annual corporate reports each year.

> As an investor, Rogers takes a big picture approach that focuses on long-term trends—a macro strategy. Long-term trends analysis is also called secular analysis. For example, a secular trend would

be high levels of student loan debt among many millennials, consequently shaping their spending habits.

> Rogers regularly reviews company insider-trading levels. Corporate insiders—management and board directors—typically know more about their companies than outside investors do. They are also often paid in stock. If they buy additional stock, it's usually a bullish sign.

> Rogers also believes in investing only in things or companies that you know something about. He says, "Most people know a lot about something, so they should just stick to what they know and buy an investment in that area. That is how you get rich."

> Like value-investing pioneer Benjamin Graham, Rogers likes to buy depressed assets with a margin of safety: that is, some downside protection to an investment. For example, the company might have a lot of cash on hand, or valuable assets that can be sold in a pinch. At the same time, Rogers also looks for positive changes taking place with the investment: what some analysts term a catalyst. A catalyst could be a new product or service or changes in government policy for example.

> Rogers's favorite informational resources include the CRB Commodity Yearbook, an encyclopedia of commodities and pricing data published by the Commodity Research Bureau in Chicago, as well as reports from the U.S. Department of Agriculture.

> Because Rogers takes a long-term approach, he focuses on changes in supply and demand. If Rogers saw a sharp rise in the price of a commodity, he would do some digging to find out what caused it. The answer might be that aging production facilities reduced supply, or newly opened mines for metals increased supply, potentially pushing prices down.

> Rogers's academic background and interest in history and politics help him connect the dots around the world to see how history

and events might affect securities prices on Wall Street or the commodities markets in Chicago.

> The fungible nature of commodities—that is, their relative interchangeability—shows why they are a cyclical asset class.

  ○ In the high-price part of the cycle, farmers who may be receiving a relatively low price for wheat will shift production to a higher-priced crop: corn, for example. The corn supply will generally increase until its price settles at an equilibrium value, at which point a price-based incentive to switch from wheat to corn will no longer pertain.

> Rogers believed that full cycles in commodities tend to last, on average, 17 to 18 years.

> Given his hedge fund beginnings, Rogers is as likely to go short on an investment as he is willing to go long. Rogers also takes pride in his contrarian streak. The crowd is influenced by mob

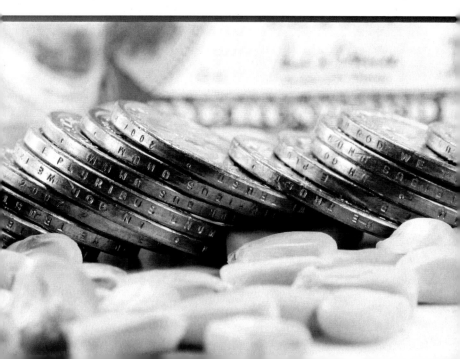

psychology and usually overshoots on the upside or downside. The contrarian can often profit as the market pendulum reverts to fair value.

> In this regard, Rogers is not afraid to bet big on countries he considers under-followed, or even unpopular. If he believes in a market, he is willing to be the first—or one of the earliest— investors in that market. This approach often enables him to get in at bargain prices.

> Rogers has 4 tests of what constitutes a good country to invest in.

  ○ Its market must be doing much better than it has done previously. This approach helps him avoid the scenario of catching a falling knife. one clue he looks for is whether the price of the market index holds its own in the face of bad news.

  ○ An out-of-favor national market with upside potential should be better off than is generally recognized, with the potential to provide a positive earnings or revenue surprise.

  ○ The national currency should be convertible. That is, the currency should be based on market prices and freely exchangeable into U.S. dollars, euros, Swiss francs, or some other widely traded currency.

  ○ It must have well enough established markets for the investor to get in and get out easily. It must be liquid. A market that doesn't trade much is illiquid, making exiting during periods of market volatility a challenge.

Conclusion

> Jim Rogers has lived the dream of many, becoming rich at a young age, and traveling around the world in search of knowledge and adventure, and he put his experience to good use. he was one of the first to invest actively in frontier markets—that is, an emerging

market for emerging markets—and he is one of the strongest advocates of global investing.

> He has done more to educate the average investor about commodities than any other person. His keen understanding of supply and demand and his relentless work ethic made this formerly obscure asset class more accessible to all of us in the general public.

Suggested Reading

Rogers, *Hot Commodities*.
Train, *Money Masters of Our Time*.

Questions to Consider

1. How would you describe the investment strategy of James Rogers?

2. Why might commodities act as a diversifier to a traditional stock and bond portfolio?

21

Transcript

Motorcycles, Gold, and Global Commodities

Many people dream about quitting their jobs and taking a trip around the world. Well, Jim Rogers retired at the age of 37, and he traveled around the world twice. The first time, Rogers crossed more than 100,000 miles—including 52 countries and six continents—on a motorcycle with his girlfriend, Tabitha Estabrook. A decade later, he topped that by traveling 152,000 miles to 116 countries with his wife Paige Parker—in a custom Mercedes. Time magazine once called Rogers the Indiana Jones of Finance. He is best known for bringing commodities—such as precious metals gold and silver; and agricultural products such as coffee and cotton, and wheat and corn—to the broad investing public.

Along with the billionaire George Soros, Jim Rogers was co-founder of the iconic hedge fund known as the Quantum Fund. And over the decade he worked there, the Quantum Fund returned an incredible 42,000% to investors. In this lecture, we'll travel around the world with Rogers to better understand his investing strategy and the global commodities markets.

In around the year 600 B.C., the Greek philosopher Thales of Miletus an area that is now part of Turkey traded one of history's first recorded derivative contracts. More specifically, Thales saw a bumper crop in olive oil, which was used widely in food, and for industrial applications— like lamp oil. So, Thales went to a number of people who controlled olive presses and offered them a small deposit in exchange for the option to use those presses, later in the year. And when the bumper crop in olives materialized, Thales was able to sell his pressing rights for a huge profit at the time. Commodities trading in the United States began to take shape in the mid- to late-1800s, as railroads started to crisscross the country. And Chicago—because it's centrally located—became home to many of the largest commodity exchanges, including the Chicago Mercantile Exchange and the Chicago Board of Trade.

Now, put yourself in the position of a farmer who plans to harvest a crop in the fall. During the spring and summer, you probably have no idea what the market price will be several months out. So, you might want to lock in the price for your crop before the fall harvest. Doing so reduces your downside risks. And with this certainty, you might be able to plan your expenses better, including whether to buy a new tractor or hire more help. Commodities can be defined broadly to include metals, oil, gas, and food. And, over the years, a large number of commodities came to be traded on organized exchanges. So today, you can trade in live animals known as livestock, including hogs and cattle. You can also trade in energy, like crude oil, natural gas, and propane. And you can trade in metals like copper, aluminum, silver, and gold.

But how, exactly, do you invest in commodities? Jim Rogers suggests four ways. First, you can buy shares in companies that produce commodities, or that provide services to these companies, mining companies, for example, or heavy-equipment manufacturers that support mines. Second, invest in countries that produce commodities. Commodity-rich countries include Canada, Argentina, Australia, and New Zealand. Third, invest in real estate in areas rich in commodities. As wealth is created in a particular country, that wealth is often spent on real estate. Lastly, you can invest in index funds, mutual funds, and futures contracts tied directly to commodities, though if you do trade futures, Rogers suggests exercising caution when borrowing to execute the transaction because there is no limit to your potential losses.

Rogers himself created one of the first commodity indexes in 1998. It's the Rogers International Commodity Index, or RICI, which is something like the Dow Jones Industrial Average or Standard & Poor's 500, except that it tracks a basket of global commodities rather than a basket of large stocks. Rogers also set up a number of commodity index investment funds. And today, most large money-management firms offer their own commodity funds. One of Jim Rogers's earliest experiences with the commodities market was his bullish call on oil in the early 1970s. Oil and gas were extremely cheap, at the time. Oil was trading for less than $4 a barrel. But Rogers realized that oil and gas supplies were being depleted; and his research showed that gas pipelines, at that time, had little in the way of reserves. So the fundamentals were in place for a rise in the price of oil.

And then in 1973, war broke out in the Middle East, and oil prices skyrocketed. Energy prices soared even higher after several Arab producers imposed an embargo on the United States and some other Western nations. Rogers is quick to point out that the spike in oil prices was not simply due to the actions of the Arab-dominated, Organization of Petroleum Exporting Countries, or OPEC. The OPEC cartel was established back in 1960, in an attempt to broadly raise oil prices. But initially, OPEC was viewed as something of a joke, due to its lack of success.

For the next decade after its formation, oil ministers would meet each year, in an attempt to raise the price of oil. But prices stayed low. And then, in the early 1970s, the supply-demand balance tilted in the favor of the producers, and prices were bound to rise, according to Rogers' analysis. That is, oil prices were bound to rise no matter what OPEC did. But the Arab oil embargo specifically—and the lack of readily available alternatives, generally—no doubt played a role in oil's massive price acceleration in the United States, and elsewhere in the West.

James or Jim Rogers was born on October 19, 1942, in the small town of Demopolis, Alabama. His father managed a plant for Borden Chemical, which makes Elmer's Glue, among other things. Jim Rogers went to Yale for his undergraduate degree and majored in history. Standing 5' 5-1/2" tall, Rogers used his size as a competitive advantage in serving as coxswain or steersman, on the Yale rowing team. While at school, Rogers landed a summer internship at the Wall Street wealth management and investing firm of Dominick & Dominick. And by the end of that summer, he knew he wanted to try his hand, one day, at making his fortune on Wall Street.

Upon graduating from Yale, Rogers received a scholarship to study philosophy, politics, and economics at Oxford University in England. He also skippered the Oxford rowing team and helped lead them to a win over their archrival, Cambridge, in an annual race that has been ongoing since 1829. So it was a big deal—especially for an American—to be at the helm of the illustrious Oxford University rowing team. Rogers reads widely. And, as a young man, he was influenced to travel in search of adventure by the Charles Dickens' novel, *The Pickwick Papers*. The fictional Pickwick Club of London forms a traveling society, in which four members journey about England, and report on their adventures.

Because the schedule at Oxford offered two 6-week breaks a year, this gave Rogers the opportunity to travel throughout much of Europe. And these excursions planted the seeds for his future as a world traveler and global investor. After graduating from Oxford, Rogers served a two-year stint in the U.S. Army, during the Vietnam War. But, his posting was to an officer's club in Brooklyn, New York, which he helped manage.

In 1970, Rogers went to work for a well-regarded Wall Street bank known as Arnhold and S. Bleichroeder, which was known for its international brokerage operation. Today, the firm is known as First Eagle Investment Management. While at Arnhold and S. Bleichroeder, Rogers met his future business partner, George Soros, who was a dozen years older than him. And the two men set up a hedge fund, the Double Eagle Fund. In time, Rogers and Soros left Bleichroeder to form the legendary Quantum investment fund, one of the best-performing hedge funds ever. At Quantum, Rogers was known for his rigorous and original research, while Soros was known more for his trading ability and his willingness to use a lot of leverage—going for the jugular as Soros put it.

An early win for the pair at Quantum was seeing the changes underway in the trash collection industry. Waste services were moving away from a municipal collection model, often dominated by organized crime, and toward a more mainstream business run by publicly traded companies, like Waste Management. The Quantum Fund was so successful that it afforded Rogers the luxury of retiring three years before he turned 40. But that didn't mean sitting at home on the couch, watching TV. Instead, he took to traveling extensively. He also taught security analysis for several years at Columbia University. He wrote magazine articles and six books. And he had his own TV program on CNBC. And all the while, Rogers expanded his interest in investing globally, with a particular emphasis on what he saw firsthand during his travels, emerging markets and commodities.

Fairly early on—and long before the idea registered broadly around the world—Rogers became convinced that the 21st century belonged to Asia, generally, and to China, in particular. He saw a geopolitical reordering of countries and economies, following a long historical pattern of the United Kingdom—once the most powerful country on earth, during the 19th century—giving way, during the 20th century, to the United States, which also dominated the world stage. Rogers wanted his two daughters to be prepared for the coming changes he envisioned. So he decided to relocate from New York City to somewhere in Asia. He initially looked at China but was put off by the pollution there. He eventually settled on Singapore for its clean environment, strong educational system, and high-quality health care. Singapore's per capita gross domestic product is among the highest in the world. And after making the move, Rogers insisted that his children's nannies speak Mandarin to them. As a result, his daughters speak Mandarin as well as they speak English.

Jim Rogers's investment performance—including that incredible 42,000% gain over the decade he was at Quantum—is not by accident or dumb luck. It is the result of enormous hard work. "Education and the necessity to work," Rogers once said, "changed my life and yanked me out of the backwater of Alabama." It is said that he didn't take a vacation for 10 years while he worked at the Quantum Fund. On a regular basis, he read forty periodicals and eight trade journals. He also devoured hundreds of annual corporate reports each year. It's no wonder that Rogers went through two early divorces—no doubt due in part to his workaholic status.

As an investor, Rogers takes a big picture approach that focuses on long-term trends. Wall Street calls this approach a top-down—or macro—strategy. Long-term trends analysis is also called secular analysis, as opposed to short-term analysis. For example, a secular trend would be high levels of student loan debt among many millennials, consequently shaping their spending habits. As we know, millennials tend to be savvy online shoppers, and seem to favor purchases on experiences, like vacations with friends, rather than accumulating a bunch of stuff. This top-down or macro approach is in contrast to simply picking good investments or stocks, which is known as a bottom-up approach.

Rogers—like Peter Lynch, the highly regarded former manager of Fidelity Investments' Magellan mutual fund—looks at company insider-trading levels, on a regular basis. Corporate insiders—management and board directors—typically know more about their companies than outside investors do. They are often also paid a lot in stock. So, if they buy additional stock on top of their stock-based compensation, it's usually a bullish sign. Rogers also believes—again, like Peter Lynch—that you should only invest in things or companies that you know something about. As Rogers says, "Most people know a lot about something, so they should just stick to what they know and buy an investment in that area. That's how you get rich." He goes on to say, "The mistake most people make is that they listen to hot tips, or act on something they don't know much about, except what they read in magazines."

Like value investing pioneer Benjamin Graham, Rogers likes to buy assets at depressed levels with a margin of safety. A margin of safety means there is some downside protection to your investment. For example, the company might have a lot of cash on hand or valuable assets that can be sold in a pinch. It might also have a long history, which perhaps would give you confidence that it can weather recession. This is in contrast to a young biotech, or Internet, company with no earnings and few marketable products. In other words, a margin of safety means that even if Rogers is wrong, he most likely won't lose a lot of money. He says, "I look down before I look up."

At the same time—and unlike Benjamin Graham, who focused on assets at a discount to value—Rogers also looks for positive changes taking place with the investment. This is what some analysts term a catalyst. A catalyst could be a new product, a new service, new management, or changes in government policy, to name a few examples. One of Rogers's favorite informational resources is something called the CRB Commodity

Yearbook, published by the Commodity Research Bureau in Chicago. The CRB Yearbook is basically an encyclopedia on commodities, and pricing data. Rogers also reads a lot of government reports. For example, the U.S. Department of Agriculture routinely issues reports on all kinds of commodities that might be of interest to investors—even frozen concentrated orange juice.

In addition, some professional investors pay more than $250,000 a year to get satellite-image-based research on the health of various crops. Because Rogers takes a long-term approach, he focuses on changes in supply and demand. For example, the widespread use of fracking techniques in the oil and gas industry has led to a long-term impact on increasing supply. But there has certainly been a lot of short-term volatility in oil prices since the advent of fracking. At one point fresh in my memory, the price of oil fell from more than $100 a barrel to about $30 a barrel, in a matter of months. If Rogers saw a sharp rise in the price of a commodity, he would do some digging to find out what caused it. The answer might be that aging production facilities reduced supply. he might find that newly opened mines for metals increased supply—potentially pushing prices down. And when he examines a weather report, he might find that cold winter meant higher prices for heating oil and gas. Or that warm winter increased Florida's orange crop, and would likely result in lower prices for orange juice.

Rogers's academic background—and his interest in history and politics—helps him connect the dots around the world to see ways in which history and events might impact securities prices on Wall Street—or at the commodities markets in Chicago, and elsewhere. To illustrate this, he cites a historic example of the American Civil War, which resulted in the cotton supply from the American South to England being cut off for a time during the 1860s. Before the Civil War, England got about 75% of its cotton from the U.S. South. So cotton prices surged not only in England but also in most regions outside of the Confederate States. And farmers, as far away as India and Egypt, responded to this signal by rotating out many of their own crops to plant the higher-priced cotton.

The fungible nature of commodities—that is, their relative interchangeability—shows why they are a cyclical asset class. In essence, high prices sow the seeds of lower prices in the future, while low prices sow the seed of higher prices in the future. In the high-price part of the cycle, farmers who may be receiving a relatively low price for wheat will shift production to a higher-priced crop, corn, for example. Now, the corn supply should generally increase until its price falls, or settles, at an equilibrium value at which there'll be no longer the price-based incentive for the farmer to switch from wheat to corn. In contrast, if the price of a commodity plummets, then—depending on the commodity—farmers, miners, or energy exploration firms are more likely to scale back production. These actions generally result in lower supply and increased prices, over time, other things being equal.

Some producers try to take basic commodity products and develop brand recognition and loyalty around them. This might enable them to generate additional demand, and squeeze out a pricing premium. Like Chiquita placing a sticker on its bananas, or Sunkist stamping its oranges. But, most commodity sellers have little success at extracting extra revenue, because they are confronted with a certain economic law of gravity that economists call perfect competition. So, given these examples, it should be easy to see that commodity prices are basically cyclical in nature. Well, you might wonder how long do commodity price cycles last? Rogers found that there are always ups and downs, but he believed that full cycles in commodities tend to last, on average, 17 or 18 years.

He had almost perfect timing back in the 1998–1999 time period when he sounded the horn that a new bull market in commodities was beginning. The crux of his thesis was that people in emerging markets—particularly in China and India, at the time—want to live like we do in the West based on his firsthand experience from his trips around the world. But Rogers's expectations were also grounded in a certain mathematical logic. In the United States, we consumed about 10 times the amount of oil, per capita, as was in the case in China and India. The same was true for many other commodities.

Now, China and India were not going to get close to U.S. consumption levels overnight. But the trend appeared to be unmistakable, as hundreds of millions of people in emerging markets around the world began to enter the middle class. Rogers also found that on an inflation-adjusted basis, commodity prices in 1998 were selling at almost Great Depression levels. A low price, plus a secular increase in demand, is a recipe for a bull market. Rogers predicted that the coming bull market in commodities would last about 15 years, an observation that proved quite prescient. But he is no permabull—by that I mean he isn't eternally optimistic.

In his 2004 book, *Hot Commodities: How Anyone Can Invest Profitably in the World's Best Market*, Rogers foresaw problems that inevitably would occur. He said, "I want to be clear that when China sneezes the rest of the world will be reaching for aspirin." Using the example of copper, he asks a bunch of questions. How much production is there worldwide? How many tons to reserves are there? Is the production in areas that might experience turmoil? Are the reserves rich with copper or only marginally productive? What are the existing inventories? how many mines exist worldwide? How productive are these mines? What is the potential supply over the next 10 years?

He goes on to ask, Are there new sources of supply? Are old mines expanding? When? How much will this cost? How much copper will this expansion produce? How long will it take before additional supplies get to the market? Finally, he asks, Are there new potential supplies? How much? How expensive to develop and then produce? how long will it be before these new sources will be available? And when will the new supplies get to market?

On the demand side, Rogers asks, What is this commodity most used for? Which of the current uses will continue? And he asks, What alternatives are available to replace it if the prices get too high? Not surprisingly, China became the driver of global copper prices—both on the way up and on the way down.

Given his hedge fund beginnings, Rogers is as likely to go short on an investment as he is willing to go long. Going short is a technique allowing you to profit from a decline in a price of an asset. It involves selling an asset first and then being obligated to buy it later. Rogers also takes pride in his contrarian streak, which means going against the crowd. The crowd is influenced by mob psychology and often overshoots or on the upside or downside. So, the contrarian—taking the other side of a trading position—

can often profit, as the market pendulum reverts to fair value. Or, as Rogers says, "If everyone thinks one way, it is likely to be wrong. If you can figure out that it's wrong, you are likely to make a lot of money."

In this regard, Rogers is not afraid to bet big on countries he considers under-followed, or even unpopular—as, at various times in history, the frontier markets of Botswana, Peru, and Mozambique have been. If he believes in a market, he is willing to be the first—or one of the earliest—investors in that market. And this approach—let's call it a first-mover advantage—often enables him to get in at bargain prices.

Rogers has four tests for what constitutes a good country to invest in. First, a country market should be doing much better than it has previously. This approach helps him avoid the scenario of catching a falling knife. It's easier said than done, but one clue he looks for is if the price of the market index of a country holds its own, in the face of bad news, like a bad GDP or unemployment report.

Second, he thinks an out-of-favor national market, with upside potential, should be better off than is generally recognized. Kind of like an undervalued stock, with the potential to provide a positive earnings or revenue surprise. Third, he wants the national currency to be convertible. That is, the currency should be based on market prices and freely exchangeable into U.S. Dollar, Euro, Swiss Franc, or some other widely traded currency. Otherwise, it's like the Roach Motel. You can check in, but you can't get your money out.

Fourth, the country must have well enough established markets for the investor to get in and get out of comfortably. It must be liquid, in trading lingo. A market that doesn't trade much is illiquid, making it a challenge to exit especially during periods of market volatility. Rogers tries to get a sense of the risks and opportunities available to his investor by his extensive travel, and by reading history and philosophy books—and not necessarily listening to the herd of Wall Street analysts.

Jim Rogers has lived the dream of many, becoming rich at a young age, and traveling around the world in search of knowledge and adventure. And he put his experience to good use. In this way, Jim Rogers has done more to educate the average investor about commodities than any other person. His keen understanding of supply and demand and his relentless work ethic made this formerly obscure asset class more accessible to all of us in the general public. Rogers, when asked by students what university degree would give them the best chance to earn a fortune in the years ahead, characteristically said, "Don't go for an MBA, get a degree in agriculture instead."

22

Private Equity Innovators: KKR, Blackstone

Private equity is the ownership of any company that doesn't trade on a public stock exchange. In Wall Street terms, private equity refers to a specific niche of investing: leveraged buyouts (LBOs) and venture capital. LBOs involve buying out the existing shareholders of a publicly traded company and delisting the firm's shares on the exchange where it formerly traded. The deal is usually paid for with debt—borrowing against the acquired company's assets—hence the term "leveraged." Venture capital, refers to investments in young growth companies.

Private Equity Fundamentals

> The two most prominent figures in the LBO world are Henry Kravis, the cofounder of the investment firm Kohlberg, Kravis, and Roberts; and Stephen Schwartzman, cofounder of the Blackstone Group. Both men became multibillionaires in the private equity market. The American Investment Council—the private-equity industry's trade group—estimates that about 2600 private equity firms in the United States invest more than $300 billion in the United States alone.

> Growth is nice, but cash is king in the leveraged-buyout business. Piling debt on a company requires cash flow to pay off the obligation. The amount of debt depends on the buyout target and the tightness of the credit markets at the time, but a rule of thumb is to borrow 3 to 4 times the amount of money that you plan to put up to complete a leveraged buyout.

> Part of the debt might be obtained from a bank, while the rest is often raised by borrowing against the target firm's assets. The more you borrow, and the more leverage you take on, the greater the investment risk.

> As a result, quite often in an LBO, the debt taken on is considered below investment grade—that is, junk bonds. As the name indicates, junk bonds have a high credit risk, and must offer investors higher yields than conventional debt. The LBO market and junk bonds grew up together during the 1980s.

> An ideal leveraged buyout target would be a firm with high free cash flow—that is, cash after expenses; a low debt-to-equity ratio; a strong competitive position in a stable industry; and a lot of cash on hand or assets that can be sold quickly, as needed to pay down debt. This kind of target acquisition leaves the buyer with opportunities both to profit on the purchase and to have an exit strategy.

> The LBO market is robust, but it has not been without controversy. During the 1980s, Michael Milken helped turn the junk-bond market into a popular way for troubled firms and corporate raiders to raise large amounts of money for LBOs and other merger-related activity when he was with the now-defunct investment banking firm of Drexel Burnham Lambert.

> As the junk bond and merger and acquisition (M&A) markets galloped forward, Milken and others were accused by federal authorities of various securities-related violations, including concealing the true owner of a security, insider trading, and tax evasion. Milken pled guilty to 6 felonies, but not to insider trading. He was sentenced to 10 years in prison, later reduced to 2 years. He was permanently banned from the securities industry, paid investors back $400 million, and paid the Securities and Exchange Commission $200 million.

Henry Kravis

> Henry Kravis was born January 6, 1944, in Tulsa, Oklahoma. His father was an engineer who set up a successful energy consulting and engineering firm in Oklahoma's oil patch. Kravis attended the prestigious Loomis Chaffee School in Connecticut, and Claremont

McKenna College, which offered strong economics and political science programs, which Kravis wanted to study.

> During his Claremont years, Kravis worked at a number of summer jobs, including research and institutional sales positions at Goldman Sachs. He graduated in 1967 with an economics degree, and that summer worked as an intern for a mutual fund called Madison.

> Kravis then enrolled at Columbia Business School for his M.B.A. After Columbia, Kravis worked in the corporate finance department at Bear Stearns, a Wall Street securities firm that was a leader in the nascent LBO industry. Kravis joined Bear around the same time as his cousin, George Roberts. Both were successful there, each of them making partner while still in their early 30s. But while Bear's leveraged buyout business was successful, they and their boss—Jerome Kohlberg Jr.—clashed with Bear's CEO, Cy Lewis.

> These tensions led the trio to leave Bear Stearns in 1976 to set up one of the first firms focused solely on LBOs. They called it Kohlberg, Kravis, and Roberts, KKR, and their most famous deal was RJR Nabisco, notorious, not only for its size, but also for epitomizing the Wall Street greed and frenzy that enveloped the market at the time.

> Kravis and KKR first discussed the idea with its CEO, Ross Johnson. Under this arrangement, Johnson would reportedly pocket up to $100 million. But Johnson partnered instead with the rival investment bank, Shearson Lehman Hutton, under a deal to take RJR private for $17 billion—$75 a share. KKR upped the offer to $20.4 billion, or about $90 a share, but the board rejected both offers.

> In the end, the RJR board accepted KKR's offer of almost $25 billion. KKR ended up earning less than 1% a year on this investment, according to some estimates. Not a disaster, perhaps, but the deal tied up a huge amount of firm capital—not to mention

management time and attention. Another 20 years would pass before Wall Street tried an LBO of that magnitude.

Henry Kravis's Strategy

> KKR's funds historically delivered strong investment returns to clients and grew to manage more than $120 billion for investors, controlling more than 100 portfolio companies with revenues greater than $200 billion a year. A number of attributes define KKR's success.

> Kravis was a pioneer. KKR's long history is not simply a track record, but a network of connections with companies, managements, investors, and financing firms that helps KKR find deals to which others do not have access.

> KKR focuses strongly on operational improvement at acquired properties, which often results in greater profitability at these companies. Improved profitability, in turn, increases the valuation multiple at which the acquired company can be ultimately sold.

> If a public company misses its quarterly earnings number, its stock gets crushed. This dynamic results in public companies sometimes overemphasizing short-term results. In contrast, private equity firms with a long-term focus, like KKR, may be in a better position to manage the firm for the long-term.

Stephen Schwarzman

> Stephen Schwarzman was born in Philadelphia February 14, 1947. He grew up in a Philly suburb called Abington and his father owned a dry-goods store that sold such products as drapery and linens. Schwartzman started working in the store on weekends when he was 15. The experience helped establish his work ethic and basic knowledge of business. It also taught him that he didn't want to work in retail sales.

> Schwarzman was his high school class president and went on to study psychology, sociology, and anthropology at Yale. Upon graduating in 1969, he found work as a securities analyst at the Wall Street brokerage firm, Donaldson Lufkin & Jenrette. He left DLJ after less than a year to complete his obligation in the Army Reserves before heading to Harvard for an M.B.A.

> After graduating from Harvard in 1972, Schwartzman joined the investment banking firm, Lehman Brothers. He was made a managing director by the age of 31 and head of mergers and acquisitions shortly thereafter. After a dozen years, Schwartzman arranged for Lehman to merge with the financial services company American Express: a combination that had the effect of forcing out Lehman's CEO, Pete Peterson, who, until then, had been a mentor to Schwartzman. Both men decided to leave and form their own firm, which they named Blackstone.

> Blackstone started as a boutique investment bank, providing advisory services to corporations. And then, in 1987, the pair decided to focus on the LBO market. Blackstone raised $830 million for its first leveraged buyout fund shortly before the stock market crashed in October of 1987. This good timing proved to be characteristic of the firm's future success.

Schwarzman Strategy

> Schwarzman is intensely competitive and known for outworking his competitors. His scrappy nature helped transform Blackstone from its startup stage to the largest private equity firm in the world, with more than $350 billion in assets under management. Schwarzman and Blackstone colleagues frequently seek buyers for the firms they acquire even before a deal is consummated.

> Schwartzman also controls his investment firm's risk by imposing a breakup fee on the target company if the transaction doesn't go through. If Equity Office Properties had walked away from

the Blackstone deal, it would have had to pay Schwartzman's firm $720 million. Schwarzman doesn't hesitate to pressure the management and board of target companies to make a quick decision on his offers.

> Technology firms often are considered unsuitable LBO targets because their products may have a short life span, and technology-intensive industries generally require a lot of research and development and capital expenditures to keep the business in good shape. That said, Schwartzman will buy companies near a cyclical bottom in earnings. One of his most successful leveraged buyouts was the German chemical firm, Celanese.

  o Blackstone offered to buy Celanese for $17 a share in 2004, but the company's management kept asking for a higher price, eventually yielding an offer of $32.50 a share, or about $3 billion, including debt. The deal terms are said to have made Schwarzman nauseous, but he met management's asking price. Schwartzman took some comfort that he was buying a solid company for less than book value, and believed that the industry would eventually rebound. Blackstone put up $650 million, and borrowed the rest.

  o About a year after taking Celanese private, the chemicals industry rebounded, and Blackstone cashed out by taking Celanese public again. The net result was about a 600% profit for Blackstone.

> Private equity firms like KKR and Blackstone have diversified in more recent years into other types of alternative and nontraditional investments. For example, they are now active in the lending and credit markets. Blackstone itself is now the largest owner of real estate in the world, according to Schwartzman, and the firm remains heavily involved in the commercial real estate space.

Conclusion

> Private equity and LBOs might seem to be part of the rarefied world of high finance, outside the realm of small investors, but the reality is that many of us belong to pension plans that have some portion of their assets tied up in private equity funds along with stocks, bonds, and hedge fund investments.

> Private equity is probably touching your life in one way or another. Many of the firms are now operating on a global scale, and their influence is felt in almost every industry and community.

Suggested Reading

Carey and Morris, *King of Capital*.
Kelly, *The New Tycoons*.

Questions to Consider

1. How would you describe the investment strategy of Henry Kravis and Stephen Schwartzman?

2. How do private equity firms try to increase returns for their investors?

22

Transcript

Private Equity Innovators: KKR, Blackstone

Private equity is the ownership of any company that doesn't trade on a public stock exchange. Now, there are millions of businesses in the United States, and only about 5,000 of them trade on public stock exchanges. So, by definition, private equity owns more than 99% of all U.S. businesses. But when Wall Street talks about Private Equity, it's usually referring to a very specific niche of investing. And that's what I'm going to talk about, leveraged buyouts or LBOs, and venture capital.

Leveraged buyouts are a form of investing that involves buying out the existing shareholders of a publicly traded company, and delisting the firm's shares on the stock exchange where it formerly traded. The deal is usually paid for with debt—or borrowing against the acquired company's assets—hence the term leveraged. When existing management leads one of these buyouts, it's called an MBO, which stands for management buyout. And in many cases, existing management continues with the firm after the LBO since it often knows the business—and the market—best. Many companies you are probably familiar with have been the subject of an LBO, at one time or another, Burger King, Dollar General, Dunkin' Donuts, Macy's, Toys R Us, and—perhaps most famously—RJR Nabisco, whose leveraged buyout was the subject of a bestselling book and popular movie, *Barbarians at the Gate*.

Venture capital, in contrast with most LBOs, refers to investments in young growth companies. Many high-profile firms such as Uber, Airbnb, and

Snapchat have received venture capital funding, early in their development. And although venture capital gets a lot of headlines, LBO investments are far larger, in terms of dollars invested in the space. The two most prominent figures in the LBO world are Henry Kravis, the co-founder of the investment firm Kohlberg, Kravis, and Roberts; and Stephen Schwarzman, co-founder of the Blackstone Group. Both men are multibillionaires in the private equity market. In this session, I'll try to shed some light on the world of private equity and LBOs, and discuss why it may be relevant to you. I'll also share some of the strategies that made Henry Kravis and Stephen Schwarzman successful. It's a very big business. The American Investment Council—the private-equity industry's trade group—estimates that about 2,600 private equity firms in the United States invest more than $300 billion in the United States alone.

Growth is nice, but cash is king in the leveraged-buyout business. If you plan to pile a bunch of debt on a company, then you'll need the cash to pay off the obligation. How much debt? Well, it depends on the buyout target, and the tightness of the credit markets at the time. But a rule of thumb is that you'll borrow three to four times the amount of money that you plan to put up, to complete a leveraged buyout. Part of the debt might be obtained from a bank, while the rest is often raised by borrowing against the target firm's assets. The more you borrow, and the more leverage you take on, the greater the investment risk. So quite often in ann LBO, the debt taken on is considered below investment grade—affectionately known as junk.

As the name indicates, junk bonds have a lot of credit risk, so it typically must offer investors higher yields than conventional debt. The LBO market and junk bond market grew up together during the 1980s. And even today, leveraged buyout targets tend to be mature firms that generate a lot of free cash flow. Free cash flow is the money a company has left over, after paying its expenses and reinvesting in itself.

One of the first LBOs was Orkin Exterminating Company in 1964. Now, that was probably a good company to do an LBO with since termites and rats are likely to be around forever. An ideal leveraged buyout target would be a firm with high free cash flow, a low debt-to-equity ratio, a strong competitive position in a stable industry, and a lot of cash on hand, or assets that can be sold quickly, as needed, to pay down debt. This kind of target acquisition leaves the buyer with opportunities profit on the purchase, to have a viable exit strategy. By exit strategy, I mean the acquired firm can be sold to another company, or be taken public again through a follow-up public stock offering.

The LBO market is robust, but it has not been without controversy. During the 1980s, Michael Milken helped turn the junk-bond market into a popular way for troubled firms and corporate raiders to raise large amounts of money for LBOs, and other merger-related activities, when he was with the now-defunct investment banking firm of Drexel Burnham Lambert. At the time, a generation of swashbuckling corporate raiders typically put down very little money down when offering to buy large, established companies with junk-bond financing—usually based all, or in large part, on the target company's own assets.

As the junk bond and M&A markets galloped forward, Milken and others were accused by federal authorities of various securities-related violations, including parking stocks—that is, concealing the true owner of a security—and with insider trading and tax evasion. The federal prosecutor who charged Milken was a man named Rudy Giuliani, who went on to become mayor of New York City and something of a celebrity in his own right. Milken ended up pleading guilty to six felonies—including conspiracy, mail fraud, and stock parking—but not insider trading. He was sentenced to 10 years in prison, later reduced to two years. And he was permanently banned from the securities industry. He also paid investors back $400 million and paid the Securities and Exchange Commission $200 million.

One controversial aspect to many leveraged buyouts is the desire of the new owners to reduce the acquired company's operating costs. This can often lead to large layoffs. And, in some cases, parts of the acquired firm are quickly sold, or spun off. At one time, it was even common for the acquirers to legally skim off surplus assets from a firm's pension fund. Today, many pension funds are underfunded—making this tactic impractical. And, in any event, most employee retirement savings plans have been shifted to defined-contribution plans, like 401ks, removing such savings as a source of takeover financing. The main point is that when management and a new owner are faced with a mountain of debt, they typically leave no stone unturned to reduce costs and wring out inefficiencies.

Henry Kravis was born on January 6, 1944, in Tulsa, Oklahoma. His father Raymond was an engineer who set up a successful energy consulting and engineering firm in Oklahoma's oil patch. Raymond Kravis was well regarded, and, at one time, served as an advisor to John F. Kennedy's father, Joseph Kennedy. Henry Kravis went to high school at the Loomis Chaffee School in Connecticut, a prestigious prep school, and then attended Claremont McKenna College in Southern California. Henry's dad had read an article in Time magazine about U.S. West Coast colleges that were like England's Oxford and Cambridge, and Claremont was among those featured. Claremont had a strong economics and political science program, which is what the younger man wanted to study. He also became the captain of the school's golf team.

During his Claremont years, Kravis worked at a number of summer jobs, including research and institutional sales positions at Goldman Sachs. He graduated in 1967 with an economics degree, and that summer worked as an intern at a mutual fund called Madison. Kravis then enrolled at Columbia Business School, in New York City, for his MBA. At Columbia, he also worked as vice president in the mergers and acquisitions area for Katy Industries, an industrial firm. After Columbia, Kravis worked in the corporate finance department at Bear Stearns, a Wall Street securities firm that was a leader in the nascent LBO industry, at the time.

Kravis joined Bear around the same time as his first cousin, George Roberts, did. Both men were successful at Bear Stearns, each of them becoming partners while still in their early 30s. But, while Bear's leveraged buyout business was successful, they and their boss—Jerome Kohlberg Jr. —clashed with Bear's CEO at the time, Cy Lewis. For example, the CEO Lewis repeatedly rejected Kohlberg's proposals to form a dedicated LBO department within Bear Stearns. Bear Stearns also had a trading culture, while LBOs often took years to turn profits. These tensions led the trio to leave Bear Stearns in 1976 to set up one of the first firms focused solely on LBOs. They called it Kohlberg, Kravis, and Roberts, or KKR for short.

KKR engaged in a number of high-profile LBOs, including Hospital Corporation of America, TXU, Playtex, Beatrice Foods, Safeway, Duracell, Toys R Us, Borden, AutoZone, and Regal Entertainment. But their most famous leveraged deal was for RJR Nabisco. The RJR transaction was notorious, not only for its huge size but also for epitomizing the Wall Street greed and frenzy that enveloped the market at the time.

Henry Kravis and KKR first discussed the idea of a leveraged buyout of RJR Nabisco with its CEO, Ross Johnson. Under this arrangement, Johnson was reportedly in line to pocket up to $100 million—a huge sum today, but truly enormous for a CEO back in 1988. Instead of doing a leveraged buyout with KKR, however, Johnson angered Kravis by partnering instead with the rival investment bank of Shearson Lehman Hutton, under a deal to take RJR private for $17 billion, or $75 a share. That offer—on October 20, 1988—put the consumer products and tobacco company in play, and set up a battle that Henry Kravis did not want to lose.

Four days later, KKR returned to the table with an offer of $20.4 billion for RJR Nabisco, or about $90 a share. But the board rejected both offers. KKR now tried to go around the board of directors by acquiring a controlling stake on the open market. It did so by making what's called a tender offer to all shareholders. That is, KKR offered to buy shares from any selling shareholder for that same $90 price that the RJR board had already rejected. In response, the CEO Ross Johnson's group upped the ante, now offering to buy RJR for $20.9 billion, or $92 a share. At this point, the company's board of directors sought to finalize all bids. But, the offers kept coming. KKR upped its earlier bid to $21.3 billion. And the CEO Johnson's group raised its price to $22.7 billion.

Then yet another suitor surfaced, with a tentative bid valued at anywhere from $23.8 billion and $26.8 billion. This was from a group led by the investment bank First Boston. In the final round of bidding, KKR offered almost $25 billion—and the RJR board now went with Henry Kravis's firm since an opposing offer from First Boston which might have been worth slightly more came with too many contingencies. With the negotiations behind it, KKR ended up earning less than 1% a year on this investment, according to some estimates. Not a disaster, perhaps. But the deal tied up a huge amount of the firm's capital—not to mention management time and attention.

Another 20 years would pass before Wall Street tried another LBO of that magnitude. Kravis—and his cousin, Roberts—eventually SPLIT with their mentor, Jerry Kohlberg due to the two younger men's penchant for large deals, and Kohlberg's dislike of hostile takeovers, which was part of KKR's toolkit. So, Kohlberg set up his own firm to focus on smaller deals.

Despite the missteps in the RJR Nabisco deal, KKR's funds historically delivered strong investment returns to clients. Unlike a mutual fund and many hedge funds, private equity pools generally exist for a finite period of time, usually about 10 years. And for that reason, private equity funds are often identified by date, like a fine wine. Each vintage starts at a specific date, and ends at a later date—a decade or so later—as the investment is wound down.

KKR grew to manage in excess of $120 billion for investors, controlling more than 100 portfolio companies with revenue in excess of $200 billion a year.

A number of attributes define KKR's success. First, Henry Kravis was a pioneer. And KKR's long history is not simply a track record, but a network of connections with companies, managements, investors, and financing firms. This network helps KKR find deals that the rest of us would never have access to. And the firm's large war chest makes even very large deals possible. One of KKR's sayings is, "Don't congratulate us when we buy a company. Congratulate us when we sell it." And this saying shapes how KKR is run.

And KKR focuses strongly on operational improvement at acquired properties, which often results in greater profitability at these companies. Improved profitability, in turn, increases that valuation multiple at which the acquired company can ultimately be sold. And KKR is not typically trying to flip an acquired company quickly, as was the case with many corporate raiders. Instead, the average holding period for a KKR acquisition is about seven years. With respect to improving operational efficiencies at acquired firms, Kravis poses the following questions to management. How do you shorten the supply chain? How do you improve waste in the product? How do you improve productivity throughout the organization? How do you improve the salesforce?

If a public company misses its quarterly earnings number, its stock gets crushed. This dynamic results in public companies sometimes overemphasizing short-term results. In contrast, private equity firms with a long-term focus, like KKR, may be in a better position to manage the firm for the long-term. KKR spells out its philosophy this way,

> At KKR we are particularly proud of our global, integrated approach. We operate as one firm, leveraging all of our businesses and partnering, across the firm, on behalf of our fund investors and the companies in which we invest. We look to partner closely and cooperatively with management teams and entrepreneurs that have a track record of success.

Stephen Schwarzman was born in Philadelphia on February 14, 1947. He grew up in a Philly suburb called Abington, Pennsylvania. And his father owned a dry-goods store called Schwarzman's, which sold products, such as drapery and linens. Stephen Schwarzman says he started working in the store on weekends when he was only 15 years old. The experience helped establish his work ethic and basic knowledge of business. It also taught him that he didn't want to work in retail sales. Schwarzman was his high school class president and went on to study psychology, sociology, and anthropology at Yale University. Upon graduating in 1969, he found work as a securities analyst at the Wall Street brokerage firm, Donaldson, Lufkin & Jenrette.

During those days of mandatory select service, he left DLJ after less than a year to complete his military obligation in the Army Reserves. And then he went to Harvard for an MBA. After graduating from Harvard in 1972, Schwarzman joined the investment banking firm, Lehman Brothers. And there he came to be viewed as a rising star. He was made a managing director at the age of 31, and head of mergers and acquisitions, shortly after that. After a dozen years, Schwarzman arranged for Lehman to merge with the financial services company American Express, a combination that had the effect of forcing out Lehman's CEO—Pete Peterson—who, until then, had been a mentor to Schwarzman.

So both men decided to leave, and form their own firm, which they named Blackstone. It started as a boutique investment bank, providing advisory services to corporations. And then, in 1987, the pair decided to focus on the LBO market. Blackstone raised $830 million for its first leveraged buyout fund shortly before the stock market crashed in October 1987. This good timing proved to be characteristic of the firm's future success, as it would've been very challenging to raise money after the crash.

Steven Schwarzman is intensely competitive and is known for often outworking his competitors, including in sports. Standing 5' 6", he would design elaborate plays on the basketball court in order to compensate for his stature. His scrappy nature also helped transform Blackstone from its start-up stage to the largest private equity firm in the world, with more than $350 billion in assets under management. Schwarzman and Blackstone colleagues frequently work to find buyers for the firms they acquire even before a deal is consummated. Blackstone's $39 billion purchase of Equity Office Properties in February 2007 is one of the largest LBOs ever, and it illustrates the point.

Prior to its sale, Equity Office Properties was controlled by the billionaire real estate magnate, Sam Zell. And Office Equity Properties was considered to be one of the largest Real Estate Investment Trusts in the world. It owned more than 500 office buildings across a number of major cities. Blackstone arranged for about $30 billion of Equity Office Properties' real estate to be re-sold to other investors, within six months of the deal closing. This was great timing for the sellers because the real estate market soon started to collapse, in what became known as The Great Recession. The remaining real estate portfolio—especially buildings held in Silicon Valley—did well, in time. Blackstone investors more than tripled their money in the Equity Office Properties LBO.

Schwarzman also controls his investment's risk by imposing a breakup fee on the target company. If Blackstone and its target agree to a deal—and, for some reason, the transaction doesn't go through—the firm that backs out of the arrangement often has to pay a breakup fee. If Equity Office Properties had walked away from that Blackstone deal after agreeing to be acquired, it would have to have paid Schwarzman's firm $720 million. Schwarzman doesn't hesitate to pressure the management and board of target companies to make a quick decision on his offers. In 2006, Blackstone had a tentative deal to buy Freescale Semiconductor—a spinoff from Motorola—for a little bit less than $17 billion.

But then, Blackstone rival KKR entered the picture and was reportedly planned to make a higher bid. So Schwarzman raised the offer by $800 million, with the caveat that Freescale Semiconductor's board had 24 hours to accept the deal, or else Blackstone would pull out. Freescale agreed, and Blackstone completed the acquisition for $17.6 billion, including debt.

Now, as it turns out, the Freescale deal wasn't a home run for Blackstone. It came before the financial markets crisis of 2007 and 2009 when asset valuations broadly were beaten down. Blackstone basically broke even about 10 years later, by selling Freescale to NXP Semiconductor. For that matter, technology firms often are considered unsuitable LBO targets because their products may have a short lifespan. And technology-intensive industries generally require a lot of research and development, and capital expenditures, to keep the business in good shape. That said, Schwarzman will buy companies near a cyclical bottom in earnings. One of his most successful leveraged buyouts was in the German chemical firm, Celanese.

Blackstone first offered to buy Celanese for $17 a share in 2004, but the German company's management kept asking for a higher price, eventually yielding an offer of $32.50 a share, or about $3 billion, including debt. The deal terms are said to have made Schwarzman nauseated. But he met management's asking price. Schwarzman took some comfort that he was buying a solid company for less than book value, and he believed that the industry would eventually rebound. And so, Blackstone put up $650 million and borrowed the rest.

Chemicals aren't like the fashion industry. They don't go in and out of style. They are essential to the global industrial economy. About a year after taking Celanese private, the chemicals industry rebounded, and Blackstone cashed out by taking Celanese public again. The net result was a 600% profit for Blackstone.

Private equity firms like KKR and Blackstone have diversified in more recent years into other types of alternative and non-traditional investments, outside of our primary discussion on LBOs. For example, private equity firms like KKR and Blackstone are now active in the lending and credit markets. You shouldn't be surprised if your next mortgage statement comes, either directly or indirectly, from a private equity firm. Blackstone itself is now the largest owner of real estate in the world, according to Schwarzman. For example, Blackstone is co-owner of Stuyvesant Town-Peter Cooper Village, Manhattan's biggest apartment complex with more than 11,000 units. And the firm remains heavily involved in the commercial real estate space, owning the Willis Tower in Chicago, which you might know better by its former name, the Sears Tower—the tallest building in the U.S.

Private equity and LBOs might seem to be part of the rarified world of high finance—outside the realm of small investors. But the reality is that many of us—including, teachers, the police, firefighters, civil servants, and others—belong to pension plans that have some portion of their assets tied up in private equity funds along with stocks, bonds, and hedge fund investments. In an interesting twist, many private equity firms are now themselves are now publicly traded companies, as a result of their own public stock offerings. So, it's possible for any one of us to buy and own shares in the very largest private equity firms, including KKR, Blackstone, and a third large and successful private equity competitor, Carlyle Group. Blackstone, KKR, and Carlyle Group trade on the New York Stock Exchange under the symbols BX, KKR, and CG, respectively.

Now, you might be wondering why companies that make a living off of private companies have themselves decided to go public. Well, it shouldn't be any surprise that a principal reason is money. The original owners can exchange their private equity for public shares, easily convertible to cash—for their own purposes, or for estate planning and charitable contributions. Further, by selling a piece of itself, the private equity firm gets a permanent source of capital for use in deals, or other business activities. KKR raised about $5 billion through its initial IPO, in May 2006. And Blackstone raised $4.1 billion from its own IPO in June of 2007.

Being public also makes it easier for private equity firms to raise additional capital through a secondary offering, should they need it. One other important advantage to taking private equity firms public is they can use the firm's stock to recruit, and reward, managerial talent. And, of course, being public provides an additional measure of publicity, potentially improving a firm's brand name.

In sum, private equity is probably touching your life in one way or another. Many of the firms are now operating on a global scale, and their influence is felt in almost every industry and community.

23

Four Women Who Moved Financial Markets

W omen, in aggregate, are better investors than men. they tend to be more patient, trade less, and have a greater focus on risk, all of which are important characteristics of successful investing, empirical studies show. Of course, not all women (or men, for that matter) invest in the same way. Four women renowned for their investing prowess are Hetty Green, Linda Bradford Raschke, Sonia Gardner, and Leda Braga. Each did it in her own unique way.

Hetty Green

> Hetty Green was once known as "the witch of Wall Street." She's also the first woman to be widely regarded for her investing skill. At the time of her death in 1916, she was worth between $100 million and $200 million—$2 billion to $4 billion today.

> She was born Henrietta Robinson November 21, 1834, in New Bedford, MA. Her father built a fortune in the shipping business. Hetty opened her first bank account at the age of 8. She was the family's bookkeeper, and she read the financial section of the newspaper aloud to her grandfather. Her father died in 1865 leaving her an inheritance of about $5 million.

> When asked about her investing strategy Green once said, "There is no secret in fortune making. When I see a good thing going cheap because nobody wants it, I buy a lot of it and tuck it away."

> Green avoided borrowing money or otherwise using leverage. Her discipline and fearlessness buying during panics—which occurred in 1857, 1873, 1893, 1901, and 1907—played an important role in her investing success. Green also amassed a real estate portfolio, acquiring 6000 pieces of property across 48 states.

> Notwithstanding her wealth, Green was known for her miserly behavior. She supposedly never turned on the heat or used hot water. She often wore the same clothes and dined on graham crackers, ham sandwiches, and small pies. Green also minimized the taxes she paid, routinely changing her residence so she couldn't be found by tax collectors. Once, when her son injured his leg in a sledding accident, Green took him to a charity hospital for free care.

Big Picture

> A brokerage account application includes various data points such as income, trading experience, gender, and marital status. University of California researchers Brad Barber and Terrence Odean, analyzed the trading records of a large discount brokerage firm between 1991 and 1997, reflecting the financial information of about 35,000 U.S. households.

> The data revealed that women investors outperformed men by 1.4% annually on a risk-adjusted basis. How actively one traded played a key role in this result. The research found that men traded 45% more, on average, than women did. Barber and Odean attribute the higher incidence of trading to the men's overconfidence in their trading ideas.

> The results were even more pronounced among single men and single women. Single men traded 67% more often than single women did; and the women outperformed the men by 2.3% a year.

> Another study found that hedge funds run by women outperformed the aggregate hedge fund index every year from 2007 to 2014. Woman-run hedge funds generated annual returns of 5.64% and a cumulative return of 59.43% compared to index returns of 3.75% annually and 36.69% cumulatively.

Linda Bradford Raschke

> Linda Bradford Raschke was born in 1959 in Pasadena, CA, and as a child, she helped her father look for patterns in the charts of stock prices. She attended Occidental College in Los Angeles, where she double-majored in economics and musical composition.

> At Occidental, Raschke also became involved in a program in which students managed a trust fund set up by a school donor. After graduation she tried to get a job as a stockbroker, but was turned down by every firm she applied to. Eventually, Raschke was offered a position as a floor trader on the Pacific Stock Exchange for a 50/50 split of the profits she generated.

> Raschke is a short-term trader with a focus on technical analysis. She trades in 20 different markets and usually is active in about 6 at any given time. She looks for patterns in security prices by analyzing historical price movements and trading volume data. Raschke believes that her most important skill is her ability to perceive patterns, an ability she attributes to her musical training.

> Discipline and concentration are related to patience, a skill Raschke believes is important for a trader. Raschke focuses on short-term strategies over periods of a couple of days to a couple of weeks. She says she believes short-term price swings can be predicted with some degree of precision because they are based on human behavior.

> Raschke especially likes one pattern based on contrarian psychology: If the price of a stock, bond, or commodity is trending up for several days in a row, then almost everyone likes it and it is ripe for a fall, so she will sell it short. Conversely, if the same asset falls for several days in a row, human psychology tends to be mostly bearish, and she may be inclined to step in to buy. This strategy is summarized in her statement that successful traders buy into bad news and sell into good news.

> She helps fine-tune her exit and entry points on contrarian trades with a formula known as a McClellan oscillator, calculated by finding the numbers of advancing and declining stocks adjusted by a moving average of prices. It provides a measure of overbought or oversold positions and helps her determine if the pendulum has swung too far in one direction.

> One of the techniques Raschke uses is a matrix that contains probabilities on historical price patterns. The first dimension corresponds to the past behavior of the asset. The second dimension is what will happen to the stock price in the future. The items inside the matrix are the probabilities of transitioning from one dimension to the other.

> Raschke's number one rule is, "Don't try to make a profit on a bad trade; just try to find the best place to get out." She also advises, "Never add to a losing position."

Sonia Gardner

> Another accomplished female investor is Sonia Gardner, who—with her brother Marc Lasry—manages more than $10 billion through their New York hedge fund, Avenue Capital Group, which focuses on distressed assets.

> Gardner was born February 16, 1962, in Morocco. A few years later, her family moved to Milford, CT, where she shared a room

with her brother and a younger sister. Their father was a computer programmer and their mother taught French at a private school.

> Gardner attended Clark University in Worcester, MA, majoring in philosophy and graduating in 1983 with honors. She went on to earn her law degree at the Benjamin Cardozo School of Law in New York. Lasry got a job managing about $50 million of the partners' capital at the New York investment banking firm, The Cowen Group, and soon he needed a lawyer he could trust.

> During their time at Cowen, Gardner and Lasry met the reclusive Texas investor, Robert Bass, who hired them to manage a $75 million portfolio of distressed assets for him. Bass also let them create a brokerage firm under the Bass umbrella, called Amroc Investments. Two years later, the pair left the Bass organization

to run their own debt-brokerage firm, which kept the name Amroc and maintained an affiliation with the Robert Bass group.

> To diversify Amroc's business, Gardner and Lasry formed the hedge fund management company, Avenue Capital Group, which they started in 1995 with $10 million in capital. Five years later, it had $1 billion under management. Gardner was initially a portfolio manager, instrumental in producing returns that enabled the firm to grow rapidly. Later, she transitioned to executive management, overseeing all operations.

> Avenue capital's basic investment philosophy is to find good companies with bad balance sheets. Further, it looks to find firms with sustainable businesses and positive cash flow, but whose financial situation is distressed.

> Avenue Capital typically commits to about 50 investments at a time. It states that it avoids leverage, and tries to keep a cash cushion of about 10% to 20% to take advantage of new opportunities and to avoid a cash crunch when liquidity dries up. Avenue Capital suffered losses of about 25% during the 2007–2009 recession, but it bounced back so strongly that it was able to return $9 billion to its investors a few years later.

Leda Braga

> Leda Braga is the founder and CEO of Systematica Investments, with more than $10 billion under management. She probably manages more money on a day-to-day basis than any other woman in the world. Braga was born in Rio de Janeiro in 1966. She earned a Ph.D. in engineering from Imperial College London, where she remained for 3 years afterward as a lecturer.

> Braga went on to join J. P. Morgan in London as part of its derivatives research team. When J. P. Morgan spun off part of the derivatives business into a firm called Cygnifi Derivatives

Services, Braga joined as the head of valuation. When J. P. Morgan colleague Michal Platt cofounded the hedge fund, Blue Crest Capital Management, Braga moved to Blue Crest, where she was a star as it grew into the largest hedge fund in Europe.

> Braga formed her own firm, Systematica, with Blue Crest initially retaining a 49% stake. Systematica trades in more than 150 markets around the world—including equities, fixed income, foreign exchange, energy, metals and agricultural commodities. Its models look not only at price data, which can be used to evaluate trends, but also such information as interest rates, currency movements, and financial statements.

> Price trend following seems to work, over time, for a number of reasons. Market psychology—be it fear or greed—tends to move in waves. Some investors extrapolate near-term to the long term, resulting in trend-following behavior. Often some investors uncover information before others and act on it, moving the price. Eventually the information becomes widely known, further reinforcing the trend.

> Systematica's models tend to be market neutral. That is, they try to be independent of the market movement as a whole. Generally, a portfolio can be made market neutral with offsetting hedge positions, such as shorting a market index or specific securities. Braga's portfolios also aim to limit exposure to other factors, such as being too big in an illiquid market.

> When a *Newsweek* reporter tried to speak with Braga awhile back for an article on women and investing, she declined to comment. A spokesperson said she preferred to speak about investing, rather than gender.

Suggested Reading

Ahuja, *The Alpha Masters*.
Fortado, "Lady Braga."
Schwager, *The New Market Wizards*.
Slack, *Hetty*.

Questions to Consider

1. How would you describe the investment strategies of Hetty Green, Linda Raschke, Sonia Gardner, and Leda Braga?

2. Why have studies found female investors, on average, tend to outperform male investors?

23

Four Women Who Moved Financial Markets

A woman named Hetty Green was once known as The Witch of Wall Street. She's also the first woman to be widely regarded for her investing skill. At the time of her death in 1916, she was worth between $100 million and $200 million. That would be $2 billion to $4 billion today. Hetty Green was born as Henrietta Robinson on November 21, 1834, in New Bedford, Massachusetts. Her father, Edward Black Hawk Robinson, built a fortune in the shipping business.

The daughter opened her first bank account at the age of eight. She was the family's bookkeeper. And she read the financial section of the newspaper aloud to her grandfather, who was nearly blind. Hetty's father died in 1865 leaving the young woman—then in her early 30s—with an inheritance of about $5 million. Initially, she used the money to buy Civil War bonds. Two years later, she married Edward Green, and the couple had two children, Edward and Harriet.

When asked about her investing strategy Green once said, "There is no secret in fortune making. When I see a good thing going cheap because nobody wants it, I buy a lot of it and tuck it away." Green avoided borrowing money, or otherwise using leverage. This was somewhat unusual at the time. In the early 1900s, it was possible to borrow $9 or $10 dollars to invest in the stock market for every $1 held in cash. Green's discipline and fearlessness buying during panics—which occurred regularly, at the time—

played an important role in her investing success. During Green's lifetime, financial panics occurred in 1857, 1873, 1893, 1901, and 1907.

In the midst of such panics, banks were often desperately in need of money. And Green lent to them at high rates of interest. She lent money to the City of New York on several occasions, including during the Panic of 1907. Green also amassed a huge real estate portfolio, acquiring 6000 pieces of real estate across 48 states. But notwithstanding her wealth, Green was known for her miserly behavior. She supposedly never turned on the heat or used hot water. She often wore the same clothes and dined on graham crackers, ham sandwiches, and small pies. Green also minimized the taxes she paid, bordering on evasive behavior. She reportedly routinely changed her residence so she couldn't be found by tax collectors.

Once, when her son Edward injured his leg in a sledding accident, Green took him to a charity hospital for care free of charge. Unfortunately, the leg wasn't treated properly and gangrene set in, forcing it to be amputated. Hetty Green's approach to investing—buying high-quality, low-risk investments during times of panic—resonates to this day, more than 100 years after her death in 1916. Most importantly, she had the discipline to stick to her strategy, a characteristic that extended to all parts of her life, sometimes to a fault.

It might come as something of a surprise, that women—in aggregate—are better investors than men. They tend to be more patient, trade less, and have a greater focus on risk, all of which are important characteristics of successful investing, as empirical studies show. Of course, not all women or men, for that matter invest in the same way. In this session will focus on four women who are renowned for their investing prowess. In addition to Hetty Green, we'll focus on the contemporary examples of Linda Bradford Raschke, Sonia Gardner, and Leda Braga. Each did it in her own, somewhat unique, way. But first, a little more background on women and investment performance.

University of California researchers, Brad Barber and Terrence Odean, analyzed the trading records of a large discount brokerage firm over the 1991–1997 time period. Various data points—such as income, trading experience, gender, and marital status—are included on a brokerage account application. And these records reflected the personal financial information on about 35,000 U.S. households. With this data, Barber and Odean discovered that women investors outperformed men by 1.4% a year, on a risk-adjusted return basis.

How actively one traded played a key role in this result. The research found that men traded 45% more, on average, than did women. Barber and Odean attribute the higher amounts of trading to the men's overconfidence in their trading ideas. The results were even more pronounced among single men and single women. Single men traded 67% more often than did single women. And these single women outperformed the single men by 2.3% a year. A different study by the alternative investments firm Hedge Fund Research found that hedge funds run by women, outperformed the aggregate hedge fund index every single year, from 2007–2014. Women-run hedge funds generated annual returns of 5.64%—and a cumulative return of 59.43%—compared to an index return of 3.75% a year, and 36.69% cumulatively.

The giant investment-management firm BlackRock has further found that women tend to be more conservative in matters of financial risk-taking than are men. They save more on a percentage basis and pay off debts quicker. A focus on loss control—and risk avoidance—are important, from an investing standpoint. Consider that a 50% loss requires a subsequent return of 100% just to break even.

Linda Bradford Raschke was born in 1959 in Pasadena, California. As a child, she helped her father look for patterns in the charts of stock prices. She attended Occidental College in Los Angeles, where she double-majored in Economics and Musical Composition. At Occidental, Raschke also became involved in a program in which students managed a trust fund set up by a school donor. And after graduating, she tried to get a job as a stockbroker but was turned down by every firm she applied to. She wound up accepting work as a financial analyst at Crown Zellerbach, a company that owned timberlands and paper mills. The corporation was located two blocks away from the Pacific Stock Exchange in San Francisco. And while the exchange opened at 7:30 a.m., her job at the paper company didn't start until an hour later. So Raschke would often talk with the traders, before work.

Eventually, Raschke was offered a position as a floor trader, in exchange for a 50/50 split of the profits she generated. She started out well in 1981, doubling her initial $25,000 stake after a few months, and then losing it after being on the wrong side of a takeover trade. She was now down $30,000, on the wrong-way trade, and she owed another $10,000 in student debt. Undeterred, she found another backer. Now, she focused on trading options and futures contracts.

Options and futures are derivative instruments. That is, they are securities whose values depend on underlying securities, such as changes in stock prices, commodities, and interest rates. Derivatives frequently involve leverage meaning borrowing, in which you invest a multiple of your trading capital. Raschke traded on the exchange floor for the next several years until she was involved in a horse-riding accident in 1986, resulting in a fractured rib, a punctured lung, and a dislocated shoulder. From that point on, she traded from her home office.

Raschke is a short-term trader—meaning an active investor—with a focus on technical analysis. She trades in 20 different markets and is usually active in about six of them at any given time. And she looks for patterns in security prices by analyzing historical price movements and trading volume data. Raschke believes that her most important skill is her ability to perceive trading patterns, an ability she attributes to her musical training. From the age of five until she was 21, she practiced piano for several hours a day every single day. Musical scores are symbols that often repeat in patterns, like a refrain—or hook—from your favorite song.

Raschke says that practicing on an instrument helped her develop personal discipline, and the ability to concentrate. Discipline and concentration are also related to patience, another skill Raschke believes is important for a trader. Raschke focuses on short-term strategies over a period of a couple of days to a couple of weeks. She says she believes short-term price swings can be predicted with some degree of precision because they're based on human behavior.

Raschke especially likes one pattern based on contrarian psychology. If the price of a stock, bond, or commodity is trending up for several days in a row, then almost everyone likes it, and it's ripe for a fall, Raschke believes. So, she will sell it short. Selling short is a technique that may enable a trader to profit from a decline in the price of a security. Conversely, if the same asset falls for several days in a row, human psychology tends to be mostly bearish, and she might be inclined to step in and buy. Raschke likens it to a rubber band that is stretched by human emotion, and then snaps back. This strategy is summarized in her statement that "Successful traders buy into bad news and sell into good news." Raschke also says,

> I think it's often more acceptable for a woman to rely on intuition than it is for a man to do so, and intuition certainly comes into play in trading. For example, when I'm watching the price quotes, I never say something like, "Oh, the market is down exactly 62 percent, I have to buy right here." Rather, I might think, "Geez, it looks like we've corrected enough and the price has stopped going down, so I'd better buy."

She helps fine-tune her exit and entry points on contrarian trades with a formula known as a McClellan Oscillator. It provides a measure of overbought or oversold positions. Basically, it helps her determine if the pendulum has swung too far in one direction.

The McClellan Oscillator is calculated by finding the number of advancing stocks and declining stocks adjusted by a moving average of prices, in an attempt to determine if a trend is about to turn around. A moving average is exactly what it sounds like. It takes the average of the price over the past let's say five days. Once six days of data are generated, the oldest observation is dropped from the calculation, and the newest one is included.

But Raschke's strategy is more complex than simply being a contrarian, at times, or a price or trend follower at other times. You might view these techniques as two tools in her trading toolbox. She also co-authored a book with Laurence Connors, called *Street Smarts: High Probability Short-term Trading Strategies* that spell out some of her trading ideas in further detail. One of the techniques Raschke uses is a matrix, which contains probabilities on historical price patterns. Mathematically, a matrix is a square or rectangular two-dimensional shaped object that contains rows and columns.

The first dimension of the matrix corresponds to the past behavior of the asset, let's say a stock. For example, maybe it went up one day in a row, two days, three days, or fell a similar number of days in a row. The second dimension is what will happen to the stock price in the future, up down, or unchanged. The items inside the matrix are the probabilities of transitioning from the first dimension, or state, to the other.

Let's try to make this concept more concrete by using the example I mentioned earlier. If the price of a stock falls five days in a row, Raschke might find that—based on historical data—the probability that the stock will rise the next day is 70%; and that the probability it will go down the next day is 20%; and that it would remain unchanged the next day is 10%. Given this probability, Raschke would buy. Of course, there is no guarantee the past is going to be like the future, but this is what technical analysts believe will happen, on average.

Raschke offers a number of risk-management tips. She says her number one rule is "Don't try to make a profit on a bad trade, just try to find the best place to get out." Raschke also advises, "Never add to a losing position." She says, "Have you taken a loss? Forget it quickly. Have you taken a profit? Forget it even quicker." Raschke ran her own investment firm for several years before retiring. She continues to manage her own trading account. At one point, the British multinational bank, Barclays, ranked the performance of her hedge fund 17th out of 4,500 funds it tracked, over a five-year period. She is the only female to have been featured by the popular author, Jack Schwager, in his series of books on traders and hedge fund managers called, *The Market Wizards*. Schwager wrote that Raschke once traded only three hours after giving birth to her daughter.

Another accomplished female investor that I'd like to introduce you to is Sonia Gardner, who—with her brother Marc Lasry—manages more than $10 billion through their New York hedge fund, Avenue Capital Group, which focuses on distressed assets. Sonia was born in the North African country of Morocco on February 16, 1962. A few years later, her family moved into a small apartment in Milford, Connecticut, where she shared a room with her brother and a younger sister. Their father was a computer programmer, and their mother taught French at a private school. Sonia and Marc attended Clark University, a small liberal arts college in Worcester, Massachusetts. She majored in philosophy and graduated in 1983 with honors. She went on to earn her law degree at the Benjamin Cardozo Law School in New York City.

Her brother Marc got a job managing about $50 million of partner capital at the New York City investment banking firm, The Cowen Group. And soon, he needed a lawyer he could trust. So, Sonia came aboard. During their time at Cowen, the pair met the reclusive Texas billionaire, Robert Bass, of the billionaire Bass brothers. Robert Bass hired the brother-sister team to manage a portfolio of $75 million in distressed assets for him. Bass also let them create a brokerage firm under the Bass umbrella, called Amroc Investments.

The name Amroc was a play on Morocco, where they were born; and their desire to appear under the letter A in the phone book—and elsewhere. Two years later, the pair left the Bass organization to run their own debt-brokerage firm, which kept the name Amroc and maintained an affiliation with the Robert Bass Group.

In the early days, Gardner and Lasry say they faced little competition in the distressed investments space, and that they regularly earned 50% a year on their capital. Gardner and Lasry also had talent, and they worked extremely hard. They were particularly strong in an area of the distressed-investing sector called trade claims. Let's say you sold a product to a firm that later went bankrupt. And let's say that the retail value of the product was $100 while your cost was $50. Technically, you are owed $100, but would you be willing to accept $70 or $80 to avoid the hassle of trying to collect in the bankruptcy proceedings? Skilled investors sometimes buy the rights to these claims at a discount, making the original creditor happy, and profiting when they collect.

In order to diversify Amro's business, the brother and sister team formed the hedge fund, Avenue Capital Group, which they started in 1995 with $10 million in capital. Five years later, it had $1 billion in assets under management. Chelsea Clinton once worked there. Sonia was a portfolio manager, initially, and instrumental in producing the returns that enabled the firm to grow rapidly. Later, she transitioned to executive management, overseeing all operations. Avenue Capital's basic investment philosophy is to find good companies with bad balance sheets. Drilling down further, it looks to find firms with sustainable businesses and positive cash flow, but whose financial situation is distressed.

One example was Six Flags Entertainment, which describes itself as the world's largest regional theme company. Six Flags operates about 20 amusement parks, and hosts around 25 million visitors a year. Unlike the Walt Disney Company—and the Universal Studios Theme Parks—Six Flags focuses on the day-trip crowd, rather than being an all-inclusive resort. Six Flags's problem a few years ago was that it entered the financial markets crisis with $2 billion in debt. Facing a $200 million installment payment, the firm filed for bankruptcy. Avenue Capital had started buying Six Flags bonds a few years earlier, at substantial discounts. In bankruptcy, bondholders are paid first, followed by preferred stockholders, and then common stockholders.

Within each category, there might be several subcategories. For example, bank debt tends to get paid first relative to the claims of other bondholders. Large debtholders also get to petition the bankruptcy court with a plan of reorganization for the distressed company. In this instance, the court sided with Avenue Capital's plan for reorganization. Not only did the hedge fund recover more than it paid for the amusement park's distressed bonds, but it was also given substantial equity in the reorganized firm. Avenue Capital typically commits to about 50 investments at a time. It states that it avoids leverage, and tries to keep a cash cushion of about 10–20% to take advantage of new opportunities—and to avoid a cash crunch when liquidity dries up. Avenue Capital suffered losses of about 25% during the 2007–2009 Great Recession but bounced back so strongly that it was able to return $9 billion to its investors a few years later.

Finally, I'd like to introduce you to Leda Braga, the founder and CEO of Systematica Investments with more than $10 billion under management. She probably manages more money on a day-to-day basis than any other woman in the world. CNBC has called her The Most Powerful Woman in Hedge Funds. Braga was born in Rio de Janeiro, Brazil in 1966. She earned a Ph.D. in Engineering from Imperial College in London, where she remained for three years afterward, as a lecturer. Braga went on to join J.P. Morgan in London as part of its derivatives research team.

When J.P. Morgan spun off part of the derivatives business into a firm called Cygnifi Derivatives Services, Braga joined the spinoff as the head of valuation. Later, J.P. Morgan colleague, Michal Platt, co-founded the hedge fund, Blue Crest Capital Management, and Braga moved to Blue Crest Capital. It grew into one of the largest hedge funds in Europe. Braga was a star employee. The BlueTrend Fund that she managed delivered returns in excess of 10% a year for more than a decade, more than double its benchmark. Braga was reportedly paid like a star, earning more than $50 million a year.

Braga then formed her own firm, Systematica, with BlueCrest initially retaining a 49% stake. Systematica trades in more than 150 markets around the world—including equities, fixed income, foreign exchange, energy, metals and agricultural commodities. And its models look not only at price data, which can be used to evaluate trends, but also a bunch of other information, such as interest rates, currency movements, and financial statements.

Price trend following also known as trend trading seems to work, over time, for a number of reasons. Market psychology—be it fear or greed—tends to move in waves. When the market is going up, and it seems like everyone is making money, and it's hard not to be bullish. In contrast, when the market is falling and fear is widespread, it's hard not to be bearish. Some investors extrapolate the near term to the long-term, resulting in trend-following behavior. Other reasons for prices to trend relate to research and price discovery. Often some investors—let's call them the smart money—uncover information before others. They act on it, moving the price. Eventually, the information becomes widely known, further reinforcing the trend.

And sometimes trends occur because of insider trading. Insider traders may legally—or illegally—access information and trade on it. For example, that information might consist of a decision about an impending merger. After the asset's price changes, or once the information becomes public, then others are likely to act on the information, as well. Trend trading sounds pretty simple on the surface, but talking about it, and implementing it is another story. That requires answers to such questions as, When did the trend start? How far can it last? Is the trend likely to reverse course? Has there been abnormal trading volume around the trend? That's where quantitative models come in.

Systematica's models tend to be market neutral. That is, they try to be independent of the market movement as a whole, be it the stock market, bond market, or other market. Generally, a portfolio can be made market neutral with offsetting hedge positions, such as shorting a market index, or specific securities. Braga's portfolios also aim to limit the exposure to other factors, such as being too big in an illiquid market. Braga says quantitative models, like her firm's, helped take the emotion out of trading. On the human or intuitive approach to investing compared to a machine or quantitative-driven strategy, Braga says, "Right now there is a place for both approaches. That is in the present. But then we have the future. Does the future hold a world where the systematic approach dominates? I suspect yes," she says.

Quantitative models don't always work, and no model—or models—are ever perfect. During a rough stretch in early 2013, Braga's BlueTrend Fund lost 17% in a little over one month. And then the fund bounced back. When a *Newsweek* reporter tried to speak with Braga awhile back about an investing article on women, she declined to comment. A spokesperson said that she preferred to speak about investing, rather than about gender.

But by whatever measure, Braga regularly exceeds expectations, whether obtaining a Ph.D. in Engineering, or riding a super fast Ducati Monster 700 motorcycle, or running one of the most successful quantitative hedge funds on the planet. Many women have, by now, had a major influence in the world of finance and investing. The late Katherine Graham, former CEO of *The Washington Post*, is credited as being a great influence on the billionaire and master Warren Buffett. After Buffett became a *Washington Post* shareholder and board member, Kate Graham provided him with an introduction to a who's who of global corporate executives and politicians.

Another example is Abigail Johnson, the CEO of Fidelity Investments in Boston, with more than $2 trillion in assets under management. Johnson has a Harvard MBA, and spent years working as an analyst and fund manager at the mutual fund company founded by her grandfather, Edward Johnson II, and turned into an investing powerhouse by her father, Edward Johnson III. And then there is Muriel Siebert, who became the first woman to hold a seat or membership in The New York Stock Exchange, after founding her namesake firm, Muriel Siebert & Company. For years, she was known as The First Woman of Wall Street.

I could go on. But the examples of Hetty Green, Linda Bradford Raschke, Sonia Gardner, and Leda Braga each demonstrate that women have made tremendous inroads—and accomplishments—in money management. And, in the years to come, I'm certain that the role of women in investing and finance will grow even greater.

24

Becoming a Great Investor

The challenge of developing your own investment philosophy and approach, as sketched by the models considered at in this course, should match your personality, skills, risk tolerance, and resources. You will need a high degree of self-knowledge and confidence to choose whether to be a growth or a value investor; whether you will actively manage your portfolio or turn it over to a professional advisor; whether to accept the risks of using leverage or avoid debt altogether. Whatever path you choose, continue to study and learn from the great investors who have gone before you.

The Chrysler Story

> Walter Percy Chrysler was born on April 2, 1875, and grew up in Ellis, IA, where his father was an engineer for the Union Pacific Railroad. Given his father's profession, it's no surprise that Walter Chrysler started his own career as a railroad mechanic and machinist before making his way into the automotive business.

> Over the next century, the Chrysler Corporation's up-and-down fortunes taught us something about how to look at the stock market—or any investment. At one point or another, Chrysler has been all of the following: a growth stock, a value stock, a distressed asset, a mergers-and-acquisitions target, a bankruptcy,

a government-owned corporation, a private equity asset, an international asset, a small-cap stock, and a large-cap stock.

> The auto industry came to signify what growth investor T. Rowe Price called cyclical growth—that is, sensitive to the macro-economy and each part of its cycle. The car makers' momentum slowed substantially as oil prices quadrupled during, and after, the oil embargo of 1973–1974, when American automakers were caught flat-footed with fleets of gas guzzling models.

> Chrysler, in particular, was on shaky financial ground by the late 1970s and hired a firebrand former Ford Motors president, lee Iacocca, to run the troubled company. Although Chrysler was losing money hand over fist—and on the verge of bankruptcy—Iacocca persuaded Congress to support the company with a loan guarantee that kept the company afloat, at least temporarily. A new lineup of vehicles, led by the fuel-efficient K-car series and the newly invented minivan, is what really saved Chrysler.

> Peter Lynch started buying Chrysler stock in 1982, reasoning that the government loan guarantee insulated Chrysler from bankruptcy and that its cash position was markedly improved by the $1 billion sale of its military tank division to defense contractor General Dynamics.

> The next seminal moment in Chrysler's history occurred when Germany's Daimler-Benz acquired Chrysler for $36 billion in 1998. Nine years later, Daimler sold 80% of Chrysler for $7.4 billion to the private equity firm Cerberus Capital Management. Cerberus thought it was buying an impaired firm at an attractive price, but the financial markets crisis and recession of 2007–2009 wiped out both Chrysler and GM, leaving them bankrupt and their common shares essentially worthless.

> Chrysler received another government bailout. Then, in a series of transactions, Fiat bought the U.S. government stake in Chrysler

for $11.2 billion, resulting in a loss of roughly $1.3 billion for U.S. taxpayers.

> Several lessons are clear from Chrysler's story. One is that picking a winner in a new and growing industry like automobiles can be very profitable, at least for a time. A second is the dynamic nature of companies and industries. Chrysler, a firm that helped usher in the golden age of automobiles, went bankrupt once—and almost twice. A third is the increasingly global nature of financial markets.

Investment Checklist

> The first item on the checklist is risk. Everyone needs a strategy to deal with risk. One aspect of a risk-management plan is to identify how much you want to earn or how much you can afford to lose. What are your upper and lower boundaries, in terms of financial risk and reward?

   ○ When you're starting out in life, typically you can afford to take on greater financial risks, even with fewer assets, on the expectation that your nest egg will grow, and you will have time to overcome any losses.

   ○ Find a level of diversification consistent with your risk tolerance. Owning a portfolio of treasury securities is not very diversified but is considered low risk. Owning a portfolio of distressed assets is also not very diversified, and the risk might be quite high. If you combine lower- and higher-risk instruments—such as growth stocks, utility bonds, and other instruments—you can develop a portfolio that is custom-blended for your personal risk tolerance.

> The second item is investment approach. Active investing refers to a strategy that tries to outperform the market. Passive investing refers mostly to index funds, which mirror the performance of a widely followed market index, such as the Dow Jones Industrial Average or S&P 500.

- Passive investing might also take a long-term buy-and-hold approach, even without trying to track an index. John Bogle, the founder of the mutual fund company vanguard, showed us that passive investing strategies often outperform actively managed mutual funds.

> Third, you'll need to know what types of financial securities you want to invest in and how actively you want to change your weights or allocations devoted to them. A wide range of investments is available for everyone—from the cautious and inexperienced to the expert and adventurous; from basic stocks and bonds to hedge funds, private equity, and even some very exotic derivative instruments.

> The rest of the questions on my checklist apply mostly to people who want to take an active role in managing their investments, rather than outsourcing the activity to a trusted advisor.

> What investing edge might you possess? The former Fidelity Investments portfolio manager Peter Lynch says, "Invest in what you know." If you think about it, you probably do know a lot about at least one slice of the investment universe—from your job, your school, your community, your family, and this knowledge might be your edge when it comes to investing.

> Do you want to be a trader who buys and sells or an investor who buys and holds? A trader typically focuses on a time horizon of less than one year, while an investor maintains a horizon of a year or more.

> You should also ask yourself whether you are a growth investor or value investor, or some combination.

- Investors like Benjamin Graham and Warren Buffett are value investors while Philip Fisher and T. Rowe Price are growth investors. In contrast, John Templeton, a pioneer of international investing, adopted a flexible approach that encompasses both, and he gave us the question: Should international securities be part of my portfolio?

> Continuing, ask yourself: large-cap, small-cap, or both? Large-cap firms are generally more stable and often pay a dividend. Small-cap firms often have less information available, but historically have had higher returns and higher risk over long periods.

> A more difficult question, requiring some deeper expertise, is whether your approach will be mostly fundamental, technical, quantitative, or some combination.

  ○ Seth Klarman is an example of a fundamental analyst who analyzes a firm's financials and understands company operations, industry, and management in great detail. Alternatively, Jesse Livermore was one of the most successful practitioners of technical analysis; an approach that focuses on finding patterns in past price movements that could be useful in predicting future prices.

  ○ Hedge fund managers James Simons and Leda Braga are quantitative investors. They don't visit companies or even care what a company does, but rather spend their time building mathematical models that predict where security prices are going.

> Ask yourself what investments mistakes you make or are susceptible to making. Market psychology, or behavioral finance, is the field of analyzing investor mistakes and tendencies—and profiting on them.

  ○ The contrarian investor David Dreman is often willing to buy what the market seems to hate—like tobacco stocks, when they were being investigated by the federal government.

  ○ Ray Dalio, who runs the world's largest hedge fund, suggests keeping a trading or investment journal detailing the rationale for your investments and their outcomes, as one way of uncovering and learning from your mistakes.

○ By contrast, other successful investors, like Linda Raschke, harness the power intuition part of their trading or investment process. If you find your intuition to be associated with some of your better investment decisions, perhaps it can be incorporated into your investment philosophy.

> Finally, ask yourself if you have the temperament to follow the rules you set up. Jesse Livermore, was a great trader, but he made and lost several fortunes over his lifetime. He said he lost money when he didn't follow his own rules. Your investment philosophy and approach should match your personality, skills, risk tolerance, and resources.

Conclusion

> One final great investor is Joel Greenblatt, who might not be a household name, but he has one of the best investment track records of all-time. During the decade when Greenblatt ran the hedge fund Gotham Capital, he generated annual returns of 50% before fees. He ultimately closed the fund and returned the profits and original capital to outside investors, but he and his colleagues continued to manage their own money, with stellar results.

> Joel Greenblatt was born December 13, 1957, in Great Neck, Long Island, about an hour from Manhattan, and attended the University of Pennsylvania's Wharton School ultimately earning an M.B.A. After one year in law school, Greenblatt realized he wasn't interested in a legal career and took a job as a risk-arbitrage and special situations analyst at a startup hedge fund called Halcyon Investments.

> He was soon doubling his money trading in his personal account, so a friend put him in touch with Michael Milken, the junk bond king. Milken offered to put up the bulk of the money for a new fund

Greenblatt wanted to manage, and he launched Gotham Capital in 1985 with $7 million under management.

> Greenblatt's most famous strategy revolves around finding good stocks that are also cheap. Greenblatt's thoughts are deep, and his logic compelling. He outlines an investing approach that combines value investing with special-situations investing. Special-situations investing focuses on nontraditional investments like spinoffs, merger arbitrage, rights offerings, long-term options, and others.

> Greenblatt provides some specific advice to improve your results. He suggests looking for businesses that institutional investors— such as pensions and insurance companies—don't want, especially if they are too small for the big institutions to own. Greenblatt also says to look at the behavior of corporate insiders: whether they are buying or selling. They know the business best.

> As we saw with both Walter Chrysler and Joel Greenblatt— your investment philosophy and approach should match your personality, skills, risk tolerance, and resources.

Suggested Reading

Greenblatt, *You Can Be a Stock Market Genius*.
Schwager, *Hedge Fund Market Wizards*.

Questions to Consider

1. After reviewing the Investment Checklist in this lecture, how would you describe your personal investment philosophy?

2. How does the case study of Chrysler relate to many of the investment strategies discussed in this course?

24

Transcript

Becoming a Great Investor

Walter Percy Chrysler was born on April 2, 1875, and grew up in Ellis, Iowa, where his father, Henry, was an engineer for the Union Pacific Railroad. Given his father's profession, it's no surprise that Walter Chrysler started his own career as a railroad mechanic and machinist, before making his way into the automotive business. Over the next century, the Chrysler Corporation's up-and-down fortunes taught us something about how to look at the stock market—or any investment. At one point or another, Chrysler was a growth stock meaning a fast-growing company, and a value stock meaning an underappreciated one.

It's been a distressed asset, and a mergers-and-acquisitions target, and a bankruptcy firm, and a government-owned corporation, and a private equity asset—and an international one. These are all investing concepts we've looked at in some detail, during this course. It's also been a small-cap stock and a large-cap stock. But, I don't want to get too far ahead of my Chrysler story.

In 1912, Walter Chrysler got a job as production manager for the recently established General Motors Corporation's Buick line of cars in Flint, Michigan. Four years later, he was put in charge of the entire Buick division. Chrysler left GM in 1919 to fix the troubled Willys-Overland Motor Company. At the time, the auto industry was a grab-bag of start-up firms, small-cap firms, and hyper growth firms and distressed firms.

A value investor, like Benjamin Graham, probably would have avoided the auto industry during the first part of the 20th century because the firms lacked operating history and most had shaky finances. Value investors like to minimize their downside risk, even if it means passing up on potentially astronomical returns. On the other hand, growth investors like Philip Fisher and Thomas Rowe Price might have been willing to take the plunge. They'd be looking for earnings growth—and quality management.

Getting back to Walter Chrysler, in 1921 he took a controlling interest in another car company, Maxwell Overland; and then formed Chrysler Corporation in June 1925, absorbing Maxwell Motors shortly thereafter. Walter Chrysler developed the automotive nameplates Chrysler, DeSoto, and Plymouth; and, in 1928, he acquired the Dodge Brothers Company, as well. As a sign of his growing prosperity, Walter Chrysler commissioned the art-deco Chrysler Building in New York City, which, at the time of its completion in May 1930, was briefly the tallest building in the world. Today, it remains one of the most beautiful buildings in the world, even though a year after its construction it would be eclipsed by the empire State Building.

Now, post-World War II America was a booming time for the auto industry, with many of the leading firms taking their place among the largest and fastest-growing firms in the U.S. stock market. But consolidation left us with the big three—GM, Ford, and Chrysler, and a few smaller competitors—followed by the golden age of the U.S. automotive industry in the 1950s and 1960s. The industry also came to signify something that growth investor Thomas Rowe Price called cyclical growth. That is, a firm that is very sensitive to the macro economy, and each part of its cycle. The car makers' momentum slowed substantially as oil prices quadrupled during, and after, the oil embargo of 1973–1974 when American automakers were caught flat-footed with fleets of gas-guzzling models. Chrysler, in particular, was on shaky financial ground by the late 1970s, and hired a firebrand former Ford Motors president, Lee Iacocca, to run the troubled company.

Iacocca was famous for introducing the Ford Mustang to the market. But he ended up being fired due to a conflict with the company's chairman, Henry Ford II. Although Chrysler was losing money hand over fist—and was on the verge of bankruptcy—Iacocca persuaded Congress to support the company with a loan guarantee. And that kept the company afloat, at least temporarily. But what really saved Chrysler was a new lineup of vehicles led by the fuel-efficient K-Cars, and its invention of the minivan. Chrysler also acquired the much smaller American Motors Corporation, which was having the same problems of surviving in the new global automotive market—but it owned the popular Jeep brand.

Peter Lynch—the famous Fidelity Investments mutual fund manager—started buying Chrysler stock in 1982, when the price was only $2 a share. Lynch reasoned that the government loan guarantee insulated Chrysler from bankruptcy; and that its cash position was markedly improved by the $1 billion sale of its military tank division to defense contractor General Dynamics. Lynch also liked Chrysler's new lineup of K-Cars and minivans.

The Chrysler investment turned out to be a tenbagger for Lynch—a term he coined to describe an investment that increases 10-fold or more from the original purchase price.

Good times never seem to last forever, though for Chrysler. The next seminal moment in Chrysler's history occurred when Germany's Daimler-Benz—the maker of Mercedes-Benz vehicles—acquired Chrysler for $36 billion in 1998. This merger turned out to be a disaster. German and American management styles clashed. And that was one of many reasons why the deal ultimately failed. Nine years later, Daimler admitted defeat and sold 80% of Chrysler for $7.4 billion to the private equity firm of Cerberus Capital Management. After accounting charges and write-downs, it appears Daimler actually paid Cerberus $650 million to take Chrysler off its hands. Cerberus thought it was buying an impaired firm, at an attractive price. But the financial markets crisis and recession of 2008–2009 wiped out two of the former Big Three—Chrysler and GM—leaving both bankrupt, and their common shares essentially worthless.

Now, Chrysler received another government bailout, this time through TARP, the U.S. Treasury-administered Troubled Asset Relief Program. Although Congress had intended TARP primarily for large financial institutions, it advanced $10.9 billion to Chrysler along with another $1.5 billion in support to sell Chrysler vehicles through a consumer loan program.

And then, in a series of transactions, Fiat bought the U.S. government stake in Chrysler for $11.2 billion, resulting in a loss of roughly $1.3 billion for U.S. taxpayers. Today, Fiat-Chrysler is a foreign owned company and trades on the New York Stock Exchange under the symbol FCAU.

There are several lessons we can take away from Chrysler's story. One is that picking a winner in a new and growing industry, like automobiles, can be very profitable, at least for a time. A second lesson is the dynamic nature of companies and industries. Chrysler, a firm that helped usher in the golden age of automobiles, went bankrupt once—and almost twice. A third lesson is the increasingly global nature of financial markets. American-made Chryslers were sold around the world, and today the company is owned by an Italian holding company. A particular class of investors—value, growth, small-cap, large-cap, distressed, international—was interested in Chrysler at various points in its history. Some of these investing buckets might not be your cup of tea. But, at every stage, the investment was someone's cup of tea.

Now, let's turn to the challenge of developing your own investment philosophy, as framed by the lessons we've looked at in this course. Here's a checklist of questions to think about. The first question that we typically want to address is risk. What is your personal risk tolerance? Everyone needs a strategy to deal with risk. And one aspect of a risk-management plan is to identify how much you want to earn—for retirement, for instance. Or how much can you afford to lose? What are your upper and lower boundaries, in terms of financial risk and reward? When you're starting out in life, typically you can afford to take on greater financial risks even with fewer assets on the expectation that your nest egg even if it's small will grow, and you will have time to overcome any losses.

You'll then want to find a level of diversification consistent with your risk tolerance. Owning a portfolio of Treasury securities is not very diversified, but is considered low risk. Owning a portfolio of distressed assets is also not very diversified, and the risk might be quite high. But, if you combine lower and higher-risk instruments—like growth stocks, utility bonds, and other instruments—you can develop a custom-blended portfolio for your personal risk tolerance.

The next question is, Do I want to take an active investing approach to my portfolio? Or a passive investing approach? Active refers to a strategy that tries to outperform the market. Passive investing refers mostly to index funds, which mirror the performance of a widely followed market index, like the Dow Jones Industrial Average or the S&P 500. Passive investing might also take a long-term buy-and-hold approach, even without trying to track an index. John Bogle, the founder of the mutual fund company Vanguard, showed us that passive investing strategies often outperform actively managed mutual funds.

Next, you should ask yourself, What types of financial securities do I want to invest in? And how actively do I want to change my weights or allocations devoted to these securities? A wide range of investments are available for everyone—from the cautious and inexperienced to the expert and adventurous; from basic stocks and bonds to hedge funds, private equity, and even some very exotic derivative instruments. And if you're interested in derivatives—which are contracts like options or futures, whose values depend on an underlying asset like stock prices or the level of interest rates, and are normally reserved for the more sophisticated investors—then another aspect of your risk-management plan will be how much leverage, or borrowed money, you intend to use.

Warren Buffett generally recommends against leverage. In one of his letters to Berkshire Hathaway shareholders, he wrote, "Unquestionably, some people have become very rich through the use of borrowed money. However, that's also been a way to get very poor." On the other hand, the hedge fund manager George Soros—who became famous for making more than a billion dollars in one day by shorting the British Pound back in 1992—said, "There is no point in being confident and having a small position."

The rest of the questions on my checklist apply mostly to people who want to take an active role in managing their investments, rather than outsourcing the activity to a trusted advisor. The first of these is, What is my edge? So, what investing edge might you possess? The former Fidelity Investments portfolio manager Peter Lynch says, "Invest in what you know." And, if you think about it, you probably do know a lot about at least one slice of the investment universe—from your job, your school, your community, your family. And this knowledge might be your edge when it comes to investing.

Another question to ask yourself is Do I want to be a trader who buys and sells actively? Or an investor who buys and holds? There is no hard cutoff between the two. But a trader typically focuses on a time horizon of less than one year, while an investor maintains a horizon of a year or more, and even decades. Warren Buffett says his favorite holding period is forever.

You should also ask yourself, Am I a growth investor or value investor, or some combination of the two? Investors like Benjamin Graham and Warren Buffett are considered value investors while Philip Fisher and T. Rowe Price are considered growth investors. In contrast, John Templeton, a pioneer of international investing, adopted a flexible approach that encompasses both. And he gave us the question, Should international securities be part of my portfolio?

You should go on to ask yourself, Am I going to invest in large-cap companies, or small-cap companies, or across both types? Small-cap firms are usually valued at less than $1 billion. Large-cap firms are anything larger than that—sometimes hundreds of times more, as in the examples of Apple and Amazon.com. Large-cap firms are generally more stable and they often pay a dividend. Small-cap firms often have less information available about them, but historically have had higher returns and higher risk over their larger peers, over long periods.

A more difficult question, requiring some deeper expertise, is this, Is your approach going to be mostly fundamental, technical, quantitative, or some combination of the above? Seth Klarman is an example of a fundamental analyst; that is, someone who analyzes a firm's financials and understands company operations, industry, and management in great detail. Alternatively, Jesse Livermore was one of the most successful practitioners of technical analysis; an approach that focuses on finding patterns in past price movements that could be useful in predicting future prices. Hedge fund managers James Simons and Leda Braga are quantitative investors. They don't visit companies or even care what a company does, but rather spend their time on building mathematical models that predict where security prices are going.

You should also ask yourself, What investments mistakes do I make, or am I susceptible to make? Market psychology, or behavioral finance, is the field of analyzing investor mistakes and tendencies—and profiting from them. The contrarian investor David Dreman is often willing to buy what the market seems to hate—like Tobacco stocks when they were being investigated by the federal government. Another famous investor, Ray Dalio, who runs the world's largest hedge fund, suggests keeping a trading or investment journal detailing the rationale for your investments and the outcomes, as one way of uncovering and learning from your mistakes. By contrast, other successful investors, like Linda Raschke, harness the power of intuition as part of her trading or investment process. If you find your intuition to be associated with some of your better investment decisions, perhaps it can be incorporated into your investment philosophy.

And lastly, you should ask yourself, Do I have the temperament to follow the rules I set up? Jesse Livermore was a great trader, but he made and lost several fortunes over his lifetime. He said he lost money when he didn't follow his own rules. So your investment philosophy and approach should match your personality, skills, risk tolerance, and resources.

Now it's time to introduce you to one more great investor before we wrap up this seminar on the *Art of Investing*. He's a man named Joel Greenblatt, who might not be a household name. But he has one of the best investment track records of all-time. During the decade when Greenblatt ran the hedge fund Gotham Capital, he generated annual returns of 50% before accounting for fees. He ended up closing the fund and returning the profits and original capital to outside investors. But he and his colleagues continued to manage their own money, with stellar results. Joel Greenblatt racked up this great performance primarily by employing a range of strategies that fall under the umbrella of special-situations investing. But before I explain special-situations investing, let me say something more about his background.

Joel Greenblatt was born on December 13, 1957, in Great Neck, New York. That's an affluent part of Long Island, about an hour from Manhattan. Early on, he developed an interest in betting on dog racing and horse racing, rather than the stock market. But one particular race taught him a lasting lesson. It featured a dog whose best time was 12 seconds faster than any other dog running that day. And yet the handicappers put the odds on him winning at 99 to 1. Greenblatt thought he had a sure thing. And the dog finished dead last. It turned out that the dog's best time was on a much shorter. Now, Greenblatt realized he needed to do more research before betting or investing—and that you can't always take things at face value.

Greenblatt went to college at the University of Pennsylvania's Wharton School where he learned about the value-investing legend, Benjamin Graham. Later, while getting an MBA—also at Wharton—Greenblatt and two of his classmates tested one of Graham's strategies, called net-net. The net-net strategy basically looks to buy companies that are trading for less than the value of the firm's current assets, minus all of its liabilities. Well, Greenblatt found that Graham's net-net strategy still worked years after Graham had died. So, in the summer—between finishing his MBA and heading out to law school—Greenblatt raised $250,000 from family and friends and used Graham's net-net strategy to return a 44% profit over the next two or three years. After his first year in law school, Greenblatt realized he wasn't interested in a legal career, and he took a job as a risk-arbitrage and special situations analyst at a start-up hedge fund called Halcyon Investments.

This was in December 1981. Greenblatt said he was soon doubling his money, trading in his personal account. So, a friend put Greenblatt in touch with Michael Milken, then the junk bond king at the Drexel Burnham Lambert investment-banking firm. Milken offered to put up the bulk of the money for a new fund that Greenblatt wanted to manage. With this, Greenblatt launched Gotham Capital in 1985, with $7 million under management. Greenblatt's most famous strategy is detailed in his personal best-seller, *The Little Book that Beats the Market*. It's geared mostly towards kids and teens though it has a wide following among adults as well. The basic idea revolves around finding good stocks that are also cheap.

Professional investors are also interested in another book he's written called *You Can Be a Stock Market Genius*. It's a bold title, but Greenblatt's thoughts are deep, and his logic is compelling. Here, Greenblatt outlines an investing approach that combines value investing with the term I mentioned earlier, special-situations investing. Special-situations investing focuses on non-traditional investments like spinoffs, merger arbitrage, rights offerings, long-term options, and others. I'll explain each of these in a moment.

A spinoff is one of the most common examples of special situations investing. It occurs when a company is spun out of an existing firm into its own separate stock. Why spinoff? Well, sometimes the sum of a company's parts is greater than the whole, and the market can't do this basic math. This may arise when one part of the business is growing faster than another. The company itself might be neither a growth firm nor a value firm. But, by splitting the enterprise in two, growth investors will gravitate towards the faster-growing side, while value-oriented investors migrate towards the slower growing, cheaper valued side of the business.

Greenblatt has also made money trading long-term stock options, known as leaps. The acronym stands for Long Term Equity Anticipation Securities which is a long way of saying, you better look before you leap. More to the point, options can provide the opportunity to leverage or multiply the value of your investment. Buying a call option on a stock is a bullish bet. Buying a put option on a stock is a bearish bet. Traditional exchange-traded options expire in nine months or less. And one problem with buying options that last less than a year is that you might be right about the direction of a stock over the long-term, but not within that time window. By comparison, leaps are good for up to three years. And leaps are traded on about 2000 different stocks.

Here's another one. In some cases, a company might directly issue an option-like security to investors called warrants. These sometimes last up to five or 10 years. But leaps and warrants alike give you a chance to magnify your gains—and losses—with leverage. Greenblatt has been successful with another type of specialized instrument, as well, called rights offerings. Sometimes, companies offer new stock to their current shareholders at a slight discount of about 3 to 5% to the traded market value. These shareholders usually know and like the company. They may be less likely to sell or flip a new offering, making the discount offer worthwhile from the firm's perspective.

So, one of Greenblatt's favorite strategies is to identify a company trading at a discount to its fundamental value that also plans on making a rights offering. It's like a double discount. Risk arbitrage, also known as merger arbitrage, is another tool in Greenblatt's investing toolbox. Let's say that before a merger deal is announced, the target company is selling at $40 a share. And the next day, a bidder offers to buy it for $50 a share. Because there is a chance the deal could fall apart, the company shares might still trade at $48 or $49 for a while, until it's clear that the deal will go through. The size of the spread also relates to the time-value of money, since it could take several months for the deal to close. When the deal does close, the arbitrage trader—the arb—will capture the spread of $1 or $2. However, if the deal falls apart, and the stock falls back to its $40 pre-merger price, the arb trader would lose $8 or $9 a share.

Greenblatt is not a big fan of a regular merger arb trade. But he does get excited about something called contingent value rights, or CVRs. These are common in the healthcare and biotech mergers. Let's say a bidder is unsure of the value of a future drug in a biotech company's pipeline. Rather than having a potential deal break down, the two parties might agree to issue a CVR, or contingent value right, tied to the drug in question. This way, if the drug is a blockbuster, pre-merger shareholders are entitled to a premium beyond the deal price. Now, CVRs often generate their own trading market even though they are often small in value compared to the original stock. And a lot of investors dump their CVR rather than waiting to see what the outcome is. For Greenblatt, this can be an opportunity, bringing to mind the old saying, "One person's trash is another person's treasure."

Greenblatt became famous in the investing community for his concentrated portfolio of special-situation stocks. A good example is the spin-off of Marriott some years ago, involving the separation of the company's hotel management business from its hotel ownership. Back in 1993, the hotel-management business was spun out into a new business called Marriott International, which initially was believed to account for about 85%– 90%

of the value of the combined firm. In turn, the hotel ownership part of the business—which had a lot of debt—was rechristened Host Marriott, and was expected to account for the 10%–15% of total value.

Most institutional investors wanted to keep the management business and sell the hotel real estate business. First, they thought Marriott International was the better strategy. And second, they thought that Host Marriott could end up being too small for them to hold. But Greenblatt thought better. He noticed that the parent company's chief financial officer, Stephen Bollenbach—who masterminded the spinoff—was to become the CEO of the Host Marriott part of the business supposedly the laggard piece of the company. And the Marriott family was retaining a 25% stake in the hotel ownership company that Bollenbach planned to lead. Fast forward to the time when the spinoff was executed and the stock of the new Host Marriott business initially plunged, from the pressure of institutional selling. But then it tripled from this depressed value only four months later.

Greenblatt provides some specific advice to further improve your results. He suggests looking for businesses that institutional investors—such as pensions and insurance companies—that they don't want, especially if they are too small for the big institutions to own. Greenblatt also says to look at the behavior of corporate insiders, whether they are buying or selling. They know the business best. But again—as we saw with both Walter Chrysler and Joel Greenblatt—your investment philosophy and approach should match your personality, skills, risk tolerance, and resources.

Bibliography

Ahuja, Maneet. *The Alpha Masters: Unlocking the Genius of the World's Top Hedge Funds.* New York: John Wiley & Sons, 2012. This excellent book contains chapters on Bill Ackman, Daniel Loeb, David Tepper, Sonia Gardner, and Marc Lasry, detailing their backgrounds and providing information on their investment strategies.

Bernstein, Peter. *Capital Ideas: The Improbable Origins of Modern Wall Street.* New York: Free Press, 1991. An interesting and easy to read book that describes the origins of modern portfolio theory, as well as the backstories of their creators.

Bodie, Zvi, Alex Kane, and Alan Marcus. *Investments.* 10th ed. New York: McGraw Hill Education, 2013. This is the most popular investments textbook used in college courses. It provides a good academic foundation for the topic.

Bogle, John. *Common Sense on Mutual Funds: New Imperatives for the Intelligent Investor.* New York: John Wiley & Sons, 1999. This is perhaps the best of the books Bogle has written on investing. In this book he makes a strong argument for using low cost, index mutual funds as the foundation for almost everyone's portfolio.

Burton, Katherine. *Hedge Hunters: Hedge Fund Masters on the Rewards, the Risk, and the Reckoning.* New York: Bloomberg Press, 2007. This book profiles a range of well-known hedge fund managers and includes a chapter on James Chanos, providing some insight into his investment strategy.

Carey, David, and John Morris. *King of Capital: The Remarkable Rise, Fall, and Rise Again of Steve Schwarzman and Blackstone.* New York: Crown Business, 2010. This book discusses Schwarzman's background and his journey from an investment banker at Lehman Brothers to cofounding Blackstone.

Dalio, Ray. *Principles*. Westport, CT: Bridgewater Associates, 2011. This is the handbook given to all Bridgewater Associates employees. It describes Dalio's personal philosophy and approach to business management. It is freely available for download at Bridgewater's website, www.bwater.com.

Davis, Jonathan, and Alasdair Nairn. *Templeton's Way with Money: Strategies and Philosophy of a Legendary Investor*. New York: John Wiley & Sons, 2012. This book provides information on John Templeton's background, as well as his investment strategy. To support its case, the book cites several letters written by Templeton.

Dreman, David. *Psychology and the Stock Market: Investment Strategy Beyond Random Walk*. New York: American Management Association, 1977. This is David Dreman's first book. He makes an argument that it is possible to "beat the market" by being aware of market psychology and following a contrarian investment strategy.

————. *Contrarian Investment Strategies: The Next Generation*. New York: Simon & Schuster, 1998. This book lays out Dreman's investment strategy in further detail. It features a list of 41 rules that summarize his investment strategy and views on the stock market.

Fisher, Philip. *Common Stocks and Uncommon Profits*. New York: Harper & Brothers, 1958. This bestselling book outlines Philp Fisher's approach to investing in growth stocks, as well as his "scuttlebutt" method for finding information on companies.

Fortado, Lindsay. "Lady Braga: Meet the Most Powerful Female Hedge Fund Manager in the World," *Bloomberg*, February 26, 2015. Accessed September 2, 2016. http://www.bloomberg.com/news/articles/2015-02-26/leda-braga-s-bluetrend-delivers-a-top-hedge-fund-performance. This Bloomberg article profiles Braga and her fund, Systematica Investments.

FTSE Russell. "The Russell 2000® Index: 30 Years of Small Cap," FTSE Russell, March 2014. http://www.ftserussell.com/sites/default/files/research/the_russell_2000_index-30_years_of_small_cap_final.pdf. This white paper discusses the history of The Russell 2000 Index, the first small-cap stock market index.

Gannon, Geoff. "Warren Buffett: How to Make 50 Percent a Year in Micro Cap Stocks," GuruFocus, January 13, 2011. http://www.gurufocus.com/news/119442/warren-buffett-how-to-make-50-a-year-in-micro-cap-stocks. This article cites Warren Buffett's comments on why it may be easier to achieve high returns trading small-cap stocks.

Graham, Benjamin, and David Dodd. *Security Analysis*. New York: Whittlesey House, McGraw-Hill Book Company, 1934. The original "bible" of securities analysis. This landmark book helped establish the field of value investing.

Graham, Benjamin, and Jason Zweig. *The Intelligent Investor*. Rev. ed. New York: Harper Business Essentials, 2003. Warren Buffett has called this book the best book on investing ever written. This edition is revised by Jason Zweig, who also works as a reporter for *The Wall Street Journal*. Zweig adds interesting commentary to the revised edition and discusses Graham's principles in the context of modern times, such as the Internet bubble of the late 1990s.

Greenblatt, Joel. *You Can Be a Stock Market Genius: Uncover the Secret Hiding Places of Stock Market Profits*. New York: Simon & Schuster, 1997. This book details Greenblatt's approach to special-situations investing, including topics such as spinoffs, merger arbitrage, rights offerings, long-term stock options, and other investment opportunities.

Greenwald, Bruce, Judd Kahn, Paul D. Sonkin, and Michael van Biema. *Value Investing: From Graham to Buffett and Beyond*. New York: John Wiley & Sons, 2000. This excellent book features a discussion with a range of value investors and includes a chapter on Seth Klarman, detailing his investment strategy.

Gross, William. *Bill Gross on Investing*. New York: John Wiley & Sons, 1998. This is Bill Gross in his own words, describing his background and investment philosophy.

Hagstrom, Robert. *The Warren Buffett Way: Investment Strategies of the World's Greatest Investor*. New York: John Wiley & Sons, 2004. This bestselling book provides some insight into Warren Buffett's investment strategy. It is a quicker read from the more comprehensive biographies by Roger Lowenstein and Alice Schroeder.

International Working Group of Sovereign Wealth Funds. "Sovereign Wealth Funds: Generally Accepted Principles and Practices, 'Santiago Principles.'" London: International Working Group of Sovereign Wealth Funds, October 2008. http://www.iwg-swf.org/pubs/eng/santiagoprinciples. pdf. This white paper outlines the Santiago Principles, a set of 24 voluntary guidelines for sovereign wealth funds, partly designed by the International Monetary Fund, and whose signatories include China, Qatar, Singapore, Russia, and the United States.

Jones, Paul Tudor. "Perfect Failure: Commencement Address to Graduating Class of the Buckley School," June 10, 2009. Accessed September 1, 2016. https://www.scribd.com/doc/16588637/Paul-Tudor-Jones-Failure-Speech-June-2009. In this commencement speech to a group of ninth graders, Jones discusses learning from failure and details the time he got fired from working for commodity trading legend, Eli Tullis. The experience of being fired caused Jones enormous pain, but he eventually used it as a source of inspiration as he developed his enormously successful trading career.

Kelly, Jason. *The New Tycoons: Inside the Trillion Dollar Private Equity Industry that Owns Everything*. Hoboken, NJ: John Wiley & Sons, 2012. This books discusses the evolution of the private equity industry and its key characters, including Henry Kravis and Steven Schwarzman.

Klarman, Seth. *Margin of Safety: Risk-Averse Value Investing Strategies for the Thoughtful Investor*. New York: HarperCollins, 1991. This is Seth

Klarman's take on value investing. The out-of-print book is so revered by investors that used copies on Amazon.com often sell for more than $1000.

Laing, Jonathan. "The King of Bonds." *Barron's*, February 20, 2011. No current biography of Jeff Gundlach is available. This *Barron's* cover story discusses Gundlach's background and his split from TCW and provides some glimpses into his investment strategy.

Lefèvre, Edwin. *Reminiscences of a Stock Operator.* New York: John Wiley & Sons, 1923. Those interested in the exploits of the younger Jesse Livermore should consider this book.

Loomis, Carol. "The Jones Nobody Keeps Up With." *Fortune*, April, 1966, 237–47. This article on A. W. Jones brought hedge funds perhaps their first mainstream attention. Before the article, hedge funds were a somewhat unknown niche in the investment universe.

Lowenstein, Roger. *Buffett: The Making of an American Capitalist.* New York: Random House, 1995. This is one of the earlier biographies on Warren Buffett and perhaps the best.

———. *When Genius Failed: The Rise and Fall of Long-Term Capital Management.* New York: Random House, 2000. This is a fascinating book that, as indicated by the subtitle, describes the rise and fall of Long Term Capital Management. Insight is provided into the principles of the firm as well as its investment strategies.

Lynch, Peter, with John Rothchild. *Beating the Street*. New York: Simon & Schuster, 1994. This is Peter Lynch's second book and provides further details on his background and investment strategy.

———. *One Up On Wall Street: How to Use What You Already Know to Make Money in the Market*. New York: Simon & Schuster, 1989. This is Peter Lynch's first book and likely his best. In it, he discusses his background and investment strategy.

Mallaby, Sebastian. *More Money than God: Hedge Funds and the Making of a New Elite*. London: Penguin Press, 2010. This book provides an excellent history of the hedge fund industry, and the first chapter features A. W. Jones.

Markowitz, Harry. *Portfolio Selection: Efficient Diversification of Investments*. New York: John Wiley & Sons, 1959. In this book, Markowitz details his approach to selecting portfolios. He was awarded a Nobel Prize for his work on portfolio theory in 1990.

Orchard, Freddy. *Safeguarding the Future: The Story of How Singapore Managed Its Reserves and the Founding of GIC*. Singapore: Government of Singapore Investment Corporation, 2011. http://gichistory.gic.com.sg/download.html. This e-book discusses the founding of Singapore's sovereign wealth fund, one of the earliest and most successful.

Patterson, Scott. *The Quants: How a New Breed of Math Whizzes Conquered Wall Street and Nearly Destroyed It*. New York: Crown Publishing Group, 2010. This book discusses the background and provides a sketch of the trading strategies of many of the top quantitative investment managers. The part of the book related to James Simons and Renaissance Technologies is most applicable to this lecture.

Proctor, William. *The Templeton Touch*. New York: Doubleday, 1983. This book provides a good overview of John Templeton's investment strategy. It lists 22 "maxims" or principles of Templeton's strategy.

Rogers, Jim. *Hot Commodities: How Anyone Can Invest Profitably in the World's Best Market*. New York: Random House, 2004. In this book Rogers makes a strong case for a secular bull market in commodities. He also discusses various ways of investing in commodities.

Rostad, Knut. *The Man in the Arena: Vanguard Founder John C. Bogle and His Lifelong Battle to Serve Investors First*. New York: John Wiley & Sons, 2013. This book provides insight into Bogle "the person" as well as his evolution from the CEO of an actively managed firm, Wellington, to the founding of Vanguard, the firm most responsible for the index fund revolution.

Rubython, Tom. *Boy Plunger: Jesse Livermore—The Man Who Sold America Short in 1929*. Northamptonshire, United Kingdom: The Myrtle Press, 2015. This book details the rise and fall of Livermore over his lifetime.

Schroeder, Alice. *The Snowball: Warren Buffett and the Business of Life*. New York: Bantam Books, 1998. This massive biography of Warren Buffett is the only one where he cooperated extensively with the author.

Schwager, Jack. *The Market Wizards: Interviews with Top Traders*. New York: HarperCollins, 1989. This is the first of 3 successful books that feature interviews with top investment managers. Paul Tudor Jones is featured in one chapter, and Schwager's questions provide some insight into Jones's investment strategy.

———. *The New Market Wizards: Conversations with America's Top Traders*. New York: HarperCollins, 1994. This is the second of 3 successful books that feature interviews with top investment managers. Linda Bradford Raschke is featured in one chapter and is the only woman to appear in the series.

———. *Hedge Fund Market Wizards*. New York: John Wiley & Sons, 2012. This is the third in a series of excellent books that focuses on interviews with top money managers. This particular book features interviews with Ray Dalio and Joel Greenblatt, covering their backgrounds and investment strategies.

Slack, Charles. *Hetty: The Genius and Madness of America's First Female Tycoon*. New York: Harper Perennial, 2005. This book is a biography of Hetty Green, arguably the first woman widely known for her investing skill. Green was an active investor from the mid-1800s until her death in 1916.

Soros, George. *The Alchemy of Finance: Reading the Mind of the Market*. New York: John Wiley & Sons, 1987. This is a somewhat theoretical book in which Soros articulates his Theory of Reflexivity, which argues that prices affect the fundamentals of an asset and that financial markets are prone to a series of boom and bust cycles.

Stevens, Mark. *King Icahn: The Biography of a Renegade Capitalist*. New York: Dutton, 1993. This book discusses Icahn's background, his deals, and his investment philosophy as articulated in what has become known as the "Icahn Manifesto."

Train, John. *Money Masters of Our Time*. New York: HarperBusiness, 1993. This book profiles 17 great investors, including chapters on George Soros, Thomas Rowe Price Jr., and James Rogers, whose backgrounds and investment strategies are covered.

Image Credits

Page No.